VYGOTSKY'S SOCIOHISTORICAL PSYCHOLOGY AND ITS CONTEMPORARY APPLICATIONS

COGNITION AND LANGUAGE
A Series in Psycholinguistics • Series Editor: R. W. RIEBER

A Continuation Order Plan is available for this series. A continuation order will bring delivery of each
new volume immediately upon publication. Volumes are billed only upon actual shipment. For further
information please contact the publisher.

This book is dedicated to my mother,
to whom I owe the better part of
my sociohistorical psychology

Preface

The social character of psychological phenomena has never been easy to comprehend. Despite the fact that an intricate set of social relations forms our most intimate thoughts, feelings, and actions, we believe that psychology originates inside our body, in genes, hormones, the brain, and free will. Perhaps this asocial view stems from the alienated nature of most societies which makes individual activity appear to be estranged from social relations. One might have thought that the emergence of scientific psychology would have disclosed the social character of activity which naive experience had overlooked. Unfortunately, a century and a half of psychological science has failed to comprehend the elusive social character of psychological phenomena. Psychological science has evidently been subjugated by the mystifying ideology of society.

This book aims to comprehend the social character of psychological functioning. I argue that psychological functions are quintessentially social in nature and that this social character must be comprehended if psychological knowledge and practice are to advance. The social nature of psychological phenomena consists in the fact that they are constructed by individuals in the process of social interaction, they depend upon properties of social interaction, one of their primary purposes is facilitating social interaction, and they embody the specific character of historically bound social relations.

This viewpoint is known as sociohistorical psychology. It was articulated most profoundly and comprehensively by the Russian psychologists Lev Vygotsky and Alexander Luria during the 1920s and 1930s. Unfortunately, their work has remained marginal in the Soviet Union and in the West, unable to penetrate into mainstream psychological science. The present book attempts to demonstrate that sociohistorical psychology is a valid view of psychological phenomena which can redirect psychological science toward fruitful future development.

While psychologists occasionally touch on the social character of psychological phenomena, they fail to fully comprehend it or appreciate its centrality. One reason for this failure is that psychological phenomena are intellectually fractured into separate faculties and components. This fragmentation relegates social character to being one component of one or another faculty. Social character is thereby prevented from being central to all psychological functions. In other words, the asocial view of psychology is supported by an atomistic view.

Appreciating the social character of psychology therefore requires replacing this atomistic view with an integral conception of all psychological phenomena as having a common social basis and character. Such an integral, comprehensive conception constitutes a paradigm. I hope to demonstrate that employing sociohistorical psychology as a paradigm will provide a coherent understanding of diverse psychological functions including cognition, perception, emotions, memory, language, personality, and psychological dysfunction. Furthermore, the paradigmatic use of sociohistorical psychology will advance the discipline of psychology to a more profound comprehension of its subject matter and a more effective application of this knowledge to practice.

A work of this scope cannot be written without substantial help from other people. Among the many individuals who have contributed in numerous ways I would like to express special appreciation to the following for their invaluable assistance: Roy D'Andrade, Michael Cole, James Wertsch, Norris Minick, Theodore Sarbin, Solomon Asch, Bill Livant, Bud Andersen, Gus Bagakis, Phil and Elaine German, Bernard Ratner, Tom Langehaug, David Bakhurst, Derek Edwards, Mark Kaplan, Josh Weinstein, Susan Frances, Kim McCreery, and Bob Robbins.

I am especially indebted to Edith Gold, John Mandes, and Lumei Hui for their painstaking editorial assistance.

Contents

We are so little accustomed to treat social phenomena scientifically that certain of the propositions contained in this book may well surprise the reader. However, if there is to be a social science, we shall expect it not merely to paraphrase the traditional prejudices of the common man but to give us a new and different view of them; for the aim of all science is to make discoveries, and every discovery more or less disturbs accepted ideas. . . . The reader must bear in mind that the ways of thinking to which he is most inclined are adverse, rather than favorable to the scientific study of social phenomena; and he must consequently be on his guard against his first impressions.

Emile Durkheim, Preface to *Rules of Sociological Method*, 1938

Introduction

This book develops sociohistorical psychological theory into a paradigm that speaks to today's psychological issues. Sociohistorical psychology was founded by the Russian psychologist Lev Vygotsky and his colleague Alexander Luria and is inseparable from their work. I take Vygotsky and Luria's main concepts (which have been lucidly explained by other scholars such as Wertsch, Cole, Scribner, Van der Veer, and Valsiner) and unify them into a coherent paradigm that is applied to numerous psychological topics in order to demonstrate its contemporary validity. This demonstration is accomplished by a twofold exposition. On the one hand, I show the importance of sociohistorical concepts for elucidating specific psychological phenomena including cognition, perception, personality formation, emotion, memory, developmental processes, and psychopathology. On the other hand, I reciprocally demonstrate how research into these phenomena substantiates the truth of sociohistorical psychological concepts. Such support suggests that sociohistorical psychology is an appropriate paradigm for the discipline and can provide the integral concepts which the field so desperately needs.

Vygotsky himself sought to provide such a comprehensive paradigm, and his writings constitute a significant foundation for it. However, the brevity of his career precluded a full-fledged psychological system based on empirical observation growing out of theoretical propositions (Cole, 1979). My project is to realize this vision by systematizing Vygotsky's rather fragmentary ideas, extending them to new areas, drawing out their implications, empirically substantiating them, defending them against alternative theories and data, and modifying them to enhance their validity. Of course, this book is only a step in this direction. It cannot hope to be a definitive vindication of sociohistorical psychology because the amount of material that needs to be evaluated is far too great. No one

1

book can review the entire discipline of psychology and demonstrate convincing support for one theory throughout all the subfields. Nor is one author sufficiently expert in all the subfields to accomplish this interpretation. My task is to suggest the framework within which such a vindication can proceed and to take the first step in garnering the necessary evidence. Others are certainly welcome to scrutinize the paradigm with the aid of other evidence.

I am not attempting an exegesis of Vygotsky's work. Rather, I seek to employ his ideas as the springboard for a sociohistorical psychology which has yet to be completed. Although Vygotsky is unquestionably the guiding light of this project, the point is to move beyond his words and to demonstrate their application throughout the field of psychology. While the book draws its strength from a reciprocal movement between Vygotsky and other psychologists—centrifugally casting Vygotsky's concepts outward to numerous areas of psychology and centripetally drawing these areas into Vygotsky's orbit—the outward direction is perhaps the more important of the two. The Vygotskyian center is less important in itself than in its otherness, as it reaches beyond itself to illuminate distant territory. It is not a monument to itself but a resource for others.

The tenets of sociohistorical psychology which I shall explain and substantiate begin with the premise that *psychological phenomena are humanly constructed as individuals participate in social interactions and as they employ tools (technology).* Rather than being impersonal by-products of natural stimuli or intrapersonal products of purely individual decisions, psychological phenomena are fundamentally interpersonal products. That is, psychology is stimulated by social and technological goals and it is socialized by existing social practices and technological instruments. The form as well as the content of psychological activity has a social character which generally reflects broad social-historical practices, not just interpersonal family relations.

Sociohistorical psychology additionally maintains that all psychological phenomena are moments of social consciousness and have a social, conscious character. In human adults emotion, sensation, and perception are not natural processes as they are in animals and human neonates. Human psychological phenomena depend upon and are infused with social concepts and language. Moreover, the organization of these conscious phenomena vis-à-vis each other is socially constituted. This socially constructed character of consciousness is socially changeable. It is neither immutable nor individualistically altered. Change requires a social analysis of psychology's form and content, but it also requires praxis that alters the underlying social relations. An important tenet of sociohistorical psychology is that *humans actively transform themselves as they transform their social and natural world.*

Vygotsky's emphasis on psychology's constructed character does not disregard biological influences. On the contrary, Vygotsky, and especially Luria, were students of neurophysiology. One of their paramount contributions was to demonstrate the importance of biology for psychology without dissolving social consciousness into biological processes. According to sociohistorical psychology, biological phenomena provide a general, potentiating substratum for mental phenomena rather than directly determining them. This leaves psychological activity as something to be built up from, rather than reduced to, a biological substratum. Psychology is therefore a new functional system that operates according to distinct principles. In fact, social consciousness is only possible to the extent that biological mechanisms loosen their directing function and recede into the background as a general substratum.

The fact that psychology is socially constructed means that it is not a direct by-product of internal physiological mechanisms or of external physical stimuli. Quite the contrary, socially constructed psychological activity *mediates* the impact of internal and external stimuli—by selectively attending to, interpreting, hypothesizing, inferring, synthesizing, and analyzing them (Toulmin, 1978).

A final Vygotskyian tenet, if it may be called that, is the notion that psychological phenomena are dialectically interrelated. This primarily means that they interpenetrate each other's quality or character. Each phenomenon reaches inside the others so that they are *internally* related rather than independent.[1] The ramifications of internal relatedness make it the indispensible philosophical underpinning of sociohistorical psychology in a number of respects. Most obviously, the fact that a thing takes on the quality of its relations and circumstances is why psychological phenomena manifest cultural variation. Sociohistorical psychology is only possible if phenomena are open to absorbing social features, and this possibility is uniquely emphasized by dialectics (Vygotsky, 1989, p. 54). We shall see that the failure of most psychological approaches to fully appreciate the social character of psychology entails an insufficient appreciation of dialectics. Psychological phenomena are erroneously postulated as having inherent properties that are external to social life when, in fact, their properties embody social life.

Internal relations also allow for a given psychological function to vary qualitatively according to different stages of development. The different processes which are in effect at different stages of development impart fundamentally different characteristics to functions at various periods. Acknowledging qualitative changes in memory, perception, emotion, and motivation over phylogenetic and ontogenetic development is central to Vygotsky and Luria's thought. They state that both phylogenetic and ontogenetic development involves primordial characteristics becoming permeated by, subsumed within, and transformed by advanced features. Primordial "lower" characteristics do not retain their original nature and simply coexist, side by side with advanced, higher features. It is erroneous to generalize from animals to humans or from infants to adults, because the primitive processes have no analogue in human adults. Whatever functions they had in animals or human infants are completely altered as they become integrated into higher processes, lose their primitiveness, and take on social psychological features. Even psychobiological disturbances at different stages of psychological development will have quite different consequences by virtue of the different related functions in which they are embedded (Luria, 1966, pp. 56ff.).

Yet another aspect of sociohistorical psychology that hinges on dialectical principles is the notion that diverse psychological phenomena are internally related. For example, Vygotsky (1987, p. 50) emphasizes the fact that emotions and the intellect are unified in a dynamic, meaningful system. Far from existing as independent functions, as Western psychology has traditionally maintained, emotions and cognition are mutually interdependent. Emotions are constituted by cognitive appraisal of events and thus depend upon cognition for their very quality. Conversely, cognition is intrinsically permeated and affected by emotion. Every nervous public speaker knows how anxiety can block clear thinking and memory. Cognition and perception stand in the same kind of interlocking, interdependent relationship. Expressing the interdependence of perception and cognition Vygotsky (1987, p. 297) said that perception is "an immediate fusion of the processes of concrete thinking [cognition] and perception such that the two functions are inseparable. One function works within the other as its constituent." Striking differences in the perception of optical illusions, spatial relations, personal attributes, art works, and other phenomena testify to the cognitively mediated nature of perception. In fact, Gregory (1970, p. 59) declares, "Perceiving is a kind of thinking. We have examples of ambiguities, paradoxes, distortions, and uncertainties in perception as in all other thinking" (cf. Bruner, 1973, chap. 1; Rock, 1983, 1984). Language and thought stand in a similar dialectical relationship. As Vygotsky outlined in the first and seventh chapters of *Thinking and Speech*, language and thought reciprocally constitute each other in an "internal unity." Language objectifies, completes, and informs thought just as thinking creates language and produces its meaning. Doctrines which separate language and thought, and doctrines that conflate the two both miss the fact that "the two processes manifest a unity but not an identity" (Vygotsky, 1987, p. 280; cf. Schaff, 1973, chap. 4).

While dialectics emphasizes that an element is never self-contained or homogeneous, and that it is always more than itself through its involvement in, and dependence on, others, neither is an element ever collapsed into its relationships and indistinguishable from other phenomena (Hegel, 1965, p. 166). In fact, without differences there would not be phenomena to be related. The individual element is always distinguished from the others with which it is unified. The individual is itself *and* more than itself (Kosok, 1970). As Hegel often insisted, dialectical relationships are differentiated unities or unities of differences. Vygotsky emphasizes this point in his discussion of language and thought. He rejects identity theories which collapse the distinction between language and thought as much as he rejects atomistic theories that divorce the two. Whereas atomism overlooks the interdependence of language and thought, identity theories overlook the distinction between them (*Thinking and Speech*, chap. 1). Similarly, "Child development is a unitary, but not uniform, an integral, but not homogeneous process" (Vygotsky, 1987b, p. 88).

Vygotsky's view of consciousness's relation to experience also embodies this dialectic of difference and relationship (difference-in-relation). He says that consciousness derives from particular, circumscribed experience, yet it is always an elaboration, generalization, or idealization of experience. It is not a mere replica of given experience as empiricists maintain. On the other hand, consciousness's distinctiveness is not a separation from experience as nativists tend to believe. Putting this in modern psychological terms, Bruner aptly said, consciousness "is attained neither by an unfolding of mysterious inner structures nor by the gradual accretion of shaping through reinforcement" (Bruner, 1973, p. 294). As an explanation of consciousness, "Empiricism is impossible, nativism is miraculous" (Bruner, 1983b, p. 34). Consciousness is experiential yet more than experience. It forms a differentiated unity with experience.

The interpenetration of phenomena (or facets of phenomena) means that each is intrinsically part of a larger unit that includes others. Consequently, phenomena (or facets) are dynamically interacting parts within a whole rather than independent, homogeneous, inert, temporarily engaged atoms. The dynamic contradiction between integrated yet differentiated moments leads to change, which is another main tenet of sociohistorical psychology that is generated by dialectical principles. Change is inescapable in a system where elements are continually affecting each other. For as A affects B, A is also changed by B. But then the changed A reacts again on the changed B which produces additional changes in both of them. Such a dynamic is intrinsically nonmechanistic because there can be no such thing as A unilaterally changing B. This is especially important for sociohistorical psychology's understanding of the relation between the individual and society which is often construed mechanically. Dialectically speaking, social relations are not external to the individual. Rather, just as they influence his very core, social relations are themselves constituted by individual acts as these are coordinated in a concerted fashion.

Dialectics is only a general formulation about interrelatedness. The specific organization of elements depends upon their actual properties. As Asch has told us, one element is more powerful in one configuration of traits while another is more powerful in another set. Similarly, the relationship between consciousness and experience is quite different from that between consciousness and biology. Whereas experience stimulates the form, content, and level of development of consciousness, biology simply provides a general potential for consciousness without any of the detail that experience provides. Consciousness's relation to and difference with each of these is a function of their specific human properties. Consciousness is related to, and different from, both of them but in different ways.

In the eyes of conventional social science, the foregoing principles may appear unpalatable. This is not surprising considering that Vygotsky explicitly sought to radically redirect the discipline of psychology away from traditional viewpoints and methods. I hope to demonstrate that these integral tenets accurately express the character of perception, cognition, memory, personality, emotions, developmental processes, and psychopathology. Even the foregoing brief description of Vygotsky's concepts makes it obvious how far-reaching they are. They concern nothing less than essential characteristics of human nature in relation to social life and biology.

Because Vygotsky's tenets are so far-reaching, verifying and extending them requires drawing on anthropology, history, philosophy, sociology and biology, in addition to psychology. I hope to demonstrate that the above disciplines, taken together, illuminate phylogenetic, ontogenetic, and historical developments which verify and extend the tenets of sociohistorical psychology.

A comprehensive viewpoint such as sociohistorical psychology, which unifies the diversity of psychological phenomena into a coherent framework and integrates psychology with social and biological sciences, may be illustrated in Figure 1.

The relationships depicted in the diagram are reciprocal. Psychology utilizes the various social sciences to understand the social context of

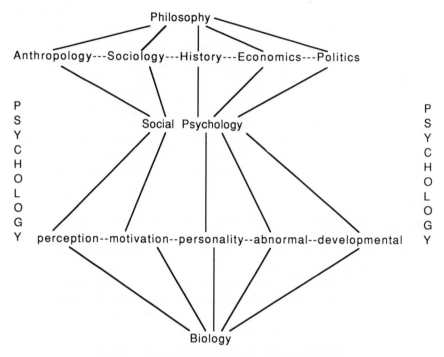

Figure 1. Psychology in relation to other disciplines.

people's thinking. But psychology contributes to the other social sciences by illuminating the mental processes involved in politics, economics, class structure, crime, education, other cultures and historical eras. Psychology also provides crucial evidence regarding philosophical positions such as idealism, determination, and dialectics.

The portion of Figure 1 labeled "PSYCHOLOGY" indicates that the discipline of psychology is fundamentally social psychology, and that all of the particular specialities such as child psychology, adolescent psychology, abnormal psychology, personality, prejudice, industrial psychology, and so on must be informed by a social perspective. Social psychology is the guiding framework for all the specialities rather than being one speciality among others as it is presently conceived. Biology's position at the bottom of the diagram is not meant to connote its priority over other disciplines. Quite the contrary, biology illuminates the uniquely human physical processes which constitute a general, potentiating substratum on top of which, so to speak, psychological activity is constructed.

The thrust of sociohistorical psychology to situate psychological phenomena within societal relations is unique. For a variety of reasons, society has been radically expunged from most psychological inquiry. It is no exaggeration to say that despite manifold differences among psychological schools of thought, they are all united by a common tendency to sanitize psychology from societal issues. The ways in which this is (unwittingly) accomplished are as ingenious and variable as the psychological schools themselves. Asocial formulations include various forms of nativism and biological reductionism, sophisticated "interactionism" between biology and culture, mechanical cognitive models, abstract descriptions of interpersonal interactions and group processes, humanist individualism, and methodological empiricism. All of these approaches, however informative they may be regarding certain aspects of psychological functioning, divorce psychological phenomena from specific social systems.

For example, the cognitive revolution that has swept psychology during the past three decades perpetuates the intraorganismic focus bequeathed to psychology by its biological heritage.[2] In Pepitone's words, the cognitive revolution "centers research and theory on thinking, judgement, perception, language, intelligence, and other processes in the individual mind. The social structural relations and cultures in which all human individuals exist play little or no part in cognitive theory and research" (Pepitone, 1986, p. 246; cf., Shweder, 1990, p. 18). This asociality is prominent in mechanical models of cognition which treat consciousness as if it were just a particular stage of processing in an automatic flow of information (Neisser, 1976, p. xiii). Perversely, it was only after cognition had begun to be mechanically simulated by computers that mental terms became accepted into psychology (George Miller, 1983). This mechanical interpretation obscures the fact that "culture penetrates the habit systems that govern automatic, and 'intuitive' information processing, evaluative judgments, and customary conduct" (Pepitone & Triandis, 1987).

Pepitone (1976, 1981, 1986) and others (Steiner, 1974; Cartwright, 1979; Hogan & Emler, 1978) have observed that even social psychology has become increasingly asocial. The study of small groups, organizational processes, and social influences on attitudes which comprised the field two or three decades ago has shifted toward endemic cognitive models of attribution, attraction, and attitude change.

Empiricism also obscures psychology's full social character despite its recognition of environmental influences on psychology. Empiricism's atomistic decomposing of wholes into parts denies reality to social systems and it thereby denies any coherent social character to psychology.

Social life is reduced to isolated, singular factors, and the interconnectedness which unifies them and constitutes their social character is obscured. Family, schooling, the media, work, and even social class are treated by empiricists as variables which quantitatively affect the level of psychological phenomena in the same way that physical stimuli do. There is little illumination of the full social character of these institutions or how it is reflected in psychological functions. As Urie Bronfenbrenner (1979) complained about this approach:

> to the extent that we include ecological contexts in our research, we select and treat them as sociological givens rather than as evolving social systems susceptible to significant transformation. Thus, we study social class differences in development, ethnic differences, rural-urban differences—or, at the next level down, children from one- versus two-parent homes, large versus small families—as if the nature of these structures and their developmental consequences were eternally fixed and unalterable . . . (pp. 40-41).
>
> Social class has typically been treated as a linear variable rather than analyzed in systems terms as an ecological context. To do so would require examining the settings that are implicated in the operational definitions of socioeconomic status and the roles, activities, and relations in which persons entering these settings necessarily become engaged (p. 245).

This need to elucidate psychology's societal character is the motive for resurrecting sociohistorical psychology as a paradigm for today.

Notes

1. Perhaps the most vivid and thorough demonstration of internal relations in psychology is Solomon Asch's brilliant study on forming impressions of personality (Asch, 1946). He found that a given personality trait has a different connotation depending upon the other traits with which it is configured. The trait, in other words, takes on the character of its relationships. The coldness of a person who is also intelligent, skillful, industrious, determined, practical, and cautious is perceived as ruthless. However, the coldness of an intelligent, skillful, sincere, conscientious, helpful, and modest person is perceived as a superficial coldness resembling formality, without the sinister connotations of the first individual. Conversely, cold colors the other traits so that a cold intelligence has a different quality from a warm intelligence. Asch concludes, "the characteristics forming the basis of an impression do not contribute each a fixed, independent meaning, but their content is itself partly a function of the environment of the other characteristics, of their mutual relations."

   In the dialectical interpenetration of qualities, some of the elements are more influential than others. For instance, Asch found that "cold" had a great effect on the quality of the other traits, whereas "polite" had less effect. In addition, the importance of an element varies with the context of other elements. In one grouping, "warm" played a central role in affecting the content of the other traits; in another configuration, "warm" was only a peripheral trait which had little impact on the others.

Since phenomena (or their facets) take on the quality of the relationships in which they stand, any character that the constituents may intrinsically possess is significantly modified in particular relationships. This means that a phenomenon's character in a concrete context cannot be deduced from its abstract character viewed in isolation because the latter condition lacks the very relationships that constitute (define) the element-in-context. In other words, the concrete is not simply the sum of abstract properties; the concrete is a unique configuration of interrelated parts whose character grows out of the interaction. In the first chapter of *Thinking and Speech*, Vygotsky (1987, p. 46) applies this kind of analysis to speech sounds. He argues that spoken sounds have a unique sound quality by virtue of being linguistic signs. In other words, these sounds are imbued with a unique linguistic quality that natural sounds lack. Speech sounds cannot be understood as abstract sound juxtaposed onto speech, they can only be understood in their own right as distinctive kinds of sounds quite unlike natural sounds. Concrete speech sounds cannot be deduced from abstract "sound" because the latter lacks just what is unique to speech sounds.

2. The pioneers of psychology's subdisciplines (Wundt, James, Hall, Galton, Pavlov, McDougall, Cattell, Kraepelin, Freud, Münsterberg, Piaget) were all doctors, physiologists, or naturalists who sought to extend biological formulations to psychology. In contrast, the other social sciences (sociology, history, economics, political science) grew out of a direct concern with social problems, and, initially at least, sought a comprehensive understanding of social life. In America, the social sciences were differentiated out of the American Social Science Association. Founded in 1865, the Association's purpose was the advancement of education, prison reform, civil service reform, the Freedman's Bureau, public health, infant welfare, prevention of crime, and the study of history, law, political economy, and sociology. At the 1884 convention of the ASSA, those members especially interested in history joined with other parties to found the American Historical Association, under the sponsorship and support of the ASSA. At the next year's convention of the ASSA in 1885, economically minded social scientists formed the American Economic Association. The AEA and AHA held a joint convention for many years, and at the 1903 meeting the American Political Science Association was established. Two years later, at the jointly held convention of the AHA, AEA, and APSA, the American Sociological Society was founded. The ASS was brought into existence mainly by AEA members who were dissatisfied with the specialization that had led economists to neglect social problems and philosophical questions (Oberschall, 1972, pp. 187-251; Silva & Slaughter, 1984).

1

Human Psychology's General Features

It is valid to speak of a "worm nature," an "ant nature" or even a "bird nature" but not of a "human nature," for man can have whatever nature the conditions of his rearing and social situation permit.

T.C. SCHNEIRLA

The Mediated Nature of Human Psychology

It may seem odd for a renowned biologist such as Schneirla to have made the above statement because obviously humans do have a distinctive biological nature. Indeed, in the article in which the quotation appeared, "Psychology, Comparative" (in Schneirla, 1972, pp. 30-85), Schneirla contrasts human neuroanatomy with that of lower animals'. The absence of human nature that he refers to concerns human *activities*, not their biology. His point is that humans are unique in not having any *specific* species-wide, identifying forms of behavior.

As Schneirla points out in his article, the reason humans have no specific psychological nature is that biology has a radically different influence on human and animal behavior. Biology directly determines most of animal behavior, which is why members of the same species (possessing a common biology) have common characteristic actions. Human biology, however, has an indirect, nonspecific influence on behavior, which means the same biology does not produce common, characteristic acts. As Schneirla explained, among higher animals, "maturation alone provides few specialized adaptive behavior mechanisms, whereas large repertoires of relatively stereotyped behavior are found in the lower groups. Among [the highest] mammals as a rule, the general adaptive pattern

11

is initially unformed or very loosely formed" (Schneirla, 1972, p. 220, 55).

Human biology constitutes a broad *potential* for perceiving, thinking, feeling, personality, tool use, social communication, and interaction; however, this potential does not naturally or automatically realize itself in given forms and contents (Lerner, 1984). Pannekoek (1953, p. 9) is therefore correct in saying that "the biological laws which govern animal life have with man largely receded into the background" Cooley (1922, p. 19) captured this idea in a vivid metaphor:

> Roughly speaking, the heredity of the other animals is a mechanism like that of a hand organ; it is made to play a few tunes; you can play these tunes at once, with little or no training; and you never play any others. The heredity of man, on the other hand, is a mechanism more like that of a piano: it is not made to play particular tunes; you can do nothing at all on it without training; but a trained player can draw from it an infinite variety of music.

Sociohistorical psychology recognizes the crucial importance of biology for psychology, and it is not at all "antibiological." Biological characteristics such as the need for stimulation, activity, and social contact, as well as extremely slow growth and prolonged dependence after birth, plus a disproportionately large brain cortex are all indispensable for psychology—in a paradoxical manner. The effect of our unique biology is to *minimize* the *directive* function of biology on psychology. Biology is important for psychology because it *withdraws* itself from strict control over behavior. Biology motivates the development of consciousness not in the positive sense of directing its formation but in the negative sense of absenting itself and requiring that consciousness develop itself in order to replace biological determination (Montagu, 1957, p. 37). Among humans, biology functions abstractly and does not generate the concrete reality of who does what, where, when, how, and why (Sahlins, 1977, p. 15). Human psychology is characterized by a reduction *of* biological determinants rather than a reduction *to* biological determinants.

The absence of biological determinants of activity means that, in Sartre's terms, man is, psychologically speaking, initially non-Being who acquires Being. Other beings begin with a more definite Being which saves them from the struggle to acquire it. The human need to acquire a being which is not inborn means that infancy provides few clues about adult being. What the adult will become is something that he must determine for himself; it is not the extension of a pre-given being.

If our biology dictates anything, it is that we are free to constitute our own activity. As Vygotsky noted, "Most basic is the fact that man not only develops [naturally]; *he also constructs himself*" (Vygotsky, 1989, p. 65). This self-construction is enabled by two unique features of human

biology. In the first place, the number of human activities under biological control is greatly reduced in comparison to animals. For instance,
while animals innately fear certain things, fear is not innate to humans.
It is learned through experience (Izard, 1983, p. 306). Secondly, the few
endogenous human psychobiological functions that exist possess a general rather than a specific character. The specifics are provided by experience rather than nature. As Durkheim (1938, pp. 106-108) correctly
insisted, the contribution of human nature to social psychological functioning "consists exclusively in very general attitudes, in vague and consequently plastic predispositions which, by themselves, if other agents
did not intervene, could not take on the definite and complex forms
which characterize social phenomena."

For example, hunger provokes us to decide whether to eat, what
to eat, how to obtain it, how to prepare it, how to eat it, and how to
allocate it among other hungry people. Hunger, per se, does not mandate
that we will attempt to eat or what we shall eat, whereas it does determine
these facets of animal eating. "What people *can* eat is biologically determined; what they *do* eat is quite another matter" (Levins & Lewontin,
1985, p. 262). Even naturally tastey foods such as sugar are not naturally
eaten, but are eaten because of social psychological reasons. These social
psychological reasons which dictate the consumption of sugar include:
whether resources will be allocated to produce sugar, whether sugar is
judged as healthy or unhealthy, whether a fat body which results from
a sugar-rich diet is socially valued or devalued, whether the stimulating
effects of sugar on bodily energy are socially desirable or undesirable,
and social customs regarding the time that sugar is eaten—before, during,
after, or in between meals. Such social psychological considerations determine whether sugar is eaten, how much is eaten, when it is eaten,
and by whom it is eaten. As Mintz (1985) says in his anthropology of
sugar, the predisposition to sweetness is inarguable, but "it cannot possibly explain differing food systems, degrees of preference, and taxonomies of taste—any more than the anatomy of so-called organs of speech
can 'explain' any particular language" (p. 18).

The entire range of infantile psychobiological needs are similarly
comprised of general needs such as the need for stimulation, regularity
of experience, opportunity for practicing skills, exposure to language,
attachment, and social encouragement to build self confidence. These
needs do not intrinsically mandate any necessary, fixed manner of fulfillment. There is no certain schedule of cuddling, kissing, spanking, holding, or deprivation of privileges in order to become gratified and
productive adults. As Kagan (1986) said, "Environmental niches are neither good nor bad in any absolute [i.e., biological] sense." Different cul-

tures opt for different practices and these become the *individual's socially constituted needs*.

Even meeting the psychobiological requirement for attachment, say, does not ensure normal psychological functioning if the kind of attachment is discrepant with social norms. For instance, a girl who establishes close attachment to parents who promote passivity, fear of boys, and a noncompetitive attitude toward schoolwork will be vulnerable to conflict and anxiety when she becomes an adolescent (Kagan, 1984, pp. 63-64). Thus, not only do social relations determine the manner in which psychobiological needs will be fulfilled, but additionally whether their fulfillment ultimately leads to psychological happiness.[1]

The difference between human and animal activity is that animal behavior is primarily (not entirely) a biologically determined, immediate response to stimuli whereas human behavior is a constructed response. Animal biology determines the individual's sensitivity and also its response. Response is naturally associated with a stimulus according to biological dictates. Human biology does not establish any natural sensitivity, responsiveness, or necessary connection between the two. Instead, an inventive, constructed act *mediates* between stimulus and response because no biological mechanism establishes a direct, necessary stimulus-response connection (Pannekoek, 1953; Leontiev, 1981, pp. 203, 301-309, 419-426; Luria, 1978d, pp. 275, 278; Schneirla, 1972, pp. 46, 52, 231, 263, 915). As Hallowell has noted, "The psychobiological structure that the hominid evolved is one in which intervening variables which mediate between immediate stimuli and overt behavior came to play a more primary role" (Hallowell, 1962b, p. 250). Mediations rather than natural sensitivity determine the impact that both internal and external stimuli have on the organism (cf. Lowith, 1971, for a good historical discussion of mediation).

There are three kinds of mediations: consciousness (or mental activity), social cooperation (sociality), and tools (technology). Consciousness is a relatively encompassing awareness of things and actively processes information. It analyzes, synthesizes, deliberates, interprets, plans, remembers, feels, and decides. Genuine consciousness is also aware of its own state and activity; it is, in other words, self-conscious. Sociality is coordinated, joint activity (not merely sequential behavior) with other individuals that includes cooperation, detailed communication, sharing, taking care of others, sacrificing for others, molding oneself as one interacts with others, and understanding other individuals' intentions, goals, thoughts, and feelings. Tools are physical implements which are utilized to augment the natural powers of the physical organism. Consciousness, sociality, and tools organize our sensitivity to stimuli, our perception, comprehension, and memory of them, and our responses to them.

Symbolic interactionists have described the mediated character of consciousness with particular clarity. They point out that stimuli become symbols invested with meanings and values. Humans do not respond to bare physical characteristics, we respond to symbolized features of things. Moreover, symbolization does not merely represent things as they stand independent of man; it selectively emphasizes and de-emphasizes various properties as they pertain to human purpose. This active organization may be said to symbolically construct a world. Such a symbolic construction is prerequisite to materially constructing and reconstructing the world. For, things can become material artifacts because they are symbolic artifacts, invested with changeable human meaning.

The individual does not confront things as a solitary consciousness. He is a member of a social community and relies upon other people for material, behavioral, and psychological assistance. The individual fashions his response to stimuli from materials, behavioral patterns, concepts, aspirations, and motives which have been socially organized. This social mediation of stimuli is expressed in the Russian term *predmet* which denotes the nature of an object as it is defined by the system of social actions in which it is incorporated and through which it enters into a particular relationship with the acting subject. *Predmet* is distinguished from the term *vesch* which denotes a thing independent of human intentionality (Minick, 1985, p. 116).

The social acts which constitute *predmet* and define things are not purely intellectual or semiotic. Nor are they fanciful exercises in generating metaphors or narratives about things, as Ken Gergen and certain other social constructionists maintain. The constituting social acts are fundamentally practical interactions which organize the material, social, and psychological existence of human beings. Emphasizing the social activity which generates symbolic constructs led sociohistorical psychologists to refer to their doctrine as activity theory. This term approximates the Marxian concept "praxis" which construes thought as inseparable from practical social action (Volosinov, 1973; Leontiev, 1981).

Tools and instruments similarly organize human sensitivity to, perception, comprehension, and memory of, and responsiveness to things. Tools thus comprise the third mediation between stimulus and response.

Conscious, social, and technological mediations comprise man's distinctive being. As Hockett (1960, p. 96) said, "incipient language, incipient tool-carrying and toolmaking, [and] incipient culture started leading the way to a new pattern of life, of the kind called human."[2]

The absence of biological specification of sensitivity and responsiveness leaves these unrestricted. They are canalized by man himself as he constructs consciousness, sociality, and tools, not by any natural tendency. Being self-constituted through mediations is what distinguishes human sensitivity and responsiveness from biologically dictated, animal analogues. Since mediations canalize human sensitivity and responsiveness, mediations are the true subject matter of psychology.

Consciousness, sociality, and technology do not simply supplement the biological mechanisms which determine animal behavior. Consciousness, sociality, and tools do not interact with biological determinants in the sense of each contributing some percentage of influence to behavior. Instead, consciousness, sociality, and technology supplant biological determinism. Biological processes of course continue unabated in the presence of mediations. However, these processes lose their determining power over activity. The genes, hormones, sense receptors, and peripheral nervous system which determine the behavior of low organisms continue to exist in higher organisms but they do so in a new form. Biological determinism is thus superceded (*aufgehoben*) by mediations and this is why they exist. They would have no place if organismic determinants mandated sensitivity and behavior. Consciousness would not exist because a determined organism would have neither the need nor the possibility to think, decide, or understand. A consciousness that can engender novel images, plans, instruments and behavior in a genetically dictated organism would be an oxymoron. In Gellner's picturesque terms, "A chained being has no use for the capacity to conceptualize alternative paths to freedom" (Gellner, 1989, p. 520).

Sociality is also only possible given the diminution of natural guidance mechanisms. As Geertz (1966, p. 7) observed, it is "only because human behavior is so loosely determined by intrinsic sources of information that external [cultural] sources are so vital" (cf. Baldwin, 1913, p. 23; Ogbu, 1987). Geertz goes on to say, "We live in an 'information gap.' Between what our body tells us and what we have to know in order to function, there is a vacuum we must fill ourselves, and we fill it with information (or misinformation) provided by our culture" (Geertz, 1973, p. 50). "We are incomplete or unfinished animals who complete or finish ourselves through culture—and not through culture in general but through highly particular forms of it" (ibid., p. 49).

In addition, humans complete and extend themselves through tools, which would be impossible for a biologically determined organism. Such an organism would be physically prepared (fated) to survive through its organismic sensitivity, genetically programmed response repertoire, and bodily strengths. With all of its behavior harnessed to a biological straightjacket, this creature would be incapable of expanding its afferent and efferent powers through auxiliary, unnatural instruments. Nor could such a constrained organism utilize tools to expand its behavioral repertoire.

Biology makes psychology possible; consciousness, sociality, and technology make it actual. These *mediations constitute psychology* in the absence of natural constituents. As Bruner and Sherwood (1981, p. 27) said, "While the *capacity* for intelligent behavior has deep biological roots . . . the *exercise* of that capacity depends upon man appropriating to himself tools and techniques that exist not within his genes but in his culture." It may also be said that while the questions posed by human biology may be essentially the same, culture constitutes distinct answers to those universal questions (Kluckhohn, 1953, p. 520).

Human biology has a general function while mediations comprise the specific details of psychology. This reverses animal nature where biology contains most of the specific ingredients which experience simply elicits. Unfortunately, many psychologists have misapplied the animal model to explaining human activity.

According to this misconception, social experience triggers off predetermined psychological factors such as cognitive skills, personality traits, moral concepts, behavioral tendencies, and predispositions to psychological dysfunction. Environmental stimulation thus has a threshold effect in the sense that when stimulation exceeds a necessary threshold it can switch psychological functions on, and below the threshold it switches them (or leaves them) off. Stimulation does not constitute specific properties of psychological phenomena. It doesn't even correlate with the level of psychological development. As long as the threshold for stimulation is exceeded, the precise level of excitement has little effect on the level of psychological functioning because the latter is determined by endogenous factors. Noam Chomsky holds this position in asserting that variations in exposure to language all culminate in roughly the same linguistic competence. In another formulation of the same basic position, Arthur Jensen believes that similarities in experience will culminate in different levels of intelligence because the latter are determined by intrinsic capacity.

Actually, this whole conception of experience as being a mere threshold effect is wrong. *Biology* has the threshold effect such that once basic biological requirements for nourishment, stimulation, and security are met—once the biological threshold has been crossed—specific determination of psychological functions lies in social experience (Kagan, 1984, p. 109). Given normal biology, variations in this area have a small affect on psychological functions.

The mediations which differentiate (distance) the human organism from the natural world paradoxically enhance our sensitivity, comprehension, objectivity, adaptability, and freedom (Scheler, 1961, p. 37). Animals' natural filters constrain sensitivity and reactivity. It is only when these natural filters are eliminated that organisms can become fully aware of things and implement a wide range of actions for dealing with them (Montagu, 1957, chaps. 2, 22; Scheler, 1961, p. 37; Leontiev, 1981, pp. 203-207). Only when nature is expelled from inside the organism as a determinant of activity, i.e., only when the organism is differentiated or distanced from nature, can the organism comprehend and master nature. Being dominated by nature precludes understanding it; being submerged in the world prevents having a world. Paradoxically, awareness and transformation of nature are inversely proportional to the determining power that nature has over the organism's activity.[3] Whereas animals are objects of nature, nature is an object for humans.

Consciousness, sociality, and technology do not simply coexist while acting independently. They are interdependent, inseparable, and mutually reinforcing. For example, consciousness can only develop in an infant who is protected and guided by a social support system. Without such social protection and guidance, the neonate would have to survive on its own shortly after birth. It would have to be biologically equipped with innate sensitivities and action patterns rather than be able to gradually acquire consciousness.[4] Only social organisms can afford to give up natural, rigid guidance mechanisms and have the luxury of developing consciousness (Baldwin, 1913, pp. 70-73). This means that consciousness is a social phenomenon (Wald, 1975b, pp. 85-86; Durkheim, 1953; Washburn & Hamburg, 1965b).[5] The cornerstone of sociohistorical psychology is that consciousness only develops through participating in practical social activity. This emphasis resurrects the original meaning of consciousness which is "knowing something with others."

Conversely, consciousness is a *sine qua non* of sociality. In addition, tool use is indispensable for consciousness and sociality, as well as reciprocally depending upon them.

In a book on psychology consciousness will naturally be the focal point on which the other mediations converge. This will be accomplished by a twofold exposition which demonstrates (1) the social and technological origins of consciousness, and (2) the nature of consciousness that generates sociality and technology. The consciousness that is formed by social and technological influences, and the consciousness which creates sociality and technology is the consciousness which psychology investigates. The most complete demonstration of the interdependence of consciousness, sociality, and technology employs both positive and negative examples. That is, it describes how the advanced state of each relies upon advanced levels of the others; and how the rudimentary state of any one mediation impedes the development of the others. The following discussion will therefore describe the continuum from primitive, or non-existent, mediations to advanced levels. This continuum will portray a richly textured picture of the interdependence of consciousness, sociality, and technology across a broad range of gradients. Such a gradation of consciousness, sociality, and technology is nothing less than evolution itself because evolution is the development of these interdependent mediations.

The entire course of evolution is one of increasing emancipation from natural, organismic determinants of behavior in favor of active, voluntary mediations. This is what accounts for evolution proceeding toward greater organismic flexibility, intelligence, uniqueness, creativity, and volition, and away from simple, stereotyped, automatic, species-wide behaviors (Montagu, 1957, chap. 8; Lerner, 1984; Bruner et al., 1966, p. 320; Schneirla, 1972, pp. 30-85; Scheler, 1961; Luria, 1932, pp. 401ff.). Yet even the highest nonhuman primates continue to be primarily determined by organismic biological processes which severely limit their scope. It is only in humans that nature has been fundamentally transcended as the determinant of life activity. While plasticity and intelligence have roots in evolutionary development, their human form nevertheless represents a qualitative leap in comparison to subhuman animals. As Marshall Sahlins (1959, p. 68) said, "Humans don't continue animal nature but replace it." This is what makes human psychology distinctive from biology, whereas animal "psychology" is part of biology. It will become evident that mediations are not simply improvements in natural abilities, they constitute a radical metamorphosis of these abilities.

To make the complexity of this story manageable, we will first take up the interdependence of consciousness and sociality. The relation of tool use to consciousness and sociality will be addressed in the next section.

The Interdependence of Consciousness and Sociality

Rudimentary Consciousness and Sociality of Animals

Rapidly developing, biologically determined organisms possess neither consciousness nor sociality. Consciousness is precluded by instinctual sensitivity and responsiveness because "the animal is involved too deeply in the actualities of life which correspond to its organic needs and conditions ever to experience and grasp them as objects" (Scheler, 1961, p. 39). Innate sensitivity, antedating and detached from the empirical world, is rigid and circumscribed. It only registers single, superficial features of things as attractive or repulsive, and is not conscious of their real character (Scheler, 1961, pp. 15-21, 45). Such sensitivity is devoid of consciousness that could remember, think about, or even feel things. Describing instincts' lack of consciousness, Merleau-Ponty (1963, pp. 104-105) said, "the stimulus is reflexogenic only to the extent that it resembles one of the dimensionally limited objects of a natural activity; and the reactions which the stimulus evokes are determined not by the physical particularities of the present situation, but by the biological laws of behavior."

Instinctual organisms are insensitive to other creatures as well as objects and this makes them asocial. Instinctual organisms are asocial because their sensitivity and responsiveness to other creatures are involuntary rather than being conscious understanding and concern. In other words, lacking consciousness is a defining characteristic of asociality. For instance, ants' attacking of intruders is not based upon genuine concern for the livelihood of the nest members, but rather is an inflexible reaction to the unusual scent of the invader. If the invader is protected in the nest until that scent disappears and it acquires that of the nest, it will be ignored by the workers even while it feeds on the inhabitants. Conversely, when the scent is put on some of the nest members, the worker ants will attack and devour them.

The same lack of genuine social interaction characterizes the dancing of bees which helps their mates locate sources of pollen. This too is a blind instinct rather than purposeful communication and cooperation. For, if the nest is empty when the bee returns, it will perform the dance anyway. Even birds' feeding their young is a blind, unfeeling instinct rather than concern for the youngsters' well being: "A [pigeon] which feeds young regularly on the nest will neglect them when they are off the nest even if close by. Evidently the young have a very simple meaning for the mother bird, rigidly dependent on the nest locus (at least in the early stages of incubation) and much below the level of maternal perception in monkeys, in which mothers feed and protect their young under a variety of conditions" (Schneirla, 1972, pp. 60-61).

Although low organisms coexist in groups, occasionally act in unison, and derive certain benefits from others' presence, genuine social concern, social learning, and interaction are absent. Lauer and Handel (1977, pp. 26) are therefore correct in concluding that, "despite their apparently complex social structure, the insects provide little, if any, comparative insight into human social life." In Baldwin's terms, instinctive groups are entirely different from "reflective social groups" (Baldwin, 1911, chap. 1).[6]

The absence of consciousness necessitates the absence of sociality, and vice versa. Sociality and consciousness can only emerge as instincts recede and permit experience to register fuller characteristics of things. Baldwin succinctly expressed the interdependence of sociality and consciousness and their mutual antagonism to endemic mechanisms when he said, "as soon as there is much development of mind, the gregarious or social life begins; and in it we have a new way of transmitting the acquisition of one generation to another, which tends to supersede the action—if it exists—of natural heredity in such transmission" (1896, p. 301). The mutual development of consciousness and sociality in animals reaches its highest level in nonhuman primates.

The importance of nonhuman primate social life is manifested in a strong disposition toward social contact (Harlow, 1959, 1963), important forms of social protection (Hinde, 1983), and significant forms of social learning (Harlow, 1959, pp. 41-43; Tolman, 1927, p. 22). Youngsters learn from group members which foods to eat and which to avoid, the location of appropriate food, the boundaries of the home range, friendly vs. predatory animals, tolerable distances to maintain between groups, communication (e.g., warning cries), grooming (picking parasites from the hair of another member), how to interact with group members (e.g., appropriate and inappropriate displays of aggression, forming of dominance hierarchies), and even sex role behavior such as mating and caring for the young.[7]

Sociality generates intelligence by amplifying the amount of information that an individual can and must process (compared with what it could acquire on its own) and by presenting individuals with complex social relationships and spontaneous behaviors which must be understood, anticipated, and accommodated. Sociality extends the mere *sensing* of details (which exhausts the capability of low organisms) to *perceiving* essential characteristics (Schneirla, 1972, p. 59).

Evidently, social life is more important for stimulating intelligence than the demands of the physical environment are. Nonhuman primates live in bountiful settings with easy access to food. In these conditions, physical survival does not require great intelligence. However, predicting and adjusting to the behavior of conspecific group members does. For instance, knowing that an individual will be aggressive or submissive depending on whether one of its allies is present, requires understanding and adjusting to the varying social contexts that differentially affect individuals' behavior. This is the reason a positive correlation exists

across species between social complexity and individual intelligence
(Humphrey 1976, p. 316; Asch, 1952, p. 119).

While social interaction stimulates consciousness's sensitivity and
knowledge, it also depends on consciousness. Complex, shifting social
interactions can only be implemented by a willful consciousness that
acts, understands, anticipates and remembers. Sociality and consciousness
are two moments of a spiraling whole, they are not independent, self-
contained, externally associated elements. There is no boundary demark-
ing the two because they interpenetrate. Sociality and consciousness
sustain each other. Sociality is a conscious concern for others and consciously directed interactions with them. Conversely, consciousness is consciousness that is stimulated by, formed in, and permeated by the crucible
of social relations.

Although nonhuman primate consciousness and sociality are significantly advanced relative to lower animals, the continued biological dominance of behavior precludes substantial development in these two areas.
Constrained by this biological limitation, apes remain fundamentally an-
imalistic and thus qualitatively different from humans (Kohler, 1956, p.
237). The biological mechanisms that prepare and preclude learning in
lower animals (Seligman 1970; Rozin, 1976) continue to determine what
primates can and cannot learn (Schiller, 1952, 1976). Although the range
of learnable phenomena is greater in nonhuman primates than among
lower animals, learning is not a generalized ability as it is for humans
(Washburn & Jay, 1968, p. 207). Animal culture can only teach new
behaviors that are consistent with natural dispositions. Culture therefore
only supplements animals' nature, and has a modest role in influencing
their behavior (Dewart, 1989, p. 176).[8]

Innate determinants of primate consciousness inhibit its intentionality (worldliness, objectivity) and limit it to perceiving fairly immediate
spatial, temporal, and conceptual relationships (Kohler, 1956, p. 242).
As Schneirla (1972) put it: "To be sure, a chimpanzee can be taught
human activities such as using utensils, yet the circumstances of training
and of use indicate a limited perceptual and conceptual command over
the adjustments and a performance more rigidly bound to specific sensory properties and motor routines than in man" (p. 78). Animals cannot
truly comprehend essential properties and relationships, and this failure
makes their problem-solving simple and discrete, relative to man. As the
noted biologists Yerkes and Nissen (1939) concluded: "It is our opinion,
based upon the results of varied and long-continued training experiments, that symbolic processes occasionally occur in the chimpanzee;
that they are relatively rudimentary and ineffective . . ." (p. 587).

The intellectual achievements of Kohler's, Harlow's, and Premack's apes do not contradict this assessment because their achievements were only obtained by a handful of subjects under systematic training by humans in highly constrained, carefully arranged situations, replete with prompting by the experimenter. These arrangements were frequently so conducive to learning and problem solving that intellectual abstraction might not even be required. Recognizing this contamination has led the Premacks to qualify their assessment of apes' intelligence (Premack & Premack, 1983, p. 147). Even if the laboratory demonstrations are genuine, they have never been replicated by apes living independently in their natural habitats, which makes these achievements unrepresentative of apes' intellect.

Primate social interactions are as biologically constrained as their consciousness is. For instance, the extent of social interaction is biologically fixed in each species: it is minimal in the orangutan (which roam individually), unstable and changing in other species such as chimpanzees (where group composition changes daily), and stable only in certain others such as macaque monkeys and gorillas. The distribution across species and gender of particular social behaviors such as aggression are also selected through evolution and are biologically fixed. Aggressive behavior is grounded in a complex biology which provides for a corresponding temperament as well as a supportive bodily physique (Washburn & Hamburg, 1965b, p. 614; Hall, 1968b, p. 160).

While social learning is a vital source of information about appropriate social behavior, such learning complements the learners' genetic predispositions. Indeed, the constraints on learning—or "learning what comes naturally" (Kaufman, 1972)—dictate that its outcome will exhibit uniformities throughout a species. These uniformities are more striking than the unique behaviors which accrue from individual experience. In certain cases, social treatment of offspring is largely a reaction to natural differences in the offspring's behavior. This is true of rhesus mothers' differential treatment of males and females (Poirier, 1973, pp. 26-27).

The fact that the overall pattern of primate social life is biologically mandated does not mean that primate sociality is undifferentiated. Numerous social roles and shifting alliances are not incompatible with essential determinism of nonhuman primate behavior. Biological direction means that the alliances are motivated to satisfy biological needs such as access to food and reproductive opportunities (Hinde, 1983, p. 289). Moreover, the mechanisms which guide the formation of alliances are primarily endogenous and involuntary. Differentiated behaviors are primarily rooted in natural, involuntary mechanisms rather than in voluntary decisions. This basis ensures that these, and only these, types of behavior will occur, however numerous they may be.

Fascination with the complexity of primate social relations should not obscure its limitations. Apes cannot conceptualize or voluntarily transform the overall structure of their behavioral norms. Certain ethologists overlook the natural basis of primate sociality and they assume that differentiated behaviors must rest upon quasi-human psychological processes. For example, deWall (1982) asserts that chimpanzee social relations are similar to human political intrigues and are founded on rational strategies, self-awareness, and the calculated exchange of favors. However, such claims rest upon the logical fallacy of assuming common underlying psychological processes from superficially similar behavior. In fact, quasi-human psychological functions (thoughts, emotions, language) have not been proven in nonhuman primate social encounters. Quite the contrary, the foregoing evidence on chimpanzee cognition (which will be supplemented by additional evidence below) suggests that chimps are incapable of such psychological operations. Moreover, primate sociality does not share other crucial features of human sociality such as concern for others, sharing, cooperating, linguistic communication, and profound self-transformation through social intercourse.

Determined social interactions, coupled with a rudimentary consciousness, cannot embody the understanding, concern, and flexibility necessary for true sociality. Kohler vividly describes the shallowness of concern that apes have for the distress of their mates as he observes that attention is only paid to another's distress if it is immediately apparent to the sense organs of the members. Removal from direct contact makes any interest on the part of the others vanish altogether.

> More than once I established that the temporary (or permanent) disappearance of a sick (or dying) animal has little effect on the rest, so long as he is taken out of sight and does not show his distress in loud groans of pain, as, indeed, chimpanzees, so rarely do. This corresponds to the lack of concern of the group in the healthy ape that is segregated, as long as he does not whine too miserably. . . . *Unquestionably, their interest today in some fruit which they buried yesterday, is greater than that taken in one member of the group who was there yesterday and who today does not come out of his room any more.* (Kohler, 1956, p. 253; emphasis added)

Monkeys' and apes' fundamental "egoism" is illustrated in Washburn and Jay's (1968) description: "An individual simply eats what it needs. After an infant is weaned, it is on its own economically and is not dependent on adults. This means that adult males never have economic responsibility for any other animal, and adult females do only when they are nursing" (p.225). Isaac (1978) concurs in observing: "The chimpanzees' behavior falls far short of active sharing: I suggest it might better be termed tolerated scrounging. Vegetable foods, which are the great apes' principal diet, are not shared and are almost invariably consumed by each individual on the spot" (p. 92). Experimental laboratory studies similarly have found that "every case of sharing was from subordinate to dominant; dominants never gave food to subordinates. Therefore, 'food sharing' here is a function of previous dominance competition and actually indicates monopolization, not pooling, of a limited supply" (Sahlins, 1959, p. 64). Occasional instances of food sharing occur (deWaal, 1982, p. 200); however, they do not constitute a regular, systematized mode of life.

Primates' lack of true sociality is evident from the fact that their social organization arises as a result of individual actions without concern for the group per se. For example, a dominance hierarchy emerges from the individual competition of males; however, there is no formulation of an overall plan to compete, nor is there a conscious effort to maintain competition because of its value to the group.

Given the foregoing nature of primate interactions, it is not surprising that joint actions such as cooperative problem solving are rare and difficult to teach:

> economic teamwork and mutual aid are nearly zero among subhuman primates, including anthropoids. Spontaneous cooperation—as opposed to one animal helping another—has not been observed among them. Chimpanzees have been trained to solve problems cooperatively, but fail to do so without tuition. Monkeys apparently cannot even be taught to cooperate . . . (Sahlins, 1959, p. 64)[9]

As with food sharing, occasional instances of mutual aid, such as one chimpanzee holding a branch steady while its companion climbs up, are extrinsic to the main course of life so that they only constitute a marginal advance of primate sociality beyond a rudimentary level.

The joint impoverishment of consciousness and sociality is expressed in their common manifestation in language. Language represents the unity of consciousness and sociality because, as Vygotsky (1987, p. 49) said, language is the organ of thought and the organ of social communication. Since language objectifies consciousness and sociality, its development corresponds to theirs. Primates' primitive language reveals a good deal about their truncated consciousness and sociality, and about the restrictive influence of biological determinism.

Nonhuman primate communication consists of natural bodily and vocal expressions in direct response to events. These expressions, in turn, directly stimulate behavioral responses in other members of the species. Such biological reactions contrast with human communication which consists of invented sounds that express symbolic concepts about things. Human words cognitively mediate things rather than being immediate by-products of them.[10] Animals have a direct attachment to things in the sense that things are important for satisfying an immediate need. Terrace (1987) calls this an acquisitive relationship to things and he points out that such immediacy precludes reflecting on and communicating about objects. The direct biological bond between animal and world precludes the development of consciousness and language. Animals do not *have* a world stretched out before them which they can denote. Animals are submerged *in* a world which they cannot comprehend or denote.

Primates' rudimentary consciousness prevents significant language development by precluding the construction of general, abstract symbols, or words (Schneirla, 1972, p. 78). The biological basis of animal communication directs utterances toward denoting the organism's internal condition rather than external conditions. As Washburn and Moore (1980, pp. 177-178) state: "In nonhuman primate communication, messages are limited, fixed in number, and are primarily concerned with the inner state of the animal sending the message. Primates cannot talk about the world but only state, in effect: 'I am afraid, desirous, worried, comfortable,' and the like. Even these messages cannot be qualified by such simple additions as, 'You are afraid; I was afraid yesterday.' Nonhuman communication has no nouns and no syntax" (cf. Lancaster, 1968, p. 444; Leontiev, 1981, pp. 201-203).

There are a few calls given by nonhuman primates that convey some information about the environment—such as different calls indicating different predators, which lead to different defensive maneuvers by the group members—but these are rare. Primate language is so integrally part of natural bodily gestures, postures, and facial expressions that it has not become a differentiated symbolic function. Indeed, the sound primarily calls attention to these bodily reactions: "Many field and laboratory workers have emphasized that vocalizations do not carry the major burden of meaning in most social interactions, but function instead either to call visual attention to the signaler or to emphasize or enhance the effect of visual and tactile stimuli" (Lancaster, 1968, p.442). Consequently, "a blind monkey would be greatly handicapped in his social interactions whereas a deaf one would probably be able to function almost normally" (ibid., p.442). Just the opposite is true for humans.

Primates' limited sociality precludes language because it obviates the need for word symbols to direct joint activity and represent objects which are not immediately present. As Etkin (1962, p. 140) put it, the need for word symbols "does not operate to any considerable extent in the lives of group-living primates today since each animal is a self-sufficient economic unit. . . . The social organization of contemporary apes therefore does not favor . . . language development."

While primates' rudimentary sociality precludes language development, this linguistic incapacity reciprocally interferes with sociality. The absence of clear linguistic symbols representing reality, and the subjective nature of animal vocalization, obviates the social function of genuine language. Primate communication cannot specify to a conspecific what or how to act, and it is therefore incapable of constituting behavior. It only triggers off an endemic tendency in the other to act, a tendency that is naturally, rather than socially, constituted. Primate communication is additionally understandable only to a small group of members who are familiar with each other and who sense the relation between the sound and the emotional expression it articulates. "Communication rarely occurs between strangers, but for the most part is between animals that have known each other as individuals over long periods of time" (Lancaster, 1968, p. 440).

A few noteworthy psychologists have made great claims about apes' language ability (and abstract thinking, in general); however, these have been repudiated by a sober assessment of the actual accomplishments and the contrived training and testing procedures.[11] These critiques have led many of the early proponents to significantly reduce their claims. Terrace's (1979, 1980) retraction is perhaps the most formidable, admitting after himself training a chimp to use sign language that "our detailed investigation suggests that an ape's language learning is severely restricted. Apes can learn many isolated symbols (as can dogs, horses, and other nonhuman species) but they show no unequivocal evidence of mastering the conversational, semantic, or syntactic organization of language" (1979, p. 901). The Premacks' later work also reduces their earlier claims. Whereas in 1972 they were asserting that chimp Sarah's understanding of sentence structure was equivalent to that of a child's, in 1983 they state that:

> even the brightest ape can acquire not even so much as the weak grammatical system exhibited by very young children. . . . While we find evidence for semantic distinctions, distinctions in the meaning of words, syntactic distinctions are not within the capacity of the chimpanzee." (Premack & Premack, 1983, p. 115)

Certainly, chimps are incapable of learning and using grammar which is the essence of language (Chomsky, 1980). It is misleading to call the learning of word symbols "language" because they are only the formal properties of language. Far more crucial to the definition of language are the complex grammatical processes by which the symbols are manipulated and understood. Apes' failure on this point invalidates the claim to language. And the lack of genuine language testifies to primates' conjoint lack of consciousness and sociality.

Human Consciousness and Sociality

In contrast to animal sociality and consciousness which are rudimentary because of their dependence on natural determinants, human sociality and consciousness are advanced because they reciprocally reinforce each other without interference from biological determinants. Consciousness can flower because it can fully accept the stimulating power of sociality, and sociality is advanced because it is consciously created and directed by consciousness instead of following stereotyped natural constraints. Human consciousness is great because it is social, and social life is great because it is conscious. To become advanced, sociality—i.e., social concern and understanding, communication, and planned, extended, conjoint action—requires consciousness. Conversely, consciousness requires the social stimulation of complex social relations, knowledge amassed by other individuals, symbols derived from social communication, and deliberation that is necessitated by considering the desires and responses of others. Social consciousness and conscious sociality are two sides of the same coin.

Consciousness is indispensable for true sociality in that the latter is a system of social norms which are planned, maintained, and symbolically communicated through language (Bernard, 1924, p. 111; Kaye, 1982, p. 151). Sociality additionally presupposes mutual understanding of intentions, desires, needs, thinking, feelings, and personality—all of which are obviously conscious. The conscious underpinning of social relations enables humans to act *with* and *for* others in addition to reacting *to* others as animals do. Primates and other animals may engage in similar actions simultaneously, such as hunting in packs. However, each still remains bound up within his own perspective and acts to satisfy his own need/pleasure. Only humans can fit themselves to a common perspective which transcends and guides them.[12] And only humans can genuinely care about and feel morally obligated to others (Fishbein, 1976, p. 135). Consequently, "[Systematic] food sharing exists in no primate other than man" (La Barre, 1973, p. 29).

Genuine sociality is a profound interpenetration of individuals such that each is a formative influence on the other. Genuine sociality is not mere coexistence of individuals but mutual constitution of individuals by each other. Lesser forms of sociality include primitive communication, modeling, and stimulating of sequential behaviors, but real sociality entails fashioning one's entire individuality (personality, consciousness, and behavior) from interaction with others.

These constituents of sociality presuppose that conscious understanding has replaced endogenous, instinctive, behavioral programs. Taking the perspective of other people, gearing one's action to theirs, and sacrificing one's immediate pleasure for the interest of social harmony are antithetical to biogenetic programs. Natural determinants preclude a social orientation because they filter all stimulation through the individual's innate mechanisms, and they dictate that things are noteworthy only insofar as they contribute to the individual's survival needs. This is precisely the reason for the absence of animals' social concern that was described above. It is only because human sensitivity and responsiveness are *not* biologically constrained that we can transcend our individual needs and standpoint to understand others, learn from and be influenced by them, and interlock ourselves with them. In contrast to animal biology which acts "centripetally," focusing all things on the individual organism, human biology acts "centrifugally," fostering sensitivity to other individuals and shifting our psychological center of gravity away from ourselves to self-in-relation-to-others.

Culture and society only exist to the extent that they are not genetically determined and transmitted. Ernest Gellner describes this with great clarity as he emphasizes the humanly constructed character of culture.

> A community is a sub-population of a species which shares its genetically transmitted traits with the species, but which is distinguished from that wider population by some additional characteristics: these in some way or other depend on what the members of that community or sub-population *do*, rather than on their genetic equipment. It shares a series of traits which are transmitted semantically: what is reproduced is behavior, but the limits imposed on that behavior depend on markers carried by the society and not by the genes of its members. Cultural behavior is not dictated genetically, and cannot be reproduced either by some genetic *Diktat*, or even by a mere conjunction of genetic programming with external nonsocial stimuli. Hence its boundaries or limits must be defined by something or other in possession of the community within which this reproduction of behavior takes place. Such non-genetic delimitation of boundaries of conduct or of perception, in the keeping of a community, is about as good a definition of *meaning* as we possess. Meaning, culture, community—these notions interlock with each other. (Gellner, 1989, p. 514)

Sahlins is thus correct in distinguishing human from animal society in terms of the conscious, voluntary nature of the former.

A comparison of subhuman primate and primitive society must recognize
the qualitative difference between the two. Human society is a cultural society;
the organization of organisms is governed by culture traits. The social life
of subhuman primates is governed by anatomy and physiology. Variations in
human society are independent of, and are not expressions of, biological
variations of the organism. Variations in primate society are direct expressions
and concomitants of biological variation. (Sahlins, 1959, p. 55)

It follows that "Culture is not a product of biological evolution although the capacity to develop and maintain culture is" (Dobzhansky,
1964, p. 93).

If consciousness is indispensable for sociality, sociality is equally central to consciousness. Sociality generates consciousness in two comple-
mentary ways: (a) Sociality acts as a *goal* (or "final cause" in Aristotle's
terminology), the realization of which spurs consciousness to develop.
In this case, consciousness extends itself *in order to* accomplish the social
goal. (b) Sociality also acts as an established *force* (or, "efficient cause"
in Aristotle's terminology) on consciousness. Here, consciousness develops *because* of existing social influences. The distinction between the two
is not always plain because they typically operate jointly. However, it is
important to acknowledge the difference in principle between teleological
and causal social influence because their impact on consciousness differs.
Sociality-as-telos is man's constituting of himself as he pursues his social
goals. Man constitutes himself as he constitutes and reconstitutes society.
Emphasizing this telos acknowledges the creative activity involved in personal and social relations. Treating society only as a given, causally im-
pacting on its members, ignores its origin and possibility for change.

One example of teleological social influence on consciousness is the
manner in which social intercourse spurs the invention of *symbols*. Symbols are, of course, necessitated by communication which, among humans
must be specific and refined in order to compensate for the absence
of natural sensitivity and responsiveness. In other words, animals' natural
dispositions can be elicited by crude communicative acts because the
organism already knows what to do. Human communication, in contrast
must tell the individual what to do and how to do it because he has
no biological guidance. But in addition to this biological necessity for
human communication, coordinating the social division of labor that
characterizes human life also requires refined communication. Coordinating separate activities requires encoding events in the form of symbolic representations which can be kept in mind while individuals are
physically apart. When the group members reunite they can discuss their
separate experiences, plan new activities, remember and implement these

during ensuing divisions of labor. The invention of symbols is thus inspired by the need to communicate about social interaction.[13]

Interaction and communication with others incites people to make their intentions and meanings explicit so they can be recognized by others. Inchoate ideas and feelings must be organized, systematized, and objectified in order to be identifiable to others. This objectification turns ideas into concepts which can be managed and manipulated by the individual himself. Acting for others thereby fosters *conceptual thinking* on the part of the individual.

The fact that symbols must transcend individual experience with particular things means that symbols are necessarily abstract. That is, they denote general rather than specific properties of things. Communication across division of labor requires abstracting out idiosyncratic properties of events which are unknown to absent group members and representing general properties which are known. I have not seen the particular bear you encountered, but I know what bear is in general because I have seen other bears which resemble yours. To communicate with me you must communicate in general, abstract terms which are common to both of our experience despite the many differences involved. The incentive to develop abstract symbols spurs the development of abstract thought, and this means that *abstract thought* is socially inspired.

Intelligence is also socially generated in a number of ways. Most obvious is the fact that social interaction extends the source of information from the individual's own experience to the experience of all the group members. Understanding, organizing, and remembering the sheer amount of socially provided information requires an expansion of the organism's intelligence. The vertically and horizontally structured *cognitive classifications* which organize complex information into manageable formats (Berlin, 1978) are thus generated more by social information than by physical experience. Even more important than the vast increase in quantity is the complexity of social information. As numerous social scientists have observed, it is the complexity of social life rather than the physical environment which stimulates intelligence. This is why social animals are more intelligent than lower, nonsocial animals. Richard Leakey states that social intelligence is *prerequisite* to intelligence about the physical world. In his words, "learning about the environment (which demands a certain intelligence) means living in a stable [social] milieu (which demands at least an equal and possibly greater intelligence): as social intelligence increases, so too will the ability to learn . . ." (Leaky & Lewin, 1977, p. 189).

Nicholas Humphrey (1976) similarly points out that primitive man's struggle for physical survival was not sufficiently challenging to incite high intelligence. Far more inspiring was the challenge of constructing and coping with human social life (cf., Asch, 1952, p. 177). The need to devise, plan, regulate, coordinate, and communicate social norms in the absence of biogenetic behavioral programs was a major incentive for developing the requisite intelligence. Moreover, the absence of genetic behavioral constraints subjected human action patterns to individual variations, prevarications, and transformative struggles—which also motivated an augmented intelligence for coping with such complexity. In this regard, the need to decipher intentions behind behavior stimulated the general ability, so central to intelligence, to discern *essences* that underlie appearances.

Questioning given information and assumptions in order to reach counterintuitive truth is surely another vital aspect of intelligence. Such questioning is spawned by social interaction in which individuals probe each other's behaviors, ideas, and motives. This interpersonal query generates intrapersonal intellectual questioning. As Sacks (1989, p. 64) states, "The origin of questioning, of an active and questioning disposition in the mind, is not something that arises spontaneously, or directly from the impact of experience; it stems, it is stimulated by communicative exchange—it requires *dialogue* . . ."

Devising and revising social relations also spurs the development of such key conscious functions as *deliberation*. The opinions, intentions, and needs of numerous individuals must be synthesized and evaluated in order to devise a common, mutually acceptable plan. This promotes reflecting and formal reasoning. As Parker (1985, p. 92) argues, "the invention and manipulation of kinship terminologies and associated rules of exogamy, descent, residence, and so on, requires formal reasoning, and such reasoning abilities were selected in part because they facilitated these self-serving inventions."

Social intercourse also promotes *self-control* because the individual must restrain his own desires in the interest of social coordination. Self-control, in turn, is vital for the development of *volition* because genuine volition requires that one consciously command one's activity in line with one's purposes. Unrestrained impulsiveness is not volitional because the subject is not in command (Luria, 1932, pp. 401ff.). Since willfulness presupposes self control, and self control is a function of social restraint, it follows that *social restraint promotes willfulness*. This, of course, runs counter to popular belief which polarizes social interaction and volition as antithetical. However, a social analysis suggests that the two are actually interdependent.

Social interaction also fosters *intentionality*, or goal-oriented striving (Meacham, 1984). Intentionality must be greatly extended as direct action of an individual is refracted through social mediations. For the intention of achieving a goal is greatly complicated by having to pass through a social body. Numerous subgoals of attracting others' attention, convincing them to participate, and earning money, are indispensable extensions to the original intention. Social intentionality is much more sophisticated than individual purposefulness.

In one of his more social comments, Piaget suggests that *logic* is stimulated by interpersonal communication and argumentation. Under pressure of argument and opposition one pays attention to his mode of thought and analysis because he must justify himself to others. Conversely, anyone who thinks for himself exclusively will not trouble himself about the reasons and motives which have guided his reasoning (cited in Kitchener, 1981, p. 265; cf. also Durkheim & Mauss, 1963, p. 82). Now the extent and sophistication of argumentation is a variable feature of social interaction, and logical reasoning depends upon these societal characteristics as well.

Ed Hutchins's (1980) investigation of inferential reasoning among Trobriand Islanders illustrates the grounding of logic in complex property rights (although this is not Hutchins's primary concern). The Islanders' complex rules of land use include "owners" temporarily allocating use rights to disenfranchised leasers, a system of payment for the rights, a legal system governing the inheritance of use rights over generations of leasers, rules by which the original owners can reclaim their land from the leasers, and rules by which the owners can permanently transfer their land to others. In addition to basic rules, there are many extenuating circumstances which are included in the legal system. Property disputes are resolved through logical argumentation which incorporates knowledge of this complex socioeconomic system of rules.

Evidently, a simpler social system devoid of institutionalized argumentation would entail simpler logical reasoning. For instance, if all the land was held in common and could never be allocated to individuals, there would simply be no complex normative system to understand and logical reasoning would be minimized. Or, where property was so privatized and production so self sufficient and isolated that little socioeconomic intercourse existed, logical reasoning would quite likely receive little encouragement. This social condition characterizes the Ojibwa Indians where "no institutionalized means exist for the public adjudication of disputes or conflicts of any kind. There is no council of elders or any forum in which judgment can be passed upon the conduct of individuals" (Hallowell, 1976, p. 411). We would expect that the absence of defending behavior to oneself or to others would minimize the development of logical reasoning. Logical reasoning should also be minimized in a system where disputes are settled by force for there would be no need to justify one's action.[14]

Sociality not only stimulates psychological functions teleologically, it also acts causally in the sense of instructing individuals how to observe, feel, think, and solve problems.[15] The teleological and causal effects of sociality typically occur together.

The joint importance of causal and teleological sociality for cognitive functioning is demonstrated by a wealth of research. Piagetian-type cognitive skills are dramatically enhanced by social instruction and modeling. When children who knew how to conserve on Piaget's water-pouring task explained the principle to nonconservers, 65% immediately learned to conserve (Doise & Mackie, 1981, p. 67). In addition, children who receive training in playing with blocks, dominoes, and tinker toys score higher on visual ability tests than children who do not receive such training. The prevalent superiority of boys over girls on field articulation tests disappears as girls receive training with the task materials (Sherman, 1978, p. 167; Halpern, 1986, p. 133). Discrimination and recall also improve dramatically when socially provided verbal designations are attached to things (Luria, 1961, pp. 10-11; Luria, 1969, p. 147, Bandura, 1986, pp. 57, 455; Bandura et al., 1973, 1974; Craik & Tulving, 1975). A remarkable example of this is the case of "S.F." whose ordinary ability to recall 7 digits shot up to a phenomenal recall of 80 digits, after 250 hours of practicing a mnemonic system (Chase & Ericsson, 1981).

Luria (1978c) has demonstrated how children's abstract thinking can be enhanced by adult training procedures. Employing a sophisticated design in which sets of six-year-old identical twins received different training, Luria presented some subjects (the "E" Ss) with detailed models of objects and then asked the children to duplicate them from a collection of pieces. Other subjects (the "M" Ss) saw only the outlines of models and were instructed to construct these from parts. Two and one-half months later, the M Ss had learned to become far more imaginative and creative than the E Ss. 86% of them successfully improvised building a model when several parts were unavailable. Only 13% of the E Ss were successful. M Ss solved all the problems on an embedded figures test, compared with only 20-40% of the E Ss. The M Ss correctly drew inverted figures 83% of the time in contrast to 25% for E Ss. Finally, given the opportunity to freely build models, M constructions were more complex and imaginative than the Es. Moreover, the M Ss utilized a plan whereas the E Ss proceeded haphazardly and in piecemeal fashion. This experiment demonstrates that training individuals to attend to structure rather than isolated details fosters imagination, creativity, planning, analysis, self-reflection, and self-control. The effects of two and one-half month's training were evident on tests conducted one and one-half years later.[16]

The dependence of psychological functioning on sociality is negatively demonstrated by the 30 or so reasonably authenticated cases of feral children who lived in nature apart from other people and who, when discovered, evidenced no human psychological functions. Indeed, such complete social deprivation made later years of painstaking socialization ineffective in humanizing them (Caldwell, 1968). These cases demonstrate that the inanimate environment which the subjects inhabited is an impoverished stimulus of psychological functioning (Newson, 1979, p. 207). Childrens' tremendous cognitive and emotional growth can only be attributed to complex social interactions.

Within modern society, systematic psychological differences among social classes and cultural groups (Ogbu, 1987) are further testimony to psychology's dependence upon social relations. Jerome Kagan goes so far as to state that social class is the most significant influence on psychological functioning. He cites several studies which unanimously found that social class is the only robust predictor of a child's IQ and reading skill. Biological variables such as attentiveness and activity level did not predict cognitive performance (Kagan, 1978a, pp. 206, 229-230; Kagan, 1984, p. 102). Bee et al. (1982, p. 1152) arrived at the same conclusion in stating that, compared with psychophysiological measures, "at most ages the total HOME [family environment] score was the single best predictor of IQ or language."

Dramatic improvements in cognitive skills pursuant to socially mediated stimulation constitutes further demonstration of sociality's effect on psychology (Fujinaga, 1983). Cases in point are Genie (Curtiss, 1977), Isabelle (Brown, 1965, p. 249), and Luria's (1968) twins. Additional evidence comes from the overcoming of perinatal trauma by supportive home environments (Werner & Smith, 1982; Werner, 1989; Gollnitz et al., 1990), and the dramatic enhancing of IQ scores produced by Binet,[17] Freeman (in Dennis, 1973, p. 108), Dennis (1973), Skeels (1966), Palardy (1969), Rosenthal and Jacobson (1968), Fleming and Anttonen (1971), Schiff (1978), Ceci (1990, chaps. 4, 5), and the Milwaukee project (Hunt, 1979). Kagan and Klein (1973) report that poor Guatemalan rural children, retarded in speech, memory, and perceptual inference ability because of restricted experience, achieved levels comparable to middle-class Americans when they were encouraged to explore their environment and interact with adults. Hunt (1980) found that not only does socially mediated enrichment improve lower-class children's cognitive abilities relative to a non-enriched lower-class control group, it also elevates certain skills above *middle-class* children who do not attend enrichment programs. The initial advantage which middle-class subjects enjoyed because of their generally stimulating environment was quickly overcome by the special attention given to their lower-class counterparts.[18]

One of the most crucial ways in which sociality forms consciousness is by providing the tool necessary for consciousness's objectification. This tool, of course, is *language*. If any one idea is central to Vygotsky and Luria's writings it is that socially provided language constitutes thinking, and consciousness in general. Language does not merely express thoughts, it forms them. This is difficult to see from the perspective of an adult speaker because his thinking precedes speaking and his language seems to have a purely expressive function. However, this appearance is only maintained by disregarding the individual's history. A sociohistorical analysis discovers that the individual's present thought was formed by linguistic activity. The order in which we exercise thought and language scarcely reveals the order in which we develop them (Dewart, 1989, p. 88). Luria (1974, p. 9) went so far as to state that "speech is thought's most vital cultural tool." Vygotsky similarly said that thought is born through words: "Speech does not merely serve as the expression of developed thought. Thought is restructured as it is transformed into speech. It is not expressed but completed in the word" (1987, p. 251). Thought is only formulated to the extent that it can be articulated in a linguistic medium. "Ideas and perceptions have only a shadowy, intangible and spiritual existence. . . . The word gives substance to a conception; and only through the word the vague feeling is turned into a precise thought . . ." (Pannekoek, 1953, p. 49; cf. Merleau-Ponty, 1973).

Social language provides us with objectified symbols which can be considered, manipulated, reorganized, and refined. Language is therefore the indispensable tool for conscious functions which require symbols such as deliberation, self-control, planning, volition, imagination, prediction, intelligence, abstract thinking, and mnemonic aids for active recall (Luria, 1978d, p. 275; Tikhomirov, 1978; Tinsley & Waters, 1982; Lee, Wertsch, Stone, 1983; Lee & Hickmann, 1983).

Language not only objectifies thought, it objectifies experience in general by making it explicit. As Dewart (1989, p. 168) explains, "The incidental result of the assertive communication of experience is that one makes present to oneself the experience that one communicates." Human language is a meta-communication about experience which makes experience present to the communicator. The human statement, "I am happy" objectifies and delineates the happy state, and enables it to be comprehended and savored. In contrast, animal communication, such as a cat purring, is an element of its contentment which comes and goes with the experience and which cannot aid in understanding, recalling, or manipulating it. Being differentiated from experience, language makes experience explicit. "Learning to speak amounts, thus, to developing an 'insight' into one's nature as an experiencer and speaker, and into the nature of reality, the objects of experience and speech" (Dewart, 1989, p. 225).

Language promotes abstract thinking by categorizing things together. This categorization highlights general features which transcend particular differences and can exist in innumerable specific forms. Describing the manner in which language fosters abstract thought, Luria (1982, p. 38) said, "The word takes one beyond the world of sensory experience and leads to rational experience." Luria maintains that

> the word becomes a tremendous factor which forms mental activity, perfecting the reflection of reality and creating new forms of attention, of memory and imagination, of thought and action. The word has a basic function not only because it indicates a corresponding object in the external world, but also because it abstracts, isolates, the necessary signal, generalizes perceived signals and relates them to certain categories; it is this systematization of direct experience that makes the role of the word in the formation of mental processes so exceptionally important. (1968, p. 12)[19]

The abstraction conveyed by one person's use of a symbol is greatly enhanced when several individuals use it. As long as a child identifies the word with one speaker he cannot use it freely to refer to objects unassociated with that person. Only when symbols are emancipated (abstracted) from social as well as physical particularity do they acquire stable object reference (Luria, 1982, p. 47; Kaye, 1982, pp. 151, 182.) Detaching language from a given speaker enables the child to use it more readily himself for it helps him to realize that it is not a single person's property and that he too can be a speaker.

The centrality of language for higher mental functions is negatively revealed by individuals who have been deprived of language. Oliver Sacks' extraordinary account of deaf people who have not been taught sign language points up the terrible impoverishment in cognitive functioning which ensues from language deprivation. His case, Joseph, for example, had been born deaf but was not diagnosed as such until four years old. His failure to talk or understand speech during these early years was attributed to retardation and autism and consequently no effort was made to teach him either verbal or sign language. After four years, he was considered retarded in addition to being deaf and he was not taught sign language even at that point. It was only when he entered a school for the deaf at eleven years of age that he began to learn sign language. Sacks explains that Joseph's language deprivation denied him symbolic functioning. This includes an impoverished memory and imagination, an inability to hold abstract ideas in mind, weak deliberation and planning, and confinement to a preconceptual, perceptual world. Sacks' description is worth quoting at length to pinpoint what Joseph could and could not do cognitively at eleven years old:

> Joseph was unable, for example, to communicate how he had spent the weekend—one could not really ask him, even in Sign: he could not even grasp the *idea* of a question, much less formulate an answer. It was not only language that was missing: there was not a clear sense of the past, of "a day ago" as distinct from "a year ago." There was a strange lack of historical sense, the feeling of a life that lacked autobiographical and historical dimension, the feeling of a life that only existed in the moment, in the present . . .
>
> Joseph saw, distinguished, categorized, used; he had no problems with *perceptual* categorization or generalization, but he could not, it seemed, go much beyond this, hold abstract ideas in mind, reflect, play, plan. He seemed completely literal—unable to juggle images or hypotheses or possibilities, unable to enter an imaginative or figurative realm. (Sacks, 1989, p. 40)

Language's role in fostering sophisticated mental activity is not confined to a general facilitating function. Language actually structures the form and content of consciousness. C. Wright Mills put it well when he said,

> The meanings of words are formed and sustained by the interactions of human collectivities, and thought is the manipulation of such meanings . . . The patterns of social behavior with their 'cultural drifts,' values, and political orientations extend a control over thought by means of language. . . . Along with [i.e., through] language, we acquire a set of social norms and values. A vocabulary is not merely a string of words; immanent within it are social textures—institutional and political coordinates. Back of a vocabulary lies sets of collective actions. . . . Vocabularies socially canalize thought. (C.W. Mills, 1963, pp. 433-434)

Symbolic interactionists took this position and claimed that language endows things with meanings or makes them significant in a way that they would not otherwise be. Language organizes the natural properties of things in a socially meaningful way. As G. H. Mead said, "language does not simply symbolize a situation or object which is already there in advance; it makes possible the existence of the mechanism whereby that situation or object is created" (cited in Strauss, 1956, p. 180).

Sapir and Whorf maintained even more forcefully that linguistic terms and grammar constitute the "program and guide for the individual's mental activity, for his analysis of impressions, for his synthesis of his mental stock in trade" (Whorf, 1956, p. 213; Sapir, 1951, pp. 160-166; cf. also Lakoff, 1987, p. 110). In contrast to animal communication which only elicits natural response tendencies, linguistic symbols are the concepts which constitute our mental schemas, and they therefore determine perception, emotion, sensation, learning, and all other psychological processes: "We see and hear and otherwise experience very largely as we do because the language habits of our community predispose certain choices of interpretation" (Sapir, 1951, p.162).

Sapir and Whorf's incisive articulation of language's molding of consciousness complements Vygotsky's and Luria's viewpoint. Whereas the latter were concerned with the formal relation between language and thought, Sapir and Whorf emphasized the particular form and content that thought acquired from specific phonological and grammatic structures. In other words, Vygotsky and Luria investigated the manner in which language fostered abstract thinking, deliberation, conceptualization, and volitional mentation. Sapir and Whorf probed the concrete form and content that particular languages imparted to consciousness. Vygotsky and Luria were led to study the phylogenetic and ontogenetic development of language to understand its formal properties; while Sapir and Whorf were led to study cultural and historical forms of language to comprehend its concreteness. Sapir and Whorf's approach is a necessary complement to Vygotsky and Luria's and must be incorporated into sociohistorical psychology (Lucy & Wertsch, 1987).

One major contribution that Whorf made, which paralleled one of Vygotsky's key insights, was to distinguish bare sense data from linguistically mediated, psychological significance with the terms "lower" and "higher" processes, respectively. He stated that ordinarily we never experience bare sense data because these are always organized and subsumed within psychologically meaningful, higher processes of interpretation. The higher processes override and mold lower sensations as the case of perceptual constancy clearly demonstrates. It is possible to artificially isolate physical attributes of things and minimize the higher processes. The resulting bare sensation will reflect the lower sensory functions. However, this de-psychologized, abnormal activity cannot then be construed as psychology (Whorf, 1956, pp. 267-268; Brown & Lenneberg, 1954, p. 465; Schaff, 1973, p. 191; Stern, 1990).

This distinction is exemplified in the difference between perceiving just noticeable differences (j.n.d.'s) between stimuli and perceiving the stimuli's quality. J.n.d.'s of color, for example, would be a lower process because they reflect the physiological limit of the eye's ability to discriminate color. It's not a matter of what the colors look like, but simply whether they are perceived (discriminated) at all. This is a physiological, not a psychological, phenomenon. Perceiving quality—what the stimulus looks like—is a higher level psychological process that includes cultural-linguistic distinctions.

The truth of this distinction is demonstrated in Kay and Kempton's (1984) study on language and color perception. When subjects were asked to distinguish just noticeable differences between colors, language had no influence. But when the task involved judging the similarity of color—i.e., which two colors in a triad appeared similar and which appeared different—language affected the perception. Colors encompassed by one color term were perceived as similar whereas colors denoted by different terms appeared dissimilar.

Congruent with Sapir-Whorf, the higher level task followed linguistic distinctions, it was unrelated to, and unaffected by, the j.n.d.'s between the stimuli: Where the j.n.d. distance was close but two colors were denoted by different terms, the colors were perceived as dissimilar. Conversely, where the j.n.d. distance was great but the colors were denoted by the same linguistic term, they were perceived as similar. The lower process only functions in artificially isolated circumstances where higher processes are prevented from operating. Where social psychology does operate, it overrides lower processes and depends upon distinctive culturally derived principles. Thus, the more than 7,500,000 color discriminations ("just noticeable differences") which all humans can make are named and perceived by English speakers as less than 4,000 categories, of which only about eight occur very commonly (Brown & Lenneberg, 1954).

Kay and Kempton's experiment demonstrates that language does not simply affect the naming of colors, it structures the manner in which they are seen. They are seen as looking alike or unlike according to linguistic categories. Another vivid demonstration of the linguistic-cognitive structuring of perception is Tajfel and Wilkes's (1963) experiment on the perception of length. Subjects were asked to judge the length of 8 lines which differed from each other by a constant ratio of 5% of length. In one condition the lines were classified into two categories by superimposing the letter 'A' on lines 1-4 and 'B' on lines 5-8. This linguistic-conceptual categorization distorted the judgement of lines 4 and 5. The association of line 4 with the group of short lines and line 5 with the taller category led to exaggerating the difference in their lengths. The perceived difference between lines 4 and 5 was greater than it actually was, and also greater than the difference that was perceived between any of the other adjacent lines. When the 8 lines were presented sequentially without any imposed categorization the distortion was eliminated.

While the Sapir-Whorf hypothesis is usually tested by comparing the cognitive processes of speakers of different languages, another striking test compares users of spoken language with users of sign language. Because sign language has certain unique properties which distinguish it from spoken language, it should, according to the Sapir-Whorf hypothesis, generate corresponding cognitive differences. In fact, because the differences between sign language and speech are greater than those between the most diverse spoken languages, the cognitive differences between deaf individuals and speech users should be greater than the cognitive differences amongst different speech users (Sacks, 1989, p. 73). This is indeed what the data indicate.

Sacks (1989, pp. 97-101, 107) reports that the visual, spatial character of sign language sensitizes deaf people to the spatial character of things and results in superior performance on visual-spatial tests. On tests such as perceiving a whole from disorganized parts, recognizing subtle variations in facial expression, mentally rotating figures, or separating (parsing) continuous movement into discrete frames, deaf four-year olds outperform hearing high school students. Deaf individuals also evidently utilize visual-spatial forms of memory—that is, given complex problems with many stages, the deaf tend to arrange these, and their hypotheses, in logical space, whereas the hearing arrange them in temporal order (cf. Bellugi et al. 1990).

A Social Model of Psychology

Social interaction does not simply "facilitate" behavior by releasing or augmenting natural tendencies as is the case in low organisms (Beach & Jaynes, 1954, pp. 253-254; Denenberg, 1969, p. 106). Social interaction actually produces new, elaborate, advanced psychological processes which are unavailable to the organism working in isolation (Vygotsky, 1989, p. 61; Blumer, 1969, pp. 8, 10; Doise & Mackie,1981; Lichtman, 1982, chap. 3). As Asch stated: "In society men produce new, important things. It is obvious that they transform their material surroundings, but it is equally true that they transform their own nature and bring into existence new psychological forces. These are a function both of the potentialities of individuals and of joint effort" (Asch, 1952, p. 136). Because psychological functions are only formed in and through social interaction they are, in Durkheim's words, social rather than individual facts.

Durkheim's elaboration of social facts in *The Rules of Sociological Method* has enormous relevance to the sociohistorical conception of psychology. Durkheim explains how social facts are irreducible to individual processes in the same way that any whole is irreducible to its separate parts. Just as the properties of water only reside in the organized configuration of hydrogen and oxygen and not in their individual qualities, so psychological phenomena only reside in the socially organized interaction of individuals, not in individuals' independent character. Of course the individual plays a role in the genesis of psychological phenomena, but only insofar as he is a social being infused with social relationships. Psychological phenomena are created and enacted by individuals and nothing other than individuals. However, these individuals are socially active and it is the social organization that enables them to be psychological. In the same way, water is nothing but hydrogen and oxygen, but it is not the sum of their independent, endemic properties; rather, it is the result of their particular organization and would not exist apart from this structured interaction.

The fact that human nature is socially constructed means that "man is not born human. It is only slowly and laboriously, in fruitful contact, cooperation, and conflict with his fellows, that he attains the distinctive qualities of human nature" (Park, 1915, p. 9).

Luria (1982, p. 27) was thus eminently correct in stating that "we should not seek the origins of abstract thinking and categorical behavior, which mark a sharp change from the sensory to the rational, within human consciousness or within the human brain. Rather, we should seek these origins in the social forms of human historical existence." For, as Pannekoek (1953) said:

> the whole of our capacity for abstraction and thinking is rooted in the community in spite of the individual form of its appearance. . . . Because for the common purpose the community learned to communicate by means of sounds, therefore the individual acquired words with which at later stages he could think out his personal activity and thus could indicate it by names. They all came forth from the source of the common spirit. . . . The higher mental development of the individual must be traced back to the development of the community, and not the other way round.
>
> Consciousness in man as an isolated being would not have been able to develop beyond the stage of vague perceptions, as we assume to be the case with animals. . . . Living together in a society is the nucleus and foundation for all mental development and for all human culture. This shows the shortcomings of philosophical opinions and systems which start from the individual and from individual consciousness. A philosophy which considers thinking to be a merely individual process can only incompletely approximate its essence. Reality is turned upside down when the philosopher proceeds from his own individual consciousness as a basic fact and then, along the way of critical doubt, endeavors to prove logically the existence of his fellow-men. He is not aware that the simplest facts of thought from which he starts out, already possess a collective character; that in the first abstractions he is dealing with, a society, a human community has already made its deposit; that each word, each conception and each thought which he experiences in himself

and which he accepts as that which is "given," has been inspired by community life. Each personal consciousness is the individual form through which the mental life of the community, which is its collective process and collective possession, gains expression. (pp. 51-52)

While humanism is an important corrective to naturalism, it must be supplemented by sociohistorical psychology which explains the social origin and character of consciousness. Without the crucial social element, consciousness is left ungrounded and empty.[20] Sociohistorical psychology therefore supersedes both naturalism and humanism as an adequate explanation of human psychology. In opposition to the *impersonal* notions of naturalism and the *intrapersonal* notions of humanism, sociohistorical psychology maintains an *interpersonal* conception of psychology. In Luria's (1978d) words, "Perception and memory, imagination and thought, emotional experience and voluntary action [cannot] be considered natural functions of nervous tissue or simple properties of mental life. It [is] obvious that they have a highly complex structure and that this structure has its own *sociohistorical* genesis and has [thereby] acquired new functional attributes peculiar to man" (p. 275; emphasis added).[21]

The key point of sociohistorical psychology is placing psychology squarely within the domain of social life and employing social consciousness as a mediation of natural processes rather than deriving directly from them. All impinging stimulation on the individual, whether from external or internal sources, is mediated by socially constituted consciousness.[22] This consciousness is differentiated into various functions which devolve around cognitive schemata. This is what makes them all "higher" social psychological functions. The manner in which socially derived cognitive schemata mediate between stimuli, psychological functions, and action, may be diagrammed in Figure 2.

Figure 2 depicts the main tenets of sociohistorical psychology as follows. Culture engenders consciousness (both teleologically and causally). Consciousness thus possesses a social character in the sense that its form, content, and level of development reflect its formative social relations. In other words, consciousness embodies and utilizes socially provided means for functioning. Social consciousness mediates the impact that stimuli have on the individual. Mediation by social consciousness (*predmet*) means that neither external stimuli (objects, other people, events) nor internal stimuli (such as hormones) have a direct impact on consciousness. Instead, there is a two-way interrelation in which stimuli are assimilated into consciousness and also provoke consciousness to adjust to them. The socially derived interpretation and organization of stimuli determine psychological functions such as perception, emotion, motivation, needs, recall, and sensation. Recall, motives, perceptual, emo-

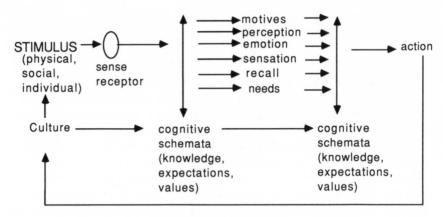

Figure 2. Socially derived cognitive schemata as mediations between stimuli, psychological functions, and action.

tional, and sense experience reciprocally provide information which modifies the cognitive schemata. The revised schemata decide how to act on the emotion, perception, sensation, memory, or motivation.[23] This action alters the physical and social world.

This dialectical relation between culture and activity, in which culture forms activity but is also its product, is an important corrective to the crude caricature of socialization as mechanically stamping impressions onto a passive recipient. Actually, social influence—both causal as well as teleological—generates unique individuals possessing active consciousness that selects, abstracts, analyzes, synthesizes, deduces, generalizes, judges, chooses, and acts on objects and institutions. Social experience imparts general knowledge and skills which can be evaluated, re-conceptualized, and used for an unspecified number of purposes (Merleau-Ponty, 1973, pp. 33-36; Bandura, 1986, p. 48).

Language occupies a distinctive position in Figure 2: it is both an aspect of culture in that it embodies and transmits cultural values, and it is an aspect of individual consciousness employed in thinking and speaking. This dual character of language epitomizes the dialectical relationship between sociality and psychology. Social language shapes consciousness but language is also generated by, and represents, consciousness. Like all objectifications, language has a dual character of forming and externalizing consciousness (Berger & Luckmann, 1966).

Although Sapir, Whorf, and Vygotsky emphasized the formative power of language on consciousness, it is also obvious that words reflect and concretize ideas. Far from language having a one-way influence on consciousness, language and thought dialectically develop together in the course of social interaction. In Vygotsky's words, "The relationship of thought to word is not a thing but a process, a movement from thought to word and from word to thought" (Vygotsky, 1987, p. 250). Vygotsky emphasized that thought is not identical to language but transcends and generates language. Thought is an amorphous whole much greater than particular words in which it is articulated. "Thought can be compared to a hovering cloud which gushes a shower of words" (ibid., p. 281). Thought is never completely expressed in words. "The two processes manifest a unity but not an identity" (ibid., p. 280).

Social institutions (mores) share the same dialectical spiral with consciousness that language does. If, for the sake of argument, we begin with an existing society, it obviously contains numerous problems, contradictions, and possibilities. Individuals detect these and devise new ideas about how to act differently. Old institutions are superseded by new consciousness which creates new institutions. Of course, the specifics of this dynamic vary historically. Who makes the changes, how widespread they are, and the extent of their difference with the status quo are all variable. In some societies, effective new ideas, action patterns, and social institutions are primarily created by a small number of elite rulers and managers; in other societies the changes are fashioned more democratically.

Some changes in consciousness and behavior may be superficially antagonistic to the status quo while remaining fundamentally compatible with it; other changes may be more radical. Regardless of the details, people do create new forms of consciousness, behavior, and institutions out of the status quo. Although these are motivated and made possible by the status quo, they are nonetheless genuine creative acts of imagination, intention, and practice. As such, they are self-constituting acts which produce history.

Sartre's book, *Search for a Method*, is probably the most thorough exploration of this dialectic. On the one hand, Sartre grasps the social grounding of all acts. He correctly states, "the most individual possible is only the internalization and enrichment of a social possible" (1963, p. 95). However the social possible is only revealed through individuals' thoughts and actions (Hauser, 1982, p. 41 & *passim*). Sartre goes on to cite Engels's classic comment that men make their history on the basis of real, prior conditions, but it is *the men* who make it and not the prior conditions. "Otherwise men would be merely the vehicles of inhuman forces which through them would govern the social world. To be sure, these conditions exist, and it is they, they alone, which can furnish a direction and a material reality to the changes which are in preparation;

but the movement of human praxis goes beyond them while conserving them (Sartre, 1963, p. 87).

In his *Critique of Dialectical Reason*, Sartre argues that every individual act "incarnates" prior conditions. He means by this that the act embodies prior conditions, yet it simultaneously fleshes them out in idiosyncratic ways (Aronson, 1987, pp. 54ff.). Individuals reorganize or "totalize" their life circumstances and this is always a creative act, regardless of how superficial or ineffective it may be. Sartre explains how becoming a boxer totalizes together the violence of the individual's lower class life, his desire to escape from that class, the economic fact that boxing earns money and so offers the possibility of escaping the lower class, the boxer's physical qualities, the audience's desire to observe violent fighting, and the community of other boxers who affect his likelihood of success. The individual coalesces all of these conditions in deciding to box and in implementing the decision in action.

Possibilities for thought and action do not come conveniently packaged, waiting to be selected like groceries on a shelf. People struggle to develop thoughts and actions, and each invention *reveals* what society is like *by creating* a portion of society. It is only after the struggle that we can see what the society is really like, what its strengths, weaknesses, contradictions, and possibilities are. Consciousness reveals society not only through contemplation but through praxis. It reveals the present by creating a future: consciousness transforms the present into the past where it is amenable to historical analysis. Such genuine achievement testifies to consciousness's creativity and freedom, however much it embodies social influences. Contextualized freedom is not unfreedom (as romantic individualists believe), it is the only freedom given the internal connectedness of things.

Consciousness and sociality continually create and stimulate each other, yet each creation outruns and influences its creator: Socially formed consciousness employs its powers to invent and satisfy desires which controvert established social practices. And social relations which consciousness originally forms to further its own ends wind up demanding its conformity to institutionalized action patterns. This conformity limits consciousness's further flexibility and calls for it to transform those institutions in order to develop. Social consciousness is truly freer than animal behavior, but this freedom is not pure, it is social freedom. Its freedom is always bounded by a social context and can only advance by advancing society in ways that are historically possible and fulfilling.

This dialectical relation between consciousness and sociality includes a third element, tool use. The interconnection of these three mediations is the topic of the next section.

The Interdependence of Consciousness, Sociality, and Tool Use

As the third mediation between organism and world, tools are intimately related to the other two, consciousness and sociality. Like the others, tools are artificial constructs that transcend our physical organism and enhance its powers. Human development is only possible via unnatural mediations which, in contrast to physical organs, can be improved. As Wundt (1921) pointed out, "Man is primitive so long as he is essentially limited in his immediate means of support to that which nature directly offers him or to the labor of his own hands" (p. 121). Tools not only augment our strength, but the universality of action as well. In contrast to animals which are restricted to specialized acts appropriate to particular organs, humans have an unlimited range of potential skills by virtue of the unlimited variety of instruments they can invent (Pannekoek, 1953, p. 91). We are uniquely suited for this because our biology is a universal, potentiating, capacity for extrabiological inventions.

Tools so epitomize extrabiological inventions that Vygotsky (1978, chap. 4), Luria (1928), Leontiev (1932, 1981), and Bruner (1966, p. 81) analogize mental constructs to tools. They liken consciousness to a tool in order to highlight its artifactual character: symbols and concepts overcome the limits of natural sensitivity just as tools overcome natural strength. As Luria (1928, p. 495) describes it:

> instead of applying directly its natural function to the solution of a definite task, the child *puts in between that function and the task a certain auxiliary means,* a certain manner, by the medium of which the child manages to perform the task. If he wishes to remember a difficult series, he invents a conventional sign, and this sign, being wedged between the task and the memory, assists in the better mastering of task. The direct, natural use of the function is replaced by a complicated cultural form.

These signs can be physical cues, such as tying a string around one's finger, or they can be symbolic words repetitively rehearsed in order to enhance memory. Both kinds of signs are tool-like artifacts for implementing a goal.

Luria (1928) goes on to classify stages of children's thinking according to their use of symbols and other "auxiliary" means of problem solving. The earliest stage he terms "pre-instrumental," followed by "pseudo-instrumental," and culminating in "real instrumental" thinking.

Of course, tools are not only analogous to conscious symbols, they stand in a real relationship with consciousness. Montagu argues, "it seems highly probable that the development of physical tools went hand in hand with the development of mental ones. Tools, physical or mental, open up a world of unlimited possibilities for development . . ." (1962, p. x). Tools expand the possibility of developing consciousness by tremendously expanding the range of possible activities for consciousness to invent, direct, and understand. Tools provide a great range of directions for consciousness to take, each one leading to different sensitivity and comprehension. In contrast, biological specialization of organs that occurs in animals confines consciousness to one corresponding domain rather than expanding it to encompass many domains. As Pannekoek (1953, pp. 12-13) said: "Instead of the manifold organs of the animals, each appropriate to its own separate function, the human hand acts as a universal organ; by grasping tools, which vary for different functions, the combination hand-tool replaces the various animal organs."

The general consciousness that is associated with tool use is necessarily a voluntary consciousness that decides how, when, and which tools to use. In contrast, specialized animal organs, capable of only limited, stereotyped activity, have no place for voluntary, creative, consciousness. Instead, a pre-ordained connection holds between behavior, bodily structure, and temperament. This connection is broken with the advent of mediations just as the natural underpinnings of behavior and personality are superceded. The consciousness associated with tools is as artifactual (in the sense of being constructed, implemented, and voluntarily controlled) as the instruments themselves. For example, the aggressive temperament that selectively employs tools of destruction has as little natural basis as the tools themselves do. It is illogical to suppose a biological aggressive instinct which then deliberately invents and employs weapons. A consciousness that controls tools is equally capable of controlling itself.

Tools amplify cognitive abilities in the same two ways that sociality does—teleologically and causally. The goal of transforming objects into tools (teleologically) stimulates reflection about objects' properties more than direct consumption of things does. As Dewey stated, "Only when things are treated as *means*, are marked off and held against remote ends, do they become 'objects'" (Dewey, 1902). Tool use further stimulates thinking because of the flexibility it imparts to action. The fact that we can instrumentally transform objects in numerous ways spurs our imagination of novel uses for things. Tool use also stimulates relational thinking between the instrument and the goal: the individual considers what kind of instrumental objects can be employed in what manner to achieve the goal (Luria, 1978a, p. 105; Pannekoek, 1953, p. 15).

Tool-inspired, relational thinking tremendously proliferates the amount of information the organism must process since enormous permutations of relationships become possible: any object may be considered in relation to any aspect of other objects and any combination of other objects. Media technology also expands the amount of information which impinges on the individual's consciousness, and writing implements (including paper) facilitate the recording of vast amounts of information which the brain alone cannot retain. Before recording instruments were invented, the mind of early man was greatly taxed by the necessity of remembering countless detail. Tales abound of the amazing memories possessed by our early ancestors which far surpass that of modern peoples. Freed from such tediousness by recording devices, civilized man is able to reduce the power of his memory and devote more of his brain and mind to more abstract, intellectual reasoning (Pannekoek, 1953, pp. 97).[24]

Wald (1975a) argues that writing, being less personal than face-to-face speech, and less natural than speech is more difficult to master ("Anyone can speak, but not all can write"). Consequently, the process of inventing it stimulated complex thought. And because writing is also more abstract than speech (Wald, p. 56), the desire to invent it spurred the requisite abstract thinking. It is significant that the history of writing, from pictograms to the letters of the alphabet, is not only the history of more abstract graphic representation, but also marks the development of more abstract and general ideas about reality (Wald, 1975a, p. 51). Goody (1977, p.110) similarly argues that writing technology has profoundly altered cognitive processes and is a major factor in the development of modern scientific, mathematical, logical thinking. Written numbers can be manipulated in a much more complex manner than words can, and writing thus potentiates higher mathematics in a way that would be impossible with oral communication (Goody, p. 12). Specifically:

> the invention of a notation is clearly a prerequisite for the kind of highly abstract, decontextualized and arbitrary procedures that are typically represented by the [mathematical] formula. One of the particular aspects of the formula that enables us to carry out computations is the ability to retain the balance or equality between the two sides by performing the same operations on each. . . . There is no non-visual way of doing this; the process depends upon spatial manipulation. Speech alone cannot do it; writing can. The visual-spatial mode [that is empowered by writing technology] permits the development of a special kind of manipulation. (Goody, pp. 122-123)

According to Goody, writing also fosters a generally critical mode of thinking that is vital to science and that could not occur in the absence of writing. For writing allows one to distance oneself from the recorded message and thereby rationally scrutinize it. The speaker, in contrast, has no objective record beyond his memory on which he can deliberate (Goody, p. 37). This kind of critical analysis makes one aware of contradictions in the record and enhances a sense of logic and argument. In addition, the formalization of propositions, abstracted from the flow of speech, leads to the syllogism and advanced logical reasoning. "Symbolic logic and algebra are inconceivable without the prior existence of writing" (Goody, p. 44). Finally, Goody argues that writing technology enhances the ability to categorize and recategorize information. Preliterate people do, obviously, employ classificatory systems, however these are comparatively few (e.g., kinship, plants, animals) and more implicit than explicit. Classification is made explicit and greatly expanded by being able to list and hierarchically order things in writing (Goody, pp. 105, 115).

Berry and Bennett (1989), and Scribner and Cole (1978, 1981) dispute these claims after having experimentally found minimal effects of writing on cognition. They argue that most such claims have failed to isolate literacy per se from other variables. Benefits attributed to writing and reading could therefore have been confounded with the influence of schooling, commerce, and perhaps even upper class position. While further research is needed to determine the impact of writing instruments on cognition, it is obvious that tools have enhanced other modalities of consciousness such as aesthetic sensitivity by potentiating music, painting, sculpture, and other arts.

Automation has had at least as great an impact on stimulating consciousness as simple tools have. Sacks (1989, p. 95) observes that the ease with which personal computers allow information to be spatially transformed (relocated, rotated) has led to an expansion of the ability to cognitively transform topological space. This ability was distinctly rare in the pre-computer age. Automation has additionally diversified and elevated many job skills, and it has increased leisure time, all of which affords great opportunity for enriching thought. Automation has also stimulated peoples' interests and desires by holding out the almost unlimited possibility of products. Of course, automation has had many deleterious effects on consciousness because of the social misuses to which it has been put, however these should not obscure its existing benefits and its enormous emancipatory potential.

Tool use fosters consciousness by imparting a sense of mastery of things. The tool user develops the attitude that he can use things to serve himself. To use objects is to impart a use to them, to make them do what they don't do naturally, to make them "for-oneself" rather than "in-themselves." This stimulates purposiveness and intentionality.

Tool use also spurs abstract thinking. Using objects instrumentally entails freeing them from a particular locale and moving them to another set of relationships. This spatial and functional decontextualization requires a consciousness that is not situation-bound. Consciousness must have some inkling of future possibilities, i.e., of the possibility that if "A" *were* brought over here it *could* be used in such and such a manner to *bring about* "B." And when the premonition is not entirely successful—when the object fails its intended purpose—the craftsman must be willing to systematically experiment in order to achieve the correct fit (Parker, 1985, p. 94).

Tool use stimulates abstract thinking in several ways. First, the need, goal, or problem is conceptualized in general, categorical terms. For instance, a "distance must be bridged." Objects are then sought which possess the necessary property, also conceived abstractly. One looks for "a long object" where length is the criterion property, abstracted from other features: we look for any suitably long object, not this particular object. Both the problem and the instrument are conceived in abstract terms in order to conjoin these two very different things. In terms of immediate appearance, there is no resemblance between the problem situation (e.g., a bolt that is immovable) and the instrument (a wrench). Matching a tool to the problem requires an abstract equivalence of the object's and the tool's properties. For example, the strength of the tool-object is compared with the heaviness of the goal-object, or the delicacy of the tool is matched against the fragility of the objective (cf. Koffka, 1959, pp. 209-212).

Another aspect of consciousness that is causally and teleologically fostered by tool use is self-control and the ability to postpone immediate need-satisfaction. The tool user does not directly or immediately satisfy his need. Rather, he must first find or make the appropriate tool with which to obtain the goal-object. He uses tools to transport and process the goal-object before it is consumed. Bernard (1942) expresses this self-control well when he states:

> Man was the first animal to be domesticated, and his domestication was the product of that discipline and regularization which came with the invention of mechanical instruments and processes and their use as a means to a more effective individual or collective adjustment to nature and to culture. When man began to invent instruments of hunting and fishing, he not only increased the quantity of his food supply but he subjected himself to greater regularity and discipline in labor. The non-producing gatherer gleans from nature only when he is hungry, but the hunter must work between meals and on rainy and cold days in order to produce the weapons of the chase. This labor is exacting, and each increase in the skill of workmanship is accompanied by greater discipline of hand and brain and closer application to his task. (p. 735)

Foresight motivates humans to work even when not impelled by biological need, in order to prepare for the time when that need will arise. Such preparation and temporary postponement of satisfaction lead to much greater, or at least more regular, satisfaction later on.

Once technology is institutionalized, it acts causally as well as teleologically. It structures the manner in which information comes to people—as pictorial representations on the media or as live encounters, as witnessed from the back of a camel or from an airplane. It determines the speed at which information is received and the multiplicity of tasks that can be performed simultaneously. Teaching children to use writing, drawing, painting, and musical instruments forms their consciousness accordingly to the implements' imperatives. The representations that are produced encourage representational thinking and imagination. In other words, representational products such as pictures are models for representational, symbolic thinking. People think symbolically because symbols have proven representational value.

While tools generate consciousness, they are dialectically dependent upon it also. As Isaac (1978) notes, only the development of truly human consciousness and culture in *Homo sapiens* about 40,000 years ago enabled tools to be used and manufactured significantly.

> The earlier tools from the period under consideration here seem to me to show a simple and opportunistic range of forms that reflect no more than an uncomplicated empirical grasp of one skill: how to fracture stone by percussion in such a way as to obtain fragments with sharp edges. At that stage of toolmaking the maker imposed a minimum of culturally dictated forms on his artifacts. . . . There is marked contrast between the pure opportunism apparent in the shapes of the earliest stone tools and the orderly array of forms that appear later in the Old Stone Age where each form is represented by numerous standardized examples in each assemblage of tools. The contrast strongly suggests that the first toolmakers lacked the highly developed mental and cultural abilities of more recent humans. (p. 104)

The interdependence of consciousness and tools is manifested in their correlation over the course of phylogeny. Animals deficient in consciousness also lack tools, while advanced consciousness is associated with sophisticated tool use and manufacture. Animals up through lower mammals are essentially incapable of using tools. Birds occasionally use a twig to probe insects or larvae out of wood, or they hold a small pebble in their beaks to pound some item of food. However, these cases are exceptional and occasional rather than regular. Moreover, the "tools" are extremely simple and are quite closely tied to the accompanying bodily action. The tool does not facilitate new actions. For example, the pebble is incorporated into the bird's natural pecking motion and does not significantly extend the animal's power. In addition, lower animals' use of objects is quite spontaneous and impulsive, caught up in a moment of excitement or need, and then abandoned. There is no sustained, deliberate use of tools, and no comprehension of the instrumental function, per se.

For example, birds can learn to pull on a string that will open a door. However, they do not comprehend any means-end relationships and instead mechanically peck at the string as a thing unto itself. After the "pulling habit" has been learned, if the string is moved the bird fails to follow it to the new location and continues to peck at the old position despite the absence of the string (Schneirla, 1972, p. 67). With the conscious functions necessary for genuine tool use missing, objects cannot be used instrumentally; and without tools, consciousness cannot develop. Lower animals are dominated by natural functions and fixed in given ecological niches. They cannot stand back from nature, process it (i.e., comprehend, analyze, generalize, deduce, remember, or even feel it), or transform it.

Dogs manifest somewhat greater ability to understand and use tools. In comparison with birds, they more readily learn to pull on the aforementioned string. And they pursue it when it has been moved to a new location. Monkeys and apes, of course, manifest the most sophisticated tool use among animals, although differences between the two species should not be overlooked. Monkeys' tool use is restricted to situations where the instrumental property of an object is obvious. For instance, "monkeys will not employ a stick or a rake in order to attain fruit, unless the tool is placed in a proper position as, for instance, the rake already behind the fruit and its handle within easy reach. If the tool is less favorably situated it is never used" (Koffka, 1959, p. 212). Apes can grasp more distant and indirect means-ends relationships, and they can more drastically transform objects in order to make them suitable to novel situations (Ladygina-Kots, 1969, pp. 45-51).

Jane Goodall has found apes to strip leaves off a twig to make it fit into tiny crevices, and Kohler's apes are legendary for their manipulation of objects. Perhaps the most startling use of tools by an animal was demonstrated by Rafael, a twelve-year-old chimp studied in the 1930s by one of Pavlov's colleagues, Vatsuro (Ladygina-Kots, 1969, pp. 66-67). Confronted by a container of burning alcohol which blocked access to food, Rafael reportedly learned to pick up the container, take it over to a water tank, open the faucet, pour water into the container, and thus extinguish the fire. As if this were not sufficiently astonishing, in the absence of water, Rafael would urinate into a container and pour the urine on the fire to extinguish it!

These accomplishments certainly reflect some diminution of natural constraints on activity and an overcoming of the natural order of things. Apes have a comparatively sophisticated consciousness that perceives rather abstract relationships among things, imagines novel properties and relationships, and alters things in line with an imposed purpose. On the other hand, these accomplishments remain rudimentary in a number of ways. First of all, they are for the most part achieved under specific training and prodding (Kohler, 1956, p. 101) in highly artificial, simplified, structured situations which are conducive to finding a solution to the problems that have been arranged.[25] Even with all of this assistance, only a handful of apes manage to achieve success on complex problems. In addition, their tool use remains clumsy, irregular, imprecise, simple, and limited to manipulations that closely follow the obvious contours of the problem situation.[26] Leontiev (1981, pp. 306-307) correctly concludes that all of these limitations indicate that apes lack the fundamental cognitive capacity to use tools, however much they may occasionally successfully manipulate one or another instrument: "Although apes can develop particular actions with simple implements, the principle of implement activity itself is beyond their reach."

The reason for apes' rudimentary tool use is that, as we have seen in the preceding sections, they remain governed by natural organismic controls which preclude significant technological mediations. Although these controls are less powerful than among lower animals, they, nevertheless, exert a powerful inhibitory influence on apes' comprehension and manipulation of objects. Most of apes' tool use is rooted in innate behavioral tendencies. Ladygina-Kots (1969, pp. 50, 61) has observed that apes' ability to break off branches and other objects from larger wholes and then use the parts as tools derives from a natural propensity toward breaking branches for use in nest-building. Given the presence of a tree with branches, apes will have little difficulty breaking off a part which is the first step toward finding a long tool. Schiller (1976) further notes that apes have a natural tendency to tear or break things when frustrated, and this propensity surely aids them in appropriating a branch as a tool. Thus, "that a chimpanzee breaks off a branch if excited has nothing to do with his desire to get at the food" (p. 236). The obtained stick is then brought to bear on the distant object because of another natural tendency rather than intelligence: apes naturally probe and poke with objects and this tendency easily develops into hitting at the distant objective placed out of reach. These comments are not meant to deny all intelligence to apes, but rather to show its limitation by natural tendencies. Intelligence and tool use only flourish in man where natural controls are absent (Hallowell, 1962a, pp. 238-240; K.R.L. Hall, 1968a).

With the interdependence of consciousness and tools, and consciousness and sociality having been discussed, it only remains left for us to indicate the interrelationship of tool use and sociality.

Tool use and sociality stand in the same dialectical relationship as tool use and consciousness. On the one hand, tools profoundly affect society and actually constitute its indispensable precondition. For tools enabled primitive man to kill and dismember game larger than what he needed for his own individual survival, thus making food sharing possible (cf. Engels, 1876/1964). In addition, early tools were used for transporting surplus food (including meat, fruits, and vegetables) to a home base where they could be distributed to group members. "Without devices for carrying foodstuffs there could not be a division of labor and organized food sharing" (Isaac, 1978, p.102). Finally, tools raise productivity to a point which creates the leisure time necessary for conducting complex social activities such as social planning, distribution of products, educating the young, and care for the aged.

On the other hand, sociality contributes to tool use. There must have been some initial social concern for supporting others and sharing food with them, which inspired primitive man to utilize tools for killing large game and transporting it back to the home base (cf. Lovejoy, 1981, who points out that socialized eating acted as a selective pressure for anatomical changes such as bipedalism which freed the hands for carrying food back to the home base).

Community goals and practices also provide the impetus for devising specific instruments as Bernal (1954) makes clear in his social history of technology. Instruments then transmit these social practices to individuals, thereby molding their psychology. Norbert Elias (1978) explains how eating utensils perform just such a function. According to Elias, contemporary eating utensils reflect individualized social relations and a modern sense of privacy. Eating instruments are interposed between the individual and the common food supply in such a way as to force a separation upon people which parallels broader socioeconomic relations. A serving spoon or fork transfers food from a serving dish onto the individual's plate. From there, he uses his own utensil to carry the food to his mouth. The elaborate set of culinary mediations between group and individual may be diagrammed as follows:

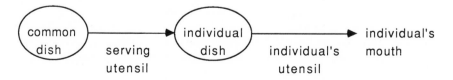

These culinary mediations transmit privatized socioeconomic relationships into the most private, personal act of eating with one's family at home. The instruments separate each individual's contact with the common food source (serving plate). They make it physically difficult and aesthetically repulsive to directly contact food that has been touched by another person. As such, culinary tools instantiate an entire sensibility of personal space, respectable behavior, and emotionality. By separating individual bodies from common contact, these instruments effectively decree that bodily functions of another person, as well as food that has been in contact with another person's body, elicit embarrassment and revulsion. Expressing the psychology that is embodied in eating utensils, Elias stated, "The fork is nothing other than the embodiment of a specific standard of emotions and a specific level of revulsion" (p. 127).

Medieval society had no such system of privatized socioeconomic or personal relations, and this was reflected in the eating utensils. Eating was communal, as individuals shared the few available utensils including forks and glasses. The same piece of food was even shared as partially eaten food was returned to the serving plate to be finished by someone else. Individuals were thus directly connected together rather than separated by eating tools. People took food by hand from the serving plate and brought it directly to their mouths; plates were uncommon. Communal eating habits entailed the public expression of bodily functions. Individuals wiped their hands and blew their noses on the tablecloth, cleaned their teeth with the communal knife, belched and spit freely. It was only with the rise of private, capitalist, socioeconomic relations that modern 'civilized' eating habits arose. Their physical objectification in the fork became widespread only after the sixteenth century (Elias, 1978).

These changes in eating technology were paralleled in the structure of houses. Medieval houses typically consisted of large common rooms in which many functions occurred. Aries (1962) tells us that the feudal living room not only served as an entertainment area, but an eating and sleeping area as well. At night, beds would be erected and everyone present, including guests, would sleep in the same room. Bourgeois architecture, in contrast, segregated individuals in separate rooms, and segregated different activities in different rooms. Modern architecture structured an entire sensibility of personal space, respectable behavior, and corresponding emotionality (Clark, 1976).

In conclusion, tools, sociality, and consciousness are interconnected and mutually dependent. Each is both cause and effect of the others; neither could exist without the others. Any rise of one stimulates the

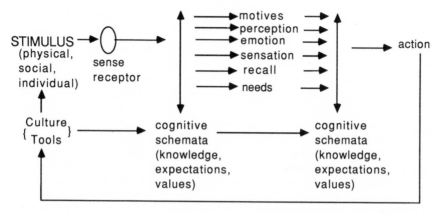

Figure 3. Cognitive schemata, derived from society and technology, as mediations between stimuli, psychological funcions, and action.

rise of others which, in turn, facilitates the one's own growth. None of the three emerged full-fledged prior to the others; they all gradually developed through a process of reciprocal interaction.

The main implication of these dialectical interrelations for psychology is that consciousness forms in, and embodies the form of, social relations and technology. The capacity for consciousness does not develop autonomously. Instead, consciousness requires participation in social and technological activity. This practical activity shapes consciousness's form, content, and level of development. A full depiction of consciousness in relation to technology as well as culture is diagrammed in Figure 3.

Figure 3 summarizes the tenets of sociohistorical psychology as follows: Culture and technology foster consciousness teleologically and causally. Consciousness therefore embodies the character of its formative cultural and technological mediations, and its form, content, and level of development reflect cultural and technological mediations. This social consciousness mediates the impact of impinging stimuli. Emotions, sensations, motives, needs, perception, and recall are integral parts of social consciousness and are imbued with its social, conscious character. Finally, individuals act on the stimulus world through the intermediaries of technology and social institutions.

The remainder of this book is devoted to verifying this social psychological model.

Notes

1. Freudian psychoanalysis is therefore incorrect to insist that parents treat psychosexual needs in certain particular ways, and to condemn other manners as pathogenic (cf., Orlansky, 1949, and Chapter 6 below).
2. See the entire issue of *Scientific American*, Sept. 1960, for articles on these aspects of human evolution.
3. The fact that volitional consciousness is necessary for comprehending the world means that subjectivity and objectivity are correlates, not antagonists as commonly supposed. Objectivity depends on and enhances subjectivity, just as subjectivity depends upon and enhances objectivity: comprehending the full range of an object's properties and its relationships with other objects requires an agent who interprets, deliberates, analyzes, modifies and tests things. Conversely, individuals can only develop and realize their subjective purposes if they possess objective information. Humans' advanced consciousness means that we are more objective *and* subjective than animals.

    The fact that objectivity and subjectivity are correlates, not antagonists frequently escapes psychologists who seek to explain intelligent behavior in natural terms devoid of subjectivity. Behaviorists, for example, explain the objective acquisition of knowledge in terms of direct stimulus-response associations; psychobiologists and sociobiologists posit more biological determinants of human knowledge. However, all attempts at explaining the acquiring and processing of information in natural or mechanical terms are erroneous because natural and mechanical mechanisms are antagonistic to objective comprehension.
4. The inverse relationship between speed of maturation and the level of cognitive achievement is confirmed in rats where artificially accelerated neural maturation leads to impaired intelligence (Gould, 1977, p. 351).
5. The importance of social protection for consciousness is proven by the fact that animals raised in protective captivity develop more sophisticated consciousness than conspecifics (of the same species) raised in natural conditions where they face pressures of survival. Socially protected, or "ecologically released" (emancipated), animals evidence more learning, greater variety of action, and better problem solving ability in contrast to naturally reared conspecifics who are dominated by a small number of fixed action patterns (Chiszar, 1981, p. 89).
6. T.C. Schneirla arrives at precisely this conclusion in discussing ants' social life and communication. Comparing the synchronized marching of ants to human social behavior, Schneirla and Piel (1948) state: "Men, too, can act as a mob. These analogies are the stock-in-trade of the 'herd instinct' schools of sociology and politics . . .

    "We are required, however, to look beyond the analogy and study the relationship of the pattern to other factors of individual and group behavior in the same species. In the case of the army ant, of course, the circular column really typifies the animal. Among mammals, such simplified mass behavior occupies a clearly subordinate role. Their group activity patterns are chiefly characterized by great plasticity and capacity to adjust to new situations. This observation applies with special force to the social potentialities of man. When human societies begin to march in circular columns, the cause is to be found in the straitjacket influence of the man-made social institutions which foster such behavior. The phenomenon of milling, it turns out, has entirely different causes and functions at different levels of social organization. The differences, furthermore, so far outweigh the similarities that they strip the 'herd instinct' of meaning.

"The same reservations apply to the analogies cited to support the superorganism theory of 'communication.' Among ants it is limited to the stimulus of physical contact. One excited ant can stir a swarm into equal excitement. But this behavior resembles the action of a row of dominoes more than it does the communication of information from man to man. The difference in the two kinds of 'communication' requires two entirely different conceptual schemes and preferably two different words.

"As for 'specialization of functions,' that is determined in insect societies by specialization in the biological make-up of individuals. Mankind, in contrast, is biologically uniform and homogeneous. Class and caste distinctions among men are drawn on a psychological basis . . .

"Finally, the concept of 'organization' itself, as it is used by the superorganism theorists, obscures a critical distinction between the societies of ants and men. The social organizations of insects are fixed and transmitted by heredity. But members of each generation of men may, by exercise of the cerebral cortex, increase, change and even displace given aspects of their social heritage."

7. Poirier (1973, pp. 26-27) and Hinde (1983, pp. 154-159) report several fascinating accounts of how aggression is socialized in monkeys. In the first place, mothers treat male and female infants quite differently. Males are punished and rejected while females are restricted and protected. This leads males to be more independent, playful, and aggressive. Furthermore, rhesus monkeys evidence an extremely high correlation between a juvenile's position in the dominance hierarchy and that of its mother's position. For both male and female offspring, the correlation with their mother's rank is greater than 0.77. One reason for this is that infants observe and imitate their mother's aggressiveness or timidity. Mothers high in the dominance hierarchy protect their infants bravely without cowering, screaming, or retreating. Low-ranking mothers express these timid reactions frequently.

Even more interesting is the fact that lineage determines the manner in which other members of the group treat the young even in the absence of the mother. High-ranked lineage juveniles are frequently protected by other adults besides the mother, whereas middle- or low-ranked monkeys rarely receive such protection. Finally, the latter are frequently threatened by other monkeys in contrast to the high-ranked which are rarely threatened. As monkeys mature, males engage in competitive struggles with other males, and their individual strength determines their success and later position in the dominance hierarchy. Females, on the other hand, maintain the rank that accrued to them as a result of their lineage, and their rank consequently remains highly correlated with that of their mother's. Female rankings are obviously much more stable than those of males.

Miller et al. (1967) experimentally demonstrated the crucial importance of social experience for monkeys' perception of emotional gestures in others. Ingeniously modifying the instrumental conditioning avoidance paradigm, Miller presented a conditioned stimulus preceding a shock which could be avoided by making a bar press during the CS-UCS interval. However, the CS and UCS were presented to one monkey while the bar press had to be made by a second monkey who could only observe the first one's facial expressions but not the actual presentation of the CS itself. Socially reared "responder" monkeys had no difficulty detecting the "stimulus" monkey's expression to the CS onset and making the appropriate avoidance response 77% of the time. Socially isolated monkeys, however, had great difficulty *discerning* the "stimulus" monkey's expression and therefore only made avoidance responses 7% of the time.

Interestingly, when isolates served as stimulus monkey for normal subjects, they were fairly *expressive* about the CS onset, for the normal responders made avoidance responses 62% of the time. (And isolates were fully capable of learning the usual avoidance paradigm when they were directly presented with the CS-UCS contingency and had to make the avoidance response themselves.)

8. The following lengthy description by Washburn and Hamburg (1965a) illustrates some of the natural constraints on learning:

> In Nairobi Park, Devore had begun to study a large group of more than 80 baboons, which could easily be approached in a car. A local parasitologist shot two of these baboons with a .22 rifle, and 8 months later this group was still "wild" and could not be approached, even though the animals must have seen cars almost daily in the interval. The adaptive function of such behavior is striking: danger is learned in one trial and this kind of learning will not extinguish for a long time. It takes many, many neutral experiences, probably over years, to extinguish one violent experience. It should be especially noted in the baboon incident described above that it is very unlikely all the animals in the group saw the shooting; the experience of some of the animals became part of the whole group's adaptive behavior. In contrast to this, it has been found by the Japanese, who not only have provisioned monkeys but also have deliberately introduced new foods and studied their adoption, that it may take months for a new, pleasant food habit to spread to all the members of the group. In the case of fear, survival is at stake and a minimum experience produces maximum result. In the case of a new eating habit, it is probably even advantageous that a new food be tried slowly. Adaptation under natural conditions shows clearly why it is essential for fear to be quickly learned and hard to extinguish. (pp. 3-4)

Human learning, in contrast, shows no particular directedness due to natural influences. We learn to enjoy new foods as quickly as we learn to fear dangers. And conversely, we can use reason to understand the causes of danger, and to quickly overcome many fears.

Poirier (1973) notes another interesting naturalistic feature of subhuman primate learning which is absent in humans, namely its sex-typing. "Nilgiri langur infants and males are more apt to accept new foods than females, suggesting that adult males are less conservative in their behavioral patterns (and therefore perhaps more adaptable) than adult females. Females seem to be more conservative in their behavior. This may be adaptative, for an adventurous female not only risks her own life, but her infant's also" (p. 23).

9. Lauer and Handel (1977) amplify this description of unsuccessful cooperation among chimpanzees:

> It is among chimpanzees that the highest level of cooperation, other than that achieved by humans, has been experimentally observed. But it exhibits only the barest beginning of teamwork as we know it in man. . . . [E]ven this was achieved in an artificial experimental setting which needed the planning of the human experimenter. Two chimpanzees were taught separately to pull a weighted box with food in it to within their reach by means of an attached rope. The box was then made too heavy for either one to move by its individual efforts. Two ropes were attached and the two chimps were placed in the same cage. At first the two chimpanzees pulled without reference to one another and did not learn to cooperate even when occasional simultaneous pulls resulted in moving the box. The *experimenter* was able to induce cooperation by giving a signal that each had separately learned as a cue to pull the rope. After coordination was established, the signal was no longer needed to achieve cooperative efforts. (pp. 27-28; emphasis added)

Kohler (1956) provides some amusing descriptions of apes' inability to cooperate when no human guidance is offered. In fact, he concludes that, "Mutual obstruction is more frequent than cooperation" (p. 152). "It is only rarely that one animal *helps* another, and when this happens, we must carefully consider the meaning of such action. . . . The 'help' he offers at the critical moment is simply *a heightening of his already indicated participation in the process*; and interest in the other animal can play only a very secondary part, for Sultan is a pronounced egoist . . ." (p. 149).

Sometimes the behavior of the animals resembles collaboration in the human sense, without, however, being genuinely so. In one instance, three apes managed to collectively push a box nearly underneath a hanging objective. However, it was apparent that each was only doing what it would have individually, although it did so simultaneously as the others also pushed. The absence of genuine cooperation is described by Kohler:

> [The box] was still at a little distance when Sultan bounded upon it and then, with a second spring, secured and tore down the fruit. The others received no reward, but then, *they had worked for themselves* and not for Sultan,

who had good reason to take a sudden dash forward, for otherwise he might
have been 'done out of it.' (ibid., p. 151; emphasis added)

10. The emotional-expressive, rather than symbolic, nature of nonhuman
primates' communication has a neuroanatomical as well as a social basis.
For example, monkey sounds are evoked principally from the limbic system
of the brain which also mediates emotional and autonomic behaviors.
Human language, in contrast, is localized in the neocortex where it is intimately connected to symbolic activity and placed under volitional control
(B. Robinson, 1972).

11. Many psychologists and linguists argue that the test situations were structured in such a way that did not rule out the possibility of nonlinguistic
strategies accounting for apes' linguistic achievements. The analyses of Herbert Terrace (1979, 1980), and the articles included in Sebeok and Sebeok's
(1980) volume raise a host of problems associated with the studies. These
include errors in recording/classifying responses, imprecise description of
procedures followed, ambiguous data (e.g., failure to specify the referents
of numbers in tables), partial presentation of data—Premack claims that Sarah
learned 130 symbols, but only presents 48 of them [Sebeok & Sebeok, 1980,
pp. 392-393])—and subtle prompting by the experimenters which may indicate the correct answer (ibid., pp. 34-36). Thus, many of the results reported
are not replicated when neutral experimenters are used who do not know
the symbolic system or who are less emotionally involved with the animals
and the entire project (ibid., pp. 41-44).

12. This cooperative process is detailed by Solomon Asch. In his book *Social
Psychology* (1952), which brilliantly elucidates psychology's social character,
Asch describes the joint activity of two boys carrying a log:

> A first condition is that each should have the goal in mind and understand
> the effort needed to overcome the difficulty. With this common goal and
> understanding the two apply themselves *jointly* to carrying the log. What does
> this statement mean concretely? It means that the boys are fitting their actions
> to each other and to the object and are involved in a give-and-take requiring
> considerable sensitiveness. The two do not apply force in succession, or in
> opposite directions; they bring a common force to bear simultaneously. If
> one moves somewhat faster or swerves slightly, the other adapts his movement
> correspondingly. There is an immediate, direct communication between them
> through the object. . . . Here is a unity of action that embraces the partic-
> ipants and the common object.
>   This performance is a new product, strictly unlike what each would do
> singly and also unlike the sum of their separate exertions (although physically
> one can represent the present instance as an addition of forces). . . . We
> have not a mere addition of forces, but an organization of effort. (Asch,
> 1952, pp. 173-4)
>   In such instances the essential factor is the presence of *different and com-
> plementary actions executed simultaneously and with reference to each other*. This is
> the fundamental form of cooperation. (ibid., p. 175)

13. The social basis of communication is reflected in the etymology of communicate which derives from the Latin *communicare* and *communis*, meaning "to share in common."

14. Of course, property rights and negotiation are only certain societal features which stimulate logical thinking. They are not intended to be exhaustive, and other societal features such as kinship may also stimulate logical thinking, even in the absence of complex property rights and negotiated arbitration.

15. Actually, direct instruction of youngsters is more characteristic of humans than of nonhuman primates where indirect modeling is the rule (Poirier, 1973, p. 22; Kaye, 1982, p. 97).

16. The social improvement of cognitive functions confirms their functional autonomy from biological processes. For improvement is achieved without any biological intervention. This supports Vygotsky's insight that higher cognitive operations are the most educable. "The more elementary, and consequently the more directly biologically determined, a particular function is, the more it eludes the guiding hand of education; moreover, the higher a function or a structure is in evolutionary terms, the more educable and re-educable it is" (Vygotsky, 1987b, p. 93; Leontiev, 1981, pp. 132-155).

17. In his 1909 book, *Modern Ideas About Children*, Binet lashed against the "brutal pessimism" and the "deplorable verdicts" of those conceptualizing individual intelligence as a fixed quantity. Binet argued for an optimistic conception of intelligence as augmentable by training which he termed "mental orthopedics." Binet gleefully reported the success of one such memory-enhancement exercise:

> I remember when the deputies [of Parliament] visited our classes and assisted in this exercise. Some, intrigued, asked to try the experiment themselves; and they succeeded very much less well than the little patients—to the astonishment, laughs, mockeries of their colleagues. . . . In reality all could be explained. Our deputies had not taken account of the intensive training our students had received. (cited in Fancher, 1985, p. 79)

18. Although certain of the foregoing studies are methodologically flawed (H. Spitz, 1986), the bulk of them do demonstrate the preponderant effect of experience on cognitive ability.

Studies marshaled in support of the hereditarian position have been soundly criticized by Montagu, 1975; Lewontin, 1984, chap. 5; Kamin, 1974; Bowles and Gintis, 1972; Jencks, 1972; Kagan, 1978a, chap. 8; Schiff and Lewontin, 1986. One criticism in particular concerns the flawed methodology of a series of studies on identical twins separated early in life, and raised in separate homes. Because the IQs of pairs of twins were found to be highly correlated, despite the fact that their environments were different, this was taken as proof that IQ is inherited. Long ago, Hunt pointed out a fatal flaw in the design which invalidates any conclusions drawn from the correlation of IQs. That is, "The fact that twins are reared separately need not mean that their encounters with the environment differ appreciably in any psychologically significant way." "From an investigative standpoint, it is unfortunate that twins are seldom placed in homes that differ much in any way" (1961, p. 20). In other words, twins reared in separate homes can quite likely face similar circumstances if placed in families of a common culture. Kamin's (1974) painstaking examination of the adoption studies revealed that wherever any information was inadvertently provided by the researchers, it indicated substantial similarity in the actual home environments of the two twins.

A 1937 study by Newman, Freeman, and Holzinger was exceptional in that it did deliberately ascertain the social characteristics of the adopted families. These characteristics were correlated with the adoptees' IQ: Twins reared in similar environments showed a correlation of 0.91, whereas for those reared in less similar environments the coefficient was 0.42 (Montagu, 1975, p.121). The educational level of the adopted families was particularly highly correlated with adoptees' IQ. The *difference* (discrepancy) between two twins' IQs, and the *difference* in their educational opportunity (educational level of adopted parents) correlated +.79! Thus, given a constant gene pool, variation in educational opportunity can account for substantial differences in individuals' IQ (Hunt, 1961, pp. 19-20).

An improved variation of the typical adoption studies is to study families which have adopted a child and which also have their own natural child. Here, the environments of the two children are obviously similar although their genetic makeups are different. If the correlation between the mother's IQ and that of her natural child were higher than that between her IQ and the adopted child, we would be justified in concluding that genetic relationship is a stronger determinant of IQ than environment. Two recent studies employed this design and found no significant difference between the two correlations. One of the studies used black children adopted into white families. Even here, the correlation with the adopted mother was similar to that between the mother and her natural child. Thus, children reared by the same mother resemble her in IQ to the same degree, whether or not they share her genes (Lewontin, 1984, pp. 112-114).

Peculiarly enough, all of this evidence has failed to dislodge the hereditarian bias of most American psychologists, since 70% of them continue to believe that IQ is genetically determined (to some degree or another) (Snyderman & Rothman, 1987, p. 140).

19. Premack makes the identical point concerning the importance of language for abstract thinking in apes. He says:

> Once the chimpanzee has been exposed to language training, it can solve certain kinds of problems that it cannot solve otherwise. Specifically, it can solve problems on a conceptual rather than a sensory basis. For example, while the normal chimpanzee can match, say, half an apple with half an apple, or 3/4th cylinder of water with 3/4th cylinder of water, it is only after it has been language trained that it can match, say, 3/4th an apple with 3/4th cylinder of water, that is, match equivalent proportions of objects that do *not* look alike . . .

> Language training does not enhance all mental abilities but only those of the kind indicated. . . . Chimpanzees exposed to language training are not generally superior but superior only on a specific kind of task. (Premack, 1984, p. 182; Premack, 1983)

20. Humanistic psychology's failure to comprehend the social character of psychology is reflected in the notion that society simply aids the individual in actualizing his own inner needs and abilities rather than constructing those needs and abilities. According to Maslow,

> Man is ultimately *not* molded or shaped into humanness, or taught to be human. The role of the environment is ultimately to permit him to help him to actualize *his own* potentialities, not *its* potentialities. . . . Creativeness, spontaneity, selfhood, authenticity, caring for others, being able to love, yearning for truth are embryonic potentialities belonging to his species-membership just as much as are his arms and legs and brain and eyes. . . . A teacher or a culture doesn't create a human being. . . . Rather it permits, or fosters, or encourages or helps what exists in embryo to become real and actual. The same mother or the same culture, treating a kitten or a puppy in exactly the same way, cannot make it into a human being. The culture is sun and food and water: it is not the seed. (Maslow, 1968, pp. 160-161)

In one sense it is certainly true that everything man does is rooted in his capacity. However, this is mere tautology, and Maslow is saying more than this. He means that all of the aforementioned competencies exist not simply as capacities, but as tendencies which have an intrinsic intentionality and direction. Thus, we do not simply have the capacity for authenticity, we actually want to be authentic and intrinsically know how to be. In the same way, the seed is not merely the capacity to become a plant, it contains the information and the direction about how to become so. The environment simply nourishes these innate tendencies in humans as in plants.

It is curious that a humanist such as Maslow—who emphasizes the unique creativity of man—winds up with a decidedly naturalistic view of people in which human beings are comparable to plants!

21. Symbolic interactionism also favors interpersonal rather than impersonal or intrapersonal explanations of mind and self (cf. Blumer, 1969, p. 4). Drawing on this position, C.W. Mills (1963, pp. 429-430) said, "The stuff of ideas is not merely sensory experiences, but meanings which have back of them collective habits."

22. As Sahlins said, "Reference to the world is an act of classification in which realities are indexed to concepts in a relation of empirical tokens to cultural types" (Sahlins, 1985, p. 146).

23. Of course the cognitive schemas which mediate psychological operations are acquired through experience and are not present in infancy. As we shall discuss in Chapter 4, neonatal perception, sensation, and emotion are innately determined, unmediated reactions to stimuli. Socialization establishes cognitive schemas which transform these reactions into higher social-psychological functions and eliminates their natural character. From then on, per-

ception, sensation, and emotion are never "pure" processes independent of cognition. They are differentiated from, add information to, and modify consciousness, but are never independent of its schemas. Their dialectical relation to cognition takes the following form as articulated by Neisser (1976, p. 43):

> Perception does not merely serve to confirm preexisting assumptions, but to provide organisms with new information. Although this is true, it is also true that without some preexisting structure, no information could be acquired at all. There is a dialectical contradiction between these two requirements: We cannot perceive *unless* we anticipate, but we must not see *only* what we anticipate. . . . The upshot of the argument is that perception is directed by expectations but not controlled by them.

24. Unfortunately, contemporary pedagogy has failed to keep pace with these developments and continues to insist on individual memorization rather than encourage the resourceful seeking of collaboratively stored information.

25. For instance, in Kohler's experiments where apes had to fit sticks together in order to make a long enough tool to reach a piece of food, there was only one possible way to put the sticks together. When Vatsuro provided Rafael with more possibilities of combination, he was far less successful: When one of the sticks had 3 side holes in addition to the hole in the end, Rafael first inserted the second stick into the side holes, forming a T-shaped object which was too short to reach the objective. Only after many errors did Rafael finally succeed in joining the two sticks end to end—which Kohler's chimp had done immediately. Even then, Rafael did not immediately retrieve the objective, but left the new tool aside. This, coupled with the fact that on later tests he repeated all the previous errors over again, indicates that he had not comprehended the character of the problem or of his solution (Ladygina-Kots, 1969, pp. 62-63).

26. In Kohler's words:

> Even sticks that have already been used often both by Tschego and Koko seem to lose all their functional or instrumental value, if they are at some distance from the critical point. More precisely: if the experimenter takes care that the stick is not visible to the animal when gazing directly at the objective—and that, vice versa, a direct look at the stick excludes the whole region of the objective from the field of vision—then, generally speaking, recourse to this instrument is either prevented or, at least, greatly retarded, even when it has already been frequently used. I have used every means at my disposal to attract Tschego's attention to the sticks in the background of her cage and she did look straight at them; but, in doing so, she turned her back on the objective, and so the sticks remained meaningless to her. (1956, pp. 35-36)

Similarly:

> One fact must be noted in reference to the breaking off of pieces from boxes, etc.: not everything that is obviously "*a part*" for man, is so for the chimpanzee. If a box be left with only its lid, and if this half consist of

separate boards, the chimpanzee will not always behave in the same way, whichever way these "parts" are put together. If the separate boards are nailed to the box in such a way that they make an unbroken surface, i.e., the joints not noticeable, the chimpanzee will not easily see "possible sticks" there, even if he be in urgent need of them; but if the last board towards the open half of the box is nailed in such a way that a small space or crack separates it from the next, it will be immediately torn off . . . [Humans] will dissolve visual wholes of much greater firmness [i.e., coherence, unity]; or, to be more exact, under the same objective conditions, visual wholes are probably more easily analyzed by the adult human than by the chimpanzee. Man is more likely to see "parts" when he needs them, than the ape. (ibid., pp. 99-100)

2

Psychology's Concrete Social Character

Sociality and technology are not simply general underpinnings which yield an amorphous consciousness. Quite the contrary, sociality and technology exist as specific social-technological systems which endow consciousness with particular form and content. Consciousness only emerges in the struggle to comprehend, create, and transform a particular social, technological, and physical reality. Accordingly, consciousness's activity and organization are thoroughly imbued with that reality. The features of psychology that were described in Chapter 1 are only abstractions that have been intellectually lifted from sensuous life activity. The statement that "thought is stimulated by language" is a summary description of the fact that different kinds of language exist which stimulate quite different kinds of thinking. The summary description is abstract in the sense that it extracts a common quality from the different instances. The instances are concrete in that they are integrated configurations of numerous real properties. While abstractions are real in the sense that different particulars do have common qualities, abstractions must always be recognized as emanating from concrete particulars; they do not exist in and of themselves.[1] Beneath the serene, imperturbable homogeneity of abstractions lies a vibrant, discordant concreteness. The comfortable, secure feel of invariant abstractions is only the external shell of a most unstable, variable lived struggle to produce concrete phenomena. Accordingly, psychological abstractions such as thinking, feeling, perceiving, learning, and communicating must be grounded in sensuous life activity. Psychology is the psychology of real, living individuals engaged in a definite mode of social life and intercourse with nature. Psychological functions are not independent of practical life. As Vygotsky (1989, p. 65) said, "It is not thought that thinks; a person thinks."

69

Expressing the sociohistorical nature of psychological phenomena, Luria said that consciousness is "not given in advance, unchanging and passive, but shaped by activity and used by human beings to orient themselves to their environment, not only in adapting to conditions but in restructuring them" (Luria, 1976, p. 8). "Cognitive processes (such as perception and memory, abstraction and generalization, reasoning and problem-solving) are not independent and unchanging 'abilities' or 'functions' of human consciousness; they are processes occurring in concrete, practical activities and are formed within the limits of this activity" (Luria, 1971, p. 226; cf. D'Andrade, 1981; Pepitone & Triandis, 1987). Since psychological phenomena are tools for aiding our adaptation and development, they must be fashioned in accordance with the particular environments in which they function. This chapter will demonstrate that people in different societies literally feel, think, sense, perceive, remember, and construe their individuality differently. The following examples will validate the sociohistorical model, depicted in Figures 2 and 3, that culture structures psychological functions through constructing the cognitive schemata on which these functions depend. In this way culture organizes both the form and content of psychological functions.

The Social Constitution and Variability of Content

Color Perception

Color perception reflects distinctions and concepts that are important to a definite socio-technological mode of life. The cultural distinctions and concepts that are embodied in color categories determine the colors' appearance or quality. For instance, green for Navahos is a large category which encompasses English green, blue, and purple (Ervin, 1961; cf. also Lenneberg & Roberts, 1956; Berlin & Kay, 1969, for other examples of categorization systems). Green, blue, and purple look similar to the Navahos, whereas they appear categorically different to us. Cultural concepts and categories are not posterior to some primordial, nonceptual sensation and perception. Quite the contrary, concepts and categories determine the sensed and perceived appearance of colors, as depicted in Figure 3.

Culturally generated differences in color perception were convincingly demonstrated by Luria (1976). He compared backward Russian farmers with administrators working on large, complex collective farms in the 1930s. Color perception was ascertained by presenting 27 colored skeins of wool and asking the subjects to categorize them. The administrators readily formed 7-8 groups of similar hues, and even complied with the request to reorganize the colors into five groups. The small farmers, however, found categorization extremely difficult, complaining that the colors were not the same and could not be grouped together. They formed a large number of small groups which were not even organized strictly according to hue, and included skeins of different color but similar brightness. When the farmers were requested to form five groups, none complied.

The farmers' discomfort over the categorization task was precipitated by their perception that the skeins did not appear similar to one another. In contrast, the administrators perceived them as similar. Although all subjects saw the colors, they saw them differently in the two societies.

The cultural differences in color perception are linked to linguistic differences in color terminology. Luria found that 60% of the peasants' color names were object names such as peach, spoiled cotton, cotton in bloom, decayed teeth, calf's dung, pig's dung. The administrators' color terms were predominantly (84%) decontextualized words such as blue and red which are disconnected from any specific object. The linguistic distinctions which segregate the color of pig's dung from cow's dung and tie them to different things promote perceptual distinctions. In contrast, generic color terms such as brown enable cow's dung and pig's dung to be categorized together as shades of brown.

Important confirmation of language's shaping of color perception is obtained from interesting experiments comparing bilingual with monolingual subjects. It has been found, for example, that bilingual Zunis categorize the color spectrum in a manner intermediate to monolingual Zunis and monolingual Americans (Lenneberg & Roberts, 1956, p. 30). Groups of bilingual Navaho subjects similarly categorized colors intermediate to monolingual Navahos and monolingual Anglos. Interestingly, each bilingual group reflected the predominance of its mother tongue in skewing the color perception toward that culture. Thus, English-dominant bilinguals categorized colors more in the manner that Anglos did, whereas Navaho-dominant bilinguals categorized colors more like the monolingual Navahos (Ervin, 1961).

Linguistically mediated cultural differences in color categorization involve far more than breadth. The entire concept of color varies, leading to highly discrepant perceptions. For instance, the Dani people in Indonesian New Guinea have two color terms which apparently mean something akin to light and dark. However, their use of the terms indicates that they mean something completely different from our sense of light and dark. Dani light and dark do not correspond to measurable brightness. When Heider and Olivier (1972) asked Dani subjects to name various color chips, the color chip 10 G (green) with a brightness of 8 was called "dark" while the chip 5 R (red) with a brightness of 3 was called light—despite the fact that 8 is measurably brighter than 3. The attributes which the Dani include in their concept of light and dark are therefore quite different from what we include. Their categorization system is not simply broader than ours, it is orthogonal to ours.

Another interesting example of this orthogonality is the Hanunoo of the Philippines. Conklin (1955) reports that the Hanunoo have a color system founded on entirely different attributes from ours. They have four basic color categories: Dark-black includes the range covered in English by black, violet, indigo, blue, dark green, dark gray, and deep shades of other colors. Light-white encompasses English white along with light shades of many colors. Red refers to our red, orange, and yellow. Green includes the English green, yellow, and light brown. In addition, however, these color categories also encompass achromatic features of things. Red includes dryness or desiccation and green includes wetness or succulence. Consequently, a shiny, wet, brown section of newly cut bamboo is called "green," not "red," although "red" ordinarily refers to brown things. Evidently, the Hanunoo do not organize colors together according to the same dimensions that we do. Whereas we see colors as varying according to hue and brightness of light, the Hanunoo have an entirely different scheme. Colors for them do not vary along these dimensions but rather along other dimensions which include the kind of object to which the color refers. They literally perceive colors according to categories of objects. In contrast, object-type has no impact on our color perception because we have abstracted color from object. The experiments of Kay and Kempton and Tajfel and Wilkes, described in Chapter 1, should be recalled as demonstrating the real perceptual effects that cognitive structures have. Color perception is not directly given by the stimulus properties. Rather, light wavelengths are symbolized (organized) as psychologically meaningful stimuli (*predmet*) and are perceived and responded to as such. Color is a socially constructed "secondary property" of light.

Auditory Perception

Auditory perception similarly embodies cultural distinctions and classifications. Discussing the cultural organization of auditory perception, Sapir observed:

> In a musical tradition which does not recognize chromatic intervals, "C" sharp would have to be identified with 'C' and would be considered as a mere deviation, pleasant or unpleasant, from "C." In our own musical tradition

the difference between "C" and "C sharp" is crucial to an understanding of all our music. . . . In still other musical traditions there are still finer intervallic differences recognized, none of which quite corresponds to our semitone interval. In these three cases it is obvious that nothing can be said as to the cultural and aesthetic status of a given tone in a song unless we know or feel against what sort of general tonal background it is to be interpreted. (Sapir, 1974, p. 41)

Olfactory Perception

Olfactory distinctions and the psychological threshold for odors are socially constructed. Alain Corbin's (1986) fascinating account demonstrates shifts in the perception of, and reaction to, odors among the various classes of French society between 1750 and 1880. Bourgeoisification of the sense of smell parallels that of eating customs described in Chapter 1 (Mitzman, 1987). In contrast to the early eighteenth century acceptance of odors emanating from omnipresent refuse, excrement, stagnant water, unwashed bodies, and even corpses in open vaults, a great intolerance for these smells developed after mid-century. Socially mediated cognitive schemas which associated bodily odor with filth altered olfactory sensations after 1750. Smells that were formerly either unnoticed or else experienced as pleasant, became perceived as noxious. The very quality of the olfactory sensation changed. Further demonstrating the social construction of smell is the fact that this transformation only occurred among the elite classes. The masses persisted in enjoying the smell of "foul" things which did not smell fetidly to them. In fact the masses recognized that the bourgeois sense of smell mandated, as well as reflected, a reorganization of social life and they opposed this. The masses aligned themselves against the bourgeoisie's deodorization practices and they continued to collectively sleep in beds, show no aversion to excrement and bodily functions, use "foul" language, and avoid bathing.

On purely sensory tests conducted in artificial, laboratory-like conditions, members of both classes may have been equally capable of detecting odors. However, as Sapir and Whorf point out, the perceptual experience was different, and this is the domain of psychology.

Size Constancy

The perception of size constancy also varies across societies. Investigating size constancy over a distance of 3 to 12 meters, Winter (1967) found that African Bushmen were far more accurate than other cultural groups. The order of accuracy was Bushmen (whose perception only deviated 0.21 cm. from perfect size constancy), followed by European employees in the South African scientific organization "National Institute for Personnel Research" (1.14 cm. from perfect size constancy), followed by Bantu N.I.P.R. employees (1.57 cm. from perfect size constancy), and European optometry students (2.76 cm. from perfect size constancy). A cultural, rather than a racial (i.e., physiological) explanation of these differences is called for by several salient facts. First of all, European N.I.P.R. staff members outperformed European optometry students despite similar racial stock. Secondly, Bantu N.I.P.R. members scored similarly to their European colleagues despite enormously different racial backgrounds. Finally, individual differences in size constancy performance among the Bushmen corresponded to different social experience. The few Bushmen who scored poorly in size constancy had had more Bantu and European contact than the Bushmen who were accurate (Winter, p. 56).

Although Winter does not offer a cultural explanation for the differences in size constancy, it is reasonable to assume that optometry students performed poorly because their scientific analytical attitude (which would be especially prominent when they serve as subjects in a perceptual experiment) leads them to isolate visual properties of things and to disregard the contextual cues that enhance size constancy. Size constancy is the result of a complex estimation that utilizes size and distance cues. Social experience affects reliance on these cues and the judging process that yields the perception of size constancy. It is well known that experimentally removing contextual cues eliminates constancy, and the analytical attitude of the optometrist would produce this kind of effect. This explanation could explain the kindred fact that art students, who also employ a trained, analytical perceptual perspective, tend to have significantly worse size constancy perception than other individuals (Winter, p. 45). Certainly, some kind of social experience is at work to engender size constancy differences within and between populations of people.

Spatial Perception

Another example of social experience affecting perceptual processes is male-female differences in spatial perception. Gender differences in this area reflect social roles which determine access to various kinds of experience. In Western societies, male superiority on spatial tests (such as recognizing a form embedded in a larger figure) is moderate; in other societies, such as Mexico, males perform far better than females; while in some societies, such as the Eskimos, there is no difference (Sherman,

1978, p. 141). These variations hinge on socially induced adult sex roles regarding male-female inequality. Where women are consigned to a rather sheltered environment and dependent upon men, they fail to develop spatial skills (at least those types measured by current spatial skills tests) to a high degree. On the other hand, when "despite [sexually] different social and economic roles, Eskimo women and children are in no way treated as dependent in the society," there was no significant difference on spatial tests (Berry, 1966, p. 225; Brooks, 1976).

These examples testify to the fact that,

> human space perception is biologically rooted, but the level at which it functions in the individual is not reducible to innate capacities or maturational development. The process of socialization contributes experiential components which must be considered. Some of these acquired components of space perception are a function of the cultural milieu in which the individual has been reared. The cultural patterns of different societies offer different means by which spatial perceptions are developed, refined, and ordered. (Hallowell, 1955, pp. 201-202)

Conceptual Categorization

Conceptual categorization also bears the imprint of socially provided language. Carroll and Casagrande's (1958) classic experiment demonstrates the congruence between language and concepts. The authors presented sets of three pictures to Hopi Indians and white Americans, and then asked the subjects which two were most closely related and could be classified together. For example, one set showed a man pouring fruit out of a box by holding it upside down (picture A); a coin dropping out of a man's pocket as he pulled out his handkerchief (B); and a man spilling liquid from a pitcher as he fails to concentrate on the glass into which he seeks to pour it (C). The Hopi language does not distinguish between pouring which accidentally results in spilling, and intentional pouring. Therefore it was hypothesized that Hopis would not emphasize the distinction cognitively, and would classify pictures A and C together as instances of pouring. "Anglos," on the other hand, conceptually and linguistically emphasize the distinction between accidental and intentional, and were therefore predicted to classify dropping and spilling together (B and C), in contrast to pouring. Most subjects in each group acted as expected, and also used the predicted reasons in explaining their choices.

Of course, language is not the only social influence on psychology. Other social experiences also affect psychological content, sometimes overriding linguistic distinctions. This is why words' etymologies are often anachronistic curiosities with little relevance to contemporary conceptualization. The fact that our word *Thursday* originally referred to a day that commemorated the god, Thor, is irrelevant to our modern, standardized sense of time (see below). While language is obviously not omnipotent in its influence, the foregoing examples demonstrate that its power to shape conceptual meaning is considerable.

Emotions

The social content of emotions is difficult to fathom because they are typically regarded as either the most personal or the most natural of psychological functions (cf. Chapter 4 and Ratner 1989a for a review of the naturalistic theory of emotions). However, emotions are as much a social psychological phenomenon as cognition, perception, and memory. This has been articulated by a school of thought known as "social constructionism" (cf. Harre, 1986; Shweder & LeVine, 1984; Kleinman & Good, 1985; Solomon, 1980; Averill, 1980a,b; Hochschild, 1979; Super & Harkness, 1982; Hallowell, 1955, chap. 13; Lazarus et al. 1970; Lazarus, et. al., 1980; Lewis & Michalson, 1983; Lutz, 1986b, 1988; Vygotsky 1987 "Emotions and Their Development in Childhood"). Social constructionists emphasize the inextricable interdependence of emotions on thinking, perceiving, and memory. Since the latter three functions are social phenomena, the emotions dependent upon them must also be. Averill explains the relationship between culture, consciousness, and emotions in a way that matches perfectly our model as diagrammed in Figure 2. He said: "The emotions are viewed here as transitory social roles, or socially constituted syndromes. The social norms that help to constitute these syndromes are represented psychologically as cognitive structures or schemata. These structures—like the grammar of a language—provide the basis for the appraisal of stimuli, the organization of responses, and the monitoring of behavior" (Averill, 1980b, pp. 305-306).

Emotions depend on a social consciousness concerning when, where, and what to feel as well as when, where, and how to act (cf. Lutz & White, 1986 for a summary of research into these social aspects of emotion.)[2] The culture provides a "niche" or "ethos" which is a set of guidelines for feeling. These feeling rules delineate emotional "rights and duties" and they derive from and support legal, moral, and social codes. Emotions are so socially functional that violating feeling rules is tantamount to developing a new social ideology and a new social system. For instance, the feminist demand for women to feel and act more assertively is nothing less than a demand for women to take on new social roles. As social ideologies and social systems change, they bring about new emotion norms (cf. Cancian & Gordon, 1988; Stearns & Stearns, 1986; Stearns, 1989).

A few emotions, such as joy, sadness, fear, and jealousy, have analogues in animals and human infants. But whereas "emotional reactions" in these organisms stem from natural processes, adult human emotions lose their natural, spontaneous basis and become mediated by social consciousness as described in Figure 2. Although the natural analogues to these emotions are interesting, and indicate an original natural basis, emotions in human adults are qualitatively different from their counterpart in organisms devoid of social consciousness. The analogy between them is consequently extremely inexact. For instance, "jealousy" among animals or human infants is a spontaneous desire to obtain a desirable object for oneself. It is rooted in a primitive, instinctual survival tendency. Adult, human jealousy, in contrast, presupposes a concept of exclusive ownership, a future-oriented premonition of losing something important and even losing self-esteem. All of these coalesce into the jealous feeling that one's lover loves another person. And they are absent from infantile and animal "jealousy." The fact that adult human jealousy is constructed from social concepts introduces the possibility of intra-species variation in jealousy, in contrast to the species-wide uniformity which characterizes biologically determined jealousy among animals and human infants. Cultures lacking appropriate concepts should not experience jealous feelings.

With feelings dependent upon social concepts, feelings can only be as universal as the concepts they embody. And concepts are only as similar as their societies. Consequently, "affects, whatever their similarities, are no more similar than the societies in which we live . . ." (Rosaldo, 1984, p. 145; cf. also Armon-Jones, 1986b, p. 66). Even universal emotions such as joy, sadness, and fear will evidence significant variation as a function of cultural particularities (Lutz, 1988, chap. 7).[3]

While a few emotions have natural analogues, most emotions, including shame, gratitude, obligation, anger, pity, regret, admiration, hatred, scorn, vengeance, love, and guilt, do not. Their lack of natural analogues should make their social character even more evident.

Anger, for example, presupposes a notion of intentional responsibility for a misdeed, since if I believe that the act was not the person's (or the group's) fault, I would not be angry at him. I might be disturbed that the misdeed occurred, but I would not feel anger. This is the case when someone inadvertently bumps us, whereas when they deliberately push us we do feel angry. Similarly, when our infant spits up on our shirt we are disturbed but not angry because we know it was an involuntary act. Thus, what distinguishes the feelings of anger and frustration is the concept of personal intention. Entire cultures, such as the Eskimos, evidently lack anger, according to Solomon (1984), because they do not blame individuals for their actions. They feel annoyed and even act violently, yet this is not equivalent to anger. Solomon takes pains to point out that the Eskimos do not merely suppress anger, they apparently do not feel it. As Armon-Jones (1986b, p. 80) observes, "an emotion must be generated before it can be prohibited" and the absence of appropriate concepts forestalls the generation of certain emotions.

Solomon's conclusion regarding the absence of anger among Eskimos is, of course, controversial and stands in need of confirmation. Even if it turns out to be repudiated, the possibility certainly exists that entire peoples may not experience anger—if they believe, for example, that misfortune is fate which must be accepted, or if they believe that misfortune is a test of their forbearance or a virtuous sign of humility. This possibility is easier to imagine if we disabuse ourselves of the reified notion that anger and other emotions are things (dispositions) intrinsic to our being, just waiting to be elicited. Once emotions are understood to be constructs which are invented to serve human purposes and are dependent on cognition, interpretation, and perception, variations in emotionality will appear quite plausible. If anger is discovered to be universally present among all of the world's people, this is because they have developed similar social concepts which foster the emotion, not because anger is naturally based.

Where anger does exist, it takes on different qualities depending upon the specific social concepts and practices at play. Rosaldo (1984) describes some unique expressions of anger among the Ilongot people of the Philippines which are based upon certain distinctive notions of anger. Because the Ilongots have a great fear of anger's potential to disrupt social relationships they immediately dissipate anger in order to ensure continuous amicable relations. One technique is to simply forget the anger. Rosaldo emphasizes that the Ilongots do not repress anger but literally forget it. It does not dwell within them, surreptitiously motivating indirect hateful acts. It is utterly squelched. Thus, Ilongot anger is not the same as ours but simply expressed differently. The different expression corresponds to a different notion of anger. The Ilongots consider anger as something quite tangible and controllable, whereas we regard anger as ineluctably part of our self which we have a right and a need to express, and cannot simply shut off as though it were alien to us. We can repress the anger but it continues to exude from our personal indignation. It appears inconceivable that we could distance ourselves from this facet of ourself (Lakoff & Kovecses, 1987). In other words, we consider anger personally, as part of our self which we must deal with in some way. The Ilongots, in contrast, view anger in terms of its social implications and summarily terminate it when the situation demands such action.

Our personalized conception of anger dictates our requirements for assuaging anger. For example, we typically require an apology which involves the other person recognizing and atoning for their responsibility in antagonizing us. Anger for us is directed at the other person's self; we are angry about his character, that he could have caused us harm. This, of course, requires that we have a concept about a person's character. Societies which do not recognize psychological character would obviously feel no disappointment over it, would not insist that the person acknowledge their personal failing, and would be content with a compensation that simply offset the injury. This is true of the Kaluli people of New Guinea. Instead of demanding a personal, heartfelt apology and an admission of fault, their anger is dissipated after receiving a simple compensation such as a sum of money (Schieffelin, 1985). The different requirements that different peoples have for assuaging anger correspond to different interpretations of the causes of anger, and all of these aspects make anger different for different cultures.

Shame is another emotion whose social constitution is manifested in different cultural colorations. The Ilongot people of the Philippine Islands and the Japanese exemplify such a contrast in their sense of shame. Rosaldo (1984) observes that in Japanese and other hierarchical societies, shame functions as a social restrainer to prevent individuals from violating social rules. One feels shameful when one has broken a rule, and the shame refers to a weakness of character: the individual has not controlled himself sufficiently to live up to the social standard. Shame has none of these connotations or functions for the Ilongots. In their egalitarian society, they normally want to accept social standards and do not have to be controlled through shame. Shame is felt when one is incapable of meeting social obligations because of old age or physical infirmity. Thus, shame has nothing to do with an antisocial, malevolent character which has to be psychologically punished and inhibited. Quite the opposite, it is manifested by socially oriented individuals who are prevented from social participation by impersonal forces. In both cases, shame reflects the failure to meet social obligations, but the function, connotation, and specific reasons for shame are significantly different (cf. Heelas, 1986, p. 238, for a similar analysis of guilt among the ancient Greeks).

Love also manifests qualitative variations in different social arrangements. For instance, South American Yanomamo women measure their husbands' concern and love in terms of the frequency of beatings and burns they inflict (Heelas, 1986, p. 251). Evidently, love for these women is expressed through physical pain, which, to our way of thinking, is normally anathema to love. Western romantic love is predicated on gentleness and consideration. It is a sensuous, passionate, personal, special attraction which develops quickly. This kind of personal relationship is unique to a particular set of social relationships. These include an individualized social system which emphasizes individual rights and fosters a highly individualistic notion of the self. The social system also dichotomizes personal and public domains so that the personal is more expressive, honest, emotional, supportive, and enduring than the impersonal, calculating, impenetrable, competitive, materialistic, transient, frustrating public arena. This socially structured contrast between two entire domains of life imbues romantic love with a mysterious, intense, irrational, almost magical quality that is uncommon among other social systems.

Romantic love was even uncommon in the United States during earlier eras. Mary Ryan (1983, p. 42) tells us that young women in colonial times devoted little of their psychic energies to falling in love. Certainly they had neither the time, the incentive, nor the socialization to cultivate the extravagant sentiments of romance. The economic priorities which dominated family life meant that "a woman's love for her husband, and his in return, became a 'duty,' a 'performance,' not a rarefied emotion" (Ryan, p. 47). Rothman (1984, pp. 31, 102ff.) similarly concludes that eighteenth century middle-class Americans eschewed romantic love which the gentry had endorsed. However, as both a cultural ideal and an individual expectation, romantic love was taking hold among the middle class by the turn of the nineteenth century. Lawrence Stone's monumental study of premodern family life in England documents the same conclusion. Stone (1977, pp. 272-284) found that, despite the flood of poems, novels, and plays on the themes of romantic and sexual love in the eighteenth century, such sentiments played little or no part in the daily lives of men and women. Only after 1780 in England did romantic love become a major motive in courtship and marriage, and only among the propertied classes.[4]

A practical orientation toward family life not only precluded romantic love, it also precluded maternal love as well. Mothers were concerned with helping infants physically survive and directing them to become responsible, productive family workers. As Ryan put it, "An elaborate mystique of motherhood did not grow up around the time-consuming and oft-repeated physical ordeal of childbearing. The biological intimacy of mother and child did not ordain an instinctive emotional attachment between the two" (p. 49). Quite the contrary, Puritan ideology regarded newborns as inherently depraved creatures who had to be disciplined ("broken") by stern, unapproachable, vigilant mothers. Maternal love as we know it—characterized by a warm, effusive attachment to the infant which included a sense of psychological fulfillment for the mother—did not develop until the nineteenth century when capitalist socioeconomic relations placed women, children, and the family in an entirely new social position.

This does not mean that Puritan mothers felt no love for their children. On the contrary, Evangelical mothers experienced a sense of love and affection for infants and took pleasure in observing them, despite being extremely suspicious and distant (Greven, 1977, pp. 28-31). However, the fact that affection was diligently controlled and infused with distrust makes it different from modern maternal love. Asch's study of personality, cited in the Introduction (Footnote 1) demonstrates how such qualitative change in attributes occurs when they are combined with different elements. John Gillis (1988) is quite correct to caution against assuming that modern love is the only form of love. Other forms must be acknowledged, not denied. This means that love throughout history is modulated, it is not uniform. While some general caring about others is undoubtedly universal, the concrete quality that love has at any particular time and place is extremely variable.

These examples make it clear that emotions are not given, thing-like phenomena which are simply displayed in different behaviors in different circumstances. Such a superficial view presumes an arbitrary relationship between the emotion and the situation, and it implies that the emotion is indifferent to the circumstances in which it is felt. The truth of the matter is that an emotion is felt in a particular situation only because it is appropriate to that situation. Americans feel shameful when we are responsible for a social faux pas because our shame embodies a sense of personal failure. Ilongot shame lacks this sense and that is why it is not felt in those kinds of situations. Conversely, we do not generally feel shameful when we grow old because aging is not our fault and our shame embodies the notion of personal fault. Different situations engender different kinds of shame, not the same kind of shame. Emotions are internally, not externally related to circumstances.

One's conception of an emotion includes the situations to which is it applicable. The emotion is not something separate which can be arbitrarily attached to any circumstance. Rather, the emotion is designed to respond to that particular kind of circumstance. To know an emotion is to know the kinds of situations it refers to, and, conversely, these situations define and constitute the emotion itself. There is a necessary, not a contingent, reason that the emotion is expressed in particular situations and in particular acts. The emotion is internally related to the situation and its behavioral manifestation. This is why Geertz (1984a, p. 135) says, "You can no more know what *lek* is if you don't know what Balinese dramatism is than you can know what a catcher's mitt is if you don't know what baseball is."[5]

Emotions are also internally related to language. With emotions dependent upon concepts, and concepts tied to language, it follows that emotions depend upon language. In a provocative extension of the Sapir-Whorf hypothesis to emotions, Heelas (1986) states, "Differences in [linguistic] representation are actually differences in construction" (p. 258). Representing different emotions is, after all, why the different terms exist. According to Heelas, the tremendous variation in the number of emotion terms across cultures—some cultures having no emotion words, English has 400, and Chinese has 750—corresponds to real distinctions in emotional experience. Thus, the absence among the Ilongots of a linguistic differentiation between anger and irritation means that individuals do not feel two distinct emotions (p. 259). Because Ilongots do not emphasize the individual's responsibility for hurting another, the hurt one feels as a result of another's action is not differentiated from the irritation one feels about impersonal frustrations.

Another example of linguistic terms expressing emotional and conceptual relationships concerns the Ifaluk people in the Western Pacific. According to Lutz (1988, chap. 5), the Ifaluk have one emotional term, *fago*, which encompasses the English terms: compassion, sadness, love, respect, and gratitude. The single Ifaluk term represents a global concept and feeling which, in the United States, is differentiated into several concepts and corresponding feelings. The difference in emotional structure between the Ifaluk and Americans is so great that Lutz required extensive enculturation before she was able to understand and begin to feel what fago really connotes. While each of fago's components has counterparts in American emotionality, their integration has no Western analogue. It was therefore extremely difficult for Lutz to comprehend how the same term, concept, and feeling could refer to another person's illness, death, separation, suffering, beneficence, politeness, and love.

Yet, as Lutz explains, such a global emotion is intelligible given the Ifaluk life conditions. For example, under the harsh conditions in which the Ifaluk live, and the intense interdependence on one another that this hardship necessitates, separation typically causes suffering because of the loss of support that separation inflicts. Because separation is so closely associated with real suffering and danger, separation elicits a feeling of compassion concerning the inevitable difficulties that will ensue. In America, with its different socioeconomic structure, children leaving home temporarily or permanently do not inflict economic hardship on their parents (usually, quite the opposite), and consequently separation does not elicit compassion, although it may elicit grief. Our emotional differentiation of grief and compassion therefore reflects our particular life conditions. Of course, for us separation occasionally entails suffering but not often enough to solidify the association in our emotional, conceptual, and linguistic structures. In the same vein, the harshness of Ifaluk life imbues their love relationships with impending suffering, and this leads to conjoining love, grief, and compassion in a way that is foreign to us. Again, our love does sometimes occasion sorrow through misdeeds or unfortunate accidents, however normally love and sadness are contrary experiences which leads to their emotional, conceptual, and linguistic differentiation.[6]

Now the culturally mediated position that an emotion has in the configuration of other emotions affects its quality. For instance, Lutz (1986a) found that the Ifaluk regard disappointment as closely related to fright since both connote an unexpected bad occurrence. Americans do not generally associate disappointment with fright and, indeed, regard them as quite disparate. Because the "horizon" of related social-psychological phenomena pervades an emotion and qualifies it, the same emotion in a different position or in a different configuration will take on a new quality. It follows that our sense of disappointment is significantly different from the Ifaluk's. This difference would be obscured by an isolated description of disappointment in the two cultures.

The socially mediated quality of emotions reflects the fact that emotions serve complex communicative, moral, and cultural purposes. The complex meaning of each emotion is the result of the role emotions play in the full range of peoples' cultural values, social relations, and economic circumstances. Emotions are not reified entities (or states) which naturally exist inside all individuals independently of their life activity. Emotions are constructed by people in their conjoint social life activity and embody the character of this sensuous activity. This is what makes emotions eminently human phenomena (Lutz, 1988, chap. 1).

Needs

As suggested in Chapter 1, the biological needs for food, sex, shelter, and support are extremely general, and carry no mandate concerning necessary means for satisfaction. Instead, the manner in which these needs are released and satisfied is socially determined. Hunger and sex drives are utilized for social purposes and infused with social practices which far transcend their biological character. Sex, for example, can be used for reproduction, love, gaining and expressing power, compensation for loneliness, proof of one's attractiveness, or to earn money. Even the intensity and periodicity of the sexual drive is socially constructed. For example, in contrast to our sexually driven culture, the Grand Valley Dani culture of West New Guinea cultivates little need for sex. The Dani have remarkably little premarital sex, and after marriage they wait two years before having intercourse. They abstain from sex for five years after the birth of a child, all with no sign of stress or unhappiness (Heider, 1976). Since the physical act has become social-psychological, "a study of the physical act itself, its biological preconditions, its evolution, its similarity to that behavior in other animals, or the regions of the brain that influence it, will simply be irrelevant to the human phenomenon" (Levins & Lewontin, 1985, p. 263).

Rather than biological needs mandating their own goal object, socially mediated objects structure our biological needs. Human need is not indifferent to its object but is integrally dependent upon it. The object that satisfies a need simultaneously shapes the need. An exquisite article of clothing that promises to warm the body against cold cultivates a particular need for clothing that is different from the need for a coarse item. Since objects constitute needs, a culture which produces and distributes exquisite products thereby cultivates a refined need and sensitivity. Producing humane goods is a significant way that society can humanize its citizens (Lichtman, 1982, pp. 86-95). Even on the level of survival needs (food, clothing, shelter), then, society does not simply serve, but actually shapes (constitutes, in part) the individual's needs.

In addition to biological needs being socialized into psychological motives, other social-psychological motives are produced that are unrelated to survival. The need for intellectual inquiry, logical consistency, romantic love, sexual chastity, fabulous wealth, a certain physical appearance, privacy, and particular consumer products are all entirely cultural.[7] These cultural needs are valid in their own right and are not by-products of biologically prior, species-wide needs.

The reductionist bias, which dominates such diverse theorists as Freud, sociobiologists, and classical conditioning behaviorists, leads to disparaging novel, culturally variable higher needs as superficial derivatives of a universal, constant biological core (Asch, 1952, chap. 11). Actually, survival needs are displaced in importance by the proliferation of nonbiological needs. As Asch said, "To survive as humans they must have concerns other than those of surviving" (1952, p. 339). Preteceille and Terrail (1985) point out that while primitive societies may have geared production toward fulfilling survival needs, modern society has reversed this process and creates needs in the interest of economic advance. Today, therefore, "The needs that production satisfies are the needs of production itself, the demands of its reproduction" (Preteceille & Terrail, p. 39). The natural theory of needs is thus a political anachronism as well as scientifically erroneous.

Biological reductionism is entirely at odds with the way in which social psychological needs surpass and alter biological needs (Asch, 1952, p. 341). For example, Freud's notion of a biological id presumes that natural drives have a life of their own which continues to motivate behavior despite social opposition. Social forces may stifle the id from expressing itself but they never extinguish its primordial desire for certain preordained objects of satisfaction. However, the fact that needs are socially organized repudiates Freud's conception of natural needs.

Freud's picture of endogenous antisocial impulses conflicting with social demands is false. If all adult needs are socially constructed, they cannot be intrinsically antisocial. Needs, desires, and actions which contradict particular social demands are the product of other social tendencies. For instance, the conflict between sexual desire and sexual repression that preoccupied Freud reflected two contradictory social demands. It was not a conflict between an intrinsic sexual drive and social repugnance for sexual expression. Intense sexual desire was stimulated by the hedonic materialism of nineteenth-century European capitalism. Sexual excitement was the inevitable accompaniment to upwardly mobile middle class life that emphasized individual expression and choice, and took pleasure in material comforts. Intense sexuality was not endemic to individual biology as the subdued sexuality of the Dani people demonstrate. On the other side, nineteenth-century social repression of sexuality was also not endemic to social life, as Freud contended. It reflected the restraint necessitated by the earlier social order that was based on the frugal accumulation of capital. Nineteenth-century Europe and America was a period in which this older social order was becoming superceded by the new one, and this social conflict was represented in the conflict between sexual expression and repression (Birken, 1988). The conflict between sexual stimulation and sexual restraint was thus entirely a conflict between two social needs. The triumph of unfettered materialism and individualism over preindustrial frugality unfettered sexual desire as well and eliminated the social demand for sexual repression.

This social modification in the need for sex rendered Freud's central antagonism between sexual desire and sexual repression obsolete. It also transformed the psychological processes by which sexual desire was dealt with. Sexually repressive society did not wish to admit the existence of sexual desire and so it repressed awareness of sexual desire in the individual. It not only repressed sexual expression, but also repressed awareness of this repression (Laing, 1969). In Freud's unhappy phrase, sexual desire was rendered unconscious. However, contemporary society channels sexuality in other ways. It allows awareness of sexual desire and employs conscious means to regulate sexual expression. We are now aware of sexually desiring someone, and we consciously decide whether to pursue or renounce this desire. We do not employ intrapsychic defenses to deal with sexual desire, we employ conscious choice in the same manner in which we decide whether or not to steal an expensive object that we cannot afford to buy. In other words, the social organization of our needs entails social differences in mental processes for handling these different needs. Unconscious, intrapsychic defenses are not natural, inevitable ways of regulating needs. Regulating needs can take many forms ranging from unconscious to conscious.

The so-called maternal instinct is another need which is socially derived rather than natural. This maternal need to feel an intense, sentimental attachment with infants, coupled with an intense concern for the baby's material and psychological welfare, is not at all universal, as Nancy Scheper-Hughes (1990) demonstrates in her anthropological investigation of poor mothers in Brazil. These mothers, who witness about one-half of their children die before the age of 5, evidence few of the maternal reactions that are evident among middle-class mothers. The poor Brazilian mothers prepare themselves for the likely death of their babies by developing a set of understandings and expectations which preclude the intense, sentimental attachment characteristic of middle-class mothers. The Brazilian mothers wait several years before accepting the child as a viable, individual person. Before this time, during the infancy years, infants remain unnamed and unbaptized. In addition, they are rarely held or picked up. Moreover, infants are construed as less human and less valuable than older children and adults. No effort is made to attribute to the small baby such human characteristics as consciousness, will, intentionality, self-awareness, and memory. Infants are consequently seen as incapable of real human suffering. Similarly, the mothers are slow to personalize an infant by attributing specific meanings to their cries, facial expressions, their flailing of arms and legs, their kicks and screams. Nor are they accustomed to scanning an infant's face to note his or her resemblance to family members. The infant, in short, does not have an individualized self that would make its death unbearably painful.

The mothers so expect their babies to die that malnutrition often elicits rejection rather than succorance. Mothers generally assume that sickly babies are doomed to die anyway and are not worth trying to save. Curiously, allowing such infants to die arouses sympathetic approval from others, while efforts to save young children are met with hostility and surprise. When a child does die, its burial site is not marked. No prayers are recited, no priest attends, and the grave is never visited again. Mothers do not express any guilt for deaths that are hastened by severe neglect. Nor do mothers express grief over the death of their infants. Death is tranquilly accepted as being the will of god. Mothers' crying is inhibited by the belief that the baby's soul must climb to heaven, and the path will become slippery and unnavigable if it is made wet by the mother's tears.

Of course, it is possible to assert that the Brazillian mothers really do have natural maternal feelings toward their living and dead infants and that sentimental love, remorse, and guilt are simply repressed and made unconscious. However, there is no evidence to support this assertion, and it remains a hollow, ethnocentric presumption that all mothers are just like ours'. A more plausible conclusion which is supported by the available evidence is that the maternal need, with its accompanying behaviors and emotional reactions, is absent from the Brazillian mothers. The mothers' explanations and understandings of infant mortality are not defensive rationalizations which mask natural maternal needs and emotions. Rather they preclude the formation of such needs and emotions in the first place. Maternal attachment to children and grief over losing a child rest upon socially mediated cognitive understandings, they are not natural. Support for this statement comes from the fact that Scheper-Hughes' Brazillian mothers did manifest an attachment to, and grief for, *older* children. Older toddlers are incorporated into the family, are expected to live and to contribute to the family's material and psychological well-being. This socially mediated cognitive expectation allows feelings of attachment to form. Death at this point surprises the mothers, disrupts their social and psychological attachment, and causes feelings of loss and remorse. Death of a last born child also produces grief because it frustrates an important socially derived need for the mother to have a relationship with this child: In a world of dire poverty, with its inevitable material, social, and psychological insecurity, the last born child represents perhaps the last opportunity for a mother to have an intimate relationship. Death of this child is especially traumatic because of the tremendous loss it represents *in this particular social psychological circumstance*.

The Social Constitution and Variability of Form

Although some psychologists challenge the social variation of psychological content and insist on certain content universals (their position will be considered momentarily), social variation in content is accepted by most scholars. Accordingly, psychologists have directed their quest for universal laws into studies of process, structure, or form. Process is severed from socially variable content and is presumed to be biologically mandated, universal, and basic. As Shweder (1990, pp. 4-5) has critically summarized the field:

> General psychology assumes that its subject matter is a presupposed central (abstract and transcendent = deep or interior or hidden) processing mechanism inherent (fixed and universal) in human beings, which enables them to think (classify, infer, remember, imagine, etc.), experience (emote, feel, desire, need, self-reflect, etc.), act (strive, prefer, choose, evaluate, etc.) and learn.
>
> The aim of general psychology is to describe that central inherent processing mechanism of mental life. Since the central processing mechanism is presumed to be a transcendent, abstract, fixed, and universal property of the human psyche, general psychology has the look, taste, and smell of a Platonic undertaking. For it is that presupposed central and inherent processing mechanism that is the true object of fascination in general psychology and not all the concrete, apparent, variable, and particular stuff, substance, or content that is operated upon by the processor or may interfere with its operation.
>
> It is a necessary step in the general psychology enterprise to distinguish intrinsic (internal) psychological structures and processes from extrinsic (external) environmental conditions, to procedurally abstract and analytically withdraw the knower from what he or she knows, and to insist on a fundamental division between the processing mechanism of the person versus his or her personal or group history, context, stimulus and task environment, institutional setting, resources, beliefs, values, and knowledge.

This bias is evident in the main areas of research concerning laws of learning and memory, stages of cognitive development, universal grammar, group processes, schizophrenic thought processes, and communication. In all these cases the "how" is independent of and more important than what is experienced or accomplished (Zinchenko, 1984).

However, dichotomizing form and content is erroneous because it illogically derives them from separate, antagonistic sources. In fact, psychological processes do not exist in a pristine sanctuary cut off from real life activity. Instead, processes depend upon and reflect real life activity as much as content does. Culture is not the superficial content which lies outside of an intrinsic central processing mechanism; culture is the machinery of the processor itself. As such, psychological processes admit of significant social differences. In Luria's (1976, p. 8) words, "The structure of mental activity—not just the specific content but also the general forms basic to all cognitive processes—changes in the course of historical development."

Decontextualized vs. Contextualized Mental Processes

Perhaps the most important manifestation of this change in psychological processes is in abstract thought. The level of abstraction may be regarded as a process because it involves the manner in which content is assimilated. Content that is grasped as bounded by a particular context, as having a specific function within that context, and limited to that familiar context has a certain form by virtue of the way it is construed. On the other hand, content that is decontextualized and construed as properties that can be interrelated in numerous, unfamiliar, formal ways, has a different form. Psychological processes may be regarded as occupying differing positions along a continuum which is contextualized, functional, and empirical at one extreme, and decontextual, formal, and theoretical at the other. As we shall see, the position that a psychological process occupies on this continuum is a function of social structure. Of course, the entire range of abstraction is relative to man, and is qualitatively more sophisticated than any animal consciousness. Even the most context-bound human thought is far more abstract than animal consciousness in that it entails language, symbols, and concepts.

In general, traditional subsistence societies (also known as primitive, without any pejorative connotation implied), characterized by little division of labor, little or no formal schooling, and minimal commercial trade, engender contextualized, functional, empiric thinking. In contrast, modern societies, characterized by extensive, complex division of labor, formal educational institutions, and extensive commerce, engender decontextualized, formal, theoretical thinking. This may be seen in peoples' concept of time, number, measurement, personhood, color, shape, as well as their use of logic and memory.

Time Sense. For example, traditional peoples sense time to be associated with particular events (Whitrow, 1973; Capek, 1973). According to this "Relational Theory," time is measured by "a rice-cooking," or "the frying of a locust." In addition, time is considered to be influenced by different heavenly bodies such as "Sun-day," "Moon-day," and "Saturn-day." However much the different kinds of time may be organically linked, for the premoderns each time period has a qualitatively heterogeneous sense.

In contrast, modern time is typically divorced from particular events and is qualitatively homogeneous. We do, of course, make qualitative distinctions in time, such as daytime and nighttime, however these are thoroughly permeated with the idea that time itself is homogeneous throughout. Daytime and nighttime are felt to be composed of the same time units despite the fact that different events occur in the different periods. Modern time's qualitative homogeneity permits quantitative division, in contrast to primitive time whose qualitative heterogeneity precludes quantitatively equivalent units.

Whorf (1956, p. 58) notes that the Hopi do not abstractly conceptualize time per se. And Hallowell (1955) similarly observes that time for the Ojibwa Indians of North America refers to particular events such as "When I was young," rather than to abstract temporal units. The Kpelle of Liberia likewise emphasize the qualitative nature of time periods which are associated with particular events, and this renders quantitative commutation among periods impossible. In other words, although the Kpelle distinguish days and weeks—a week is the period of time leading up to a market day—they cannot calculate the number of days in a week because there is no common unit that can be added. Years also have no precise quantitative referent, but denote only events such as "the year I was born." Consequently, people do not normally count weeks of years, nor do they know their age as the sum of individual years passed. Until recently, the Kpelle had no abstract word for time, and have only borrowed one from English (Gay & Cole, 1967, pp. 71ff.).

Color Perception and Conceptualization. Color perception and conceptualization are similarly tied to particular objects among primitive people, whereas they are decontextualized in modern society. The earlier discussion of Luria's research on color described the object-related color vocabulary of the peasants in contrast to the abstract color terms used by the administrators. The manner in which colors are associated with or dissociated from objects affect what the colors look like relative to each other. Other cultures have separate names denoting "the gray of the horse" and "the gray of the dog" but no notion for "gray" by itself. These cultures are "not sensitive to the same color of different things, but to the different things with the same color" (Wald, 1975b, p. 128). Conklin (1955, p. 341) similarly observed the absence of an abstract word for color among the Hanunoo and he noted how difficult this makes abstract discussion of the phenomenon.

Shape Perception and Conceptualization. Luria found that the perception and conceptualization of shape is construed along the same continuum of abstraction as color. The administrators employed formal names such as circle and triangle. They designated figures made up of dots and incomplete shapes as "something like a circle." In contrast, the farmers assigned no geometrical designation to any of the figures. They designated all of them with the names of familiar objects. Thus, a circle was called a plate, a watch, or a moon; a square was a mirror, a door, or an apricot drying board. The peasants construed a triangle composed of crosses as crosswork embroidery, a basket, or stars; they described a triangle made up of little half-circles as a collection of fingernails. Not once did they call an incomplete circle a circle; it was almost always either a bracelet or an earring. Likewise, they perceived an incomplete triangle as a stirrup.

The culturally derived concepts of shape produced different classifications just as they affected color categorization. The administrators categorized figures on the basis of their geometrical properties—e.g., all types of triangles together, all kinds of quadrangles regardless of contour. The farmers, on the other hand, classified figures according to the objects they resembled. Thus, a square and a truncated triangle were both categorized as window frames, while a square perceived as a window and a rectangle perceived as a ruler were said to be unrelated (Luria, 1976, pp. 32-39).

Logic. Another difference in level of abstraction that Luria discovered involved the use of logic. Formal logic is abstract in that it requires recognizing the relationship between premises according to their own stated characteristics, independently of their actual truthfulness and their correspondence to one's personal experience. In view of the more decontextualized, formal, theoretical thinking of the administrators already described, it is not surprising that they manifested a greater facility for deducing conclusions than the farmers. When presented with syllogisms, the farmers failed to grasp the premises in general, abstract terms and failed to relate them deductively. They were usually befuddled by the request to draw a conclusion from the premises. Occasionally, they attempted to guess about the conclusion from direct knowledge unrelated to the major premise. E.g., "There are no camels in Germany. The city of B. is in Germany. Are there camels there or not?" Answer: "There probably are. If it's a large city there should be camels there" (p.112). The peasant's difficulty concerned forming theoretical, hypothetical, deductive judgments divorced from immediate experience. This, of course, parallels their contextual view of colors and shapes which tied them to familiar, particular objects.

Scribner's (1975,1977) contemporary cross-cultural research confirms Luria's results. Primitive peoples answer logical problems at a chance level of correctness. They don't understand or remember the sense of syllogisms, and their answers are based on personal experience rather than on following theoretical premises. However, success increases dramatically upon exposure to formal education. Schooling in any culture, even traditional ones, fosters abstract thinking that is crucial in formal logical deduction (cf., Tulviste, 1979 for additional evidence). Evidently Mills was correct in suggesting that "principles of logic are the abstracted statements of social rules derived from the dominant diffusion pattern of ideas" (Mills, 1963, p. 429). Reasoning is thoroughly dependent upon a "socially derived logical apparatus."

Measurement and Quantification. Measurement and quantification lie along the same socially generated continuum of abstraction as the foregoing phenomena. Primitive people generally associate quantity with quality and do not detach number from the thing being quantified. Quantification per se is therefore impossible. The Melanesians, for example, have a word for ten coconuts (*buru*) which is entirely different from the word for ten fish (*bola*). They have several distinctive notions to denote the same number ten whenever it has to do with different things. "They are less interested in numerical identity and much more in the qualitative distinction between fish and coconuts" (Wald, 1975b, pp. 128-129). The Ojibwa Indians have a similarly context-bound notion of quantity. Measurement does not take the form of abstract quantitative units, but rather consists of ambiguous categories such as "long," "small" which are specified by referring to particular objects; e.g., something is "taller than the trees," or it is further away than "the jagged rock." The Ojibwa do not have any common units applicable to all classes of linear measurement. "There is no means of bringing linear concepts of all kinds into a single unified category of spatial attributes because the units of measure expressing the distance traveled on a journey, for example, are categorically distinct from those applied to the length of a piece of string" (Hallowell, 1955, p. 206).

Damerow (1988) reports that early Babylonian arithmetic symbols were similarly context-bound. The simplest numerical notations from 8000 B.C. (which, interestingly enough, predated written letters by some 4,000 years), and even more sophisticated quantitative symbols which came into being around 3000 B.C., were all used only in specific situations. They had no general use or meaning. Some were used to designate discrete objects, others for objects of mass consumption, others for grain. In addition, each notational system was grounded in a different base value which minimized commutation. A further contextual complication was the fact that certain symbols had one meaning in one context and another meaning in a different context. Two symbols used to measure discrete objects indicated a relation of 1:10; but when used to measure grain the same symbols denoted a relation of 1:6.

Cole and his colleagues (Cole, Gay, & Glick, 1968) found the same context-bound measurement among the Kpelle of Liberia. In the first place, quantification and measurement are uncommon—the Kpelle rarely know their exact ages; if one asks them how far it is to the neighboring town, a typical reply would be, "not far," and gross quantitative categories such as "large" and "small" are more common than refined quantities. In the rare instances where the Kpelle utilize measurement, they have separate metrics for each situation. They cannot transpose from "handspan," used to measure a table, to "armspan," used to measure rugs, to "footlength," used to measure a floor.

Memory. Evidently, memory also functions at a more or less abstract level according to social relations. Primitive people's memory is extremely context-bound in the sense of recalling material in terms of its relationships to other things. Modern people, in contrast, are able to remember decontextualized material which has little reference to related information. This difference was reported by Cole and Bruner (1971), who found that, in contrast to Americans, Kpelle rice farmers in Liberia perform very poorly on free recall tasks. Even when the words to be remembered denote familiar objects in Kpelle life, the number of words recalled is small, there is no evidence of semantic or other organization of the material, and there is little or no increase in the number recalled with successive trials. Presented with a list of 20 familiar words, Kpelle subjects recalled 9 on the first trial and 10.8 on the fifth trial. In contrast, American college students went from 13 to 19 words (Cole & Gay, 1972, p. 1071). Free recall is so difficult for Kpelle that even when the words are carefully chosen as belonging to indigenous conceptual categories—which should give them an intrinsic organization and enhance recall—free recall, clustering, and improvement over trials was minimal (Cole & Gay, 1972, p. 1077).

Kpelle memory only improved when the material was embedded in a distinctive context, that is when free recall was no longer required. One method was to incorporate words into folk stories. Another contextualizing method was to physically place objects near chairs and then ask Ss to remember the items. This second method improved recall to more than 14 words averaged over 5 trials.

Obviously, Kpelle memory requires a concrete context whereas Americans achieve excellent recall even with decontextualized material. The memory process is thus socially variable. Regardless of the content, Kpelle require the material to be embedded in a certain contextualized form in order to remember it well. Even familiar material that is devoid of some concrete context is difficult to remember.

Cole and Gay speculate that perhaps such concrete cuing has spatial organization counterparts in other areas of Kpelle thought. Their hypothesis that Kpelle memory depends upon spatial cues in a way that is quite foreign to American memory is rendered plausible by research that compared memory processes in Aboriginal and Anglo children. Whereas the Aborigines remembered displays by visually recalling the spatial positions of each object, Anglos were more likely to employ verbal strategies of naming objects and describing their positions. To remember the displays, the Aborigines silently concentrated upon their fixed visual image, in contrast to the Anglos who verbally repeated their descriptions to themselves during the observation period (Laboratory of Comparative Human Cognition, 1983, p. 326). Memory processes thus evidence significant cultural variation.

Two additional examples of memory's following social (interpersonal) rather than natural (impersonal) principles concerns the serial position effect and the primacy-recency effect.

While American subjects typically evidence a serial position effect in free recall (remembering the first and last stimuli better than items occupying a middle position in the series), the Kpelle subjects showed a flat curve in which early, middle, and late items were remembered equally well (Cole & Gay, 1972, p. 1078). Actually, the serial position effect is subject to social violation within Western culture as well as across cultures. Stimulus materials that are culturally meaningful will be recalled in the middle of a series; they do not have to be positioned at the beginning or end in order to be recalled well. For example, in a test of recall of American presidents, American subjects, presented with a chronological list of names which was then removed, remembered Lincoln very well despite the fact that his name appeared in the middle of the sequence (Roediger & Crowder, 1982). Thus, cultural salience rather than natural process determines what is remembered. The serial position effect holds, at most, only in artificial experiments devoid of culturally significant material.

The primacy-recency effect evidences similar cultural variation. From research in Mexico and Morocco, Wagner (1982) found that primacy recall—the recalling of information that is perceived early in a sequence—only "developed with age for schooled subjects, and in a somewhat diminished form for nonschooled children who lived in an urban setting. Rural, nonschooled subjects showed little primacy effect [ability] and no increase in recall with age. Wagner's explanation emphasizes the importance of schooling in enhancing primacy recall by encouraging rote memorization through verbal repetition to oneself. This is plausible because the subjects with good primacy recall also employed the mnemonic strategy of verbal rehearsal. "Verbal rehearsal appeared to be used regularly only by older schooled subjects" (p. 120). Significantly, the influence of social factors such as schooling was far stronger than personal factors such as family and demographic background. The latter "were found to be of little help in predicting memory performance when schooling and urbanization were controlled" (p.121). Moreover, recency recall—the remembering of most recently perceived information—was not enhanced by schooling, perhaps because recent information is so easily remembered that no specially learned mnemonic strategies are necessary.

The foregoing research into memory processes confirms the sociohistorical contention that they, like all psychological processes, are grounded in the real social life of people. They do not comprise an isolated mental function but depend upon the content of what people deal with and the socially structured manner in which they deal with it. In the words of one of Vygotsky's Russian colleagues:

> Memory processes must be understood as processes that constitute the content of a specific action. They must be understood as remembering [that is] responsive to and functioning in a particular task.
>
> The subject does not appear as the bearer of associative or conditioned-reflex connections in these actions. Still less does he appear as the source of "mental activities" or "functions" that merely manifest themselves differently accordingly to the conditions under which they appear. The subject is the subject of life, the subject of a specific action in which one of his diverse links to reality is realized. (Zinchenko, 1984, p. 76)

Personhood. The conception that people have of their own personhood ranges from the Western, abstract self-concept, divorced from social relations, to the self as nothing more than particular social roles. To contemporary Westerners, personhood is a generalized concept that is intrinsic to individual existence: everyone is a person regardless of his particular social roles. A one-day-old infant is as much an individual as an adult is, and the extreme claim is even made that an embryo is an individual. Western friendship is also a purely personal relationship based upon mutual liking for the individuality of the other. It does not require or cement any particular social roles. In fact, friendship is considered to be a purer, more genuine relationship than the congruence of common social roles. "This is my friend" signifies a more meaningful relationship than "this is my classmate."

Premodern societies do not believe in such abstract notions of self, and instead regard the individual in terms of his particular social relationships. Homeric Greece, for example, not only had no general concept of person, but also lacked a generic term for man or woman. There were only words for young man, old man, maiden, married woman, and other such descriptors indicating particular social relationships (Simon, 1978, pp. 56-61; cf. Pepitone, 1986; L'Armand, Pepitone, & Shanmugam, 1981; Amir & Sharon, 1987; J. Miller, 1984, for additional cross-cultural differences in person perception). The Gahuku-Gama people of Highland New Guinea also cannot conceive of a self or a personal relationship apart from social structural terms. Interpersonal relations are not conceptualized as relationships between persons but rather between players of social roles. Along the same lines, personhood among the Lugbara of Uganda is an achieved, not an ascribed status. Only people of certain social positions are worthy of such a title. Among the Tallensi of Ghana personhood is similarly conferred by society rather than regarded as intrinsic to the individual. Personhood is only validated at the death of the individual, for this is when social roles and obligations have been completed and the person is most socially defined. Personhood, or identity, is the culmination of a whole life and is defined in terms of social criteria.

Personhood in the West, by contrast, is ascribed to all individuals, even to infants prior to any significant social life (La Fontaine, 1985). In contrast to premodern societies where children are not ascribed personhood, and may even lack a name, Western infants and children are regarded as the most precious and purest individuals whose individuality has not been "corrupted" by social life.

The Social Basis of Abstraction

With the level of abstraction of psychological functions varying dramatically across societies, it is evident that a social basis determines this variation. Durkheim perceptively expressed the idea that although abstract thought is decontextualized, it definitely depends upon a social context. He said: "If logical thought tends to rid itself more and more of the subjective and personal elements which it still retains from its origins, it is not because extra-social factors have intervened; it is much rather because a social life of a new sort is developing" (cited in Collins, 1985, p. 54).

The social and technological influences that differentiate decontextualized and contextualized psychological functions include division of labor, commerce, and formal education. As Hallowell explained it, the particularistic thinking of the Ojibwa Indians, and primitive people in general, is a function of their primitive division of labor: "In such a simply organized and individualistic society, where articles are manufactured only for domestic use and not for sale, there is no demand for the application of standard measurements to any article produced . . .

Each person constructs for himself and measures for himself or other members of his immediate household group. No truly objective standard is necessary" (Hallowell, 1955, p. 214). There is thus no need for general quantitative measures, including those of distance and time. Mathematical operations are similarly confined to particular usages rather than possessing general applicability.

The need to transcend local contexts and develop general, abstract, standards only emerges under the impetus of interaction among diverse populations occupying disparate positions in a division of labor. Particular usages and functions, familiar to immediate experience, are overridden by general principles and features that must be available to diverse participants in widespread interactions. Communication beyond the bounds of face-to-face contact sparks the need for written messages which has been identified by Goody and Wald with abstract thinking (cf. Chapter 1).

Leontiev (1932, pp. 60-63) adds that abstract thinking is fostered by stable, organized social life. He states that in comparison to primitive hunting and gathering societies, settled, productive societies demand a generally more sophisticated, farsighted, and rigorous consciousness in order to participate in the more systematic organized production process. Whereas nomadic existence is relatively spontaneous, collecting what nature provides and then moving on to new territory, ongoing production requires long-range planning and husbanding of resources plus complex understanding of the interrelation among diverse positions in the comparatively extensive division of labor. Settled peoples have a more disciplined labor than nomads, and they must accordingly discipline their thinking. The more sophisticated tool use characteristic of settled societies also entails more sophisticated instrumental, sequential, interrelational thinking.

The need to teach abstract, decontextualized thinking, so necessary for many everyday interactions, is fulfilled by creating specialized schools to educate students apart from any specific, practical context. Without formal education, thinking is contextual because, as Bruner (1965) observes among tribal people, "one virtually never sees an instance of 'teaching' taking place outside the situation where the behavior to be learned is relevant. Nobody 'teaches' in our prepared sense of the word. There is nothing like school, nothing like lessons." In such societies, "it is almost impossible to separate what one does from what one knows." Knowledge and thinking are therefore obviously tied to specific, immediate situations.

Small, face-to-face society allows individuals to have extremely similar experiences, and this similarity contributes to the particularistic, immediate nature of knowledge and thinking. Advanced society differs from this in that, "there is knowledge and skill in the culture far in excess of what any individual knows. And so, increasingly, there develops an economical technique of instructing the young based heavily on *telling out of context rather than showing in context.* In literate societies, the practice becomes institutionalized in the school or the 'teacher'" (ibid., my emphasis). Knowledge, learning, and thinking necessarily become abstract as they are "freed from the immediate ends of action, preparing the learner for the chain of reckoning remote from payoff that is needed for the formulation of complex ideas." "It is no wonder then, that many recent studies report large differences between 'primitive' children who are in schools and their brothers who are not: differences in perception, abstraction, time perspective, and so on" (ibid.).

Scribner and Cole (1973) similarly maintain that schooling emphasizes universalistic skills and principles. These transcend the immediacy of any specific task, teacher, culture, or environment. Thus, we learn reading, writing, and mathematical skills to use in a variety of unspecified situations, whereas unschooled children learn to use practical tools for particular purposes. Education emphasizes abstract principles which are filled out by interchangeable examples, in contrast to everyday observation which builds up from particular experiences which are rarely systematized into formal principles.

In addition to school, division of labor, technology, and stable socioeconomic systems all fostering abstract thought, mention must be made of the importance of commerce for this way of thinking. By commerce we mean more than simply interacting across positions in a division of labor. Commerce involves exchanging commodities according to some principle of equivalence. This equivalence is a value on which different objects can be compared; as such it is abstracted from their quality. Different qualities are then compared in terms of an abstract, homogeneous value.

Mere transactions across divisions of labor do not necessarily involve exchange of equivalent values since they can include the distributing of commonly owned products without any quid pro quo principle. The quid pro quo of commercial exchange greatly intensifies the abstraction inherent in mere transactions across division of labor because it replaces heterogeneous quality with homogeneous, decontextualized quantity (Haug, 1986, chap. 1). That quantification is spawned by commerce is demonstrated by the rise of mathematics to facilitate commercial transactions. This is true of Greek mathematics (Wilder,1973; Thomson, 1955, chap. 12), Babylonian mathematics (Damerow, 1988), and Renaissance mathematics (Swetz, 1987).

Saxe (1982; Saxe & Posner, 1983, p. 295) found the influence of commerce on mathematics in primitive people as well. As commerce and currency were introduced into a New Guinea highland group, their indigenous crude counting system was replaced by increasingly sophisticated arithmetic concepts including a base structure. Saxe (1988) also found that uneducated ten-year-old children learned arithmetical operations during their apprenticeship in selling candy on city streets. Their participation in these simple commercial transactions produced more sophisticated mathematical skills than were achieved by urban children outside the candy selling enterprise. Rural children, exposed to even less commercial activity, had the lowest arithmetic skills. Gay and Cole (1967, p. 75) similarly observed that whereas Kpelle people normally are quite inexact about measurement and quantification, precision increases substantially in commercial activities. Length, money, and volume are all quantified where a commercial need is felt.[8]

Commerce not only fosters the abstract quantification of objects. It also fosters the abstract quantification of people. Especially when commerce is motivated by private profit, workers tend to be treated as a mere cost of production, as anonymous bodies to be relocated, discarded, and replaced in accordance with profit considerations. Workers are valued more for their abstract labor power than for their personal needs or qualities. Businessmen are similarly valued for their wealth rather than for the particular kind of business activity that generated it. The very freedom to operate any enterprise for considerations of profit rather than justifying the enterprise in terms of some particular social benefit de-emphasizes content: the right to choose is more important than the content of the choice.

Abstract labor power which is the measure of workers, and abstract value which is the measure of objects in capitalism are themselves measured by the time expended in their production. Objects' value depends upon how long it takes to produce them, and workers' value similarly depends upon the time necessary to train (produce) them. This time that measures abstract labor power and value must itself be abstract. It must be homogeneous, standardized, quantitatively divisible time that can compare different objects' production time and different workers' training time. It must be insensitive to qualitative differences. In his classic historiography of time, E.P. Thompson (1967) describes how capitalist production relations spawned the modern notion of abstract time. He shows how time also became capitalized as currency which was spent, wasted, and accumulated.[9] (cf. Goldstein, 1988)

The abstract thinking that increases with the transition from isolated village life to commercialization (Cole & Scribner, 1974, p. 122) not only includes quantitative measurement systems and standardized time, but also abstract colors and shapes which encompass a great variety of particulars. It additionally includes modern people's ability to reclassify categories according to new principles, and to use formal logical principles for deducing conclusions from unfamiliar premises. Finally, socially mediated abstract thought entails theorizing about all kinds of distant, "impractical" possibilities and relationships, and justifying action by appeal to necessary, rational principles. In contrast, traditional thinking that corresponds to simple, restricted social intercourse is more situation-bound and has difficulty reconstructing categories. It also has difficulty drawing abstract logical deductions about unfamiliar issues (Luria, 1971). Finally, traditional thinking works within the status quo on activities of immediate, practical importance, without seeking any justification of action beyond traditional custom (Gay & Cole, 1967, chap. 12).

Now, the existence of significant psychological differences between primitive and modern people does not mean the differences are absolute. Modern people are not necessarily more abstract than primitives in every single psychological activity. As Michael Cole and his colleagues argue, many abstract processes are only exceptionally utilized by modern man who normally employs the same contextualized thinking and remembering as primitives. How often, they ask, do we engage in free recall without reference to some cue or context, or without referring to some written record? How often do we engage in scientific thinking to disambiguate variables, distinguish causation from correlation, and establish lawful relationships that are inaccessible to everyday experience? How often do we engage in syllogistic deduction as opposed to generalization from experience? (Cole, 1988; Cole, Sharp, Lave, 1976; Cole & Scribner, 1977, p. 269; D'Andrade, 1989). Actually, a strong social basis exists in capitalist countries for denigrating logic and promoting what Jules Henry (1963) calls "fuzzy mindedness." By this he means the acceptance of all kinds of pseudo-associations and illogical conclusions of the kind fostered by advertising. Cole is thus correct to argue that occasional, circumscribed abstract psychological processes must not be overgeneralized to imply an absolute difference with primitive people.

Cole explains that a genuine sociohistorical psychology should investigate the particular cultural requirements for abstraction and ascertain the particular domains in which abstract psychological processes are exercised. Sociohistorical psychology should not presume wholesale psychological differences corresponding to social structural differences; it must empirically investigate exactly when, where, and what kind of abstraction is demanded. In many cases, modern society only fosters abstraction in certain domains with other areas adequately handled by contextual, functional, empirical cognition. Cognition is not a homogeneous activity whose singular nature encompasses every task. Rather cognition is a kind of practice (praxis) which consists of certain kinds of socially constituted activity (processes) and knowledge applied to certain socially specified purposes and tasks (Scribner & Cole, 1981, pp. 236-237; Laboratory of Comparative Human Cognition, 1983; Ceci, 1990). Cognitive operations are sometimes so confined to certain domains that they must be painstakingly learned in new areas (Saxe & Posner, 1983, p. 311). Levy-Bruhl's conception of the historical heterogeneity of thought thus has vital relevance for sociohistorical psychology (Tulviste, 1979, 1987).

While cognitive operations are not intrinsically general, they may become generalized if society requires them. Despite their emphasis on domain specificity of cognitive processes, Scribner and Cole (1978, 1981) also raise the possibility of "domain generality" under appropriate social conditions. In their discussion of the Vai people of Liberia, Scribner and Cole trace the restricted psychological effects of literacy to the limited importance literacy has in that culture. The authors then suggest that as literacy practice expands, the associated cognitive operations may be applied across a range of tasks and contexts (1978, p. 458).

Social determination of cognitive generalization is evident in the case of conservation. Whereas premodern people manifest a specialized ability that is confined to certain objects (e.g., clay) and modalities (volume or quantity, for example), modern people evidence a much more general conservation ability. To illustrate, a comparison of children from four linguistic-cultural groups in New Guinea revealed great inconsistency among the groups on four Piagetian conservation tasks. Groups that were superior on conservation of length were inferior on conservation of quantity and area. Significantly, these inconsistencies persisted into sixth grade. Thus, in New Guinea, cultural requirements for specialized skills dictate that school does not produce a uniform cognitive competence across tasks (Shea et al., 1983). In contrast, modern people easily conserve across modalities such weight and volume (e.g., 1/4 pound of butter = 1/2 cup).

Mathematical operations are similarly context-dependent among traditional people but are generalized among modern people. For example, some Dioulans of West Africa understand the commutative relationship in addition problems (e.g., $38 + 46 = 46 + 38$) but not in multiplication problems (e.g., $6 \times 100 = 100 \times 6$) (Saxe & Posner, 1983, p. 305). Even within traditional societies, individuals occupying commercial roles learn to generalize mathematical operations over a greater range of problems than individuals outside the commercial sector. Saxe (1982) found that older Oksapmin adults who were uninvolved in the money economy could add numbers of coins and arrive at a correct sum, but they could not subtract. Traders, on the other hand, were equally adept at both operations. The traders' social life activity thus spurred them to learn reversibility of cognitive operations whereas the peasants' life activity did not stimulate this competence—which repudiates Piaget's contention that it naturally develops in children between seven and eleven years of age. Furthermore, the peasants employed different strategies for addition depending on whether the objects were present or whether the addition was to be done mentally, out of sight of the actual objects. Traders, on the other hand, employed similar strategies for both kinds of problems.

Modern society manifests similar social class variations in the demand for generalization of certain cognitive competencies. Where using proper grammar is essential for successful action, as in the middle class, school-taught grammar is readily generalized to everyday activities. However, in the lower class, where the opportunity for success is negligible regardless of the correctness of one's grammar, school-taught grammar remains confined to the classroom and shows no generalization. Where the demands and structure of modern society pervade all socioeconomic classes, the lower class manifests cognitive generalization as well as the upper classes. For instance, all classes share the modern abstract conception of time—as decontextualized, homogeneous, divisible, and linear—throughout all sectors of life. Our decontextualized notion of time is not confined to certain atypical domains, it is general to most domains.

Number and measurement is likewise generally abstract for virtually all classes of people in modern society. Number almost always has an abstract identity that is differentiated from objects and is commutable across them. Color has a similarly abstract identity. We have very few context-bound colors such as "coral." Even "orange" has been severed from its object source and the latter is rarely conjured up by the color term. These instances of abstract thought are not exceptional or restricted, they are normal and typical. Modern culture demands such generality in these practices, although it does not demand such generality in free recall, deductive logic, and scientific thinking.[10]

The task of concrete psychology is to empirically investigate the particular level of abstraction of particular psychological processes in particular social psychological domains. Generality and particularity of abstract processes are empirical matters that derive from concrete societal relationships.

If the generality of individual concepts and abilities, such as number, time, color, free recall, deductive reasoning, and personhood is socially constituted, then the generality of cognitive operations, which encompass the full spectrum of individual concepts and abilities, is also. Piaget's notion of an intrinsic uniformity to cognitive stages, which encompasses the manner in which all things are thought about, is therefore quite misguided. Piaget is so wedded to the notion of endogenous, uniform, cognitive stages that he explains irregularities in cognitive development as due to the blocking of natural tendencies. Feldman and Toulmin (1976, pp. 452-453) make the important observation that the term "decalage," which Piaget uses to denote a lack of uniformity in cognitive processes, has the sense of a blockage or wedge. The use of this word suggests that if artificial obstacles could be avoided, cognitive stages would naturally be homogeneous in the sense of governing the entire range of an individual's thinking. It is only because this natural tendency is blocked by some unnamed, external factor, that cognitive stages manifest irregularities.

Feldman and Toulmin suggest that contrary to Piaget's formulation, cognitive processes form in thinking about particular things. Decalage is therefore entirely normal because we think about different things in different ways. There is no preordained thinking process which naturally tends to encompass the entire spectrum of thought objects. Rather than uniform stages being blocked and having to become unblocked to achieve their "natural" cohesiveness, uniformity is only achieved under the press of social demands. Cognitive homogeneity is a social product that must be positively constructed. It is not a natural tendency which will flower through avoiding social pressures.[11]

Variation of Mental Processes along Other Dimensions

Although discussion of psychological processes typically focuses on the dimension of contextual-decontextual thought, many other dimensions are equally important. If psychological process is defined as the manner or form in which information is construed, then atomism-holism is certainly an important dimension that encompasses diverse content. Atomism construes things as discrete self-contained bits which are simply added together. Holism construes things as integrally related parts whose manner of integration determines the parts as much as the parts determine the whole. Yet another kind of psychological processing concerns the superficiality or depth of comprehending information—that is, whether appearances are taken for granted or penetrated to fathom essential properties and relationships. Another form of thought that may be considered as falling within the rubric of psychological process is whether or not events are construed as humanly constructed and changeable or given like things (i.e., reified).

All of these processes are socially constituted and they dominate different domains of the psychological life space in different societies. *Atomistic, fragmented thought* dominates Western cognition but is quite exceptional in other societies (Whorf, 1956; Horkheimer, 1974, chap. 1; Horkheimer & Adorno, 1969, *The Concept of Enlightenment*). Therefore cognition is neither intrinsically atomistic as empiricists believe nor intrinsically holistic as Kantians believe. Atomism and holism are functions of social life.[12]

Superficial and profound thinking are also social products. Identifying characteristics of our society which foster superficial thinking in everyday life, Jules Henry (1963) criticizes the trivializing function of infantile, misleading, frivolous advertising. The Frankfurt social philosophers indict insensitive, superficial cultural institutions (media, art, and news reporting) for lowering the intellectual level of modern man (Horkheimer & Adorno, 1969, *The Culture Industry*). Marcuse's (1964) critique of industrial society brings out important ways in which it promotes one-dimensional, conformist thinking. More orthodox Marxists have shifted the focus from industrial society to capitalist commodity production as responsible for undermining a farsighted, organic understanding of life and promoting a superficial concern with immediate, palpable, material phenomena. With education, for example, increasingly regarded as a commodity to be exchanged for a high salary, students lose intrinsic interest in studying and they participate in a superficial, utilitarian manner. Of course, superficial thinking is not unique to our society. It is promoted by different social practices in other societies. Many of these practices have a common origin and require a general solution. An important, widespread social feature that fosters superficial thinking in everyday life has been identified by Erich Fromm. His analysis also illuminates a contrary social feature that must be brought about in order to foster profound everyday thinking. Fromm (1980, p. 4) states:

> We cannot find the truth as long as social contradictions and force require ideological falsification, as long as man's reason is damaged by irrational passions which have their root in the disharmony and irrationality of social life. Only in a society in which there is no exploitation, hence which does not need irrational assumptions in order to cover up or justify exploitation, in a society in which the basic contradictions have been solved and in which social reality can be recognized without distortion, can man make full use of his reason, and at that point he can recognize reality in an undistorted form—that is to say, the truth. To put it differently, the truth is historically conditioned: it is dependent on the degree of rationality and the absence of contradictions within the society.

According to Marx's *Capital* and Lukacs's *History and Class Consciousness*, under commodity exchange social interaction is dictated by rules governing the exchange of products. With personal, social decisions increasingly subordinated to commercial ones, the human constitution of society and technology becomes obscured. Everything appears to happen because of the market, and we lose sight of the fact that the market is a particular, humanly constituted phenomenon in the first place. Commodity production thus fosters the illusion of *reification* or fetishism—that social relations, artifacts, and even human traits have thing-like properties independent of human activity. However, reification is actually a social phenomenon: the interpretation of events as natural and unsocial is entirely due to the structure of a particular social system. The social system has obscured its own sociality and human constitution (Leontiev, 1981, pp. 244-272).

Psychological form is not confined to particular ways of thinking. The entire *structure of consciousness*, including the relationship of emotions, cognition, memory, personality, and motivation, has a culturally mediated form which deserves far more investigation that it has received. Erich Fromm's and Jules Henry's insightful observations illustrate what is involved. Fromm and Henry argue that modern Western man is, in everyday life, ruled by his desires rather than reason. Tracing this to a consumerist orientation, Fromm and Henry state that modern man expresses his impulses and acts on whims, in contrast to the nineteenth-century orientation which subjected desires to calculated scrutiny and control. This means that the relationship between emotions, motivation, and reason has changed over the past century. Whereas previously the ego, to use Freud's metaphor, stood guard over the id and moderated its impulses, today the id overwhelms ego functions. Modern impulsiveness does not refute the cognitively mediated nature of emotions discussed above, it simply means that cognitively mediated emotions are freely expressed rather than constrained. That this change is socially dictated confirms the cultural character of emotions, motives, and needs, and their relation to cognition. Such a change in the relation of psychological functions reflects the fact that "the relation of psychological functions is. . .linked to real relations between people" (Vygotsky, 1989, pp. 57, 69-70).

Notes

1. Criticizing abstraction which loses sight of its constituent particulars, Hegel emphasized the importance of a dialectical integration among the two. Only

this integration, which he called the true Concept of a thing, is concrete. In his inimitable words,

> Now, as regards the nature of the Concept as such, it is not in itself an abstract unity at all over against [i.e., separate from] the differences of reality; as Concept it is already the unity of specific differences and therefore a concrete totality. So, for example, ideas like man, etc. are prima facie not to be called 'concepts,' but abstractly universal ideas, which only become the Concept when it is clear in them that they comprise different aspects in a unity, since this inherently determinate unity constitutes the concept. (Hegel, 1975, vol. 1, p. 108)

Hegel contended that avoiding reified, abstract universals is central to doing good philosophy. Insisting that identity dialectically encompasses, rather than excludes, differences he warned, "we must especially guard against taking identity as abstract Identity, to the exclusion of all Difference. That is the touchstone for distinguishing all bad philosophy from what alone deserves the name of philosophy" (Hegel, 1965, p. 214).

The specifications that concretize and limit the general are its determinateness (*Bestimmtheit*). Hegel emphasizes that being is always determinate being (Marcuse, 1987, chap. 3).

2. While feelings depend upon attitudes, they are not identical to them. I can have a generalized attitude of loving my mother which I do not *feel* most of the time because I am not thinking about her. When I talk to her, however, I feel the love. Similarly, if someone asks me, I can certainly say I fear snakes even though I do not normally, or at that moment, *feel* the dread. I do not walk around vividly feeling fear. I only *feel* afraid when I am in the presence of snakes.

3. The social-conceptual basis of adult human emotions does not mean that natural vestiges have been entirely expunged from the human organism. These vestiges definitely exist in babies, and the fact that certain adult facial expressions accompany certain emotional experiences might be rooted in primordial connections that have persisted to this day. However, any such natural components of human emotion will function as Whorf's "lower processes" (described in the previous chapter) which means they will be overridden by higher social-conceptual processes. Facial expressions are a case in point: As Plutchik stated, "At best there is a prototype facial pattern that may appear briefly under extreme stresses or conditions but it is quickly changed, modified, or inhibited on the basis of rules and experiences that are unique both to the culture and to the individual" (cited in Ratner, 1980a).

4. Romantic love did also exist in earlier periods in other countries. According to Lantz (1982), besides eighteenth-century England and nineteenth-century America, romantic love has been identified in ancient Rome, early Christianity, and feudalism. Common social factors in these periods account for the romanticizing of love. In addition, however, social differences in these periods generated important distinctions in the particular characteristics of romantic love. For example, medieval courtly love was typically an unfulfilled

relationship between a married upper-class woman and a suitor of lesser rank. There was little of the personal involvement and soulful sharing that became so prominent in the nineteenth century.

Romantic love has even changed considerably from the nineteenth century to today. Changes in society, the relation of the family to public life, and in notions of the self and personal relationships inevitably alter the nature of love. The former ideal of commitment has been undermined by ideals of personal freedom and change. Lovers are wary of entanglements, and they are more concerned with what they can get out of a relationship (i.e., how it will enrich their own experience) than with what they put into it for the other person. In addition, modern love has become invaded by commercial notions of terms, rights, and responsibilities which are equilibrated in order to ensure equality of exchange. Love has also become permeated by economic notions of work, so that lovers work on their relationships as on a job (Swindler, 1980).

5. Of course, the incorporating of situational variations in emotions must not be overstated. Within a given culture, the same kind of anger may be expressed in a range of circumstances without significantly altering its quality. Its behavioral manifestations can also vary considerably without altering its quality. However, there are limits to this equilibrium. Just as water remains liquid within a range of temperatures but freezes or vaporizes outside this range, so an emotion retains its essential quality within a range of situations but changes significantly in cultures with different concepts and understandings.

6. The real difference in emotional constructs that is reflected in emotional terminology makes translation of emotional terms quite precarious. This poses great difficulties for cross-cultural research and understanding of emotions. Leff (1977) points out the problem of trying to convey differentiated emotions of one culture into another culture that has an undifferentiated emotional vocabulary. For example, worry, tension, and anxiety, which refer to separate sections of the mental state examination schedule must all be collapsed into a single Chinese word.

Another difficulty involves translating between languages which express emotion in bodily terms and those, such as Indo-European, which express the cognitive experience of emotions. For example, "When translating into Yoruba, a Nigerian language, it was hard to find equivalents for depression and anxiety. The words eventually chosen, when translated back into English, came out as 'the heart is weak' and 'the heart is not at rest' " (Leff, p. 322).

The doubtful cross-cultural equivalence of emotional constructs and terms is troubling for most cross-cultural psychological research on emotions which requires subjects to label facial photographs with a single affect word. Assuming equivalence of terms when none, in fact, exists conjures up a false impression of universal emotions and emotional recognition processes. This problem of false generalization will be discussed in the next chapter.

7. Discussing the cultural constitution of the need for privacy, Moore (1984) writes, "By and large, privacy appears to be much less of a social necessity . . . in nonliterate societies than in those with a written language and some form of state." "Hence the need for privacy or protection from intrusion is not explicable as an instinctive or reflex reaction. Instead it derives from the perceived difference between benefits derived from the social order, such as protection and an assured supply of food, and the costs of maintaining the social order in the form of social obligations like sharing food and performing labor" (pp. 73, 74).

Social historians have amply demonstrated that the European feudal nobility had little, if any, need for privacy. Their homes were always open to outsiders who habitually dropped in without notice. Rooms were large, unspecialized areas where diverse activities were conducted simultaneously. Beds did not permanently lie in bedrooms, but were unfolded and set up in the living room at night. Guests often slept in the same beds with their hosts, and all the beds were close together rather than in being in separate rooms. There was no sexual privacy except for a light curtain that was sometimes drawn around a bed.

Bodily functions were also quite public, as it was common to urinate, spit, and blow one's nose on the street. Even eating was a communal activity with a common dish and utensils. It was only with the rise of the individualized bourgeoisie that modern privacy came into existence. The bourgeoisie rigidly separated the household from the outside, required appointments before visiting, specialized rooms to serve separate activities, introduced sexual privacy, and privatized bodily functions including eating (Aries, 1962, pp. 393-404; Stone,1977, pp. 253-257; Elias, 1978; Clark, 1976).

The antipathy to privacy in ancient Greece is revealed in the fact that the Greek term for idiot—"iodotes"—meant a private and separate person.

8. The economic basis of mathematical thinking repudiates Piaget's explanation of number as "an endogenous construction" which "is not learned but only exercised" (Piaget, 1971, pp. 310, 312). Piaget claimed that arithmetic derives from spontaneous, endogenous tendencies to order things in relation to each other. The tendency toward equilibrium, which involves compensating activity in one direction with activity in the opposite direction leads to reversible mathematical operations such as addition and subtraction (Piaget, 1971, p. 12). Similarly, counting springs from the tendency to pair things together.

Emphasizing the endogenous nature of these tendencies, Piaget explicitly states that "the operations of putting together, including, putting in order, and so on are in no way the products of learning . . . The sources or roots of these connections are to be found within the organism and not in the objects, so that it is impossible to speak of learning or structures or acquired habits in their normal sense" (Piaget, 1971, p. 310).

Obviously, such a nativistic formulation overlooks the sociohistorical relationships that inspire mathematical thinking and which preclude its emergence in children living in noncommercial societies. Piaget's nativistic explanation of mathematics also overlooks the systematic encouragement that parents give to children on an interpersonal level (Saxe et al., 1987).

The fact that entire populations learn math when exposed to commercial life-styles demonstrates that the capacity for mathematical thinking is universal—rather than being confined to extraordinary individuals—and simply requires a social motive to incite people to construct mathematical concepts (cf. Chapter 4 discussion of genius).

9. This analysis is borne out by the fact that standardizing of time is historically quite recent. De Grazia (1962) says that although the Egyptians and Babylonians divided the day into 12 parts, they did not pay attention to the exact "hour" and only recognized the "early" and "late" parts of the day, the "hot part of the day," and "nighttime." Before the fourteenth century A.D., an "hour" was not a uniform unit. Europeans divided the day into 12 daylight and 12 nighttime hours so that, except for the two equinoxes, the 12 dark hours did not equal the 12 daytime hours nor, obviously, was each nighttime hour equal in length to each daylight hour. (Whitrow, 1973, p. 401). Indeed, clocks only came into existence as reliable measures of time in 1500 when the hour hand alone was invented. The minute hand only became common after 1660. Even then, the round shape of clocks over which the hands repeatedly swept reflected the cyclical pattern of agricultural life. Modern digital clocks are the true reflection of our quantified, discrete, linear sense of time.

10. Generality of cognitive functions is not restricted to modern society. Wagner and Spratt (1987, pp. 1211, 1216) found that premodern Moroccan children who are taught in Quran preschools to rote-memorize Islamic names but do not spend time memorizing digits, perform as well on memory tests using digits as they do on rote-memory tests with Muslim names as the items to be remembered. In other words, practice in memorizing names generalized to digits (cf. Jahoda, 1981, for an additional example of generalization from school to everyday cognition among Ghanian tribal people).

11. Actually, evidence challenges any such homogeneity across all cognitive operations. Specifically challenging Piaget's conception of generic, coherent cognitive stages, Shweder (1982a, p. 357) said,

> The idea that children or adults are characteristically preoperational (or concrete operational, or formal operational) has taken a beating in recent years. If we examine the actual cognitive functioning of individuals across a series of tasks or problems, we discover that no single operational level is a general property of an individual's thought. Children and adults often do not apply the same mode of reasoning (e.g., reversibility) to formally equivalent problems (e.g., a conservation task) which differ in content or surface characteristics (e.g., conservation of number versus conservation of liquid quantity). By varying the content of a task it is possible to elicit either preoperational thinking from a college-educated adult or formal operational thinking from a four year old. The person who functions at a formal operational level on one task is not typically the same person who functions at a formal operational

level on a second task. Indeed, to cite but one example, Roberge and Flexer discovered that performance on formal operational tests for propositional logic and combinatorial thinking intercorrelate a mere −0.07 for eighth graders and 0.17 for adults (cf. also Cole & Bruner, 1971; Laboratory of Comparative Human Cognition, 1983, pp. 340-342; Feldman & Toulmin, 1976).

Kagan (1981, p. 118) similarly rejects "a concept like 'developmental rate' or 'developmental level' which applies to all major cognitive functions during an era of growth. Such general constructs—g being one example—are not theoretically useful and are not in accord with the relative independence we found among many of the indices of cognitive development." Gelman and Baillargeon concur with this conclusion. In their extensive review of the developmental literature they pointedly state: "In our opinion there is little evidence to support the idea of major stages in cognitive development of the type described by Piaget" (Gelman & Baillargeon, 1983, p. 214).

Cultural variations in the sequence in which cognitive abilities are exhibited further challenges the notion of intrinsic, maturationally mandated stages. Research on decentration, or the ability to adopt different perspectives, has found that it appears on different tasks at different ages in different societies. On 3 tasks of decentration—(1) sibling perspective comprehension, (2) sibling category definition, and (3) left-right orientation—Vietnamese children are successful at 7, 11, and 10 years of age, respectively. Geneva children are successful at 10, 9, and 8 years, respectively. And Hawaiian children are successful at 9, 8, and 10, respectively. The sequence is thus (1), (3), (2) in the Vietnamese population, (3), (2), (1) in the Geneva sample, and (2), (1), (3) in the Hawaiian children. An additional complicating piece of data is that Hausa children achieve decentration on the left-right orientation task as early as 6, compared to 10 in the Vietnamese population (Luong, 1986). Luong concludes that the variation in what Piagetians would consider a horizontal decalage sequence closely relates to the diversity of sociocultural rules and is a function of the sociocultural environment:

> It is no coincidence that the extremely early decentration in left-right orientation by Hausa children takes place in a system which, as a part of the Islamic tradition, attaches considerable importance to the differentiation of left and right hands and to the full comprehension of their symbolic significance. Similarly, the emphasis on the assumption of junior interactants' perspectives in Vietnamese kin term usages underlies the earlier decentration among Vietnamese children on the sibling perspective task. (pp. 26-27)

The fact that 3-year olds recognize the difference in perspective between themselves and others well before they achieve reversibility and decentration in other tasks (such as right-left orientation), challenges Piaget's hypothesis that this operation constitutes a part of the domain-free concrete operational structure that emerges at age 7-12 (Luong, p. 34; Leontiev, 1981, p. 397).

While maturation dictates a general direction of cognitive ability toward abstract and decentered thinking, there is no evidence for a fixed sequence of decentered competencies (Luong, 1986, p. 8).

Experientially derived variations in cognitive competencies do not rule out the possibility that certain competencies are intrinsically more complex and difficult to acquire than others. In these areas, a universal developmental sequence would be manifest. Decontextualized thought succeeds contextualized thought for this reason. And cross-cultural evidence suggests a universal developmental sequence for other competencies as well. Mwamwenda and Mwamwenda (1989) report several studies which find an invariant sequence: transitive inference, conservation of volume, class inclusion. This data contradicts Piaget's contention that transitivity is the most difficult and latest to appear of the three, however the data suggests that a universal sequence among the three may occur.

The notion that invariant sequences of activity can result from differential complexity of *tasks* rather than from an endogenous set of *cognitive processes* (which naturally unfold at predetermined times) is readily illustrated with examples from history. In history, literacy invariably precedes science, and hunting and gathering society invariably precedes agriculture which always precedes industrialization. It is inconceivable that mankind could have reversed this order or skipped directly from hunting and gathering to industrialization without the intermediate "stage" of agriculture. However, the sequences are invariant because each "stage" requires knowledge (and material support) that has been acquired in earlier periods. The sequences are certainly not determined by endogenous dispositions which unfold in an intrinsically predetermined order. No ineluctible destiny compels every society to develop from one stage to another (some remain at one stage) or to complete the entire possible progression and achieve the most developed state (Gellner, 1988, p. 16). Exactly the same can be said for the ontogenetic sequence of cognitive operations.

12. The way in which atomizing knowledge instantiates bourgeois social values within educational institutions is illuminated by McNeil (1986). She shows how the atomistic form in which knowledge is dispensed (and cognition is structured) co-opt disparate content within a uniform bourgeois form.

3

Psychological Universals, True and False

The Relation between General and Concrete Psychological Features

The fact that psychological phenomena are sociohistorical does not preclude the existence of universal features. However, the nature of these universals is quite different from the way they are ordinarily construed by mainstream psychologists. Universals are ordinarily conceived as a separate class of phenomena from variable features, originating in psychobiological properties of the human organism in contrast to variations which reflect socially mediated experience. Sociohistorical psychology rejects this dichotomy and argues that universal features of psychological phenomena have a social basis just as variations do. The social basis of psychological universals lies in common features of social life. What Rosaldo said about emotions—that they are similar to the extent that societies are alike—holds true for all psychological phenomena. Whereas socially relative aspects of psychology reflect differences in social life, psychological universals reflect uniformities of social existence. Some of these commonalities were described in Chapter 1 where universal aspects of social existence such as division of labor, social organization, cooperation, language, and tool use were shown to generate universal aspects of psychology such as symbolization, thought, logic, self-concept, mnemonic strategies for remembering information, volition, self-control, a broad sensitivity to things, and comprehension of things' essential features and interrelationships which are invisible to sense experience.

With psychological universals originating in social universals, the nature of psychological uniformities depends upon the manner in which all societies are alike. It is therefore incumbent upon us to answer the question, "In what ways are all societies alike?"

Certainly not at the national level, where nation-states manifest great dissimilarities; but neither at the level of socioeconomic systems. A socioeconomic system, such as capitalism, socialism, or feudalism, does provide common characteristics to the nations it encompasses. But no socioeconomic system is so universal as to encompass all societies. Even more general social features which encompass several socioeconomic systems are not universal. These features, which may be called "formal" for the purpose of identification, include formal educational institutions, the presence or absence of socioeconomic classes, the level of technology, and male-female equality or inequality in status. The fact that advanced capitalist and socialist nations are alike on most of the formal characteristics just mentioned makes them quite far-reaching. However, the existence of societies possessing different formal features—i.e., a low technological level, little formal education, minimal male-female inequality and class divisions—means that they are not omnipresent.

The search for truly universal social features must therefore locate even more general characteristics. These exist in the form of what may be called "abstract" social features. They include division of labor, social organization, language, and tool use. These are present in all societies in some form. Of course, the particular form varies and is not universal. What is universal is the *essence* of these features, not their concrete, particular existence. These essential aspects are necessarily abstract—that is, they are formless and contentless because the particular forms and contents vary so extensively. In other words, universal social features are the presence of division of labor, social organization, language, and tool use *apart from any specific qualities these have in any particular society*.

Since psychological phenomena embody social characteristics, psychological universals will have the same abstract character that social universals do. Accordingly, psychological universals are the essential aspects of symbolic thought, intentionality, emotions, intelligence, mnemonic strategies for remembering information, deductive reasoning, and personhood *devoid of any specific form and content*. Specific characteristics of these functions are socially variable and are not universal. As we know from our analysis of social features, specificity is locally circumscribed. *Universality is directly related to abstractness and inversely related to specificity.* Stated another way, specific psychological features are circumscribed within social domains. Let us demonstrate the truth of this assertion by comparing the psychological features which derive from various kinds of social features.

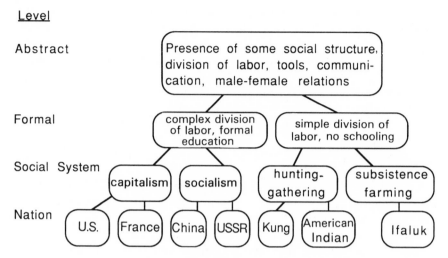

Figure 4. Levels of social organization which foster psychological similarities and differences.

The "formal" characteristics of social life engender such "formal" psychological characteristics as abstract vs. context-bound processes described in Chapter 2. Knowing that people think more or less contextually is more specific than simply knowing that they think, which makes formal psychological features more specific than abstract ones. And this very specificity distinguishes the thinking of groups of peoples which means that it is not universal across all people as the abstract features are. The psychological features which derive from characteristics of a socioeconomic system are more specific and socially circumscribed than formal features. For instance, the atomistic, reified thinking which the capitalist socioeconomic system breeds is a specific kind of decontextualized thought and it is confined to fewer societies than the formal feature is.

The foregoing formulation can be clarified by diagramming the levels of social organization and their corresponding psychological uniformities. This is shown in Figure 4.

Of course, Figure 4 is an idealized model of reality which does not come so neatly organized. In reality, a certain amount of cross-over exists among categories. For example, the formal characteristics listed do not always go together. Low technological level may be associated with class divisions, and high technological level may (conceivably, one day) be associated with minimal class differences. Many undeveloped third world countries with minimal industrialization and formal schooling are socialist systems. However, Figure 4 does identify the levels of generality of social and psychological features. It also depicts the relationship between generality and abstractness. The figure shows that the only level at which psychological phenomena are truly universal is the abstract level devoid of specific form, content, and developmental level. What Clyde Kluckhohn (1953, p. 519) said about anthropological universals includes psychological phenomena: "There are, admittedly, few genuine uniformities in culture content unless one states the content in extremely general form."

Because the world's societies are not homogeneous in their specific details, specific psychological features of emotions, memory, thinking, and language will be culturally variable. At this point in history, specific psychological features cannot be universal because social features are not. Universals must be abstract in the sense of transcending the local differences among the particulars they encompass. But this makes psychological abstractions notably uninformative (Neisser, 1982).

In contrast with physical abstractions which provide essential information about gravitation, floatation, waves, and gases, abstract psychological notions about thinking, memory, feeling, and learning are rather barren. Psychological abstractions usefully indicate the general aspects of human activity—especially in contrast to animal behavior—however, they never reveal its particularity and variety. As Clifford Geertz (1973, chap. 2) argues, generalities such as "man thinks," "man is moral," "man enjoys beauty," "man has kinship systems," "man uses language," "people have a sense of time," "humans categorize information," are neither false nor unimportant. However, they fail to disclose the richness of the concrete, particular instances from which those generalities are derived.

In his call for concrete, contextualized social science, Richard Shweder (1980, p. 268) points out the difficulty with abstract universals: "to identify universal concepts, one must empty them of all specific content. This is a difficulty because it is precisely the specific content of a concept that interacts with its universal content to produce a behavior. Focusing on universal concepts is like searching for the 'real' artichoke by divesting it of its leaves (Wittgenstein). Having divested universal concepts of any specific content, the researcher can say very little about social conduct" (cf. Shweder, 1990). This is why Vygotsky (1987, p. 91) urged, "The task of psychology is not the discovery of the eternal child. The task of psychology is the discovery of the historical child, of what Goethe called the transitory child. This stone that builders have disdained must become the foundation stone." Vygotsky (1989, p. 72) advocated studying "concrete psychology (i.e., the special here and now), not general psychology."[1]

With increasing contact and interdependence among societies, it is predictable that they will become increasingly alike. Instead of uniformities being confined to abstract levels, lower levels of Figure 4 will manifest greater similarity. As primitive societies become modernized, their formal system will become absorbed into ours, and their social systems will be coopted by one of the modern ones. Eventually, the Kung and Ifaluk will suffer the fate of the American Indians and will become nationalities within the capitalist or socialist camp. The right side of Figure 4 will become subsumed within the left side. Premodern people will then be similar to modern people not only on the abstract level, but on specific levels as well. The Kung will resemble us not simply in that we all think, feel, and communicate via language, but also in the specific ways that we think, feel, and communicate. The hitherto abstractness of psychological universals is therefore a historical phenomenon due to the existence of substantial social and technological differences among people. As history erodes these differences, universals will become more specific.

Moving up Figure 4 indicates similarities which transcend lower differences. Moving down the figure reveals differences among the commonalities. Of course, as Hegel emphasized, the universal and particular always coexist as concrete phenomena. Universals always encompass specific differences, and differences occur within the framework of universals. For example, all people engage in some form of logical thinking, however the particular level of abstraction and complexity varies. Similarly, general features of emotions such as attraction and repulsion, or pleasure and displeasure are concretized in different specific emotions. In the previous chapter we saw that mother-infant bonding and adult male-female bonding manifest substantial cultural differences. In addition, general ideas of morality, such as the formal and abstract injunctions to "avoid harming others", and to "treat people of equal status equally" are defined differently across cultures—which provides moral justification for atrocities such as slavery, foot-binding, and homelessness (Shweder, 1982c, 1990b; Fernandez, 1990).

Universal features do not stand apart from particulars. They exist in and through them and take on different coloration according to particular components (Berry, 1978, p. 98). On the other hand, particulars are not entirely cut off from each other but are linked through general commonalities. Thus, all repulsive, displeasurable emotions share a common negativity which is universally recognizable; however, the concrete modulation of this quality is socially variable and not universally obvious. Particularity and generality, difference and commonality, are all real; none is displaced by another, although they do exist on different levels.

In contrast to traditional prejudice, the concrete must be investigated *before* general commonalities are abstracted out because the general is a generalization of the concrete. As Berry (1978, p. 96) stated in an important discussion of comparative social psychology, "The search for the general or universal is only possible after wide ranges of local, specific phenomena and relationships have been observed; that is, the integration follows the differentiation of knowledge." Otherwise, we do not know how general our abstractions really are. As Margaret Mead (1963, p. 187) put it, "One cannot talk about Culture until one has systematically studied cultures." Echoing this sentiment with characteristic aplomb, Geertz (1973, p. 53) stated: "The road to the general lies through a concern with the particular, the circumstantial, the concrete" (cf. Toulmin, 1981; Kleinman, 1977, for similar analyses of this issue). If generalizations are not built up from a detailed knowledge of historically situated particulars they will be superficial descriptions of outward appearances.[2]

In addition, we cannot assume a more general level of explanation until more specific levels have been systematically ruled out. If specific social-technological factors can plausibly account for psychological phenomena, it is unwarranted to postulate universal factors. For example, the Trobriander Islanders' sophisticated logical inference can plausibly be explained by their complex system of property rights and legal negotiation. If their logical reasoning is found to be comparable to modern Americans' (which, we must emphasize, has not been proven), the explanation would lie in comparable formal features of the two social systems—i.e., in their individualized form of property allocation and their legal system of arbitration (the Trobrianders' legal system having been imposed during their colonial period by the British and Australian governments). Psychological similarities between the two peoples should not be attributed to abstract, universal social features unless the formal features can be shown to be insufficient explanations.[3]

Unfortunately, mainstream psychology approaches psychological universals quite differently from sociohistorical psychology. In the first place, universals are construed as more important than social variations. The preoccupation with discovering psychological laws, akin to physical laws, is one reflection of this preoccupation with universals. Inference statistics explicitly assume that the performance of a small sample of individuals represents the entire human population. Consequently, findings are typically presented as describing "cognitive development of *the child*," "thought processes of *the schizophrenic*," "*group* processes," or "laws of *memory*" without any qualification concerning the nationality of the individuals being described. Psychologists *presume* they are investigating and describing universal phenomena.

This predilection for universals is linguistically instantiated by calling them "basic." Among the more famous examples are Berlin and Kay's "basic colors" which refer to universally perceived colors. Rosch's designation of middle level taxonomic categories—e.g., "chair" which stands between the superordinate "furniture" and the subordinate "kitchen chair"—as basic similarly denotes a presumed universal saliency (See below for further discussion of this issue.) Finally, emotions such as fear, joy, sadness, surprise, frustration, and expectation are termed basic because they are universal, and even experienced by animals (Izard, 1980, p. 198; Ekman, 1972, p. 223; Zajonc, 1980, p. 157; Plutchik, 1980b, p. 139).[4] Employing the appellation "basic" to refer to universals implicitly denigrates socially variable phenomena (or features of phenomena) to secondary or superficial status.

Universalists such as Piaget and Chomsky certainly hold this bias. Piaget disparages variations in psychological content and speed of cognitive development as pertaining to individual differences, while the form through which all psychological content must pass is deemed central to "general psychology" (Glick in Broughton et al., 1981, p. 159). As Kitchener summarized Piaget's position, "One might say that factual knowledge is content that varies from individual to individual, but Piaget is more concerned with the form or structure of knowledge (with Kant) which is universal" (Kitchener, 1986, p. 154; cf. Mischel, 1971, pp. 346-348). Chomsky is similarly more intrigued by universal features of grammar than with individual grammars.

In addition to prioritizing universals over variations, the conventional view severs universals from variations and endows them with their own determining mechanisms. According to this viewpoint, endogenous biological mechanisms determine the universal features of psychological functions, leaving variable features to be devised in the course of practical experience. For example, presumed universal emotions such as loss or anger are construed as innately programmed, although the display rules governing time, place, and manner of expression are socially variable. In this vein, sociobiologists contend that aggression is universal by virtue of genetic programs, while the target, time, place, and method of aggressing are socially devised (E.O. Wilson, 1978, p. 114). Wilson (p. 177) goes so far as to claim that religion has a genetic basis which orients people toward religious-type behavior such as dichotomizing objects into the sacred and profane, accepting hierarchical dominance systems, and admiring charismatic leaders. The specific kind of religion that a people invent is unconstrained by such genetic programs. Schizophrenic thought is similarly biologically determined in its essential symptoms such as delusions, while the content of delusions is derived from social experience.

Psychoanalysts presume that psychosexual stages are biologically rooted, although the manner in which they are treated by parents leads to different psychological outcomes. Research on attitudes similarly postulates a natural drive to maintain consistency, consonance, or balance among attitudes which motivates attitude change regardless of content. Research on conformity, group processes, and persuasion likewise seeks laws among abstract variables (such as the number of group members, primacy or recency of the communication) which encompass any and all content.

Mention must finally be made of Chomsky's linguistic theory and Piaget's conception of cognitive development as exemplifying the bifurcation of psychological universals and social variations. Chomsky argues for a universal grammar that is biologically mandated and specifies the properties of sound, meaning, and structural organization that all human languages will have. Within these constraints, people of different cultures can construct unique phonetics, semantics, and syntax.

Piaget was similarly moved to postulate biological factors which generate universal forms of cognitive development. Although he often stated that cognitive development emerged out of interaction with the environment, the forms of this interaction were innately structured. For instance, the tendency to order objects—which eventually culminates in mathematical operations—is:

> in no way the product of learning, for the connections of inclusion, order, and correspondence intervene as previously existing conditions, and not merely as results . . . of the nervous system, of the physiological functions, or of the functioning of the living organization in general . . . [T]he sources or roots of these connections are to be found within the organism and not in the objects, so that it is impossible to speak of learning or structures of acquired habits in their normal sense. (Piaget, 1971, p. 310)

The mathematical operations which result from such endogenous ordering tendencies are necessarily construed as also innately fashioned. In Piaget's words, "number appears to be an endogenous construction" which "is not learned but only exercised" (Piaget, 1971, pp. 310, 312).

The fact that Piaget likens the sequence of cognitive development to a biological epigenesis, according to which "intellectual growth contains its own rhythms and its 'chreods' [necessary, channeled paths] just as physical growth does" (1971, pp. 18, 21), coupled with his contention that deviation from these paths is righted by a process of "self regulation," is further indication that he grounds universal developmental phenomena in biological processes. We saw in Chapter 2 that Piaget is so wedded to universal cognitive processes that he explains heterogeneity of thought as due to the blocking of tendencies toward uniformity.[5]

In contrast to biologically determined universal processes, Piaget states that their content is free to vary with individual and social experience.[6]

Sociohistorical psychology challenges this one-sided conception of psychological universals. Universals cannot logically be divorced from and prioritized over specific variations. Universals are not more important than variations. If anything, they are less informative as Geertz maintains. Dichotomizing universal and variable features is a serious logical mistake. Universals devoid of specific variations would be empty categories, like the category Man without individual men. There simply is no universal without specifics. There is no aggression apart from aggression toward particular targets, there is no memory apart from particular ways of remembering things, there is no religion apart from religions. And there is no universal grammar apart from variable grammars, just as there is no universal, endogenous logical-mathematical sensitivity apart from real logical, mathematical systems that have been created by sensuous, local activity. Humans only create socially specific psychological phenomena. They don't create "memory," "logic," or "emotions" per se. General features or categories do not antedate particulars; they rather represent real, diverse specifics. The general is actually the result of the particular ways in which individuals have constituted themselves.

Formal universals (akin to Kantian categories) devoid of specifics are not only logically impossible, they are impractical as well. A universal tendency toward aggression or anger, without specification of when, where, and how they would be expressed, would be quite maladaptive. They would produce generalized, aimless response tendencies which would only be troublesome.

Another problem with dichotomizing universals from variations is that the former are attributed to endogenous causes while the latter are attributed to acquired experience. However, biological mechanisms cannot account for abstract, indefinite reactions. Years ago, Bernard (1924, 1926) observed that biological determination consists of programs for a definite sensitivity and reactivity. There can be no program for indefinite abstractions such as maternal love which can take numerous forms. The same injunction applies to biological determination of religion, aggression, cognitive forms, and linguistic principles. These cannot be biologically determined because there is simply nothing specific to determine.

Constancies in human activity are quite different from constancies in animal behavior and these contrasts necessitate different explanatory mechanisms. Whereas animal constancies involve specific sensitivities and responses, human constancies are general forms which are shot through with variations. Biological determinants of specific animal behavior are inapplicable to human activity because they preclude the flexibility that is so highly developed in humans. Any explanation of human universals must also provide for man's psychological variability. In fact, given the interdependence of universals and variations they must both be explained in the same terms. These terms are sociohistorical.

All psychological phenomena are constructed in the course of social participation. Humans engage in historically circumscribed social relations and our psychology has the characteristics of these social interactions. But, of course, all social relations and psychological activity have some common, essential features which transcend their particular qualities. The key point of sociohistorical psychology is to emphasize that these common features do not stand on their own, they are only the common features *of* localized activity. We do not construct "social organization," "tools," "memory," "perception," "logic," "emotions," or "language." We only construct particular societies, tools, memories, perceptions, logics, emotions, and languages. The common features of tools, division of labor, social organization, speech, thinking, memory, emotions, and personality are invented by humans through a long, difficult, and ongoing struggle. They are not things standing above and beyond this inventive process.

A final error of the conventional conception of psychological universals is that it construes them too specifically. Psychologists are rarely content to admit the abstract nature of universals and the local variation among specifics. Consequently, what are purported to be psychological universals are often really socially specific features which have been erroneously overgeneralized. This conflating of particular and universal constitutes a major, prevalent error in psychological research (cf. Marcuse's *One-Dimensional Man* for the finest discussion of this in contemporary society).[7] We shall call it the error of false universals.

False Psychological Universals

Instead of rigorously distinguishing general and particular psychological characteristics, most psychologists wittingly or unwittingly smuggle particular social psychological characteristics into notions of universals. Few psychologists are content to confine their conception of universals to abstract phenomena. Most study the richer form and content of specific social psychological phenomena but persistently presume them to be universal. The universal thus becomes identified with a particular expression instead of being a generalization of various particulars (Berry, 1978). Consequently, the sociohistorical character of social psychological phenomena is obscured because it appears to be universal and natural. The result is an ethnocentric inability to understand other people's different psychology. Either the differences are overlooked and other psychologies are naively presumed to "really" be a form of our own; or the differences are halfheartedly recognized but are denigrated as aberrations which should be altered to correspond to our kind of "normal" psychology.

Both the form and content of psychology have been subjected to false universalization (Billig, 1982). Content is falsely universalized by theories which proclaim certain colors to be intrinsically more salient than others (Ratner, 1989b), by theories which contend that certain emotions are natural and universal (Ratner, 1989a), and by sociobiology which presumes that tendencies toward aggression, private property, and monogamy are genetically determined, species-wide dispositions. Psychological form or processes are also commonly subject to false universalization. This is more difficult to discern because the content has been abstracted out and the process appears to be genuinely universal. However, the level of abstraction is too low for the process to be truly universal and it surreptitiously embodies specific social elements.

For instance, decision making is typically viewed by psychologists as a process of calculating gain and loss. Psychologists' concern is not for the particular issues being decided, but for how they are rendered into profit-and-loss terms. Such rendering is presumed to be a universal feature of decision making, regardless of what the issues are. However, the calculating of exchange value is not universal, but is particular to societies where commodity exchange is prevalent. In noncommercial societies, calculating the exchange value of things and behaviors is unimaginable (Hogan & Emler, 1978; Pepitone, 1976; Fromm, 1973, pp. 163-164; Triandis, 1989). Thus, calculated, exchange-oriented decision-making is historically circumscribed despite the fact that it has been emptied of content.[8]

It is fair to say that most of the psychological processes characteristic of Western individuals have been falsely universalized. This has not gone unnoticed, and critiques have been leveled against the false universalization that plagues Kohlberg's theory of moral development (Broughton, 1985; Shweder, 1982b; Shweder et al., 1987; Sullivan, 1977; Harkness, Edwards, Super, 1981), frustration-aggression theory (Pepitone, 1976; Bateson, 1941), behaviorism (Matson, 1964; Asch, 1952, p. 150; Pepitone & Triandis, 1987, p. 486), psychoanalysis (Lichtman, 1982), attribution theory (Pepitone, 1986; Amir & Sharon, 1987), and the biomedical model of mental illness (Kleinman, 1977). It is worthwhile to examine a few examples of false universalizing of psychological processes in order to analyze the problem.

False universalizing occurs in two ways. In the naive manner, universality is assumed without evidence. This error is easy to fall into with more than 90% of psychological research being monocultural (Pepitone & Triandis, 1987, p. 476). Given this, presumptions of universality are difficult to falsify, although they are equally difficult to prove. A second, more invidious, strategy to buttress false universalization is to disregard data which demonstrates cultural variation in particular psychological phenomena and misinterpret it as indicating universality. Both of these gambits are illustrated in the following examples.

A particularly important and influential example is Piaget's universalist assumptions concerning children's cognitive processes. We have already indicated in Chapter 2 that the generality of Piaget's cognitive operations varies with social requirements and is not a generic characteristic. This qualification can be extended to other areas of Piaget's work. In the second chapter to *Thinking and Speech*, Vygotsky (1987) shows that Piaget's fundamental concepts concerning childhood thinking recapitulate Freud's primary processes. Piaget follows Freud in postulating children as intrinsically unrealistic, autistic, emotive, pleasure seeking organisms. According to Piaget, children only begin to become socialized and think realistically at seven, and they do not develop rational thinking until adolescence. Piaget argued that early egocentric thinking is evidenced in children's animism. According to Piaget, animism is a stage of thinking characteristic of two- to four-year-old children in which the child "projects" or attributes his own inner psychological qualities onto inanimate objects. For example, children believe the sun walks behind them in the same way that they move.

In contrast to Piaget's contention that animism is natural to young children, cross-cultural studies indicate it only exists in certain cultures. Greenfield and Bruner (1969), and Jahoda (1958a, b) report that in many societies young children do not think animistically. They do not assume that the world functions as they do, or exclusively for their benefit. On psychological tests of categorization, for example, only Western children classify objects in terms of how they use them; children from Eskimo and other societies see objects much more in terms of their benefit to the group. Margaret Mead (1932) observed that Manus children did not manifest spontaneous animism, or the tendency to personalize things that had not previously been given personalities by adults. In fact, sometimes Manus children *reject* the magical concepts of adult. For example, they do not believe their parents' superstition that if one's reflection falls on water, part of one's soul will leave their body. Consequently, the Manus do not take their children out in boats because the children ignore the taboo and insist on looking at their image in the water.

Mead, and Greenfield and Bruner, locate the source of animism in unrealistic thinking which stems from a protected social position segregated from adulthood: "It is only where the child's every whim is satisfied that he is led to believe his thought omnipotent" (Greenfield & Bruner, 1969, p. 637). Manus children, being encouraged to learn as much about the world as possible, are consequently not prone to magical thinking (Siegel & Hodkin, 1982, pp. 71-74). Barolo's (1979) finding of realism among lower classes of Italian children is also consistent with this explanation. Barolo found that lower middle-class five-year-old Italian children were far more realistic and less animistic than their upper class counterparts: Whereas 76% of the poor subjects gave realistic responses and only 3% gave animistic responses, only 42% of the privileged children used realistic thinking whereas 46% were animistic. The fact that upper-class children are more protected and sheltered than those of the lower classes lends plausibility to Mead's association of unworldliness with animism and worldliness with realism.[9]

Evidently, animism is "connected to the subject's sociocultural environment rather than to universal developmental laws as claimed by Piaget's theory" (Barolo, 1979). Piaget's insistence that animism is natural ignores its social character and social basis, which precludes the possibility of more realistic childhood thinking.

Other facets of egocentric thinking that Piaget falsely universalizes are the presumed inability of children below the age of seven years to understand another person's point of view, coordinate their view with others, cooperate with others, or communicate intentionally (Piaget, 1962). While Piaget construes these as biologically determined, natural limits, research unmistakenly disproves this contention. On the most elementary level, the self is a social product which cannot precede awareness of social relations.

Maureen Cox (1986) points out that the terms which a child uses to identify and refer to herself are extrapolated from their use by others: "In order to use the terms correctly to refer to herself, the child must have first understood how they are used by other people; she *then* has to reverse the roles and apply them to herself" (p. 87). For instance, the child has never heard herself referred to as "I," she only hears others refer to themselves as "I." In order to conceive herself as an individual "I," she must come to recognize a general principle that "I" refers to anyone who is speaking, and *then apply this general principle to herself* when she is speaking, or thinking. "I" must be conceived generally before it can be conceived personally. Such a general conception can only come from encountering the terms used by a variety of individuals. If the child interacted only with one adult and did not witness conversations between the adult and another person, she would have no way of discovering that "I" is not tied to a particular person as proper names are. The parent would always use "I" to refer to himself and "you" to refer to the child (Cox, p. 74). To be aware of oneself thus requires that one also (first) be aware of others.[10]

Numerous experiments have demonstrated that one- and one-half-year-old children understand other points of view, arrange objects so that others will have a clear view of them, share things, and cooperate (Cox, 1986; Gelman & Baillargeon, 1983, pp. 172-175; Rheingold et al., 1976; Hay, 1979). Children's use of language also expresses significant social awareness rather than being solipsistic as Piaget maintains (Vygotsky, 1987, chap. 2, & pp. 257ff). Even among Appalachian children, comparatively backward in language skills, "the kind of egocentric communication Piaget had described made up less than 1% of the children's language. When they intended to communicate with others, children's speech was almost always socially adaptive and clearly understandable to the listener" (Beck, 1986). Actually, children in Piaget's own experiments manifested a more developed social orientation than he was able to accept (Cox, 1986, pp. 34-35).

There is no doubt that a primitive form of egocentrism does exist among very young infants although it is different from Piaget's description. Neonates are obviously unaware of the needs of others, cannot meaningfully communicate with them, and are preoccupied with satisfying their own immediate needs. However, this state does not persist for seven years, as Piaget contends. It ends after about one year as consciousness, empathy, intentionality, and communication develop. Piaget's egocentrism only characterizes the infant who does not possess a meaningful self at all.

The self that develops is a thoroughly social self that is inspired by social interaction (Guillaume, 1971, pp. 136-137). Ensuing interactions with other people depend upon the particular social intentions that children have learned from their culture. When youngsters disregard other people's desires and insist on their own point of view, this is not a natural, immutable *inability* to consider and communicate with others; it is a socially fostered, changeable attitude—whose learning by children is proof positive that they do understand others. Like animism, unsociability in children is evidently fostered by social systems which isolate children from adult responsibilities and indulge their individual wishes (Vygotsky, 1987, p. 90). All these aspects of egocentrism emerged historically in the emerging bourgeois class which segregated and indulged its children. They were not characteristic among the European feudal aristocracy or American colonial settlers (Stone, 1977). Nor is egocentrism encouraged in Samoa where caretakers orient youngsters to respect and understand others (Ochs, 1988, p. 24).

Historical and experimental evidence is thus consistent in showing that children *can* empathize and communicate with other people, although they sometimes do not do so because of the way they are treated. Piaget mistakenly attributed a particular social disinterest to a natural, universal insensitivity. He assumed that individualism naturally precedes sociality, which is precisely opposite to their true order (Vygotsky, 1987, p. 80). Individualistic thinking is a product of social relations.

Just as childhood egocentrism is a function of social relations, not natural processes, so the transition out of egocentrism to sociability and realistic thinking is also a social rather than a natural product. The reason that Western children become more sociable and realistic at seven years is not a function of biological timing; it is the age at which Western culture determines children abandon infantile traits, enter institutionalized education, and embark upon a new stage of social life (Bruner, 1959, p. 369).

The transition to formal operational thinking evidences the same social basis: In Western society adolescence is the time when children begin to take on adult responsibilities and attendant forms of culturally necessary, propositional reasoning. Piaget's explaining this transition as dependent on neurophysiological maturation occurring during adolescence is clearly fallacious given the fact that quite young children can be trained in formal operations. Training in one experiment enabled 52% of 4-5-year-olds, and 96% of 5-6-year-olds to engage in formal operational thinking. In contrast, only 4% and 20% of their respective untrained counterparts had acquired these skills (Luria, 1982, pp. 205-206; cf. also Rosenthal & Zimmerman, 1978, pp. 243-245; Gelman & Baillargeon, 1983, pp. 175-179). These data suggest that all children possess the capacity for formal operational thought at an early age. When this capacity is realized, to what level, and applied to what domains, are cultural issues. Piaget's cognitive stages thus unwittingly reflect social stages. By unjustifiably construing them as natural and universal, Piaget naturalizes this social character and precludes any other possibility (Toulmin, 1981).

Perceptual processes similarly reflect social experience which has been obscured by misconstruing them as natural and universal. Gestalt laws of perception provide an excellent example of this problematic. It is well known that Gestalt psychologists assumed that perceptual patterns are established by, and isomorphic with, cortical mechanisms. However, researchers have found that closure, continuity, and simplicity are culturally specific rather than natural and universal. When Luria's peasants were shown incomplete geometrical forms they described them as familiar objects rather than in terms of Gestalt "good forms." Luria specifically commented on this violation of Gestalt principles. He said:

> The subjects who perceived shapes in an object-oriented fashion displayed no characteristics corresponding to those described by the Gestalt laws of structural perception. . . . The subjects judged an incomplete circle or triangle as a bracelet, or device for measuring out kerosene, but not as an incomplete geometrical figure. We have reason to think, therefore, that the laws of 'good form' and of structural continuation (or amplification) as described by the Gestalt psychologists are fully apparent only for subjects who have mastered geometrical concepts, and do not appear in people who perceive shapes in an object-oriented fashion. (Luria, 1976, p. 33)

Research by Donahue and Griffitts (1931), Washburn et al. (1934), and Henle (1942) further challenged Gestalt theory by experimentally demonstrating that identification of figures depends more on familiarity with them than on closure, continuity, proximity, and simplicity.[11]

When Gestalt laws of closure, continuity, proximity, and simplicity are operative, they must therefore be the product of cultivated attention rather than universal cortical mechanisms (Gregory, 1970, pp. 20-21).[12] Bartlett demonstrated that simplicity or complexity is actually determined by socially mediated familiarity with objects, not by objects' properties. He found that a complicated but familiar pattern was felt to be simpler and easier to recognize than an unfamiliar pattern consisting of just a few lines. In Bartlett's words, "'simplicity' in the data of perception or of memory is, psychologically speaking, almost entirely a function of interest" (1967, p. 27).

In other words, experienced objects appear simple and regular; forms appear to be regular and simple because we are familiar with them, we do not become familiar with them because they are intrinsically simple and regular; familiarity with other forms would make *them* appear simple and regular. As Merleau-Ponty said in criticizing the Gestalt principle of good form: "'Good form' is not brought about because it would be good in itself in some metaphysical heaven; it is good form because it comes into being in our experience" (1962, p. 16; Zinchenko, 1984). Notions of natural perceptual laws overlook the culturally mediated experiential basis of perceptual regularities and misconstrue them as natural, universal principles.

Color perception is also assumed to possess a "universal component." Universalists such as Berlin and Kay, and Rosch recognize the cultural differences in color boundaries presented in Chapter 2, but they contend that the "prototypes" or best examples of each color category are universally perceived. The authors postulate separate, antagonistic mechanisms for perceiving color boundaries and prototypical best examples: whereas boundary perception is governed by cultural categories, focal color perception is due to a universal biological sensitivity (Berlin & Kay, 1969, p.13; Rosch, 1975, 1978). Ratner (1989b; Ratner & McCarthy, 1990) demonstrates that this claim is untenable and that focal colors are not universal.

The search for natural, universal prototypes of experience extends beyond color to the perception of birds, vehicles, geometric forms, and facial expressions of emotion—all of which, according to Rosch (1978; Rosch et al., 1976) are structured around cortically determined prototypes of good form. Rosch further maintains that important features of *conceptual classification* rest upon endemic psychological principles. In her view, the middle level of a hierarchical classification will naturally be the most salient and distinctive. For example, a taxonomy for furniture would include "furniture" as the superordinate concept, chair (and table) as a middle-level concept, and kitchen chair, living-room chair, etc. as subordinate concepts.

Rosch theorized that the middle-level concept is most distinctive and salient—which earns it the favored appellation "basic"—because the superordinate is too impoverished while the subordinate is redundant because it overlaps so much with the basic concept. In other words, "furniture" is so vague as to provide us little information about what exactly the item is, while "kitchen chair" and "living room chair" are so similar that we don't need to concentrate on their differences. Consistent with her viewpoint, Rosch argues that the basic-level concept constitutes a prototype around which more general and more specific features are organized.

Rosch (1978; Rosch et al., 1976) found that subjects listed more attributes for basic concepts than for superordinate ones, and that the number of attributes for subordinate concepts did not significantly exceed the number for basic-level objects. This, she concludes, demonstrates that basic concepts provide the most meaningful information, more than that generated by higher concepts yet not less than that generated by lower concepts. Rosch then explains this finding as due to endemic psychological principles.

Unfortunately for Rosch, however, the data challenge this explanation. In the first place, there is no reason to assume that a sensitivity to basic-level categories is intrinsic. Research has demonstrated that basic-level categories are highlighted by parents more than superordinate or subordinate categories. This calling attention to middle-level categories easily explains any sensitivity to them that might exist. Callanan (1985) reports that parents use basic level terms much more than terms at other levels in their speech to children. Parents even highlight basic-level categories when discussing superordinate and subordinate levels. These latter levels are "anchored" in the basic level which makes the basic level appear to be foundational to the others. For example, a parent is not likely to point to an object and say, "This is a vehicle." She is much more likely to anchor at the basic level, saying, "this is a jeep; a jeep is a kind of vehicle." Callanan found that 12 of 14 mothers used basic level names more often when they taught superordinate categories than when they taught basic level categories. This certainly indicates that the basic level is the reference point of the hierarchical system.

While this kind of social experience easily explains the instances in which middle-level concepts elicit fuller responses than superordinate or subordinate concepts, Rosch's own data show that middle-level concepts are *not* always more salient than the other levels. Rosch employed nine taxonomies whose superordinate objects were tree, bird, fish, fruit, musical instruments, tool, clothing, furniture, and vehicle. For three of them the number of attributes was equally apportioned among the three levels rather than concentrated at the middle level. Thus, the supposedly natural psychological principles of categorization failed on one-third of the tests. Obviously, they are neither natural or universal.

Toward the end of her 1976 and 1978 articles, Rosch acknowledges the need for explaining cognitive categorization in terms of a socially conscious understanding of reality rather than impersonal, biological determinants. She recognizes that perception is a learned activity which reflects experience with things. Our cultural experience may emphasize certain middle-level things but superordinate and subordinate levels for other things. No one level is universally basic. For instance, our culture is knowledgeable about mammals and we have rich descriptions of individual mammals. This makes the subordinate level "basic" in this case. On the other hand, the paucity of knowledge about individual fish means that the general class "fish" is the most informative level for that object (Rosch et al., 1976, p. 432).

Another interesting example of concrete knowledge affecting categorization was one subject who had been an airplane mechanic. In contrast to the other subjects who designated "airplane" as a basic conceptual level, his descriptions of individual airplanes contained numerous additional attributes which made the subordinate concepts the basic level for him (Rosch et al., 1976, p. 430). Rosch goes on to add that such deviations will routinely occur among experts possessing detailed knowledge about particular things. It is quite imaginable, for example, that an antique furniture dealer will provide rich detail about subordinate Chippendale and Hepplewhite chairs while failing to significantly differentiate kitchen and living room chairs at a more abstract level. Rosch concludes that "The basic level of abstraction is that level of abstraction that is appropriate for using, thinking about, or naming an object in most situations in which the object occurs. And when a context is not specified in an experiment, people must contribute their own context . . . Indeed, it seems likely that, in the absence of a specified context, subjects assume what they consider the normal context or situation for occurrence of that object. To make such claims about categories appears to demand an analysis of the actual events in daily life in which objects occur" (p. 43; cf. Lin et al., 1990).

Deriving categorization from concrete life rather than from natural prototypes reverses Rosch's original position. Rather than prototypical best examples preceding and determining categorization, they are the *resultant* of encounters with numerous things. As we have emphasized earlier, general forms derive from concrete experience, they do not precede and determine it.

Rosch's original quest for *a priori* prototypes reflects an extreme individualism—wherein the individual's cognitive schemas precede experience with things and experience with other people—which was fortunately tempered by the recognition that "the analysis of objects into attributes is a rather sophisticated activity that subjects (and indeed a system of cultural knowledge) might well be considered to be able to impose only *after* the development of the category system" (Rosch, 1978, p. 42). Natural prototypes and principles have happily given way to socially constructed categories.

Strangely enough, Rosch did not emphasize or develop this social-psychological character of cognition. In fact, in her retrospective summary (Rosch, 1988) she minimizes it and reemphasizes the original notion of independent prototypes—that is, prototypes which intrinsically provide maximum information and which do not derive from their socially mediated relations to things. Rosch even enthusiastically welcomes the adoption of this notion into new areas such as information processing. Evidently, her statements about the socially mediated character of prototypes have not mitigated her earlier proclivity toward false universalism.[13]

Overuniversalizing culturally specific psychological phenomena not only plagues culturally naive psychologists and psychologists. Some psychologists who are quite sensitive to cultural variation in psychological phenomena nevertheless shy away from fully accepting these differences and exaggerate psychological commonalities. These psychologists argue that specific cognitive competencies are universal and thus posit false universals. Despite their great appreciation of sociohistorical psychology, I believe that Michael Cole and Richard Shweder are guilty of this error. It unfortunately contradicts the great potential of their work to refine and advance sociohistorical psychology as discussed above.

Curiously enough, Cole and Shweder argue for an essential universality in psychological competence with culture only dictating the domains in which this competence will be manifested. In other words, modern and primitive people have equal competence to abstract, although the areas in which this is manifested will vary. As Cole has stated on many accessions, "cultural differences in cognition reside more in the contexts within which cognitive processes manifest themselves than in the existence of a particular process (such as logical memory or theoretical responses to syllogisms) in one culture and its absence in another" (Cole, 1988, p. 147; Cole & Bruner, 1971, p. 870).

Cole (Cole, Sharp, Lave, 1976) likens cognitive operations to craft skills such as carpentry: All carpenters possess certain basic skills, although they organize and apply them differently. Some are good at making tables while others make dressers. In the same way, moderns think abstractly about certain things and perform well on certain kinds of abstract tests, while primitives organize their abstract ability in other ways. Such differences in expression must not be construed as deficits in basic competence. Invoking the carpentry analogy, Cole, Sharp, and Lave argue that a carpenter's failure to construct particular pieces of furniture is not due to any deficit in basic operations, simply to a lack of experience in organizing the basic operations in a particular style.

Cole invokes an additional argument to support a universalist position. He says that abstract thinking and memory are relatively unusual for most modern people. Moderns and premoderns alike normally engage in the same contextualized, functional, empirical thought processes. Thus, whatever differences in abstraction that may disintinguish premoderns from moderns are confined to unusual circumstances and are relatively unimportant. Far more important is the prevalent commonality that both groups share.

Cole's contention for a basic universality of cognitive processes rests on two arguments. The first postulates a universal competence that is organized and expressed differently. The carpentry analogy exemplifies this argument. In addition, a somewhat different argument postulates a universal competence for elementary cognitive operations that are employed in everyday, "commonsense" functioning, along with certain circumscribed, specialized, culturally variable cognitive competencies. According to the second formulation, these circumscribed, specialized operations, such as free recall and syllogistic logic, are rarely employed and they do not seriously compromise the far more common universal operations, however they do exist as culturally bound differences in cognitive competencies. In this case, modern people do have a competence for abstract thinking that premodern people lack, even though modern people do not often use this competence and normally operate at the same context-bound level as premoderns.

Whereas the first argument argues for absolute universality of competence with only differences in performance, the second argues for a virtually universal competence although admitting some minor, specialized exceptions. Although both the "absolutely universal" and "virtually universal" arguments (as we shall label them here) lead to the same conclusion of a basic universality in cognitive competence, they are not consistent arguments. Maintaining one competence which is differently expressed is quite another matter from claiming several competencies. This inconsistency is one troublesome point in Cole's formulation.

A second troublesome point is that both arguments contradict the relativist position of sociohistorical psychology which accepts full-fledged social psychological differences in competence. Culturally bound competencies are not limited to minor, circumscribed, specialized exceptions to a deeper, prevalent universality as the "virtually universal" argument contends. From the relativistic perspective, cognitive processes in the life world of everyday experience are as culture bound and varied as they are in specialized domains. Everyday cognitive processes are not universal. Whole sectors of the modern everyday psychological life space—color, time, number, and measurement—operate at a level of abstraction that is foreign to premodern people. Since the information that modern people encounter is more decontextualized than the material that premodern people encounter, our cognition, perception, memory, reasoning, self concept, etc. must necessarily be more abstract.

The operations that process information must operate at a level of abstraction that corresponds to that material. Cognitive processes are not independent of the material they apprehend; the processes must change in order to invent and comprehend new material. As Luria (1971, p. 226) said,

> Not only the content, but the structure of cognitive processes depends on the activity of which it is a part. Such a conception of the close ties between separate psychological processes and concrete forms of activity calls for a rejection of the non-scientific idea that 'psychological functions' are a priori data, independent of historical forms (cf. Leontiev, 1981, p. 222).

Postulating universal, everyday cognitive operations is only sustained by underestimating the extent of abstract thought in modern peoples' psychology. In fact, abstract, decontextualized thinking pervades "everyday cognition" nearly as much as it does specialized domains. Conversely, premodern everyday cognition of time, number, space, measurement, and color are context-bound in a way that is utterly foreign to modern cognition. Such major differences challenge the argument for virtual universality of cognitive processes. A dualistic dichotomizing of psychological functioning into a universal, everyday, common sense realm juxtaposed beside a culturally bound, specialized realm is unparsimonious and illogical. It is also, as we have seen, empirically untrue.

Of course, Cole is right in emphasizing that the cognitive differences between premodern and modern people are not absolute. Much of modern thinking relies upon personal experience and contextual cues just as premodern thinking does. However, these similarities are embedded in quite different configurations which imbues them with different qualities. Our relying on personal experience and contextual cues to understand and remember information must involve somewhat different operations as we are dealing with numbers, colors, time, individuality, moral issues, impersonal markets, and other information that already have an abstract character. Our personal experience and use of contextual cues concern decontextualized phenomena, which is quite different from a familiarity with localized, fixed, tangible phenomena. Consequently, similarities between premodern and modern cognition are no more absolute than the differences are. The similarities of everyday cognition are shot through with differences which stem from major dissimilarities in social life.

If virtual universality of cognitive competence is untrue, the stronger argument for absolute universality must be also. Recall that Cole recognizes differences in performance, however he contends that these reflect common underlying cognitive processes. For example, although premodern people may fail to engage in abstract thinking on certain standard tasks that are unfamiliar to them, if we make the tasks familiar to them we will find that they do engage in abstract thinking. While this point is deserving of serious attention in view of the tendency to unjustly conclude differences in competence from differences in performance, we shall see that Cole overreacts to this error and commits an opposite error of interpretation: He presumes equality of competence when none has been demonstrated and even when indications suggest real differences. Cole overestimates the extent of premodern abstract thinking so that it appears similar to modern thinking when, in fact, it remains quite context-bound. We shall examine three instances of this misinterpretation.

Cole (1988, p.149) contends that premodern people employ deductive logic as well as moderns, although in different situations. He cites Hutchins who has found instances of logical reasoning employed by Trobriand Islanders in adjudicating land disputes. From this research Hutchins concludes that the Islanders employ the same kind of logical thinking and inference-drawing as Americans (Hutchins, 1980, p. 128). However, this conclusion is open to question. It is far from clear whether these instances are comparable to modern peoples' nonsyllogistic inference processes. No judgment was made as to the complexity, abstractness, or extensiveness of the Trobrianders' inferences and this leaves their comparability to modern inference entirely open. Trobrianders unquestionably engage in inference-making, but whether their everyday cognitive processes are as abstract, complex, or extensively invoked as ours is uncertain.

In fact, the evidence presented earlier indicates significant differences in inference-drawing. That evidence demonstrated that premodern people rely upon "empiric" personal experience whereas modern people can readily draw theoretical conclusions apart from personal experience. A close look at Hutchins's examples of the Trobrianders' success in drawing inferences reveals that all of the cases involved personal experience and knowledge; none of them required theoretical conclusions. The mere fact that the Trobrianders' constructed logical arguments concerning their land rights does not prove that their logical reasoning processes parallel modern peoples.'

Tulviste (1979, p. 77) argues that similarities in reasoning between premodern and modern people are more apparent than real since "the seemingly theoretic explanations given by traditional subjects for their conclusions from familiar premises only too often coincide with some possible empiric explanations." While Hutchins's research disposes of the pernicious myth that premodern people are incapable of reasoning, it does not prove the converse argument that premodern and modern reasoning are identical. There is good reason to believe that they are not.

A second kind of data that Cole cites in support of universal cognitive competence are Kpelle measurement techniques and concepts. As we have discussed above, Cole found Kpelle measurement to be extremely context-bound, with different metrics for different objects. However, he argues that in dealing with their primary food sustenance, rice, "the Kpelle people displayed an articulated mathematical system and accuracy in estimating volume superior to that of educated Americans"

(Cole, 1988, p. 145). In contrast to the non-commutable metrics that are applied to most domains, rice measurement consists of interchangeable units: The basic unit "cup" may be aggregated into larger units called "tins" (1 tin = 44 cups) and "bags" (1 bag = 100 cups). Thus, "At least at a rough order of exactness, an interlocking scale of units of the sort that we associate with measurement exists among the Kpelle in the case of volume of rice" (Laboratory of Human Cognition, 1983, p. 319-320). This suggests to Cole that traditional measurement skills are comparable to modern abilities although they are manifested in different and more limited circumstances.

However, Cole's equating the two competencies overlooks fundamental differences. The very fact that Kpelle metrics are only commutable in one domain of measurement makes their calculating skill obviously more context-dependent than Western math. How can a single, circumscribed instance of interchangeable units used by the Kpelle be compared to the wide-ranging, generic, interchangeable mathematical principles of modern mathematics? To do so is to sever the rice measurement technique from the system of which it is a part. The error of such a comparison requires no comment.

Kpelle quantification and measurement are isolated into local contexts in a way that is quite foreign to their modern counterparts. As with logical inference, it is certainly true that the Kpelle make some calculations in some way, but they do not calculate as we do. *That* both peoples can calculate is true; *how, what,* and *when* they calculate differs.

Damerow confirms variation in mathematical thought processes with his historical observation that different stages in the evolution of Babylonian arithmetic entailed diverse cognitive operations. Rebuking the Piagetian notion of universal, ontogenetically derived cognitive processes, Damerow argues that socially evolving arithmetic techniques constrain the ontogenetic possibilities of cognitive development along definite sociohistorical lines. He emphasizes the "substantial influence of culturally transmitted representations on the emergence of cognitive structures in ontogenetic development" (Damerow, 1988, p. 150). Evidence from quantification and measurement makes universality of cognitive operations in this domain as implausible as it is in logical inference.

A final attempt to establish common levels of abstract thinking among premodern and modern people concerns memory processes. In the experiment discussed above, Cole and Gay (1972) finally discovered that the Kpelle subjects could enhance their recall if the stimulus material was changed from word lists to actual objects that were displayed in proximity to physical cues such as chairs. We concluded that this confirmed the contextual nature of Kpelle memory because the subjects performed poorly in the absence of concrete cues. Cole and Gay, however, draw quite another conclusion. They maintain that the eventual success of the Kpelle demonstrates that their memory process is substantially the same as Americans.' It simply requires an unusual situation to elicit good retrieval: "On certain accessions, and with certain cues, the Kpelle are able to recall and organize the material in a way comparable to that which American subjects display on different accessions and with other cues" (1972, p. 1083).

As with the previous examples, Cole seems to disregard striking differences in the situation which produce similar performance. The very fact that the Kpelle require concrete cuing which the Americans do not means that in these memory tests Americans engage in free recall while Kpelle recall is context-dependent. The fact that the Kpelle required a unique set of cues in order to close the performance gap with their American counterparts means that they were not engaging in the same memory process at all. Kpelle and American performance only appears similar if the results are abstracted from the circumstances in and means by which they were achieved. This, however, leads to false conclusions because it obscures the real disparate cognitive processes involved.[14]

The foregoing reinterpretation of Cole's data suggests that his argument for absolute universality in cognitive competence does not withstand scrutiny. The assumption of one given competence which is expressed in different styles and media is incorrect. Instead, qualitatively novel competencies are generated by diverse cultures. Modern abstract thinking is a qualitatively new skill whose level of abstraction and range of application transcends premodern forms. Rather than being analogous to basic carpentry skills that are reorganized and extended, the transition from contextual to abstract thought is analogous to simple arithmetic being superseded by calculus. Abstract thought is as qualitatively different from contextual thinking as calculus is from arithmetic.

The social basis of consciousness is not confined to directing basic, general processes; it engenders new processes (Tulviste, 1979). In Luria's (1976, p. 161) words, "The facts show convincingly that the structure of cognitive activity does not remain static during different states of historical development and that the most important forms of cognitive processes—perception, generalization, deduction, reasoning, imagination, and analysis of one's inner life—vary as the conditions of social life change and the rudiments of knowledge are mastered."

These novel processes are not confined to specialized domains, as the "virtually universal" argument stipulates, but pervade the everyday cognitive life world as well. Both the absolute and the virtual arguments for universal cognitive processes are incorrect. The argument for absolute universality overestimates the abstract ability of premodern people and presumes it to be as advanced as the modern level. The argument for virtual universality underestimates modern abstraction and presumes it to be as undeveloped as the premodern level. Uncomfortable with the competence differential between cultures, Cole elevates the abstract skills of premoderns and diminishes those of moderns. This creates the impression of universal cognitive processes and closes the competence gap.

However, evidence indicates that substantial social psychological differences do, in fact, distinguish premodern and modern cognitive functions. This is true in "everyday cognition" as well as in specialized cognitive domains. Cole's universalist interpretation of sociohistorical psychology curiously denies qualitatively distinctive forms of mental activity that Cole has acknowledged (Cole, 1988, p. 150). While Cole's caution about inferring differences in competence from differences in performance is well taken, it should not intimidate us from acknowledging differences in competence when the data have been derived from appropriate sources. Since Cole acknowledges this (Cole & Bruner, 1971, p. 871; Cole, 1975, p. 169), it is perplexing that he rejects the cultural differences in abstract thinking that his and other ecologically sensitive research reveals.[15]

Although psychological relativism is real, this does not imply the impossibility of cross-cultural communication. There are commonalities embodied in individual cultures which make some understanding possible. However, these psychological commonalities are indefinite and entail no specific characteristics. Consequently, while we are able to recognize that another culture has some social interactions, some concern for children by parents, some language, some logical sense, some abstract thinking, some way of remembering information and some sense of joy, sadness, and frustration, specific details are not conveyed in that recognition. Of course, it is possible for people to learn a good deal of other societies' customs and psychology. But this requires a thorough immersion in the culture and a willingness to acquire another world view.

Social psychological particulars are not transparently obvious to superficial observation because they are not contained in the universals which we all possess. Outsiders can be told about a foreign social psychology and thereby gain some notion of it; however, they cannot really comprehend it until they enter that culture. For instance, Whorf's telling us that the Hopi Indians have a cyclical sense of time gives us some rough intellectualized concept that is derived from abstractly combining our notion of cyclical with that of time. But we cannot grasp what this is in any vivid, meaningful way. We cannot really integrate the two concepts "time" and "cycle" to comprehend *cyclical time* as the Hopis understand and experience it unless we immerse ourselves in Hopi culture and language. Levy-Bruhl put it well when he said that,

> It is extremely difficult, if not impossible, for a European, even if he tries, and even if he knows the natives' language, to *think* as they do, although he may seem to *speak* as they do.
>
> When investigators noted the institutions, manners, and beliefs before them, they made use of the concepts which seemed to them to correspond with the reality they had to express. But precisely because they were concepts encompassed by the logical atmosphere proper to European mentality, the expression of them distorted what they were trying to render. Translation had the effect of betrayal. (Levy-Bruhl, 1966, pp. 433-434)

As intercourse among societies reduces their differences and augments their similarities, psychological commonalities will become more specific. People will come to have similar senses of time, color, quantification, and engage in theoretic logical deduction and free recall. But for the present, social differences are so emphatic that commonalities must be abstract rather than specific.

If relativism does not preclude communication, neither does it imply skepticism about knowing the world (Geertz, 1984). The fact that different people know the world in different ways does not mean that the world is unknowable. Different approaches to the world do not negate objectivity, they reflect the creativity involved in achieving knowledge. Although viewpoints will conflict, each may contain some portion of the truth. Moreover, certain approaches may be more truthful than others. Acknowledging this does not imply oppressing or repressing other views. It simply recognizes the beneficial cognitive processes that further comprehension, solve problems, and make life more fulfilling. The fact that certain societies have misused the claim of mental superiority to oppress others should not intimidate us from recognizing superiority where it exists. If, as Goody (1977, pp. 150-151) has said, modern scientific, logical thought is a more thorough probing into truth and gains greater control over natural forces than was achieved by premodern magical thinking, such a recognition can strengthen our resolve to avoid mysticism. We will not necessarily be driven to exterminate all those peoples who continue to believe in mysticism.

There is nothing intrinsically malevolent about recognizing advantageous differences among people. Nor does championing equality necessarily lead to treating people benevolently. Suppression has been carried out under the name of equality as much as it has been under the name of superiority. In fact, Vygotsky and Luria were suppressed under just such a democratic mantle which regarded their ideas as reactionary.

The psychological differences that divide people are real and reflect real differences in their social life. If this is troubling, it can only be altered by real changes that unify social life. Psychological equality only exists to the extent that it is supported by similarities in concrete social life. Social psychological universality must be constructed, it is not given.

Notes

1. Since universal features of psychological phenomena are devoid of form and content, they cannot be governed by meaningful laws. There cannot be universal laws governing perception, memory, language, cognition, or emotions because there is nothing specific to govern on the universal level. The abstract features that comprise the universal level are only amenable to extremely general descriptions such as were found in Chapter 1 above. But such descriptions are far from laws. Laws can only apply to concrete psychological phenomena and are therefore historically variable, not universal.

2. For instance, to establish general stages of psychological development, developmental psychologists must:

> consider separately the steps by which each of the relevant behavioral capacities—for bodily control, sequential behavior, symbolization, internalization, problem solving, etc.—is elicited and developed in the course of a child's life, and look to see in what different patterns all those various capacities are associated at one point or another in life. Only then will it be time to select 'milestones,' so as to define general 'stages' of psychological development, and, even then, there will be no guarantee that the 'stages' relevant to one psychological enquiry will do more than rough justice to other psychological changes—still less to the overall character of psychological development as a whole—if there is such a thing. (Toulmin, 1971, p. 53)

Now the path from the specific to the general is not linear. One does not suspend speculation about the general until after numerous specifics have been investigated. Instead, one properly uses the local instance to surmise possible generalizations, and then tests these hypothetical generalizations against additional specific examples. In Berry's (1989) words, an "emic" (specific example) generates an "imposed etic" (an asserted generalization) which is then tested against other emics to establish a "derived etic" (a true universal which derives from particulars).

3. It is, of course, important to avoid the opposite mistake of assuming a particular social basis when a more general basis really underlies a psychological function. Buck-Morss (1975) commits this error in interpreting Piagetian formal operations as bourgeois thinking. Actually, as Buss (1979, chap. 9) points out, formal operations are employed by people in noncapitalist societies (ancient Greece, the Soviet Union, and China, to name a few) which means

that they must at least reflect formal social characteristics, and possibly even abstract social features as described in Chapter 1.

Buck-Morss is wrong on another point, namely her characterization of formal operations as intrinsically reified and depersonalized. However much this may be true in bourgeois society which uses formal operations in certain ways for certain ends, formal operations are not necessarily reified. Even in capitalist society such diverse thinkers as Marx and Husserl (1970) have used abstractions beneficently because they have remembered the human, social basis of their abstractions. Formal operations have a far greater capacity of generating profound, comprehensive, flexible thinking than "concrete operations" do. As such they have far greater potential for humanitarian purposes. Whether this potential is realized is a social question.

4. The lure of "basic" emotions is so strong that Ekman (1972), after acknowledging that most of the elicitors and expressions ("display rules") of emotions are socially learned and variable, has avoided researching this issue and has spent his career in pursuit of a few postulated universal facial expressions. (His success is critically evaluated in Ratner, 1989a.)

Actually, identifying universal as basic is quite arbitrary. As Ortony et al. (1988, p. 25) and Ortony and Turner (1990) point out in their critique of basic emotions, toenails are universal among humans but are hardly anatomically basic. Moreover, "basic" can equally be identified with other characteristics that are unrelated to universality. "Basic emotion" has been used to denote primary, in the sense that it is a building block for other emotions. (Sometimes the basic emotions are posited as adding together to form the derivative emotion, sometimes they are posited as compounding into a new whole qualitatively different from the ingredients.) And "basic" has also been used to refer to emotions that appear chronologically early in ontogenetic development.

These competing uses of "basic" undermine its identification with "universal." But they also undermine each other's claim to be the true meaning of basic. Furthermore, no logical justification is provided for calling any of these meanings basic. Just as universal is not necessarily basic, neither is the early appearance of an emotion. Initial emotions may be temporary, or insignificant for later life, thus not basic at all. Compounding the ambiguity of the term "basic emotion" is the lack of agreement as to which emotions are, in fact, basic. Some psychologists posit only two basic emotions (Mowrer: pleasure and pain), others posit three (Watson: fear, love, rage), while others posit a large number (Arnold: anger, aversion, courage, defection, desire, despair, fear, hate, hope, love, sadness).

Psychologists have no monopoly on the penchant for human universals. Mead and Geertz criticize this proclivity among anthropologists as well. Geertz (1973, chap. 2) complains of anthropologists' preoccupation with a metaphysical entity, "Man," in the interests of which empirical "man" is sacrificed. And Mead (1963) complains of anthropologists' tendency to treat childhood, youth, maturity, and old age as biologically defined statuses, apart from the socially variable character that these have in different cultures.

5. Portraying Piaget as a naturalist should not slight his acknowledgement that cognitive growth requires physical and social stimulation. This is why Piaget rejects the idea that logic is innate. However this concession to experience does not compromise Piaget's essential naturalism. For experience only acts to trigger off endemic determinants of growth. Experience functions as a general threshold in the sense that it must reach a minimal intensity in order to elicit cognitive development. However, endemic mechanisms stipulate the path that development takes. Experience has no such specific effect. Indeed, any environment that is minimally stimulating is sufficient to elicit cognitive growth. This relationship is analogous to—and inspired by—that of a tree and its environment. While the conditions must provide at least a minimum of nourishment for the tree to grow, and while conditions affect the eventual size of the tree, what the tree will become and its path of development are internally determined. This characterization of Piaget's theory as quasi-interactionist, at best, is supported by Rosenthal and Zimmerman (1978) who state:

> We [have] characterized Piagetian and other, closely related structural positions such as Kohlberg's view of moral development as basically nativistic, a conclusion drawn by other writers (e.g., Baldwin; Bruner, Olver, & Greenfield). Piagetians often object to such labels, claiming that their theory is interactional, and adding, that just as experience is interpreted in light of existing structures, new events can also reorganize cognition. However, the impact of experience is delimited by the child's prevailing logic, whose scope, in turn, is rooted in an assumed sequence of biological development. Furth, a respected spokesman, is clear on this point: The form of the child's mental structure is neither induced by nor gradually evolves from the organization of experienced events; rather, it has biological origins. Piaget himself raised the same issue by denying that the logical features of thought can arise from experience. . . . Although new events can qualify structural content, the sequence of mental development is assumed to be invariant and irreversible. Further, a child at one developmental stage should not profit from, and may actively resist, guidance appropriate to a later stage. (p. 149)

Glick similarly notes that "Piaget has preserved the notion of organism-environment interaction as a central aspect of his account of development, but has given it the sort of twist necessary to meet the idealist requirement" (Glick in Broughton et al., 1981, p. 160). That is to say, "What Piaget was really seeking was a conception of the environment and the organism that, in a necessary interaction, would yield not random, not novel, but essentially what you might call 'fated' structures" (ibid., p. 171). Kitchener (1986, p. 80) is thus correct in stating that for Piaget cognitive development is a priori in the sense of being an inevitable outcome for all individuals. Such a universal outcome rests on endemic proclivities which structure cognitive development equally in everyone (Elbers, 1986, p. 382).

6. Not all psychologists consider universals to include form rather than content. In a few cases, specific content is regarded as universal. Focal colors, as described by Berlin and Kay and by Rosch are perhaps the most obvious example. Focal colors are specific hues and saturations that are taken as being universally salient by virtue of a natural sensitivity on the part of visual sense receptors. Since such universals of content are exceptional in psychological theory, they will not occupy our attention here. They will be discussed in the following section.

7. Marx (1973, pp. 85ff.) provides a classic example from economics of how universal and particular must be distinguished, and the danger of collapsing the distinction. Discussing production, he says that *production in general* is an abstraction, but a rational abstraction insofar as it really brings out the common element. A general feature of production is utilizing instruments. Capitalism as a particular mode of production partakes of this general element and certainly employs instruments. However, it is absurd to conclude that capitalism is a universal, natural mode of production just because it includes this general facet. While this one facet of capitalism is universal, the entirety of the capitalist mode of production, which surrounds this common feature with numerous particular ones, is definitely sociohistorical. Capitalism only appears to be eternal if we leave out just the specific quality which alone makes "instrument of production" into capital.

Throughout his writings, Marx painstakingly exposed false universalizing of culturally specific practices. One of his most trenchant critiques, as relevant today as it was in his time, condemns Hegel for universalizing alienation, when in fact alienation is peculiar to class society, and is presumably absent from classless society. Hegel conflates the truly universal human practice of objectifying activity into stable forms (artifacts, social institutions) with the historically specific alienation of people from control over those forms. This mistaken identification of objectification (*Vergegenstaendlichung*) and alienation (*Entausserung*) assumes that all objectification is intrinsically alienated. Alienation can therefore never be eliminated short of ceasing to engage in productive activity altogether.

R.D. Laing (1969, p. 58) has indicated that Marx's distinction between abstract universals and variable particulars is useful for understanding psychopathology: "Marx said: under all circumstances a Negro has a black skin but only under certain socio-economic conditions is he a slave. Under all circumstances a man may get stuck, lose himself, and have to turn round and go back a long way to find himself. Only under certain socio-economic conditions will he suffer from schizophrenia." The same holds for emotions: People everywhere experience frustration; however, only under certain socioeconomic conditions will they become angry, depressed, or violent.

The tendency to overgeneralize capitalism as a universal system of production is paralleled by the tendency to overgeneralize schizophrenia as a universal pathology, and anger or depression as universal emotions.

8. The real content that is being decided may often supercede calculations of profit and loss even within commercial societies. The immorality of a crime may outweigh the personal gain that could accrue from committing it. Thus, overlooking the social values and moral complexities which individuals are deciding about, and recasting these as simple quantities of profit and loss, does not even fully tap the decision-making process of individuals in Western society (Billig et al., 1988, pp. 8-15). Decision-making, like all psychological phenomena, is a function of concrete social values and practices; it does not obey abstract psychological laws.

9. Greenfield and Bruner also associate animism with individualistic societies and realism with collective societies. This appears to be untrue in view of the fact that the Manus are individualistic (cf. Fromm, 1973, pp. 199-200) as are lower-class Italian children. Evidently, it is the extent of indulgence and protection that children receive, regardless of individualism or collectivism, that engenders animistic thinking.

10. Fraiberg (1977, chap. 11) reports that blind children have great difficulty employing self-referential pronouns and they persist in referring to themselves with third-party terms which others use to address them. Blind three-year-olds typically refer to themselves as "her" or "him" and ask people to "give it to her" when they want something for themselves. And this deficiency persists into the school years for many blind children.

    Interestingly, blind children also have difficulty fantasizing or pretending to be different from their real behavior. They also have difficulty pretending that dolls or toys are different from their real, everyday reality.

11. Henle (1942) used two kinds of stimuli which were presented normally and in reversed form. Letters that were familiar to subjects were recognized more frequently than their mirror reversals (79% vs. 58%). In contrast, when unfamiliar Chinese and Arabic characters were used as stimuli, characters presented normally were *not* more readily perceived than their reversed images. Since a letter's closure and other organizational forms remain the same whether it is observed "normally" or reversed, and regardless of whether the character is familiar or not, Gestalt theory would predict no difference in identifiability among any of the characters. Yet familiarity obviously did enhance identifiability of "normally" presented, familiar English letters.

12. In their effort to rule out the influence of experience on perception, Gestalt psychologists have presented the famous Gottschaldt figures hundreds of times to subjects in order to induce familiarity. The simple figure was then embedded within a larger, complex figure where it was difficult to perceive. Gestalt experimentalists explained the subjects' failure to discern the embedded simple figure as caused by perceptual laws which naturally led the perceivers to focus on the good form of the larger, complex figure and to override the hundreds of encounters with the smaller, familiar, but "unnatural" one. However, such a formulation is gratuitous. An experiential theory readily explains the results by acknowledging that the smaller figure was difficult to perceive simply because it was fused into the larger figure, thereby

losing any recognizability and wholeness. Familiarity does not ensure that an object will be recognized under any and all conditions. Camouflaged, even the most familiar object will be difficult to discern. Familiarity with objects not so disguised does sensitize subjects to perceive them in novel circumstances (Braly, 1933).

13. My analysis of Rosch contrasts with Lakoff's contention that she significantly modified her notion of prototypes. I agree with him, however, in lamenting the fact that Rosch's original position has become the model for much of cognitive psychology (Lakoff, 1987, p. 137).

14. Documenting universal cognitive competence requires penetrating and systematic observation. Meaningful psychological activity in a variety of situations must be compared. Isolated, circumscribed responses provide no indication of cognitive processes or competence. Cole's argument for universal cognitive competence is unconvincing because he appeals to such responses. The same difficulty plagues Shweder and his colleagues' attempt at proving universal decontextualized thinking. Working in the area of personality attribution, Shweder and Bourne (1984) and Miller (1984) originally found that, under free instructions to describe a friend, Indians' attributions were more particularistic than Americans': Americans used abstract attributes such as friendly, intelligent, arrogant, whereas Indians employed context-bound descriptions such as, "She brings cake to my family on festival days." However, under prodding, the Indians were able to combine their particular descriptions into more abstract attributions. The authors conclude that the Indians' particularistic attributions are therefore not due to their lack of abstract thinking. Their attributions are simply the product of certain cultural conceptions of people that differ from Western conceptions. Indians and American cognitive processes are similar although the products differ.

Now, the fact that Indians can be prodded to abstract categorizing in a single experiment indicates that they are capable of some abstract thinking, but it does not prove that their abstract thinking is the same as ours. True similarity of performance and competence is only revealed over a range of situations (a social norm of reaction, so to speak); it is never evident in isolated instances. A competence to think in a certain manner that is restricted to a simple situation is quite different from that competence which can function in diverse, complex circumstances. Since Shweder failed to establish the distribution of circumstances in which Indians employed abstract thought, his pronouncement of cross-cultural equivalence is presumptuous.

Shweder's experimental methodology also makes it difficult to ascertain the abstractness of the Indian's attributions. Descriptions of personality were decomposed into simple subject-predicate-object units and compared for frequency of general versus situation-bound traits (Shweder & Bourne, 1984, p. 174; cf. Miller 1984, p. 965, who employed the same method). Such bare responses obscure the subjects' meaning and make any psychological interpretation hazardous.

Margaret Mead (1963) trenchantly criticized generalizations that are contrived from decontextualized observations and which overlook substantial social differences in phenomena. She attributed this error, in part, to premature quantification which strips events from their historical contexts in order to measure them. Unfortunately, this critique applies to Shweder's study.

It seems that Shweder has fallen into the same error that plagues his antagonists, namely, drawing conclusions about competence from limited instances of performance. Whereas his antagonists overgeneralize from differences in performance to conclusions about differences in competence, Shweder overgeneralizes from apparently similar performances to universal competence.

15. Shweder's universalism also contradicts his relativistic view of psychological processes. For instance, he distinguishes between primary, universal processes and secondary, socially variable products just as the universalist Piaget does. In fact, Shweder may be more of a universalist than Piaget insofar as he argues for a high degree of similarity between 5-year-old children and adults. Congruent with his belief in a universal competence which makes any and all psychological phenomena available to every individual, Shweder rejects Piaget's developmentalism and contends that 5-year-old children already possess adult-type mental structures (Shweder & LeVine, 1984, p. 50).

Concurring with Cole and Bruner's (1971, p. 874) thesis that ontological development involves the *transfer* of childhood skills into adulthood, rather than creating new skills, Shweder (1982) contends that cognitive differences between children and adults are quantitative, not qualitative. Shweder attacks Piaget's distinction between cognitive processes among age groups and he argues in favor of a general competence that takes different forms in different situations: "By varying the content of a task it is possible to elicit either preoperational thinking from a college-educated adult or formal operational thinking from a four year old" (Shweder, 1982, p. 357). Shweder's critique of Piaget's developmentalism thus has the ulterior purpose of establishing an even more absolute universalism.

In contrast to Harris and Heelas (1979) who emphasize the manner in which social conditions lead to truly different cognitive processes, Shweder, in his effort to banish fundamental cognitive differences, *denies* the influence of conditions such as schooling and class on cognitive processes (Shweder, 1982, p. 360; J. Miller, 1984, p. 975). He acknowledges their effect on concepts, purposes, and interests, but not on fundamental processes. Regardless of age, culture, or conditions, then, all of us are essentially identical, not simply in our abstract humanness, but in our concrete psychological functions.

4

The Development of Psychology
in the Individual

The Transition from Infantile Reflexes to Social
Psychological Functions

The process of psychology taking form in and taking on the form of sociotechnological relations is perhaps most observable in the child's ontogenetic development. The utter dependence of the infant upon a social environment makes early development a microcosm of the social formation of mind. Ontogeny also reveals the relation of psychology to biology, and the individual to society. The clarity with which all of these relationships are manifested in a given individual made developmental psychology the favorite topic of Vygotsky and his colleagues. Comparing periods of a child's life offered a perfect complement to phylogenetic comparisons of species and historical comparisons of adults.

Vygotsky's study of ontogenetic development promulgated a long line of social-psychological analysis that stretched from Baldwin, P. Janet, J. Royce, and G.H. Mead (Valsiner & Van der Veer, 1988; Van der Veer & Valsiner, 1988) to Bruner, Kenneth Kaye, and a host of contemporary developmental psychologists. For the most part this "sociogenetic" standpoint illuminates general, abstract interpersonal influences on psychological development and does not directly relate ontogeny to sociohistorical issues. It supplements the evidence on true social psychological universals that was presented in Chapter 1.[1] Although the sociogenetic standpoint does not directly relate ontogeny to sociohistorical events, its emphasis on the interpersonal rather than intra- or impersonal nature of psychological development opened the door for more concrete research into societal influences on ontogenetic development. Our discussion will follow this path from abstract to concrete social influences.

Sociogenetic psychologists take as their starting point Baldwin's view that an individual is not a socialized individual self, he is an individualized social self (Baldwin, 1913, vol. 2, chap. 6). In other words, the individual grows out of social relations, he does not precede them. Baldwin went on to elaborate a notion of social Lamarkian heredity to replace natural Darwinian heredity in the case of psychological phenomena. This notion stipulated that "the acts now possible to [the child] and so used by him to describe himself in thought to himself, were formerly only possible to the other; but by imitating that other he has brought them over to the opposite pole, and found them applicable, with a richer meaning and a modified value, as true predicates of himself also" (Baldwin, 1913, vol. 2, p. 16; Baldwin, 1898, p. 20).

Vygotsky (1989, p. 61) used almost identical words to describe the social basis of psychology: "Development proceeds not toward socialization but toward *individualization* of social functions (transformation of social functions into psychological functions) . . ." Specifically:

> Any function in the child's cultural development appears twice, or on two planes. First it appears on the social plane, and then on the psychological plane. First it appears between people as an interpsychological category, and then within the child as an intrapsychological category. This is equally true with regard to voluntary attention, logical memory, the formation of concepts, and the development of volition. . . . Social relations or relations among people developmentally underlie all higher functions and their relationships. (Vygotsky, 1981a, p.163; cf. Vygotsky, 1978, p. 57)

For instance, I relate to myself as people related to me; reflection is a carryover from interpersonal disputes; thinking involves speech and is essentially a conversation directed at oneself. Even when these social relations are transformed in the personality into psychological processes they remain quasi-social (Vygotsky, 1989, pp. 56-59).

If psychological phenomena are socially constructed, they cannot be biologically determined, and sociogenetic psychologists have emphatically critiqued naturalistic theories which reduce psychological phenomena to infantile biological processes. These processes are not denied but they are distinguished from psychological operations which constitute a new functional system. Sociohistorical psychologists maintain that infantile processes are superceded by qualitatively different social psychological functions.

In other words, natural mechanisms do determine the behavior of infants as they do the behavior of animals. However they do not determine mature, human psychology. The reason is that natural processes produce simple, stereotyped, nonconscious, involuntary, stimulus-bound, transient behaviors which are inimical to symbolic, mental, willful, self-controlled, instrumental, flexible, comprehending consciousness (Luria, 1978a, pp. 99, 126). Consciousness is a human artifact which, like material tools, is not natural. Accordingly, where natural processes predominate—in animals and human infants—consciousness is rudimentary (Kagan, 1981, p. 148). Psychology only develops where natural processes change their character from a determining role to a non-causal, potentiating substratum of activity. As biology recedes from direct control over psychology, social relations fill the void and become the true constituents of psychology (Vygotsky, 1929, p. 423; Leontiev, 1932, p. 78).

Psychology, then, has an entirely different biological basis from natural, neonatal acts. Where the latter are determined by genetically controlled, subcortical mechanisms, mature psychology is potentiated by neocortical structures which are socially mediated. Vygotsky describes the fundamental difference between "higher, social psychological activities" and "lower," natural acts as follows: "Within a general process of development, two *qualitatively different* lines of development, *differing in origin* can be distinguished: the elementary processes, which are of biological origin on the one hand, and the higher psychological functions of sociocultural origin, on the other" (Vygotsky, 1978, p. 46, emphasis added). The biological infant only becomes a psychological subject through participating in social relations. Luria (1932, p. 9-10) echoes this point as he says that

> the genesis of organized human behavior is through the development and inclusion of new regulating systems which overcome the primitive forms of behavior and transfer them to . . . a new and more systematized organization. There is every reason to suppose that the primitive forms of organization of behavior, characterized by the sub-cortical type of activity, are *completely transformed* into the processes of the highest development (emphasis added).[2]

Primordial, natural, infantile functions are not simply supplemented by mature social psychological processes; they are sometimes dispelled and replaced, and sometimes integrated into and reconstituted by them. Infantile processes therefore have no adult analogue because they cease to exist as such in the mature individual (Luria, 1966, pp. 56ff). Conversely, adult activity has no natural analogue with human infants or animals (or machines!). Luria (1932, p. 394) explained this in the following words:

> The reactive process as we know it in the normal adult human is a complicated elaboration in structure not having anything in common with those impulsive relations which we observed in the child or the reflex activity of animals. The chief difference of the [adult] reactive process from those forms of activity in the child and animals is that in the former the direct character of the motor discharge is controlled. . . . It is thus incorrect to say that the

> stimulus directly provokes the reaction [in the adult] . . . The outstanding
> feature of the reactive process is the fact that the tendency of every natural
> reflex act to discharge its excitation directly is controlled by a complex reactive
> process.

Luria's distinction between human adult activity and infant and animal behavior is endorsed by the eminent ethologist Robert Hinde who states, "When you deal with the behavior of babies, there are very obvious parallels that can be made with animal behavior. But as soon as you start dealing with the behavior of adult human beings, the complexities that are specific to the human case become more important than the parallels in many ways" (Hinde, 1983b, p. 177).

With lower and higher processes deriving from fundamentally different origins, higher functions, cannot directly grow out of lower ones. As Bruner put it, natural, automatic, neonatal functions, "in no sense are the paving blocks from which skilled programs are constructed" (Bruner, 1973, p. 293, 251; Luria, 1932, p. 20; Luria, 1963). For example, babbling is not the prototype or constituent core of speech. Nor is speech an extension of, or continuous with, babbling. While babbling precedes and, in some sense, prepares for speech, it does not directly produce speech nor continue to underlie speech. Babbling is absorbed into speech and disappears forever, just as all lower functions are superceded by qualitatively different psychological functions.[3]

This crucial disjunction between the origin and character of lower psychological phenomena, on the one hand, and those of higher phenomena, on the other, receives impressive support from Sandra Scarr's review of the developmental literature. Although Scarr is by no means a Vygotskian, her conclusions bear a striking resemblance to Luria's and Vygotsky's. She says: "Sensorimotor intelligence is qualitatively different from later symbolic operations, whose evolution may have quite a different history. . . . I propose that the natural history of sensorimotor intelligence is independent of skills that evolved later and that there is no logically necessary connection between them.

"Indeed, the empirical connection between sensorimotor skills and later intellectual development is very tenuous. Children with severe motor impairments, whose sensorimotor practice has been extremely limited, have been shown to develop normal symbolic function. The purported dependence of symbolic activity on sensorimotor action has not been demonstrated. . . . If sensorimotor and symbolic skills have different genetic bases, they could well be uncorrelated. Sensorimotor skills are best seen as a criterion achievement—that is, individual differences are found in the *rate* but not the final *level* of sensorimotor development. Symbolic intelligence has individual differences in both rate and level of achievement, and the rate of development is correlated with the final level (witness the substantial correlations between IQ at ages 5 and 15). Infant intelligence is characterized by universal attainment by all nondefective species members. Its evolution has a more ancient history than does symbolic reasoning, and individual differences do not have the predictive significance of variations in later intelligence. (Scarr, 1983, pp. 194-195)

"Differences in the rate of sensorimotor development are small, relative to later intellectual differences. The overall pattern of sensorimotor intelligence is quite homogeneous for the species, since criterion performance is accomplished in 15-20 months for the vast majority of human infants. When one compares this restricted range of phenotypic variation with the range of intellectual skills of children between 11 and 12 years, for example, it is readily apparent that sensorimotor skills are a remarkably uniform behavioral phenomenon." (ibid., p. 211)

Scarr is claiming that genetically controlled, infantile processes are substantially identical among individuals. Socially mediated, mature, psychological phenomena, on the contrary, admit of social and individual differences due to experience. Individual differences in psychology are only possible because biological determinants have been superceded. Biological determinants are common to all members of a species and thus preclude individual differences (Scheler, 1961, p. 27). Human biology does impose uniformities on activity but only at the level on which biology is relevant to activity—namely, rudimentary sensorimotor functions and the potential capacity for complex mental operations. Biology does not control specific details of adult activity and this is why they are free to vary individually and socially.

The equivalence of human sensorimotor functions is confirmed by Charles Super. His review of cross-cultural research on infancy concluded that, "Using the rather gross measure of neurological integrity and some indications of attentional behavior, cross-cultural studies find equivalence of mental functioning at birth in unstressed samples . . ." (Super, 1981, p. 28). However, these uniformities are unpredictive of later psychological functions. Thus, Kagan (1981, p. 8) notes that "most investigators have failed to find a correlation in healthy children between precocious or retarded development in any of the universal competencies that appear between 12 and 18 months of age and precocity or retardation in the same or related capacities several years later."

Numerous other investigations have arrived at similar conclusions concerning the discontinuity between rudimentary infantile functions and later psychological phenomena. For instance, Bee et al. (1982) found measures of perinatal status unhelpful in predicting later psychological functioning. For instance, Bayley scales of infant development at 12 months only correlated 0.21 with 4-year-old IQ scores. Measures of receptive language at twelve-months correlated 0.16 with receptive language at 36 months, and expressive language over the same time period correlated 0.21 (Bee, 1982, Table 4).

On the other hand, information about the family and the child's social interactions was a far better predictor of later childhood psychological functions. A composite of social factors at 12 months, known as the HOME inventory, correlated 0.54 with 36-month receptive language (Bee, 1982, table 5). A cross-cultural study by Sigman et al. (1988) in Kenya came to the same negative conclusion concerning the durability of sensorimotor operations. Bimonthly observation of toddlers from 15-30 months old revealed very little behavioral consistency. There was no significant correlation over any of the observation periods for crying or for play behavior. Smiling evidenced only minimal correlation (0.24) over a few of the observation periods, and even less than this during other observation periods.

Only vocalization evidenced moderate consistency over the entire 15 month range. Correlations of sampled talking behavior averaged 0.37 (Table 3). Interestingly enough, the reason for the consistency of talking lay in the moderately consistent pattern of verbal interaction provided by the children's caretakers. Other home variables (such as physical care, touching, and responsiveness to distress, and general social interaction) evidenced little consistency over the 15-month period, and this is why most of the children's behaviors were also inconsistent.

Research into personality also suggests a qualitative rupture between infantile mood, distractibility, persistence, intensity, and activity, and their later expressions. The 1-5 year correlation for activity, for example, is 0.16; for intensity, 0.10; for mood, 0.08; for distractibility, 0.12; and for persistence, 0.09; for adaptability, 0.07 (Thomas & Chess, 1977, p. 161). In an update of Thomas and Chess's research, McNeil and Persson-Blennow (1988) found similarly low correlations. The 6-month–2 year correlations included 0.01 on intensity, 0.12 on attention, 0.16 on distractibility, and 0.34 (the highest correlation found) on rhythm. The highest correlation between traits at 1 and 6 years was 0.26.

Kagan and Moss (1962) likewise found minimal correlations between 1-year-old traits and behavior several years later. Aggression toward the mother at 1 year and at 4 correlated only 0.14, and temper tantrums correlated 0.12 over the same period (Kagan & Moss, p. 88). Sociability (eagerness to interact, smiling) correlated 0.03 from 1-4 years (p. 173). The correlation between achievement behavior during the first 3 years and adult achievement behavior was 0.03 (p. 132), and this was representative of most behavioral correlations between these two ages. Kagan's recent work on inhibited and uninhibited temperaments has produced the same low correlations. Inhibition at 14 months correlates -.03 with inhibition at 48 months (Kagan et al., 1989, p. 842).

Such data has led Kagan (1984, pp. 100-111) to repudiate the doctrine of connectedness between infantile traits and personality. He says, "There is no more reason to assume that irritability during the first six months will leave persistent structural residues than that a child who has perspired a lot during her first three months, because she was born in North Carolina in the middle of July, will take with her into late childhood psychological remnants of the bouts of excessive perspiration" (Kagan, 1984, p. 105). Kagan has carefully explained the relationship between temperament and personality in the following words, "Temperamental factors impose a slight initial bias for certain moods and behavioral profiles to which the social environment reacts. But the final behavior we observe at age 3, 13, or 33 years is a product of the experiences to which the changing temperamental surfaces have accommodated" (Kagan, 1989, p. 12).

Kagan's findings about inhibited and uninhibited children are a good example of his point. Although these traits manifest no continuity over time in the majority of children, extremely inhibited or uninhibited children tend to preserve a modest continuity (correlation 0.50) with respect to these dimensions from 2 to 7 years of age. However, the continuity is not due to some intrinsic persistence of the traits themselves. Continuity is preserved by the environment which strengthens the natural tendencies in a variety of ways. In Kagan's (1989, p. 162) words, "the actualization of shy, quiet, timid behavior at 2 years of age requires some form of chronic environmental stress acting upon the original temperamental disposition present at birth." An older sibling who unexpectedly seizes a toy, teases, or yells at an infant who has a low threshold for arousal might provide the chronic stress necessary to transform the temperamental quality into the profile we call behavioral inhibition. On the other hand, a nonstressful environment can reduce the likelihood that such children will become inhibited later on (ibid., pp. 162-163).

The presence of anxious, fearful parents would be another significant social reinforcer of inhibited dispositions in children. This was indeed found to be the case by Kagan who reports that 2/3 of the mothers of inhibited children, compared with only 1/4 of the uninhibited, reported chronic fears, social anxiety, or panic disorder during their adult lives. Predictably, such fears and anxiety were paramount symptoms in

3/4 of the 7 1/2 year-old inhibited children compared with only 20% of the uninhibited children (ibid., p. 151).

Kagan (Kagan et al., 1990, pp. 171-172) reports greater stability among uninhibited behavior than among inhibited behavior, which he explains in cultural terms: American parents reflect the values of their society and regard bold, spontaneous, sociable behavior as more adaptive than shyness and timidity. Parental support for extraversion is the reason that less than 10% of the uninhibited children becam more timid. In contrast, 40% of the original group of inhibited children became much less timid by 5.5 years (although most of these remained shier than the original uninhibited children at 5.5 years). There was a significant gender asymmetry in the direction of change which also reflects societal norms: More boys than girls changed from inhibited to uninhibited, whereas the small number of uninhibited children who became more inhibited usually were girls from the working class. This pattern is in accord with social pressures for masculine assertiveness and feminine timidity.

Temperament and personality are two distinct orders. One is a physical kind of reactivity while the other is social psychological (Orlansky, 1949, p. 31). For example, whereas the infantile temperamental trait of reacting slowly to stimulation is a physiological characteristic devoid of psychological significance, shyness as a personality attribute grows out of insecurity concerning oneself and one's capability, previous relations with others, anticipated fears about how others will react to oneself, preferred attachments to familiar individuals, and other psychological issues. Moreover, temperament is general while personality is specific. Any given temperamental trait can be expressed in virtually any personality characteristic (Schneirla, 1972, pp. 46, 52). There is no one-to-one association between personality and temperament. Personality characters such as altruism, humility, cooperativeness, selfishness, arrogance, sense of humor, seriousness, recklessness, dogmatism, possessiveness, authoritarianism, honesty, flightiness, and flippancy have no analogue in temperamental traits. Traits such as attention span, intensity, distractibility, persistence and adaptability can be modulated into any personality character. One can be intensely cruel or kind. A short infantile attention span can eventuate in adaptability as well as distractibility. The result all depends upon how caretakers treat their infant's dispositions. A quiet baby who is stimulated will become involved in activities, whereas he will become withdrawn if neglected by parents who consider him dull (Thomas & Chess, 1977).

Ironically, temperamental traits are quite malleable if parents respect them and introduce changes gradually. It is only when parents ignore these traits and ride over them roughshod that the infant becomes fearful and resistent to change (Chess, in Plomin & Daniels, 1987, pp. 21-22). Personality is not the product of temperamental traits being rewarded and extended into adulthood. Personality is constructed by modulating temperament with a host of social and conscious phenomena which sublate temperament into a qualitatively new order of personality.

In the section on "Existential Psychoanalysis" in *Being and Nothingness,* Sartre (1956, pp. 557 ff) champions the irreducibility of individual choices to general dispositions. Sartre argues that Flaubert's choice to become a writer cannot be explained in terms of ambition, intense feeling, and other abstract qualities (such as libido or will to power). Such an explanation is specious because it completely fails to account for the specific act of writing. Sartre asks, why did ambition lead to writing rather than to painting or music or acting? There is a hiatus between the general and the specific that remains unintelligible. "The transitions, the becomings, the transformations, [by which the general yields the specific] have been carefully veiled from us."

Sartre repudiates abstract factors prior to the concrete and he argues against regarding the concrete as only an organization of abstract elements. He ridicules as logically absurd the suggestion that the individual is only the intersection of universal schemata. Instead, the individual project is a concrete choice to pursue a specific goal that is meaningful in its own right. Its manifest form and content are real and must be respected on the level at which they appear. They cannot be disregarded as by-products of a more general realm. Sartre's analysis is a vital corrective to psychologists' penchant for abstraction described in Chapter 2. Applied to personality, Sartre's argument illuminates the fact that personality attributes are irreducible to general psychobiological temperaments.

The irreducibility of personality to innate temperament is proven by systematic cultural variations in personality. Despite the fact that temperaments are probably universally distributed across societies, personality types are differentially distributed and highly skewed. We know, for example, that the so-called "Type A" coronary prone personality is systematically inculcated by industrialized society because half of adults living in such society exhibit it (Sterling & Eyer, 1981, p. 17). Regardless of the temperaments infants display, half of them will become competitive, achievement oriented, aggressive, impatient, restless, and tense adults. Type A behavior is a rare and deviant pattern in preindustrialized societies.

Margaret Mead's study of *Sex and Temperament in Three Primitive Societies* concluded that gender-linked personality is also culturally molded and highly variable. Although Mead's work has been faulted as oversim-

plified, Fausto-Sterling (1985, p. 152) reports a similar alteration of traditional gender-linked personality characteristics that was obtained in
Kenya. In the community, boys and girls are typically assigned to traditional sex-typed responsibilities. However, occasionally, due to the
makeup of a particular family, some boys are made to carry out certain
"feminine" tasks. The boys who engaged in feminine tasks exhibited a
60% reduction in the frequency of aggressive behavior compared with
the "sex-typed" boys.

Lepowsky (1990) has also documented social structural variation in
personality. Her anthropological research on an egalitarian society—
Vanatinai, near New Guinea and the Trobriand Islands—discovered that
gender roles and personality characteristics were comparable for men
and women, in correspondence with their similar social status and minimal division of labor. Male-female relations were harmonious and there
was no sense of a battle between the sexes. Rape was unknown and
wife abuse rare. Political and religious colonization has dramatically altered the social and personal relations between the sexes. New formalized
systems of power have been imposed by government and religious mis-
sionaries and their roles are filled exclusively by men. Gender roles and
personality characteristics have diverged accordingly.[4]

Within the United States, gender-linked personality traits have undergone radical social transformation. The modern differentiation of
masculine and feminine traits was unknown in colonial times. Historian
Mary Ryan (1983, pp. 51, 52) observes that "colonial culture did not
parcel out a whole series of temperamental attributes according to sex.
Women were not equipped with such now-familiar traits as maternal
instincts, sexual purity, passivity, tranquility, or submissiveness. Surely,
colonial writers took note of characteristics common to women and observed differences between the sexes, female characteristics, but these
were too sparse, muted, and peripheral to the cultural priorities to give
shape to a feminine mystique." "Colonial men and women were held
to a single standard of good behavior. In sum, the concepts of masculinity
and femininity remained ill-defined in agrarian America" (cf. Demos,
1974, p. 430).

Today also, men and women of comparable social position evidence
similar cognitive, moral, and emotional responses. In a strong refutation
of intrinsic gender personality differences (postulated by traditionalists
and feminists, alike), Mednick (1989) demonstrates that social role is the
primary determinant of personality variations between men and women.[5]

These modifications in personality, along with others to be described
in Chapter 5 below, bear out Mead's conclusion that

> many, if not all, of the personality traits which we have called masculine or
> feminine are as lightly linked to sex as are the clothing, the manners, and
> the form of head-dress that a society at a given period assigns to either
> sex. . . . Only to the impact of the whole of the integrated culture upon the
> growing child can we lay the formation of the contrasting [personality] types.
> There is no other explanation of race, or diet, or selection that can be ad-
> duced to explain them. We are forced to conclude that human nature is
> almost unbelievably malleable, responding accurately and contrastingly to con-
> trasting cultural conditions. (Mead, 1963b, p. 280)[6]

Psychologically speaking, then, being man or woman is a social construction not a biological fact. Our notion of the biological dichotomy
between man and woman is more a product of our gender ideology
than the reverse. Biological maleness and femaleness do not directly determine psychological masculinity and femininity; they are socially symbolized and are reacted to in terms of this social meaning (Ortner &
Whitehead, 1981).

In addition to gender-linked personality types being culturally
formed, the entire sense of self is socially constituted and variable. Sampson (1988), Lee (1959), Logan (1987), and Baumeister (1986) have observed that the contemporary Western notion of an individual self is
quite unusual and contrasts with more social notions of the self in other
cultures. Even Homer in ancient Greece had no terms for self or oneself
(Simon, 1978, p. 56). This is further evidence that temperaments are
organized, transformed, and overridden by social psychological forces
which are the true basis of personality.

Not only are higher and lower psychological functions discontinuous
in the sense that the lower provide no basis for the higher, the two are
actually antithetical in the sense that higher functions supersede lower
ones and presuppose their *diminution*. "It is *after* the infant has abandoned the reflex pattern of response, and after a period of diffuse [vol-
untary attending] activity, that *directed voluntary activity* begins" (Bruner,
1968, p. 35). Luria expressed this well concerning the development of
language and intentionality:

> We would argue that in order to learn the sounds in a linguistic system, the
> child must inhibit the sounds in babbling. This argument applies to many
> aspects of the ontogenesis of children's voluntary movements. For example,
> it was formerly assumed that [grasping] emerges from innate reflexes . . .
> However, it has been demonstrated that nothing emerges out of this grasping
> reflex. It cannot in any way be taken as the prototype of future voluntary
> movements. Just the reverse is true. It is necessary to inhibit the grasping
> reflex before voluntary movement appears. The grasping reflex is a subcortical
> act, whereas voluntary movement is a cortical act. The latter has a quite
> different origin and occurs only when the grasping reflex is inhibited. (1982,
> pp. 32-33)

The lower processes interfere with higher functions because they are inflexible, individually based, and nonconscious. As every parent knows from frustrating experience, guiding and teaching neonates is futile because babies only achieve plasticity sufficient for learning during the second half of the first year after subcortical instinctual reflexes lose their dominance. While socialization efforts may be constant from birth, their *effect* is variable. The effect is minimal at first but becomes increasingly forceful.

Of course, parents significantly affect the infant's general comfort and irritability from the moment of birth by frustrating or fulfilling his needs (Lock, 1978, chap. 8; Gray, 1978). Parents also enhance or retard natural responses such as smiling, vocalization (Schaffer, 1971, pp. 74-76; Super & Harkness, 1982), alertness (Brackbill, 1973; Korner & Thoman, 1970), and the infant's attention cycles.[7] However, such influence is quite different from socializing molar, conscious, psychological activities which only develop after impulsive tendencies have loosened their grip during the second year. Vygotsky (1989, pp. 67-68) described the distinction as follows: Whereas infantile reflexes are naturally prepared and can only be quantitatively affected by social relations (social relations thus being subsumed within natural programs), higher mental functions are qualitatively constituted by social relations (so that natural processes are subsumed within social relations).

Parents' initial socialization efforts do aid the child to focus attention and augment self-control. These early efforts hasten the diminishing of natural determinants and stimulate consciousness. But little positive guidance can be assimilated by this rudimentary consciousness. The qualitative difference between the neonatal period and the second year requires significantly different parenting skills. Parenting the instinctually driven infant involves ministering to *its* biological needs, whereas parenting the more flexible, socializable child entails *teaching* values and behavior patterns. A parent may not be equally adept at both of these, often being better at one than the other.[8]

Vygotsky exemplifies the antithesis between socially generated consciousness and primordial organic reactions in his discussion of attention. Describing how attention is transformed from a simple, involuntary "orientation reflex" controlled by objects in the environment, to a conscious, voluntary, psychological process, Vygotsky states:

> The importance of the organic process, which lies at the foundation of the development of attention, decreases as new, qualitatively distinct processes of attentional development emerge. Specifically, we have in mind the processes of *the cultural development of attention*. When we speak of the cultural development of attention, we mean *evolution and change in the means for di-*

> *recting and carrying out attentional processes, the mastery of these processes, and their subordination to human control. . . .* Voluntary attention emerges owing to the fact that the people who surround the child begin to use various stimuli and means to direct the child's attention and subordinate it to their control. . . . In and of itself, the organic, or natural, development of attention never could, and never will, lead to the emergence of voluntary attention. (Vygotsky, 1981b, pp. 193-194)

Confirming Vygotsky's position, Bruner (1973) describes how "In the first phase, the infant tends to be pulled hither and yon by objects in the field and particularly by movement in the periphery." Later, the baby's voluntary, psychological attention comes to anticipate objects rather than reflexively follow them. With maturation,

> The child, to use Piaget's term, seems to be using a visual schema, placing objects with respect to each other. His attention has now become biphasic in nature—directed outward to the good targets, but guided in change by primitive internalized schema. [It is] about 15 or 16 weeks that the child seems well able to detach from one aspect of the stimulus field and move to another with a plan that is geared to finding what was intended rather than coming to rest on what is merely encountered. (Bruner, 1973, p. 272)

Ostension is a form of attention which involves following another's line of pointing, indication, or reference, and studies have shown it follows Vygotsky's characterization. Ostension has a natural, primitive form which enables four- or five-month-old babies to follow the line of regard of an older individual. However, advancing ostension to include abstract referential procedures such as gestures and language (e.g., "look over there") goes beyond its natural limits and requires the maintenance of social contact between the addresser and addressee in which the former *directs* the latter's attention to things (Bruner, 1980; Murphy & Messer, 1977).

Vygotsky, Luria, and Leontiev describe how memory follows the same social transformation of a natural mechanism into a mediated psychological function. In early childhood, memory consists of direct imprints from impressions, perceptions and acts. However, by the late preschool and early school ages it is increasingly mediated by complex mnemonic techniques. "It begins to rest upon a complex system of meaning connections, is effectuated with the aid of speech, and acquires the nature of that mediated logical memory which increasingly approximates thought in its psychological structure" (Luria, 1963, p. 18; cf. also Luria, 1928). Vygotsky expresses the difference between rudimentary, natural memory and its sophisticated state by distinguishing the former's direct, automatic connecting of events from the latter's active connecting via interposed symbolic or physical mediations which serve as *reminders*. In his picturesque words: "In the elementary form something is remembered; in the higher form humans remember something. In the first case a temporary link is formed owing to the simultaneous occurrence of two stimuli that affect the organism; in the second case humans personally create a temporary link through an artificial combination of stimuli. The very essence of human memory consists in the fact that human beings actively remember with the help of signs" (Vygotsky, 1978, p. 51; cf. also Leontiev's essay on "The Development of Higher Forms of Memory" in Leontiev, 1981, pp. 327-365).

The difference in the two kinds of memories lies in the fact that elementary memory is genetically controlled whereas symbolic memory is social-psychological. It is only after genetic control has significantly loosened its grip that symbolically mediated memory can develop. As Luria said:

> the relationship of various forms of memory to genotypic characteristics *changes in the process of development.* . . . The coefficient of genotype determination of complex (mediated) forms of memory is manifested distinctly only in young children, when the very process of mediation is still inadequately developed, and when this form of memory too is still direct to a considerable degree. At later stages in development, mediated memory techniques are established, and at that time other factors, unrelated to the genotype, begin to play the leading role in variability of memory. (Luria, 1963, p. 21; cf. Luria, 1936)

The transition from elementary to higher memory depends upon social interaction. Elders encourage youngsters to remember more things more accurately through the use of verbal mediations. Fivush (1988, p. 281) states that children learn to organize their memory of events through social interaction. Social interaction forces children to structure their verbal reports of past events, and this, in turn, leads to organizing their memory of these events. Gillian McNamee (1979) describes this socializing of memory in a lucid analysis of a teacher pupil dialogue. The dialogue primarily concerns teaching five-year-old Karen the art of narrative—retelling a story she had heard five minutes earlier—but this social narration requires expanding Karen's memory so that she can remember the story which she is to tell. This is an excellent example of how a social goal (narrative) stimulates a psychological activity (memory). In the dialogue, Karen initially does not remember the story clearly. The teacher prompts her with certain facts and with leading questions. She reminds Karen of a few details but she also implores her to stretch her memory by asking, "And then what?"—"Who did that?"—"Is there anything else?" Karen is encouraged to remember more details, sequences of several events, and proper chronologies. The social pressure leads her to strain to recall, thereby improving her memory. In addition, the teacher's helpful prompting and praising of correct answers raises Karen's confidence so that she believes she can remember. After several such interactions, Karen reels off entire portions of the story unassisted.

The dialogue reveals one other skill that Karen is taught, namely logical reasoning. This turns out to be a great enhancer of memory because memory is often a reconstruction based upon logic, stereotypes, and other known necessary relationships among things rather than being a recollection of details themselves (cf. Barclay, 1973; Ross, 1989). The teacher encourages just this kind of reconstructed memory when she says: "Now, they couldn't cut his head off, they couldn't drown him, they couldn't burn him, so finally what did they try to do?" In other words, the teacher is saying, "Since X, therefore Y." "Y must have happened because X was not the case." Karen thus need not directly remember Y, she can infer it from what she remembers about X and from knowing the relation between X and Y. Interestingly, Karen immediately reproduces this kind of recall as she says, "He couldn't be fired? *So* he was ordered to go to the judge." This brief dialogue, then, socializes narration, memory, self-confidence, and logic. These are all obviously interdependent and mutually reinforcing. As Bartlett (1967) emphasized, memory is not an isolated skill but is integrally part of thinking, motivation, and social knowledge.

The sociogenetic contention of discontinuity of mental functions has been challenged recently. Summarizing the argument for continuity of functions, Bornstein and Sigman (1986) claim that the earlier research was misleading because it compared infantile *sensorimotor* performance with later childhood cognitive performance. Such disparate measures would naturally produce discontinuous results. The authors maintain that measuring infantile *cognitive* functions that are more comparable to those of childhood does reveal continuity in this area. Indeed, several experiments reported in *Human Development*, 1989, vol. 32, and elsewhere report correlations of around 0.50 between measures of infantile attention and childhood IQ. However, such correlational data do not prove any intrinsic psychological continuity between the two phenomena.

A look at what is meant by infantile cognitive processes shows them to be qualitatively distinct from childhood cognition. Infantile cognitive competence is defined simply as attending to novel stimuli and decreasing attention (habituating) to familiar stimuli. These are measured in terms of the duration of looking at familiar and unfamiliar stimuli. In contrast, childhood cognition is measured by IQ tests. On the face of it, there is no intrinsic relation between the crude act of attending to one or two novel stimuli for a few seconds and conceptual, comprehending, linguistically mediated intelligence. Vygotsky's, Scarr's, and Bruner's distinction between lower and higher functions certainly applies here. Whereas intelligence penetrates beneath superficial appearances to understand essential characteristics and relationships, mere attention to novelty is entirely concerned with just such superficial appearances. In addition, whereas intelligence involves improvising a novel organization of features (as in intellectual discoveries), paying attention to stimuli that are presented by an experimenter involves no such creativity. Even the more rote items on IQ tests are only remembered through linguistically mediated, symbolically encoded, meaningful processes. Infants' momentary looking at stimuli is a sensory function that involves none of this psychological activity.

Bornstein and Sigman are surely wrong when they maintain that decrement and recovery of attention in infants probably reflect central mental capacities (p. 256). The authors also create a misimpression about the nature of infantile attention when they use terms such as "preference for novelty." In fact, there is no indication whatsoever that infants *prefer* novel stimuli; they simply look at them. The impression that six-month-old infants are processing information and exercising volitional choice (preference) akin to intelligent children masks crucial differences between infantile and later processes.

In attempting to elucidate the basis of continuity between infantile attention and childhood cognitive processes, Bornstein and Sigman themselves admit that the two are certainly not identical or comparable. In their words, there is no continuity of identical behavior. The authors then discuss the possibility that some common underlying process accounts for the continuity of the two different behaviors. They wisely rule out intelligence, which has nothing to do with looking at stimuli. Another candidate, mental representation, fails for a similar reason: There is no evidence that infantile attention involves mental representations. Even the lowest organisms sense differences between stimuli without mentally representing them, and there is no reason to assume that sensorimotor infants engage in mental representation either. Lacking symbols and concepts it is difficult to imagine how they could form mental representations. Therefore, no tangible connection can be made between childhood mental representation and infantile attention.

Bornstein and Sigman do mention one factor that does plausibly account for a correlation between infantile attention and later cognition; however, it is not a psychological phenomenon at all. This factor is stability in the social, didactic, or material environment. Numerous studies have found that maternal didactic practices such as encouraging infants to attend to objects are stable between 2 and 12 months (r 0.50); moreover, these particular maternal activities also independently predict language outcome at 1 year and intelligence test performance at 4 years. These findings confirm the sociogenetic explanation of psychology's ontogenetic development. They demonstrate that any correlation between infantile and childhood behavior is not due to any *psychological* commonality or continuity between them, but rather to a common *social* encouraging of both. Mothers encourage infants to pay attention to things and later on they encourage learning of language and other kinds of information. Their children therefore perform well in all of these areas despite the fact that these abilities have no intrinsic commonality. Mothers might also encourage their children to be good carpenters and also to compose good music, in which case the performance correlations would also be due to *extrinsic* factors, not because carpentry and composition are *intrinsically* related.

Kagan (1984, pp. 106-107) advocates this social explanation of psychological continuity with great persuasion. He states:

> In contrast to the difficulty of using an infant's qualities to predict his or her future, a family's education, vocation, and income are excellent predictors of many aspects of a child's behavior at age ten. . . . A child's social class constitutes a continuing set of influences on development. It is this constancy in the envelope of daily events that determines the degree of stability of a psychological quality. The more stable the environment, the more likely the preservation of those properties that are adaptive in that context.[9]

In a later commentary on the relationship between infantile attention and childhood IQ, Kagan (1989b) argues that it must either be an artifact of common social structuring, or else an artifact of experimental procedures. One experimental artifact is the presence of a relatively large number of organically impaired subjects. Studies reporting significant correlations between infantile attention and childhood IQ typically contain 10-15% of subjects suffering from organic conditions (prematurity or minor brain damage). These infants show a slow rate of habituation and also lower IQ scores. The correlation between these two phenomena could thus be due to these atypical slow subjects, with the normal 85-90% of the sample exhibiting no correlation at all (cf. McCall, 1989, p. 184, for a concurring opinion on this point). Kagan pointedly rejects any intrinsic similarity in the psychological nature of infantile attention and IQ—that is, he denies that infantile attention is a form of IQ.[10]

The distinction between higher social psychological functions and elementary natural responses is further illustrated in the way objects are transferred between people. As Roger Clark (1978) describes it, the neonate initially drops an object into mother's hand either accidentally or as a mechanical repetition of the "hand-opening" his mother just modeled for him. This is not an intentional, social act of transferring something to someone, for the baby does not wait for mother to cup her hand, and then place the toy into it. His behavior is aimed solely at propelling an object toward a receptacle.

Only through prolonged social interaction does the baby come to realize that his action affects others and that his action establishes a social relationship which ultimately enhances his own life. He then purposefully initiates the act in order to solidify a social relationship. The object is *deliberately* given in a *social* transaction: the baby holds the object toward the mother, waits for her to position her hand appropriately, and then places the object in her hand. This socially and consciously directed gesture and the original impulsive act of dropping both concern the physical transfer of objects. However beyond this superficial similarity they are fundamentally different processes. "Whereas in the primitive phase the child communicates *incidentally*, in the gesturally mediated phase communication is *intentional*" (Clark, 1978, p. 249). "The gestural form, though necessarily bearing a resemblance to the previous form of the . . . act, reflects an entirely different mental organization on the part of the child" (ibid., p. 252).[11]

Even imitation, which appears to be an intrinsic tendency for internalizing external occurrences, must first be instigated by external social sources. As Bandura notes, young infants are poor imitators, and "the development of proficiency in observational learning is grounded on social reciprocation, in which interchanges are mutually fostered" (1986, p. 85; cf. Abravanel et al., 1984). Evidently, children learn to imitate adults because adults constantly model successful behavior and implore the child to "wait and watch me do it; like this." In addition, parents continually imitate their children, thereby modeling imitative behavior. Imitation of the child yields imitation by the child. Susan Pawlby (1977) found that initially mothers imitate infants about four times as often as infants imitate their mothers. Eventually children learn that adults are mimicking their behaviors and they begin to reverse the pleasant game and imitate adults. Since children cannot observe their own actions it is not clear how they are able to match them with other people's behaviors; however, experimental research has conclusively found that adult imitation does significantly stimulate children's imitativeness (Thelen et al., 1975; Kaufman et al., 1978).

Pawlby's observations suggest that:

> the ability to imitate actions does not appear suddenly in development or occur simply as a function of maturation. On the contrary, it emerges only gradually in the context of the reciprocal pattern of social interplay between mother and child as a result of the mother's intention to communicate . . .

Paradoxically, our study suggests that the whole process by which the infant comes to imitate his mother in a clearly intentional way is rooted in the initial readiness of the *mother* to imitate her infant." (pp. 219-220)

This description is equally applicable to language. Language also does not spontaneously spring from a child's natural tendency; it is fomented by the child's participation in social interaction. Language is not generated by infantile babbling, it is a qualitatively new function. While babbling precedes language, it does not produce speech nor continue to underlie it. Babbling is neither the prototype nor the core of speech. Babbling is displaced by and transformed into speech. Nor, contrary to prevalent nativistic contentions, do social relations merely trigger off endogenous language acquisition devices or provide grist for innate grammatical structures. "Teaching a child to speak is not like teaching a second language to someone who already knows how to speak; it is to convey to him the 'idea' of speech, to awaken him to the possibility of using signs in order to communicate" (Dewart, 1989, pp. 173-174). Young children not only lack knowledge of the semantic and syntactic conventions of a language in which they can speak; they seem to lack the very idea of language.

Social relations prepare the child for appreciating the entire nature of language and for acquiring all of its features. They do so by engendering intentionality, a general sense of reciprocal interaction, joint attention and reference, a common fund of shared meanings, verbal designations to express these meanings, imitation to reproduce the heard words, and an appreciation of social interaction as helpful for fulfilling one's desires. The child must want to communicate, purposely try to communicate, be able to take turns in an ongoing interaction, and possess shared meanings that can be reciprocally understood and are linguistically encoded.

For instance, social games played by mother and infants during the first year of life significantly affect language development. These games involve agreed-upon rules of interaction, encouraging joint attention to objects and events, shared sets of meanings which act as referents for more advanced communication, and linguistic structures which children pick up. The importance of social games for language is revealed in Camaioni's (1989) research. In the first place, her subjects produced their first one-word utterances *only* within conventional, structured game episodes. Language did not emerge during unstructured tactile, motoric, and perceptual stimulation. Moreover, these first words corresponded to the linguistic forms used by the mother to mark certain segments of joint action and/or attention during these games.

Adamson, Bakeman, and Smith (1990) amplified Camaioni's conclusions concerning the social basis of language. In the first place they found that words, gestures, and action formats (book reading, telephoning, imaginary eating) occurred significantly more often when the infant was interacting with its mother than when it was interacting with peers or was alone. Infants also tended to use conventionalized acts (such as pointing, showing, offering, shaking head to indicate yes or no, and utterring words) at an earlier age when with their mothers instead of with peers or playing alone with objects. Additional evidence concerning the social basis of language is the fact that infants' participation in joint object play with their mothers at 15 months correlated 0.46 with infants' vocabulary size at 18 months. This correlation is due to the ways in which mothers focused their child's attention during the interactive play. Merely calling attention to aspects of the environment by directly using it (e.g., shaking a rattle) did not significantly stimulate the infants' vocabulary. However, emphasizing the shared meaning of the object by pointing to it or speaking about it correlated 0.60 with vocabulary 3 months later. In a striking confirmation of Vygotsky's distinction between higher and lower psychological functions, Adamson, Bakeman, and Smith found that mother-child interaction only stimulated conventional language and action formats; it had no affect on nonconventionalized communicative acts such as babbling. Babbling is a natural act which is largely independent of social influence; however, genuine speech is thoroughly dependent upon social interaction.

In addition to establishing the intersubjective, cognitive, and motivational prerequisites to language, social interaction makes language accessible to youngsters by mediating its production and comprehension. Extensive research demonstrates that parents structure both their own and their child's communication in order to teach him language. Parents model correct syntax; they correct the child's syntactical, semantic, and phonetic mistakes; they "scaffold" his linguistic communication; they structure pseudo-dialogues with appropriate pauses and emphases; they set up pseudo-question-and-answer interchanges which teach how questions are asked and answered; and through intonations and inflections in their speech they model phrase units (Bruner, 1971, p. 70; Bruner 1983b; Kaye, 1982).

The importance of this kind of "language acquisition support system" is revealed in the fact that exposure to language via technological methods devoid of social intercourse, does not generate language acquisition. In one illustrative case, a boy with normal hearing lived with deaf parents who used American Sign Language to communicate. Because the boy was asthmatic, he was confined to his home and interacted exclusively in sign language. He also heard and saw English every day as he watched television; however, he did not hear English in any social interaction. At the age of three, the boy was fluent in sign language but neither understood nor spoke English (Moskowitz, 1978). This example demonstrates that social intercourse not only prepares the individual to acquire the general building blocks of language; interaction formats also serve the more limited function of providing the child with clues for cracking the grammatical procedural code of his particular native language (Bruner, Caudill, Ninio, 1977; Bruner, 1977).

The ineluctable dependence of language on social intercourse shows Chomsky's understanding of this relationship to be quite wrong. He argues that social communication is far too degraded and imperfect to provide a model for language development in children. The essentials of language must consequently be preprogrammed in an inherent language acquisition device which is simply elicited by social communication. In fact, language is so easily and universally acquired because it is indispensible to social interaction—which is vital to humans because they *lack* intrinsic behavioral determinants. Social relations do not underdetermine language, they overdetermine it. Social relations are not degraded, inadequate stimuli which require supplementation from biologically based syntactic mechanisms in order to generate language; they are sufficient to generate language by themselves. It is only because Chomsky overlooks the systematic, inexorable demands that social life places on children to learn language that rapid language acquisition appears to be natural.

Emotions are equally socially constructed rather than naturally given. Primordial, natural, involuntary reactions such as excitement, sadness, happiness, frustration, fear, surprise, anticipation, and amusement are not genuine emotions. Only toward the end of the first year do true social psychological emotions appear which are entirely different from the instinctual responses. In contrast to the initial state where excitement was naturally generated by the stimulus—derived from its intrinsic character—mature emotional responses depend upon social meanings attributed to things.

Vygotsky (1987, p. 300) stresses that only the latter are genuine emotions. In infants (as in animals), emotions are undifferentiated from perceptual, and motor responses and do not achieve the status of an identifiable phenomenon. It is only later in childhood, with the development of consciousness, that they become a differentiated phenomenon. Consciousness is thus a condition of emotions. It is the medium out of which emotions grow—as well as the medium in which emotions are integrated with other phenomena. Emotions are not primordial phenomena predating consciousness in ontogenetic (or phylogenetic) development. It is only with consciousness, or as consciousness, that emotions truly exist.[12]

For instance, love is not derived from, or continuous with, infantile pleasure. Whereas infantile pleasure of sucking, for example, is a purely physical sensation, love involves a cognitive valuation: One feels understood by one's lover, can communicate with him, and feels completed by him. Love is based on many socially derived needs and values which are absent from the infantile physical pleasure that ensues from sucking. Hate is similarly discontinuous with infantile displeasure: The psychological emotion involves cognitive interpretations based upon moral and other values which are absent in infants.

Two-year-olds think and talk about emotions before they experience and express them. My own daughter knew the word for anger at two and one-half years of age and she labeled the behavior of people as "angry"; however, she did not understand the meaning or reality of this term, nor did she express anger herself at that age (although she did express frustration). She play-acted at anger—uttering the word, grimacing, and gesturing—but did not evidence any real anger. In fact, the gesturing was quickly followed by giggles which indicated that she was surprised at her behavior and confirmed its playful quality. It was only around three years old that she finally experienced feeling anger. Love and hate followed the same path from imitated verbal and behavioral forms to internal feeling. They were socially and cognitively constructed rather than natural, spontaneous emotions.

The discontinuity between neonatal and mature emotions means that "there is danger in attributing to the 3-month-old the same affect state ascribed to the older child, whether the term used is *surprise* or *fear*. It would be wiser to use a different set of affect constructs for the opening four months, when [cognitive] evaluation is likely to be absent or, at the least, diminished" (Kagan,1984b, p. 58). Lewis and Michalson (1983, pp. 118-121, 133) similarly insist that young infants do not experience emotions because they lack the requisite cognitive structures. Consequently, "Only confusion can attach to the designation of the physical states of early infancy by emotional terms which derive their meaning from a later period of life" (Orlansky,1949, p. 33). Cognitively mediated surprise, which stems from discrepancies between events and cognitive schemata, is qualitatively different from the sensory startle that is occasioned, for example, by a loud noise (Cicchetti & Schneider-Rosen, 1984, p. 391). Socially constituted, variable, adult emotions bear as little qualitative similarity to infantile reactions as speech does to babbling.

Emotions, then, are not simply infantile reactions becoming associated with new, neutral stimuli, as Watson and other behaviorists believed. The whole reflexive association between stimulus, emotions, and behavioral expressions is "decoupled" and replaced by a social-cognitive mediations, as depicted in Figure 2 (Shweder, 1985, p. 202; Lewis & Michalson, 1983, pp. 134-137). The result is that natural, universal stimulus-emotion-behavior associations characteristic of infancy become replaced by socially (and individually) mediated emotional reactions. This replacement is necessary for the conducting of social life which, as defined in Chapter 1, is the voluntary, conjoint construction of behavior patterns. Fixed emotional processes would motivate fixed action patterns which would be highly maladaptive to the varied social and physical conditions humans encounter (cf. Ratner, 1989a, for a critique of universalist theories of emotions and the evidence marshalled in their behalf).

A final difference between neonatal sensations and emotions is the wider range of emotions. The wealth of differentiated psychological emotions has no counterpart in infantile feelings and constitutes a qualitative extension of these feelings. The few infantile feelings such as sad/uncomfortable/dislike, or happy/contented/like are grossly inadequate to explain jealousy, guilt, hatred, romantic love, scorn, or admiration. Guilt, for example, is as irreducible to sadness as the personality characteristic "dogmatic" is to the temperamental trait "persistence." The distinctive quality that emotions have is a function of the cultural concepts which inform them. The fact that these concepts are humanly produced is the reason that emotions are multipliable while infantile feelings are limited in number by fixed, natural determinants.

How individuals acquire particular emotions from their social experience is unclear, although no more so than their gleaning and reconstructing sensations, perceptions, needs, concepts, and a sense of self. Emotions are acquired in the same way that individuals learn to perceive colors, sounds, and smells, develop a sense of time, space, and individuality, and acquire felt needs for privacy, sex, and intellectual stimulation. According to Vygotsky all of these intrapersonal functions are internalized from interpersonal relationships which model, label, instruct, organize, reward, and punish behavior.[13] Caretakers structure the child's activity around certain principles, and these principles are then gleaned from the entire structure of activity (Leontiev, 1981, p. 431).

The way time is learned illustrates this process which holds for emotions as well. The child must wait "for a certain time because it's not time yet." They can only play "for a short time" because "playing for a long time makes them tired." They are asked to describe their behavior in terms of time ("Have you been awake for a short or a long time?").

Arranging activity around time and explaining events in terms of time create a sense of time in relation to life which children pick up. Time has a particular meaning, function, and properties by virtue of its alloted position in life activity. At first children mechanically insert time responses into the appropriate spaces of their activity: When mother finds her three-year-old drawing and asks how long he has been at it, he knows this requires a quantitative time response and makes up a figure: "Three minutes." Eventually this mechanical response is replaced by a concept of what time must be in order to be suitable to quantification, or in order to make a person wait or make him hurry up.

Emotions are socialized in the same manner. Children's behavior is restrained, quickened, punished, and rewarded, objects are made available and unavailable, social interactions are structured, and behavior is labeled and explained in terms of an emotional state which becomes reconstituted and felt by the child. Emotions are reconstructed by him from the position they occupy in his life activity (Lewis & Michalson, 1983, chaps. 6 and 7).

The reconstitution process is rooted in humans' extraordinary sensitivity to the quality of events. In contrast to animals which are only aware of limited, isolated aspects of things (cf. Chapter 1), humans are uniquely able to transcend their own individuality and become conscious of the full nature of things' qualities in relation to surrounding events. This is why we can glean different senses of time, color, individuality, and emotionality from the structure of life. It is also why we can empathize with other's emotional experience and incorporate it into our own. Once this kind of physical and social worldliness (objectivity) is recognized, and an egocentric notion of self is abandoned, empathic grasping of physical, social, and pyschological phenomena becomes understandable and social learning can displace nativism as the explanation for inner psychological functions.

The fact that emotions are empathically gleaned from taking the role of other people rather than being directly induced by contagion, as is true for animals, exemplifies G.H. Mead's distinction between significant symbols and natural signs. Human emotional expressions are symbols whose intentional meaning must be empathically comprehended by taking the role of the other. In contrast, animal emotional expressions—such as the tension in the body of one member who is exposed to danger—is directly transmitted to the observing animal by striking an indigenous chord. No role taking is necessary. The symbolic quality of human emotional expressions necessitates social knowledge for a correct empathic interpretation, which makes accuracy difficult to achieve. Animal emotional expressions are more readily understood because they are transparent and require little social knowledge.

Now, the sharp difference between social psychological emotions and infantile emotional reactions does not imply a complete divorce between the two. Adult joy, sadness, frustration, and fear evidence some continuity in feeling quality with their infantile counterparts. However, significant differences modulate the continuity. First of all, culture, not psychophysiological programs, dictates what events arouse adult emotions. Culture, not physical programs, also determines the behavioral expression of emotions. In addition, culture modulates the quality of adult emotions. The joy experienced while observing a beautiful painting, for example, embodies a culturally mediated appreciation of artistic skill, a contemplation of the picture's meaning, etc.

Sociohistorical psychology, then, does not deny that a few emotions have an original natural basis. However, it maintains that the natural basis of these emotions quickly becomes sublated by social processes. While certain rough analogies may obtain between lower and higher activities, these similarities cannot obscure obvious, fundamental differences. Higher functions are not simply extensions of lower ones, they are not lower processes conditioned to complex stimuli. Psychological activity transforms, supercedes, and suppresses lower functions. Natural processes are not primal forms of psychological phenomena, and higher functions are not derivative of lower ones. Higher functions (such as speech) are not pre-given as, or predetermined by, lower functions (such as babbling). On the contrary, they emerge and are formed only with the historical development of human consciousness. Psychological phenomena are not the precondition of man's formation, but its product (Vygotsky, 1987, p. 243).[14]

Culture and Socialization

The foregoing examples, supported by many others in Chapters 1 and 2, make it clear that socialization engenders psychological phenomena by *forming* them, not by stimulating intrinsic mechanisms. Socialization is not merely an external trigger of dormant psychobiological tendencies but constitutes their very essence. The sociogenetic tradition is an invaluable corrective to nativism; however, it concentrates on general features of parent-child interaction and overlooks broader, specific societal influences. A complete picture of psychology's social ontogeny must detail the ways in which the family reflects and transmits the society at large, as well as ways in which society socializes children via the media, school, and other institutions. In Margaret Mead's (1963) words, psychology should not remain content with the generalities of socialization, it must penetrate into the specifics of enculturation.

Vygotsky himself was concerned with societal influences on psychology. He criticized class stratification in Soviet society as having deleterious effects on the motivation, cognition, and education of lower-class youth. He also condemned authoritarian leadership in the workplace as crippling the incentive and creativity of workers. These social concerns earned him the enmity of the ruling bureaucrats and led to his work being suppressed.[15] Even the recent publication of his *Collected Works* has omitted his writings concerning social, political, and educational issues that bear on psychology. The *Collected Works* primarily reproduce Vygotsky's theoretical writings on general social-psychological subjects and this one sidedness fosters the misapprehension that he was disinterested in broader societal influences on psychology. A genuinely sociogenetic psychology must revive and expand the societal tone it originally had because this is what sociality concretely is.

Urie Bronfenbrenner (1979) has proposed that societal influences be pictured as surrounding the individual like a set of concentric circles ("nested Russian dolls"). The circles closest to the individual represent more immediate social relations (the "microsystem") such as family; the next circle out represents more distant social relations (the "exosystem"), with the largest encompassing circle representing the "macrosystem" of cultural values, class position, laws, etc. This model has the virtue of including multiple social layers in relation to individual psychology. However, it creates the misimpression that these layers are somehow outside the individual and outside each other. Bronfenbrenner's basic point can be better expressed in Figure 5 which pictures the various layers as interpenetrating.

Figure 5 shows the macrosystem passing through the individual's life space, which indicates direct macroscopic socialization through the media, etc. The macrosystem line also passes through the family, indicating that the family transmits (mediates) broader societal practices to the child. For instance, parents are affected by their work and reflect this in their behavior toward the child. Work relations thus bear on the child via the parents, even though the child does not directly experience this exosystem.

The societal parameters which parent-child socialization practices incarnate provide the form, content, and level of development of psychological phenomena. Of course, families vary in the manner and extent to which they transmit broad values to their children; however, the cul-

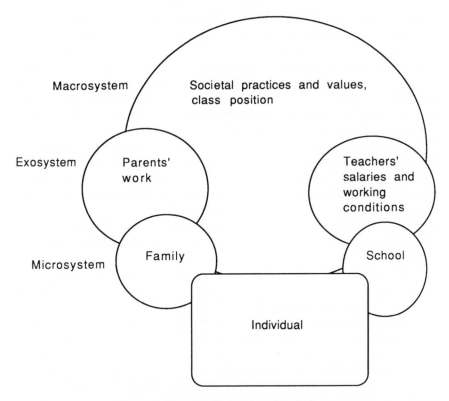

Figure 5. The individual and social relations.

ture gets through to the vast majority of youngsters. This is demonstrated by systematic cultural variations in psychological functioning.

Cross-cultural research has found that, in comparison with Western societies, non-Western societies provide far less stimulation of children and encourage far less initiative, independence, and individualism. The result is a more placid but also more secure individual. This is the conclusion that emerges from Brazelton's (1977) research on the Mayan Indians of Mexico, Kagan and Klein's (1973) investigation of Guatemalan children, Ochs's (1988) Samoan research, Schieffelin and Ochs's (1973) work among the Kaluli of Papua New Guinea, H. Geertz's (1959) observations on Java, and Super and Harkness's (1982) study of the Kenyan Kipsigis people. Brazelton's observations are typical of the others. Mayan mothers restrict their babies' early movements by swaddling and holding their infants. Babies are rarely placed on the floor and have little opportunity to crawl or even stand up. Toys are rare and social stimulation is minimal. Mayan mothers rarely attempt to elicit social responses from their infants, and rarely look at their faces or talk to them. While such restrictions do not interfere with normal psychomotor development, they do affect the quality of the children's ensuing psychology. All of the psychological concomitants of crawling and playing—including initiative, mastery, and self-confidence—are deliberately precluded by preventing psychomotor activity from occurring.

Brazelton represents the other cross-cultural investigations in observing that Mayan parents' close control over the baby's movements enables them to respond immediately to the infant *before* he can build up or express a need. There is no experience in early infancy that could foster self-motivated demand, frustration, successful achievement, or independence. The constant attention that is focused on the Mayan baby precludes any significant initiative, and it certainly minimizes crying and fussing.

In contrast, the independence and initiative allowed Western infants inevitably produces frustration and crying in the unprepared baby. Crying is allowed to persist as part of a regimen of self-reliance. The incessant push for successful, independent achievement encompasses early weaning at 6 to 9 months, early self-feeding of solid food—in contrast to the Mayan weaning at 5 years—and the granting of multiple choices to young children. These practices not only produce generally active individuals, but insecure, anxious, frustrated, self-questioning individuals as well. For instance, 90% of American 18-month-olds express separation anxiety (crying) from their mothers, whereas only 20% of communally raised Mayan (Guatemalan) children do so (Super & Harkness, 1982, p. 9).

Westerners' initiative and self-reliance are strong to the detriment of social skills and empathy. Non-Westerners evidence the opposite pattern of strengths and weaknesses. For instance, whenever Samoan children are held, the caretaker always faces them outward, looking toward others and away from the holder. Even feeding is conducted facing outward. Consequently, instead of children being oriented toward an individual caretaker, which is the result of American face-to-face cuddling, Samoan children are oriented toward the greater community through the manner in which they are cuddled (Ochs, 1988, pp. 162-3).

One manner in which socialization inculcates social norms is through language training. Such training refers to the process of teaching language rather than to the properties of language itself, which Sapir and Whorf emphasized. As the foregoing studies have demonstrated, the amount of vocalization addressed to infants evidences substantial social variation and this factor alone has important bearing on the infant's psychology. Constant verbal interaction and concern over a child's verbal competence convey an urgency about the need to master this skill. This reflects the orientation toward quick mastery of subjects which is so characteristic of Western societies but foreign to primitive cultures. Other ways in which language socialization embodies social values is the manner in which middle class American parents accommodate children's cognitive immaturity by simplifying their speech, guessing at what the children are trying to say, and helping them to formulate their intention in understandable English.

American middle-class parents are uncomfortable with the verbal "competence differential" between adult and child and they seek to reduce this gap by two strategies. One is for the adult to simplify his speech to match more closely the verbal competence of the child. A second strategy is for the caregiver to richly interpret what the young child is expressing. Here the adult acts as if the child were more competent than his speech would strictly indicate (Schieffelin & Ochs, 1983, p. 120). This child-centered language socialization fosters an "egocentric" perspective in which the child expects others to understand and respect him. American parents go so far as to ask the child whether their interpretation of his desire is correct.

Ochs (1988), Schieffelin (1990), and Schieffelin and Ochs (1983) point out that the societal parameters which structure American middle class language socialization do not obtain in other cultures such as Samoa and New Guinea. Samoan and Kaluli (New Guinea) language socialization take a different form because the societies are hierarchically organized with rights and obligations distributed quite asymmetrically. Consequently, caregivers do not indulge the interests and intentions of children. Mothers never treat their infants as partners (either speaker or addressee) in dyadic communicative interactions. Indeed, mothers rarely speak to infants or even gaze into their eyes. Caretakers do not simplify their speech to make it more understandable to older children. Nor do caretakers guess at children's ill formulated intentions or help them to better formulate their thoughts. Instead, Samoan and Kaluli adults expect children to understand them and they hold children responsible for making their utterances understandable to adults. Instead of guessing at what children mean, the Samoan or Kaluli parent will simply ask, "What did you say?" or else ignore the utterance altogether.

Despite the paucity of language training during the first few years, Kaluli and Samoan children are not left on their own to acquire language. Once a child has picked up a few words on his own he is regarded as capable of learning to speak, and instruction begins in earnest. Even at this point, however, language teaching is quite different from the Western child-centered model. Parents do correct the child's phonological or lexical form, but in a matter-of-fact manner devoid of baby talk or other kinds of speaking down. Parents also literally tell the child what to say in various situations. For instance, a mother who is dividing up vegetables among family members tells her 27-month-old to ask "Whose is it?" In addition, a mother typically does not modify her language to fit the linguistic ability of her young child; instead, her language is shaped so as to be appropriate for the child's intended *addressee* (Schieffelin & Ochs, 1983, pp. 124-126). The child may often hear simplified maternal speech when the addressee is young, however the maternal speech is not simplified *for her own child* but rather for another child.

The ways in which Kaluli and Samoan languages are socialized inculcates a sociocentric demeanor in children which reflects their inferior position in a hierarchical social system. (It must be emphasized that the different socialization practices nevertheless produce equal linguistic competence in the children of both societies.) In addition, Samoan caretakers' disinterest in their children's linguistic intentions reflects the societal emphasis on conforming to explicit, formal roles regardless of personal intention. With children's intentions undeserving of adult discourse, they become undeserving of the child's interest as well.

Samoans do not dwell on or cultivate their intentions. Nor do they justify or excuse their actions by appealing to intentions such as "I didn't mean to do it." Nor do they speculate about the motives of other people. They are more concerned about the proper enactment of behavior and its consequences than about their motives for acting. The linguistic interaction between adults and children thus perpetuates a social system which attaches more importance to appropriate behavior than to inner motives (Ochs, 1988, pp. 219-221, chap. 7).

The Western attention to motives includes a keen interest in emotions which is foreign to many non-Western societies. The manner in which American children are socialized to attend to emotions has been analyzed by Harkness and Super (1985). They observed that when a 13-month boy encounters difficulty building a model from blocks, his mother addresses his crying and labels it by saying "I know you're angry." She then indicates that this is a natural way to feel by saying, "It's frustrating to build such a tall tower." Finally, she directs her son to try building the model again, thereby actively overcoming the frustration. Such acknowledging and accepting emotion lies in stark contrast with the handling of frustration by the Kipsigis people of Kenya. Harkness and Super explain that Kipsigis mothers stifle expressions of frustration and distract the child from his frustration by talking about other things.

Describing the different socialization patterns the authors state: "In the Kipsigis scripts, the goal seems to be a quieting of the child's state, a redirecting of his or her attention to an external focus (whether food, doing a chore with the mother, or simply continuing to watch the mother at her chores) that will not be stressful. By contrast, the American mother redirects her child to confront the task that brought on the episode of crying, while directing her child's attention to his inner experience through verbally labeling and interpreting it."

Attention to children's feelings and intentions is not only unusual in non-Western societies. It was also rare in the West a few centuries ago. It was confined to the middle class and was utterly absent from the feudal aristocracy and the colonial settlers. These latter two classes had no special place for children—no baby toys, clothes, food, furniture, or rooms. Children were taught to submit to authority which demanded controlling their emotions, thoughts, and actions. Feudal and colonial children were apprenticed into adult work from an early age, and they developed few characteristics that we take for granted in children. Their submissiveness, seriousness, and realism contrasted sharply with the playful, sentimental, fantasy-oriented, animistic tendency of the sheltered and indulged bourgeois children (Stone, 1977; Greven, 1977; M. Ryan, 1983; Aries, 1962; Wishy, 1968).

The middle-class change in socialization—including permissiveness towards the child's desires, expression of emotion (especially on the father's part) toward children, encouraging of children's expression of emotions, reliance on indirect psychological techniques of discipline (such as reasoning or appeals to guilt) versus direct methods (like physical punishment or scolding)—has become prevalent because bourgeois social and technological conditions have become dominant. This modernizing effect of socioeconomic relations on socialization practices is evidenced in third world countries as well. In Nigeria and Lebanon modern socialization methods are employed by the bourgeoisie to a far greater degree than by their traditional counterparts who have been sheltered from modern conditions (Levine et al., 1967).

With the socialization of emotionality having a cultural basis, it is not surprising to find that socialization of aggression also varies with cultural requirements. Bateson (1941) reports that Balinese mothers minimize their children's aggressiveness in accordance with peaceful social norms. Taking issue with the universalistic presumptions of the frustration-aggression hypothesis, Bateson "never at any time saw a Balinese annoyed because he was interrupted in the course of some series of acts." The reason for this lack of aggressive response is rooted in cultural concepts that mediate frustration. The Balinese regard each act as important in its own sake, rather than as instrumentally leading to some distant goal. Given this social concept, an interruption is not construed as frustrating a goal beyond the activity. Consequently, interruption does not produce irritation or aggression, it is simply accepted as a sign that another activity is more momentarily propitious.

Young children who have not yet acquired this worldview do have temper tantrums. However, in accordance with sociohistorical psychology's tenets, socialization organizes and overrides such natural tendencies in line with social requirements. Bateson observes that this socialization process involves mothers damping any climactic pleasure that infants derive from their acts. For example, mothers stimulate their children, but just when a child feels excited and turns to the mother for support, recognition, or relief, the mother disengages herself. The child thereby learns not to expect any climax or reward or end state for an act, and that acts are performed for their own sake. This enculturation understandably immunizes adults to frustration.

Not only are psychological reactions enculturated to conform with social practices. Bodily functions are enculturated as well. Contemporary American children learn to control such natural functions as urinating, defecating, sleeping,[16] belching, farting, sneezing, crying, smiling (Super & Harkness, 1982, p. 8), and even breathing in socially dictated ways that are quite different from those of traditional societies. And Emmy Werner (1972) reports that culturally specific treatment of infants leads to distinct patterns of psychomotor development. Traditionally reared rural infants (living in extended families, fed on demand, sleeping with adults, participating in adult activities, and constantly being tactilely stimulated by caretakers) showed greater sensorimotor acceleration than Westernized urban infants (living in nuclear families, fed on schedule for brief periods, and sleeping alone) during the first six to twelve months.

Especially indicative of the effect of culture on psychomotor development is the fact that traditionally reared infants do not manifest a general superiority over modern children; they are only more advanced in those behaviors that are specifically taught or encouraged. For example, Kipsigi babies who are made to sit upright (by placing them in a hole in the ground with their backs supported by rolled blankets) sit by themselves much earlier than American babies do; however, they learn to crawl several weeks later than American babies because the latter are allotted three times more time on the ground practicing than Kipsigis babies (Super, 1981b).

The Nonmechanical Character of Socialization

The fact that social values and practices determine children's psychology does not mean that socialization is uniform across all individuals. Individuals occupy different social positions—including social class, local community, ethnic group, gender, educational institution attended, and birth order in the family—and consequently receive different socialization. Sociogenetic psychology recognizes individuality but attributes it primarily to the heterogeneity of social life.

If socialization is not uniform, neither is it passive. The individual's activity during socialization, and the ineradicable tension between the individual and society testify to the nonmechanical nature of socialization. Vygotsky himself forcefully opposed mechanistic conditioning as a model of socialization or learning (Vygotsky, 1977, 1979). He abhorred its attempt to bypass conscious mediations in favor of direct stimulus response links (Wertsch, 1985, pp. 20-21, 61-67, 185-187).[18] Vygotsky emphasized how socialization produces, not a replica of itself, but a creative individual consciousness. He stated that "all cultural development has three stages: development in itself, for others, and for oneself" (Vygotsky, 1989, p. 56). In other words, the natural neonatal reflexes and gestures (which occur autonomously, in themselves) are sublated by socialization (which is controlled by others) which finally yields individual, intentional activity ("for oneself") (Leontiev, 1981, pp. 294-5, 423). Socially imparted language, for example, forms our concepts, however the individual then uses ideation to invent new concepts and words (Vygotsky, 1987, chap. 7). Even parents' insistence that children follow their guidance fosters self control which ultimately promotes volition and autonomy.

The individual is always somewhat different from the social influences that act on him because he incarnates them (fleshes them out), totalizes them, and reflects upon them (Valsiner, 1988). The child engages in a "dialectic of personal growth" in which he "proves himself an inventor in the very midst of his imitations" (Baldwin, 1913, pp. 114-123). He makes something out of what he has been made (Sartre, 1963, p. 91). The individual concretizes social influences by giving them an individual twist which makes them real in relation to him.

As symbolic interactionists emphasize, social roles are not given, uniform, ideal types that are mechanically reproduced; they are taken up by the individual, made part of his life, and vitalized with a distinctive quality (Blumer, 1969, chap. 1). Turner (1962) criticizes Ralph Linton's notion of role performance because it fails to acknowledge the active process by which the individual interprets, modifies, and creates role requirements. Turner, like most symbolic interactionists, stresses the fact that, while the self is socially constituted, the very act of clarifying role requirements stamps them with a personal interpretation and is thus simultaneously an act of role modification. The variation introduced by personal interpretation and by different levels of involvement or commitment in role performance means that the individual engages in role-making as he enacts role-taking. He refracts social influences as he reflects them.

Of course, highly structured, organizational roles demand strict conformity and minimize role-making activity. But such tight restraints are more the exception than the rule, at least nowadays. Role-making includes the individual's ability to see beyond any single social sector, compare diverse social events, note contradictions, understand previous eras, deduce future trends, and glean possible alternative life styles. In Mead's terms, the individual takes on the role of the generalized other which requires abstracting essential characteristics from a variety of different models. As Mead further said, the "I" develops out of, and integrates, role playing "me's" and always transcends them to a certain extent. This continuing dialectic between "I" and "me" attests to the nonmechanical nature of socialization.

The active participation of the individual in the socialization process does not diminish the formative power of enculturation. However active the individual is in selecting, interpreting, and modifying social influences, they ineluctably shape his psychology. As Mills (1963, p. 434) cogently stated, "In manipulating a set of socially given symbols, thought is itself manipulated." The social distribution of psychological functions and dysfunctions, values, frustrations, and achievements along class, ethnic, gender, and societal lines testifies to the formative impact of social relations on psychological activity. Of course this distribution is not monolithic, and intra-group individual differences are common. However, these differences are typically variations on normative patterns; they do not create qualitatively new social values (Willis, 1977, chap. 8). This is why, despite the individuality that is fostered by capitalism, it is extremely difficult to significantly alter one's personality, cognitive processes, emotional reactions, and interpersonal relations in ways which run counter to the dominant social values. Despite the most deliberate intention to radically change psychology, prevailing values co-opt the attempt. Socialization works by co-optation as well as coercion.

Unfortunately, psychologists frequently neglect the material conditions that circumscribe peoples' possibilities, and the social changes that are necessary for fulfillment. The dialectical tension between individual and society (child and parent, student and teacher) is construed as sufficient to generate novelty, creativity, and diversity. The nonmechanical nature of socialization is regarded as a natural protection of individual freedom against social domination. Now, the dialectical tension between individual and society does introduce variation into the learning process. It makes what is learned different in certain respects from what is taught. However, these modifications are slight. Substantial creativity within a given individual and extended to a large number of people is not the result of a natural tension but requires stimulating the social, conscious aspects of higher psychological functions. For example, fostering creativity among the masses of children requires massive structural changes in the educational system, class structure, fiscal policy, and the media; it cannot be effected on the individual level alone—by presenting students with creative exercises.

Childhood play has often been idealized as a natural source of variation in, and resistance to, social norms. Kagan (1989, p. 78) aptly surmises that the popularity of play as a scientific category for children may originate, in part, in the opposition it offers to social restrictions. Numerous psychologists are enchanted with childhood play because of the free scope it gives to the individual's aptitudes, and because the spontaneous free expression of play transcends subjugation to the yoke of any necessity. Piaget construed play in this light as he said that "Imaginary play is a symbolic transposition which subjects things to the child's activity without rules or limitations" (cited in Kagan, 1989, p. 77). Play is an especially important source of freedom because it is available to all children regardless of their actual social circumstances. Play is one way in which freedom can be achieved without any attention to social reality at all—in fact, it is only achieved by ignoring social reality altogether.

Idealizing spontaneous childhood acts as creative and liberating misconstrues the true nature of creativity and liberation. It mistakenly regards creativity and fulfillment as outside social life when they are only possible for social organisms who comprehend and control their social life activities. Vygotsky emphasized that genuine creativity does not precede or lie beyond socialization, it is the *result* of socialization and therefore depends upon the kind of socialization one receives (cf. Baldwin, 1898, p. 20). Childish play is therefore not very creative because young children lack the social knowledge that is necessary for genuine creativity.

Vygotsky (1976) wrote an important essay on play in 1933 where he recognized that early play is imaginary, but not very innovative. Young children at play conform extremely closely to adult behavior and display little creativity. A two-year-old arranging her doll in the carriage imitates with unerring precision the manner in which her mother puts her in the crib. The child insists that every detail be perfect and will not accept any alteration in the doll's position. Similar conformity is evident in the fact that preschoolers' sex-typed play and their concepts of gender roles are even more stereotyped than adults'. Children, then, play *at reality* and reproduce reality, which means that their freedom is illusory. Vygotsky put it bluntly, "Play is more nearly recollection than imagination—that is, it is more memory in action than a novel imaginary situation" (Vygotsky, 1976, p. 552; cf. Vygotsky, 1990).

Vygotsky's social view of creativity is expressed in his famous debate with Piaget over the nature of individualized, imaginative speech. In contrast to Piaget, who regarded individually expressive, imaginative speech as preceding socialization, Vygotsky contended that speech is initially quite stereotyped and is only used creatively as the social conventions of language (and interpersonal relations, cf. Bruner, 1983b) are mastered (Vygotsky, 1987, chap. 2 & pp. 257 ff.; cf. Beck, 1986, for confirmation).

Luria similarly (1978a, pp. 99-101) observed that the unsocialized infant is far less flexible and creative than his older counterpart. It is only *after* being socialized that individuals can truly create new ideas and activities.[19] Higher cognitive functions, sensitivity, creativity, and personality lie within rather than outside social relations. Enhancing psychological fulfillment in these areas therefore requires fostering appropriate social relations.

Individual activity is only a necessary precondition, a bare potential, for freedom, fulfillment, and creativity. It is not in and of itself freeing, fulfilling, or creative. The individual-social tension always has a concrete character that varies considerably according to the social system. The real extent of people's freedom to comprehend and control their social world, as well as to be intellectually, artistically, and socially creative, depends on the concrete society in which they live. One's tension with the status quo—ability to distance oneself from it, reflect on, and modify it—depends upon one's involvement in it and what kind of status quo it is. Being a slave seriously undermines one's freedom despite the fact that one stands in a dialectical tension with the society (cf. Marcuse's critique of existentialist notions of freedom: Marcuse, 1973, pp. 157-190).

Capacity and Performance

The fact that psychological phenomena are free from biological determination and instead are socially constructed means that capacity and performance have no direct connection: It is not capacity that determines performance, it is the system of a child's social relations which broadly determines his psychological performance. Sociality intercedes, so to speak, between capacity and performance, and it takes determining power away from capacity. The result of biological capacity's being pushed away from any specific influence over performance is to leave capacity an extremely general, universal potential which is *socially individuated*. Just as linguistic capacity is the universal capacity for any human language without determining what that language will be or whether any individual will, in fact, acquire language, and just as the capacity for tools has the same universal, indeterminate character, so all psychological capacity is a biologically rooted general potential which is only realized through an individual's participation in concrete social relations. We all start out with essentially the same anatomical and physiological endowment (Geertz, 1973, p. 69), however we develop it into different activities according to our social experience. As Geertz put it, "One of the most significant facts about us may finally be that we all begin with the natural equipment to live a thousand kinds of life but end in the end having lived only one" (1973, p. 45).[20]

The differentiation of capacity from performance contrasts with most other psychological theories which presume a direct connection between the two. The so-called psychology of individual differences, for instance, assumes that differences in performance are prefigured in differential capacity, and are therefore fixed. On the other hand, universalists such as Chomsky and Piaget maintain that universal capacity produces a corresponding universal performance level—at least in form if not in content. Differentiating capacity from performance leads to a noncorrespondence between the two such that capacity is universal while performance is individualized as a result of unique experience.

The Social Psychology of Genius

The disjunction between capacity and performance opens up a new way of understanding genius. Genius has traditionally been explained in terms of a superior capacity for a particular faculty such as music, physics, etc. Proposing a direct link between superior performance and superior capacity makes genius a fundamentally biophysical phenomenon whose locus is inside the individual. According to conventional wisdom, the more superior the performance, the more physical and individual its cause must be. Sociogenetic psychology, on the other hand, argues that superior performance is socially mediated. We have seen that all intelligent conscious activity is a function of socially mediated symbols, tools, concepts, thinking processes, individual experience, and motivation. Since none of these elements is endemic, it makes no sense to attribute genius to "superior" biological processes (Leontiev, 1981, pp. 296-7, 305, 429).

With performance distinct from capacity, the nativistic position is untenable. Psychological activity is not rooted in particular inherited faculties; on the contrary, "the main function of consciousness is to enable the child to learn things which heredity *fails* to transmit; and with the child the fact that consciousness is the essential means of all his learning is correlated with the other fact that the child is the very creature for which *natural heredity gives few independent functions*" (Baldwin, 1896, p. 301; emphasis added). Psychological performance is fashioned out of a general potential which can take many forms. Cooley's analogy of human nature with a piano that can be plumbed for an infinite variety of melodies should be recalled as a fitting model for all psychological achievement.

Genius is irreducible to neuroanatomical properties, for example, because, aside from language, human activities have no specific neuroanatomical substratum (Luria, 1966, chap. 1; Anderson, 1983, pp. 3-5). Human activities are too complex to be captured in any particular neuroanatomical feature that is under genetic control. A high ability to comprehend physics includes the ability to understand a wealth of physical phenomena, mathematics, logic, and experimental design, as well as a vivid imagination. What specific, inheritable, neurophysiological property could generate all of this? Moreover, what could neurophysiology do to engender physics? Does it speed up the thinking process, as is often alleged? But Einstein's genius certainly had nothing to do with speed of thought. He would have been a genius however long it took him to discover relativity. It was the profundity of his theory, not its speed of development or the "number of ideas" involved, that qualifies it as a work of genius. Perhaps biology made Einstein more "sensitive" to, or comprehending of, physical phenomena? But now we are back at the original question which is how could any specific genetic factor enhance such an amorphous, heterogeneous ability?

Musical ability, such as composing music, is just as resistant to biological explanation. Once we disabuse ourselves of the reified notion that musical ability is a thing, and once we realize that it is a complex, heterogeneous skill that includes conceiving a highly structured melody, converting sounds into musical notations, structuring them within musical forms such as sonatas, symphonies, concertos, and operas, distributing the melody among various instruments (i.e., decomposing the melody into voices while simultaneously retaining a sense of the overall whole), and being familiar with the sound quality of every instrument, it becomes obvious that such a process is irreducible to genetic mechanisms. Creating music is a highly mediated activity. It depends upon considering the entire apparatus of musical instruments and forms through which the melody will ultimately be expressed. These instruments and social forms enter into the very conception of music since music is conceived in terms of these mediations—i.e., will the piece be a sonata, an opera, which key will it be in, which instruments will play it?

Creation and social expression are not separate; the mode of expression acts back on the creative process itself. Since the mode of expression is thoroughly social, the creative process is also. Creativity is not remotely analogous to any natural mechanisms like those responsible for bird "songs." In the absence of any plausible way that physiology could facilitate superior mental achievements, attributing them to cortical idiosyncrasies has no more explanatory power than invoking god's will.

Genius cannot be attributed to particular neurophysiological faculties. Just as computer programming was *invented* when it became useful, so were mathematics, music, art, science, writing, philosophy, and chess. It is as preposterous to assume a natural predisposition for these as it is to assume a neuroanatomical predilection for computer programming. Evidently, whatever skills humans need at a particular time are devised, and this presupposes an indeterminate psychobiological substratum rather than a specialized, determining one (Anderson, 1983, pp. 3-5). Damerow's (1988) history of Babylonian mathematics shows that abstract arithmetical notions painstakingly emerged from simple ones, they did not spring, full-blown, from a dormant mathematical faculty. Stressing the general cognitive underpinning of Babylonian proto-arithmetic, which was expanded to full arithmetical systems, Damerow (1988, p. 148) said: "The genesis of such [proto-arithmetical] techniques is not bound to any cognitive prerequisites of a specifically arithmetical nature, but only to the appropriate handling of the symbol function . . ." The creative historical struggle to develop mathematics from a general cognitive potential is paralleled in the life of individual geniuses who must create their mathematical ability from experience rather than inheriting it.

If the human hand is flexible to perform a virtually unlimited range of manipulations, then the brain cortex is even more flexible. The brain is no more the seat of particular, predetermined faculties than the fingers are predetermined to play the piano (Sapir, 1921, p. 9).[21]

The genius is an extraordinarily creative innovator who uses the plastic capacity we all have. This universal capacity is indicated by the ability of common people to assimilate the genius's discovery. Today's school children read, write, and understand algebra, geometry, and science, which were formerly manifestations of great genius and were only accessible to an intellectual elite. If the capacity for this knowledge were restricted to certain individuals, the vast majority of today's school children would be incapable of learning. Carrying this argument one step further, if children can master reading and arithmetic that were formerly regarded as intellectually demanding and accessible only to geniuses, it stands to reason that they could master other such knowledge like relativity physics and Hegelian philosophy if these were as necessary for surviving in our society as reading and arithmetic are. (Of course, "could" does not imply "would," since capacity does not automatically translate into performance.)[22]

Biographies of Einstein's and Mozart's lives indicate that their achievements grew out of quite common capacities. Hugh Ottaway (1980) explicitly attributes Mozart's genius to keen motivation, observation, and general receptiveness, rather than to any pre-given faculty for music. Discussing Mozart's achievement, Ottaway says:

> What that shows us of Wolfgang is a young boy's capacity for imitation, a scale that amounts to virtuosity . . . [T]he self-confident vigour presupposes an unusual degree of observation and receptiveness, an active receptiveness that insists on doing. This is a key not only to the boy but also to the youth; properly used, it should unlock our understanding of that prodigious talent which some indulgently confuse with genius, and should help us to avoid such confusion. Even Mozart had first to master his talent! This boyhood . . . active receptiveness was not confined to musical pursuits; it can be seen in the flair for languages, Italian especially, and in a well-authenticated excellence at arithmetic. (Ottaway, 1980, p. 21)

If Mozart's genius is irreducible to any special faculty, Einstein's is even less so. Far less precocious than Mozart, Einstein actually developed comparatively late. As Clark (1971, p. 27) explicitly said, "Nothing in Einstein's early history suggests dormant genius. Quite the contrary." His retarded language development led his parents to fear that he might be subnormal. And his poor school performance led teachers to predict poor prospects for his success. Einstein himself confirms the absence of any intrinsic predilection or ability for his field of mastery. And he even argues that *this absence was responsible for his later accomplishments*: "My intellectual development was retarded, as a result of which I began to wonder about space and time only when I had already grown up. Naturally I could go deeper into the problem than a child with normal abilities" (ibid., pp. 27-28).

Rather than genius being rooted in internal, organic factors, or even unique personality traits (Weisberg, 1986), it, like all normal psychological activity, depends upon social relations stimulating the development of a general, universal capacity. Of course, this stimulation should not be construed in simplistic behavioristic or interpersonal terms. In fact, genius seems to be far more affected by the macrosystem than by the microsystem of personal interactions. While there is no identifiable pattern of family relations associated with genius, there are definite historical relationships. Historical periods such as the Renaissance and Enlightenment produced an outpouring of talent in numerous fields which can only be explained in terms of broad social events. It seems that periods of social reformation provoke genius because people are incited to think anew about large questions such as the reasons for, and the means and ends of life. This searching exploration and comprehensive reformulating of inquiry is what genius is all about.

Of course, not all expressions of genius are traceable to cataclysmic social events. However, even in relatively quiet social periods, the grand, majestic, encompassing character of works of genius reflects a profound concern with life. This concern is evident in the genius's personal, social, and political statements (Goldmann, 1980, p. 103). Goldmann astutely observed that great works are the products of an exceptionally rich and insightful personality whose genius lies in expressing an aspect of life that is universally meaningful. In other words, the genius is someone who more than others transcends a merely individual sense of life and who captures a monumentally significant moment. The genius is thus simultaneously more individual and more universal than the common person (Goldmann, 1975, p. 43).

Far from genius being an individual product unfolded from mysterious inner structures, or incremental compiling of discrete, immediately reinforced behaviors (Bruner, 1973, p. 294), it is eminently social in the broadest sense. Profound thinking and feeling are not individual flukes but are intimately linked to profound social occurrences. Why, in the midst of momentous periods, individual differences in creativity are pronounced, involves numerous unspecifiable experiences which differentially link people to the world. Although these experiences are unspecifiable, they are not unspecific. Specific experience with family members, peers, school, religion, the media, etc., definitely mediate macrosystem events into the individual's life, and influence his thinking, feeling, motivation, values, and other ingredients of his talent. Parents and educators can cultivate talent on a microsystemic level, although they cannot instill the profound sense of life that macrosystem events do. Consequently, genius will perhaps always be exceptional; however, cognitive and artistic skills, self-confidence, and motivation can certainly be upgraded by enhancing the social events that are under our control.

Notes

1. Zinchenko (1984, pp. 70-71) is correct in his criticism that Vygotsky's emphasis on the formal linguistic mediation of childhood thinking (and psychological development, in general) apart from children's societal-material intercourse endowed Vygotsky's system of ideas with a certain intellectualism. In many of his writings, linguistic concepts which formed children's cognitive structures were suspended in a world of their own apart from concrete society.

2. Vygotsky and Luria's contrast between lower and higher processes resembles Whorf's, cited in Chapter 1. Both authors seek to distinguish social-psychological phenomena from natural ones. Although conceptually similar, there is a technical difference. Vygotsky's lower processes are infantile, reflexive, subcortical phenomena. Whorf's lower processes are adult, cortically mediated, sensory phenomena which are artificially isolated and deprived of social knowledge. In their own ways, both lower processes are nonsocial and nonmental. They are qualitatively different from higher processes and do not engender them. Wertsch (1985, pp. 47-48) faults Vygotsky for underestimating natural determinants of psychological development; however, Vygotsky had good reason for doing so. It should be emphasized that Vygotsky never disclaimed biological bases of higher psychological functions, he simply argued that the biological base was a general, potentiating substratum rather than a specific determiner of activity.

   The value of Vygotsky's distinction between natural-elementary and higher psychological processes is questioned from a different direction by Van der Veer and Ijzendoorn (1985). They deny any biological determination even of infantile behavior, and claim that "even processes generally thought to be 'natural' or 'hereditary' are influenced by culture" (p. 8). This, however, is quite implausible in the case of early "sensorimotor" reactions which are quite resistant to socialization—as any frustrated parent knows. Consequently, Vygotsky and Luria's distinction remains a vital one.

   Unfortunately, Vygotsky occasionally misused the term "lower" processes to mean childhood psychological phenomena such as memory which had not yet reached adult levels of maturity (Wertsch, 1985, pp. 40-48). This use of the term is quite unfortunate because the memory of 4-year-olds has nothing in common with neonatal, reflexive, nonconscious reactions, which is the original meaning of "lower" processes. It is therefore best to use a different term for childhood psychological phenomena and to confine lower processes to infantile reflexes.

   Vygotsky and Luria also occasionally stated that lower, natural reactions persist until 3-4 years of age, and occasionally even until 7, when children enter school (Luria, 1936, 1963). This is untrue because the neonatal reflexes die out toward the end of the first year, and it is at this point that natural processes give way to culturally mediated higher processes. Although Vygotsky and Luria were wrong about the timing of the transition from lower to higher processes, they were correct in emphasizing the nature of the change.

3. All doctrines which postulate qualitative continuity between infantile and mature activity are, from Vygotsky's point of view, erroneous. This includes nativism which postulates a natural continuity in personality, perception, etc., across maturational stages. It also includes behaviorism which construes adult behavior to be the continuation of reinforced infantile responses. In fact, the bypassing of consciousness in favor of immediate S-R associations renders behaviorism a form of naturalism. For Vygotsky, all direct, unmediated associations are natural because they eliminate the human element.

4. It is important to emphasize that while native men have become more powerful relative to women, they are themselves dominated by foreign authorities and are therefore less powerful relative to their pre-colonial position. "The autonomy of all individuals on Vanatinai, male and female, has declined with pacification and the hegemony of laws, courts, district offices, priests, and mission boards" (Lepowsky, p. 209). The egalitarian social structure gave men more autonomy than the hierarchical structure allows for.

5. The ontogenetic patterning of contemporary gender-linked personality traits further suggests social construction of these traits. Aggression, for example, follows quite distinctive patterns among boys and girls. Bodily aggression (physical attack) shows a *negative* correlation of 0.27 in girls from 2 to 5 years of age. However, it maintains a moderate *positive* correlation of 0.33 in boys over the same age. In contrast, object-related aggression (taking things from other people), maintained a positive correlation in boys and girls, although it was higher among boys (0.51 vs. 0.35, respectively). Both types of aggression are thus far more consistent among boys than girls. In addition, bodily aggression at age 2 and verbal aggression at age 5 correlate 0.47 among boys. However they correlate -.06 in girls (Cummings et al., 1989).

   The fact that different expressions of aggression are gender-specific suggests social patterning. What else could invert girls' bodily aggression (making aggressive girls peaceful and peaceful girls aggressive) while maintaining moderate consistency in girls' object-related aggression? What else can explain a much higher consistency in object-related aggression among boys than among girls? And what else could explain the substantial relation between different forms of aggression (bodily and verbal) in boys and the absence of a relation in girls? And what besides socialization explains the overall reduction in aggressive behavior among boys and girls from 2 to 5 years of age?

6. While Mead correctly emphasizes cultural determination of the distribution of personality types within a society, her account of the origin of personality traits is questionable. She claims that personality traits are innate and that each culture simply selects certain ones to favor as norms, and deselects others. Culture only selects from among given traits, it does not create personality types (Mead, 1963b, chap. 17).

Mead's conception of origins may be a relatively minor point in view of the heavy responsibility she grants to culture for determining the distribution of personality types and dictating norms. However, in the interest of parsimony and logical consistency, it is incumbent on us to note the error of nativism. It assumes, first of all, that personality is continuous with temperament, which sociohistorical psychology rejects. As we have discussed, culture does not simply reinforce temperamental traits, it constructs personality characteristics. Whatever natural elements may precede this construction are sublated into a qualitatively new social psychological form.

Mead's explanation is inconsistent: People who possess normative personality characteristics do so because they were born with them—they were simply lucky that the culture chose to promote these traits. However, the people who were born with other traits had to suppress these disfavored ones and learn to acquire the normative traits. Mead, then, postulates two different processes, apportioned among different sets of people, for acquiring culturally sanctioned personalities—some people inherit normative characteristics while others learn them.

A more parsimonious explanation is that all personality characteristics are culturally constructed and enculturated. Everyone who acquires the normative traits does so through learning cultural demands. Nobody is born with these traits ready made. While temperaments may be innate, these must be transformed through social experience before they become personality characteristics. This social transformation is undergone by everyone, not only by the misfits who lack the natural equipment that the culture demands. Finally, the range of personality types that transcends the favored norm in all societies is not, as Mead proposed, due to certain non-normative traits being irrepressible. It is due to the heterogeneity of culture which includes different demands, statuses, institutions, frustrations, and contradictions. Deviations are as socially derived as the norms are.

7. Kaye described the parental directing of attention as follows: "By adjusting to the on-off cycles of infant attention, mothers succeed in creating consistent, recurring mini-sequences of events, which the infant in turn responds to and comes to anticipate in consistent ways. Intrinsic processes (the cycles of attention and arousal) provide one level of organization, but adults use that to create a deeper level of organization that is extrinsic, social, and communicating—long before it is understood" (Kaye, 1982, p. 73). "[Thus,] When adults allow their own behavior to be temporally organized by the infant's, they are really assimilating his cycles of attention and arousal to the adult world's cycles of speaking and listening, gesturing and observing. So the adults' adjustment is in fact a form of socialization" (Kaye, 1982, p. 72, 151; cf. also, Newson, 1979; Brazelton & Tronick, 1980; and Cicchetti & Schneider-Rosen's excellent discussion of social relations and atypical infants).

The predominant shaping of infantile reactions by adults is also evident in crying. An infant's frequency of crying is more a function of adults' responses than of his own constitutional makeup. According to Ainsworth and Bell (1974, p. 102), "maternal ignoring [of the infant's cries] increases the likelihood that a baby will cry relatively more frequently from the second quarter onward, whereas the frequency of *his* crying has no consistent influence on the number of episodes his mother will be likely to ignore." The authors further document the fact that adults construct a pattern of crying that is not intrinsically given: "There is no stability in infant crying until the very end of the first year, and therefore no support for the view that babies who cry more than others at the end of the first year do so because they are constitutionally irritable. Mothers were found to be substantially more stable in their responsiveness to infant crying than infants in their tendency to cry (p. 100).

Early vocalization is also predominantly a function of parental encouragement rather than a spontaneous outpouring. Sigman et al. performed a regression analysis which found that social interaction measures accounted for 22% of the variance of children's 18-month Bayley verbal scores, while the frequency of toddler vocalization only accounted for 4% of the variance. "Thus, the extent of verbal and social interaction seemed to influence cognitive development regardless of the verbal skill or loquaciousness shown by the 18-month-old" (Sigman et al., 1988, p. 1259).

8. When parents erroneously construe infantile impulsive acts as true personality and as enduring desire, they prolong infantilism and make self control and social adaptability more difficult to achieve. Genuine autonomy requires volitional, deliberate control over one's acts which only comes from experiencing social restraint over one's impulses. Social restraint thus engenders autonomy and individuality, it is not antithetical to them as popular impression believes.

9. Investigation must deliberately attempt to relate psychological activity to the social context or else the association becomes obscured. For instance, investigation of psychologically disturbed young children reveals that 40% of them improve by age 9. In and of itself, this fact appears to indicate some spontaneous recovery in a minority of children, while the majority are doomed to stagnate in their misery. However, a contextual analysis which compares improvement to family environment leads to an entirely different conclusion. When context was considered, children with early problems who were from stable homes shifted toward improved status in middle childhood in 73% of the cases; improvement in children from chaotic homes was 33% (Radke-Yarrow, 1989, p. 208). The pessimistic conclusion reached when improvement is considered apart from social context is totally reversed when context is considered. The 40% rate of improvement can be nearly doubled given a beneficent environment.

10. Kagan raises another problem with these experiments. It is the extreme unreliability of measures of infantile attention. The volatility of this phenomenon makes it difficult to accept any correlation with other phenomena. For example, in a recent study by Rose et al. (1988) attention to novel

geometric forms at 6 months and at 8 months correlated an abysmal 0.03. How can it be that attention to novel geometric forms only correlated 0.03 with *itself* over a brief *2-month period*, yet correlated 0.37 with IQ some 2 1/2 years later? Rose et al.'s experiment is also undermined by the problem of defective subjects. The subjects' mean Stanford Binet scores were in the 80s and ranged as low as 59. Sixteen percent of the scores were under 70 and 46% were under 85.

11. Bruner reports on a longitudinal study in which children were observed in their homes playing a game with their mothers. He found a distinct alteration in the quality of reaching at around seven months of age. Before this age reaching was a reflexive groping at each appearance of the toy, but unrelated to the structure of the game. At 7 months, this random manipulation and grabbing stops. From then on, reaching and grasping increase and they are in tune with the structure of the game, anticipating the time and place in which the toy will appear (Bruner, 1983b, pp. 53-54).

Leontiev (1981) provides an additional description of adults' facilitating children's purposeful handling of objects by organizing and extending their awareness, self-control, and decaying reflexes:

> When an adult first tries to give a baby a drink from a cup, the touch of the liquid evokes unconditioned-reflex movements in the child that strictly correspond to the natural conditions of the act of drinking (cupping the hands as a natural water-holder) . . . The cup is not yet seen here as an object that determines the way of performing the act of drinking. The baby soon learns, however, to drink properly from the cup, i.e., its movements are reorganized so that the cup is now used appropriately to its purpose. Its rim is pressed down onto the lower lip, the baby's mouth is distended, the tongue takes up a position in which its tip just touches the inner surface of the lower jaw . . . A quite new functional motor system arises . . .
>
> The forming of this new functional system depends on the objective properties of the object itself, i.e., the cup which differs from a "natural water-holder" not only in being movable, but also in having a thin rim; the baby's use of these properties, however, is not so much determined by them in themselves, as by the actions of the adult who is giving it a drink, who presents the cup to it properly and gradually tilts it; later when she puts the cup in the baby's hands, she actively guides and corrects its movements the first time. The adult thus *constructs* a new functional motor system in the baby, partly directly by adjusting its movements (those of holding the cup to the mouth and gradually tilting it), and partly by evoking ready-made reflexes in the baby that belong, however, to other, natural "reflex assemblies."
>
> A baby's mastering of such specifically human actions as using a spoon, etc., proceeds in the same way. At first the object put into its hand is drawn into its system of natural movements; it carries a full spoon to its mouth as if it were handling any other 'non-implemental' natural object, i.e., without considering, for instance, the need to hold the spoon horizontal. Subsequently, once more through an adult's direct intervention, the movements of the baby's hand with the spoon are radically reorganized and are subordinated to the objective logic of using a spoon. (pp. 305-306)

12. The transformation of primordial sensations into conscious feelings rests upon neuroanatomical changes: subcortical centers which control infantile, automatic "emotional" reactions become subsumed by the cortex which enable social psychological emotions to develop. (Ekman & Oster, 1979, pp. 533, 537). As we shall see in the next chapter, such biological underpinnings are indispensable for social psychological phenomena to emerge although they do not *determine* that these will develop.

13. These socialization practices have been investigated in the following research: modeling (Bandura, Grusec, & Menlove, 1967; Feinman, 1982; Lewis, 1987), mapping (Laing, 1969), imputing motives to children and treating them as if these motives were genuine (Kaye, 1982; Newson, 1979; Sameroff et al., 1982; Rubin et al., 1974; Rothbart & Macerby, 1966; Condry & Ross, 1985; Will et al.,1976), and scaffolding (Bruner, 1983b). Investigation of socialization techniques is in its infancy because the behavioristic legacy of simplistic conditioning retarded investigating complex, subtle, implicit learning processes.

14. Margaret Mead (1963, pp. v-xiv) shows how natural, neonatal facts can be used as foci onto which social characteristics are unwittingly *projected*, despite the fact that these facts do not intrinsically possess such characteristics. One instructive example which epitomizes this widespread fallacy is the Mundugumor (New Guinea) belief that children born with the umbilical cord wound around their necks are natively suited to be artists.This belief leads elders to only encourage these children to paint, while other children are discouraged from artistic endeavors. The result, of course, is that only former individuals become good artists. Children born without strangulating umbilical cords never attain artistic virtuosity. Looking at the bare fact that artistic ability highly correlates with a strangulating umbilical cord lends credence to the nativistic assumption that this condition causes artistic ability. Of course, nothing could be further from the truth. Although the presence of a strangulating umbilical cord is a condition upon which artistic talent is premised, the condition is entirely a function of social beliefs. It is these beliefs that make the natural fact into a condition of psychological activity. The fact itself has no such power.

In the same way, the bone structure and musculature of the human face is socially construed as beautiful or ugly. Life style and success are highly correlated with the anatomical characteristics that underlie beauty or ugliness. However, these natural facts do not intrinsically determine life-style and success; they only do so through the significance that is bestowed on them by a social belief system.

Neonatal processes, hormones, neuroanatomy, sense receptors, and other natural phenomena have equally little determining power on psychology. Attributing causal properties to them is as misguided as Mundugumor projections are. The correlational relationship between psychology and biology is due to social, not natural, causes (cf., Jencks, 1987, for an excellent discussion of this point).

15. Luria similarly abandoned his early research on social psychology (Luria, 1974, 1976) for the politically safer study of neurophysiology. This, along with his less outspoken, though equally heartfelt, political criticisms saved him from the wrath that was heaped on Vygotsky.

16. Cross-cultural research has demonstrated that sleeping patterns are heavily socialized. The longest single episode of sleep during a 24-hour period averages around 4 hours for American babies at 1 month of age. Over the next 3 months, there is a sharp increase in maximum sleep episodes, so that at 4 months the American baby averages a maximum sleep of almost 8 hours. In contrast, the rural African baby averages 3 hours of sleep at 1 month and this duration remains stable, with no increase, for at least the first 8 months of life. As Harkness explains:

> The differences in sleep patterns between American and African babies can be readily explained by the different contexts for this behavior provided by each culture. American parents generally make major modifications in their living quarters and family life to create a separate space for the baby. At night, the baby sleeps in his or her own bed—often in a separate room. Night waking is apt to be inconvenient to parents, especially since it usually involves the complex and highly structured behavior called getting the baby the bottle. Consequently, parents are highly motivated to get the baby to sleep through the night, and this disposition is reinforced by childcare experts. The African babies, on the other hand, are constantly in the company of *other people whose activities determine their opportunities for sleep.* At night, the baby sleeps in skin-to-skin contact with the mother and may wake up to nurse at will." (Harkness, 1980, p. 9, emphasis added; Super & Harkness, 1982, p. 14)

17. Sapir observes how breathing is as socialized as religious doctrines are:

> There are polite and impolite ways of breathing. There are special attitudes which seem to characterize whole societies that undoubtedly condition the breathing habits of the individuals who make up these societies. Ordinarily the characteristic rhythm of breathing of a given individual is looked upon as a matter for strictly individual definition. But if the emphasis shifts to the consideration of a certain manner of breathing as due to good form or social tradition or some other principle that is usually given a social context, then the whole subject of breathing at once ceases to be a merely individual concern and takes on the appearance of a social pattern. Thus, the regularized breathing of the Hindu Yogi, the subdued breathing of those who are in the presence of a recently deceased companion laid away in a coffin and surrounded by all the ritual of the funeral observances, the style of breathing which one learns from an operatic singer who gives lessons on the proper control of the voice, are capable of isolation as socialized modes of conduct that have a definite place in the history of human culture, though they are obviously not a whit less facts of individual behavior than the most casual and normal style of breathing, such as one rarely imagines to have other than purely individual implications. Strange as it may seem at first blush, there is no hard and fast line of division as to class of behavior between a given style of breathing, *provided that it be socially interpreted,* and a religious doctrine or a form of political administration." (Sapir, 1974, pp. 33-34)

18. Vygotsky's antipathy to behaviorism is validated by research which thoroughly repudiates this misguided learning theory. Contrary to the S-R caricature that behaviorists endorse, learning actually is an active conscious process which far transcends simple S-R associations. Tolman, Kohler, Harlow, Menzel, and Premack have demonstrated that even animal learning acquires broad, essential information about situations, and is not confined to recording immediate sense experience. On the response side, animals draw upon any aspect of their acquired information in order to improvise novel behaviors during problem solving (Tolman, 1927).

The reified fiction that contiguity and reinforcement themselves *produce* learning is only maintained by methodically obscuring psychological activity, and it is quickly dispelled by methods which reveal the true power of this activity (cf. Asch, 1952, pp. 392-397 for an excellent discussion). Consciousness, not stimulus properties or conditioning laws, ultimately determines psychological responses. For example, Brewer's (1974) classic paper, "There Is No Convincing Evidence for Operant or Classical Conditioning in Adult Humans," shows that classical extinction of the galvanic skin response does not require repeated experience with the CS apart from the UCS (shock), but occurs in one trial when subjects *believe* that shock (the UCS) will not occur after the CS is presented. In contrast, even when the shock electrode was removed from subjects, those who continued to believe that shock would resume manifested the GSR and did not extinguish it (Brewer, p. 8).

Other instances of learning which violate conditioning principles are "backward conditioning"—where the CS is encountered after the UCS rather than before, as prescribed in conditioning theory (Brewer, 1974, p. 10)—and humans' ability to relate events over long temporal periods in contrast to conditioning's requirements that associations be instant in order to be effectively learned.

In addition, "conditioning" only occurs when subjects are aware of an intelligible relationship between events. Even Thorndike discovered that if, during the learning of a task, the subject was suddenly given a monetary reward for some reason not logically connected to his response—showing up for the experiment, for example—the "reward" had little or no effect upon the probability that the preceding response would be repeated upon presentation of the eliciting stimulus.

Recent research has further confirmed the importance of intelligibility for learning. Longstreth (1972) has demonstrated that neutral stimuli do not become secondary reinforcers simply as a function of being paired with primary reinforcers; rather they only acquire reinforcing properties if the subject expects them to bring future rewards. Similarly, when the relationship between a CS and UCS is masked, learning does not occur even when the two are presented in accordance with conditioning principles (Brewer, 1974; Dawson, 1973; Dawson & Biferno, 1973). This holds for the acquisition of GRS, heart rate, eye-blink, and verbal learning. Verbal learning and semantic activation do not occur independently of conscious awareness (cf. Holender,

1986, for a critique of semantic activation without conscious awareness). Instead, verbal conditioning is a direct function of the experimenter's expectancy as to whether it will occur, and subjects who are led to think that the experiment is testing their conformity manifest reduced verbal "conditioning" (Silverman, 1977, pp. 43-55).

Operant schedules of reinforcement also only yield predicted response patterns from subjects who are aware of the schedules, and not from unaware subjects. Uninformed subjects placed on a fixed interval schedule manifested *variable performance curves consistent with their hypotheses about the reinforcement contingencies* (Brewer, 1974, pp. 19-20; Bandura, 1986, p. 129).

Comprehension, not mere observation, constitutes learning and it requires an active, transcendent consciousness. For instance, learning the statement "Psychology is social" obviously involves far more than superficially reading and repeating this sense datum of three words (cf. Colaizzi, 1978). In fact, simply reading and repeating this statement would *not* constitute learning it. Learning this content requires transcending its immediacy, seeing it embodied in a variety of concrete examples, and understanding its ramifications. Meaning is not a discrete phenomenon, laying open on the surface of a few words or events, and available to sense impressions; it inheres in things and must be drawn from them.

Acquired knowledge frees man to use it in any manner he finds useful. Learning does not bind man to given stimuli. Just as learning to play the piano gives one the means to play any kind of piece (Merleau-Ponty, 1973, p. 96), so all learning imparts conceptions and rules for generating variant forms of behavior to suit different purposes and circumstances (Bandura, 1986, p. 46).

Objective learning thus enhances subjectivity as it depends upon subjectivity. Far from learning obviating subjectivity, subjectivity is inextricably part of learning. In fact, subconscious, instinctual animals are incapable of learning. Behaviorism's truncated view does not correspond to normal human activity, but rather to pathology where mastery of things is inhibited. Kurt Goldstein's (1963) description of patients with cortical lesions bears an unmistakable resemblance to stimulus-response accounts of behavior. These patients whose higher cognitive functions have been impaired mechanically respond to external stimuli, sense only disparate elements rather than configured structures, engage in isolated acts rather than purposeful, integrated action patterns, and are "able to take the objects only as they are given in sense experience" (Goldstein, 1963, p. 76). Indeed, "the greater the defect of the organism, the simpler are its responses to stimuli" (p. 37).

19. Arnold Hauser provides a good example of the social basis of creativity in describing how the artist builds upon what he has learned to create a new product:

> Just as a child at first only uses the language of his immediate environment, so the artist begins by imitating others, by copying and modifying his pro-

totypes. He develops usually from using a more general to a more individual formal language, follows, that is, a direction which is opposed to the widespread romantic notion of the evolution of an artist: he departs from the general idiom and approaches a personal form of expression instead of taking the opposite course. . . . Conventionalism is a force of the dialectic of artistic creation: it not only limits spontaneity but also gives it wings. (Hauser, 1982, p. 42, 37)

20. Speaking of psychological capacity, Isbell and McKee (1980) state, "Human beings universally share the same basic cognitive capacities, but nonetheless, environmental pressures and cultural selection will result in the adaptive development of specific cognitive skills, depending upon the environmental and cultural demands which confront the developing child. One source of the selection of special sets of cognitive skills is found in the culturally determined structure which mediates communication between babies and caretakers" (p. 330).

Ogbu (1987, p. 156) similarly states, "The psycho-biological foundation for human development is probably present cross-culturally, as is human malleability. However, what develops depends on cultural requirements, resulting in patterned adaptive cultural outcomes that vary cross-culturally."

Another indication of universal capacity which becomes differentiated under social influence is the fact that cognitive differences associated with socioeconomic class increase with age. Jachuck and Mohanty (1974) found that the difference score between upper- and lower-class 14–16-year-olds on Raven's progressive Matrices was twice that of 8–10-year-olds. In other words, youngsters are relatively similar in ability and become different under the impact of class social relationships.

The same transition from universal, shared competence to differentiated abilities is characteristic of gender-related psychological phenomena. Frieze et al. (1978, pp. 53-78) and Unger (1979, pp. 84ff.) conclude after extensive reviews of the literature that male-female differences in psychological competence are minimal among infants and only become evident in later childhood. For instance, sex differences are weak among infants and small children concerning social responsiveness, smiling, vocalization, dependency, attachment, fearfulness, spatial perception, nurturance, and aggression.

Even older children manifest few gender-related psychological differences on ecologically sensitive measures. Such measures must employ test items that are appropriate to the experiences of both sexes. For instance, if aggression is not only defined as physical attack, but includes psychological attack and rejection as well, girls are as aggressive as boys. Qualitative differences in expression of aggression should not obscure overall quantitative commonality. Frieze and Unger conclude that the few gender-related psychological differences which have been established are due to social psychological factors.

21. We shall demonstrate in the next chapter that the cortical neurones which are involved in higher psychological activity are stimulated in the act of developing that activity. Rather than specialized neurones preceding activity, they are specialized *by* the activity.

22. Support for this assertion comes from "idiot savants" who are mentally retarded in most respects, yet manage to excel in certain areas. These areas of excellence are stimulated by circumscribed opportunities within generally unfavorable life conditions. The limited opportunities force the individual to channel his mental functions accordingly. Great prowess is achieved in these areas because they are the sole avenues of stimulation, self-identity, satisfaction, expression, and success. Idiot savants are not possessed with any indigenous superiority; they developed their capability out of necessity. They do so in the same way that physically handicapped individuals compensate by developing other sensory capabilities to unusual heights. The handicapped demonstrate that sensory processes can be advanced by concentration and practice, and idiot savants demonstrate that cognitive capabilities can be advanced through the same means (Howe, 1989). Anybody can develop capabilities with great speed, fluency, and proficiency (i.e., "naturalness") if conditions warrant.

5

Psychology's Functional Autonomy from Biology

Previous chapters have contended that biology plays a potentiating, non-determining role in psychology, which is qualitatively different from its constraining, causal role in animal and human infant behavior. Human biology must play this role in order for psychology to have a conscious, social, and technological character. In other words, sociohistorical psychology rests upon a non-reductionistic relation of psychology to biology. This chapter elucidates such a non-reductionistic model. It also attempts to validate the model by demonstrating that specific biological mechanisms—genes, sense receptors, hormones, and the cortex—do not directly determine psychological phenomena.

Sociohistorical psychology's conception of psychology's relation to biology is a dialectical, multilevel one, roughly analogous to the relation between a television program and the television set. The physical set is indispensable for receiving the program; however, the set does not determine what the program is. The program may be satisfactory or not regardless of the tv apparatus. The principles governing the satisfactoriness of the program are qualititatively different from those governing the physical functioning of the set. The set has a threshold function in the sense that it must reach a minimum criterion of operability in order to receive the program; however, once this threshold has been crossed, the physical operation of the set has nothing to do with the program.

Improving the physical capability of the set beyond the minimal functional threshold does not improve the programming. The physical apparatus can interfere with the program but it cannot enhance it. Degrading the set degrades the program, but enhancing the set above the minimum threshold does not enhance the program. Most of the problems associated with television programs are due to weaknesses in the programs themselves, not in physical malfunctioning of the set. Furthermore, individual differences in television sets have little impact on the programs that people watch. The program may be seen in color or black and white, may be on a small or a large screen, and heard in stereo or mono, but the program is the same nonetheless. The set does not contribute a definite amount of content to the program; it contributes no content. There is no interaction between the physical properties of the set and the ideology of the program, with each contributing a fixed amount of influence to the content. The content is entirely a function of ideology and not at all dependent upon the physical apparatus. The apparatus is a necessary substratum which does not, however, affect the content. The content is functionally autonomous of the substratum.

Human biology is even less determining of psychology than television sets are of television programs. Both fulfilling and deleterious psychological phenomena are developed in their own right and are not explainable in biological terms. The vast majority of psychological disturbances occur in healthy bodies just as most poor tv programs are seen on physically adequate tv sets. The percentage of degraded programs due to malfunctioning sets is miniscule in comparison to the percentage of degraded programs which result from ideological inadequacies. Attempting to enhance psychology by advancing physiology above the minimal threshold level will be as unsuccessful as attempting to enhance programming by improving the technological capacity of the set. Finally, individual differences in physical makeup have little bearing on adult psychology.

Below a certain threshold of biological adequacy, psychology is directly affected by biology. But above this threshold, given a biologically normal individual, biological variations have minimal consequences for psychology. Psychology is functionally autonomous in that it is a new functional system that follows social psychological principles. Psychology is not independent of biology because it requires a biological substratum. However, the substratum does not strictly determine psychological functioning. Instead, there is an indeterminate relationship between the two (Margolis, 1978, p. 42). This indeterminacy is precisely what allows for consciousness to be volitional.

The qualitative distinctiveness of orders of phenomena has been cogently advocated by Alex Novikoff (1945) who stated:

> Each level of organization possesses unique properties of structure and behavior which, though dependent on the properties of the constituent elements, appear only when these elements are combined in the new system. Knowledge of the laws of the lower level is necessary for a full understanding of the higher level; yet the unique properties of phenomena at the higher level can not be predicted, a priori, from the laws of the lower level. The laws describing the *unique* properties of each level are qualitatively distinct,

and their discovery requires methods of research and analysis appropriate
to the particular level. (p. 209)

Just as biology has unique properties which have emerged from combinations of physical and chemical matter and cannot be reduced to
them, so "man's social relationships represent a new level, higher than
that of his biological makeup." Indeed, "Socioeconomic or cultural forces
come to dominate biological factors in directing man's actions." "The
concept of integrative levels, as it stresses the need to study the interrelationships between the biological and sociological, emphasizes the fact
that the two constitute two distinct levels. Blurring this distinction leads
to anthropomorphism and to mystical, often dangerous, statements about
society" (ibid.).

The qualitative differences between biology and psychology mean
that the former can never *explain* the latter. Despite the fervid hopes
of psychophysiologists, psychological phenomena such as memory, perception, emotions, language, personality, intelligence, and mental illness
will never be elucidated by even the most complete knowledge of relevant
physiological processes. As Dewey (1884) said, emphasizing the unique
irreducibility of psychology, "explanations of psychical events must themselves be psychical and not physiological."[1]

The multilevel relationship is different from multifactorial, or interactionist, models which construe biology and experience as interacting
on the same level. Although these two "factors" are acknowledged as
differing quantitatively in their influence on psychology, they are construed as qualitatively equal. In other words, they are both considered
as contributing some specific character to psychological phenomena although the "amount" of the total character that each factor contributes
may be unequal. In contrast, the multilevel model construes experientially
derived psychology as qualitatively different from biology. Biology does
not normally contribute specific character to psychology. It only provides
a neutral substratum on which psychology develops according to its own
principles.

Whereas the multifactorial, interactionist model splits the individual
into antagonistic processes of biological determination and consciousness
mediation (Dewey, 1886b), the multilevel model avoids such an incon-
gruous dualism by placing biology and psychology on different levels of
abstraction where they are interdependent but nondetermining. The
multilevel formulation which endows psychology with relative autonomy
from direct biological interference is not dualistic. It avoids the dualism
that characterizes interactionist theories.

We shall now verify the multileveled relationship between biology and psychology by examining evidence regarding the nondetermining role of genes, hormones, sense receptors and neurophysiology in psychology. Taken together, this evidence supports general conclusions regarding the overall relationship between biology and psychology.

Genes and Psychology

T.C. Schneirla tirelessly reiterated that phylogeny manifests increasing autonomy from strict biological controls, such as genes. Whereas genes directly determine the behavior of low organisms, mediating factors among mammals, and especially man, supersede genetic influences (Schneirla, 1972, p. 48). Many anthropologists have also described the autonomy of human *activity* (as opposed to anatomy) from strict genetic determination. This is especially evident historically where, as LaBarre, Kroeber, Leakey, Montagu, and Pannekoek have observed, cultural, mental, and technological changes have occurred over millennia without any significant corresponding genetic transformations. The same genetic structure obviously supports an enormous variety of activities without determining them, and therefore functions as a general substratum which engenders only the most abstract capacities, rather than particular activities. This in no way denies the importance of genotypes. Quite the contrary, it is the unique nature of human genotypes that enables psychology to be functionally autonomous.

Human adaptation and survival have an entirely different basis from animals which requires a correspondingly unique genotype. We adapt and survive through refining our technological, social, and mental mediations. This continual modification presupposes a genetic endowment, with the maximum capacity for rapid phenotypic adjustment (Dobzhansky, 1972, p. 134; Montagu, 1957, chap. 8; Montagu, 1968, p. 106; Lerner, 1984, chap. 6; Baldwin, 1913, p. 202). Human subsistence depends on intelligently devised actions, not on organismic, genetically produced, changes (Montagu, 1962, p. x). Human evolution is a process of expanding man's mastery of the environment, not genetically adjusting to it (Dobzhansky, 1960, p. 206; Levins & Lewontin, 1985, pp. 69-70; Leontiev, 1981, pp. 288-295). Animal evolution occurs by natural selection of physical, organismic traits; however, human evolution occurs by "artificial selection"—by which we mean the invention of extrabiological (technological and social) extensions of the biological organism (Dewart, 1989, p. 180). LaBarre (1955) explains the advantage that extrabiological evolution gives humans:

Machines not only can do man's flying, diving, and superhuman seeing and hearing for him, but also *they do his evolving for him.* . . . The old-style evolution by body adaptation is obsolete. All previous animals had been subject to the *autoplastic* evolution of their self-substance, committing their bodies to experimental adaptations in a blind genetic gamble for survival. The stakes in this game were high: life or death. Man's evolution, on the other hand, is through *alloplastic* experiments with objects outside his own body and is concerned only with the products of his hands, brains, and eyes—and not with his body itself . . .

It is not only the genetic freedom of man's new kind of evolution that is significant; one has to consider also the fantastic speed of it as well. It took millions and millions of years from fish to whale to evolve a warm-blooded marine mammal: but man evolved submarines from dream to actuality in a mere few centuries and at no genetic price in physical specialization. (pp. 90-91).

Animal evolution via physical specialization results in the creation of entirely new species. Human's nonbiological evolution, in contrast, leaves the biological character of the species intact (Pannekoek, 1953, pp. 88-90). By retaining all the variations within itself, the species undergoes a tremendous broadening of skills. In the animal kingdom, by contrast, skills are apportioned to different species which remain narrowly specialized. The elimination of genetic-physical evolution as a mechanism of behavioral change is thus a tremendous advantage.

Human's superior form of evolution occurs on a social rather than an individual level. "The real evolutionary unit now is not man's mere body; it is 'all mankind's brains together with all the extrabodily materials that come under the manipulation of their hands.' Man's very physical ego is expanded to encompass everything within reach of his manipulating hands, within sight of his searching eyes, and within the scope of his restless brain" (LaBarre, 1955, p. 91). The fact that human evolution is radically different from animal evolution means that evolution has itself evolved; it does not follow the same form across all species (Dewart, 1989, pp. 174-183).

Psychological and anatomical phenomena stand in quite different relationships to genes. Whereas anatomical phenomena are the product of genes interacting with the environment, (Lewontin, 1982), psychological phenomena are functionally autonomous of genetic determination. While genotypes restrict the norm of reaction of anatomical traits that is possible in different environments, genotypes do not restrict the norm of reaction of psychological phenomena. Social cooperation, technology, and consciousness enable any "normal" human genotype (i.e., any genotype within normal limits that is not diagnostically defective) to culminate in a virtually unlimited range of activity.

Mediated activity actually controls genetic determination of anatomical characteristics to a considerable extent. We consciously decide which genotypes to propagate by basing mating practices on esthetic and other social values. Our medical treatments contravene nature and save the lives of individuals with detrimental genetic mutations, allowing them to reproduce and propagate the malevolent genes.[2] Genetic engineering even opens up the ability to directly manipulate the genes themselves. Explaining the social selection of genotypes, Dobzhansky (1964, p. 96) said, "Since evolution consists essentially of responses of the species genotype to challenges of the environment, and since man's environment is chiefly that shaped by his culture, it seems to follow that human biological evolution must be directed mainly by culture." The laws of evolution which created man continue to operate in the sense that genetic mutations are selected or de-selected to propagate or eliminate physical characteristics; however, control over the laws shifts from blind adaptation via natural selection to conscious human selection. Control has shifted from lower processes determining higher ones ("bottom-up") to higher processes determining lower ones ("top-down"). Darwinian evolution is now dialectically controlled by the human species it produced.

Sense Receptors and Psychology

Sense receptors evidence the same phylogenetic transformation from bottom up to top down determination. Whereas lower animals' activity is a direct function of sensory inputs, human sensations are mediated by schemas which interpret and act on the information. Afferent physiological processes continue to function in man and underlie all of his information-gathering activity. However, they do not directly determine psychological experience. Instead, the individual selectively attends to those things in which he is interested (Schutz, 1970), seeks their meaning (Bartlett, 1967, pp. 44-46), interprets their meaning (Blumer, 1969), tests hypotheses about them (Gregory, 1970; Bruner, 1973, chap. 1; Arnheim, 1969; Schutz, 1970), attributes reasons for them (Heider, 1944, 1958), goes beyond given sensory information (Bruner, 1973; Bartlett, 1958, p. 75), assimilates sensory information to existing schemas (Piaget), and transforms sensory information (Lazarus). The individual is an active agent (Taylor, 1985a, chap. 4, 1985c) who uses, directs, and often ignores physiological afferent mechanisms to suit his own projects (Sartre; Merleau-Ponty).

Dewey's century-old statement of this activity remains valid today. He acknowledged that the physical stimulus and its attendant sense impressions are a necessary but insufficient condition for having a psychological experience. The reaction does not come *from* the stimulus, although it would never come *without* it. The response depends upon the physical antecedent for its occurrence, but for its content and nature, the response depends upon something else—namely, the mind. Although stimuli and their sense impressions call upon the mind to operate, the mind functions actively. Consequently, "the act is not determined by its immediate antecedents, but by the [organism's] end" (Dewey, 1886c). "What the sensation will be in particular at a given time, therefore, will depend entirely upon the way in which an activity is being used. It has no fixed quality of its own" (Dewey, 1896).

In his critique of empiricism, Dewey (1886a,b) trenchantly repudiated the notion that consciousness is built up from preexisting, independent sensations. He argued instead for a "top-down" model in which "the explanation of the simplest psychological fact—say, one of perception, or feeling, or impulse—involves necessary reference to self-consciousness. Self-consciousness is involved in every simpler process, and no one of them can be scientifically described or comprehended except as this involution is brought out" (1886b). This involution involves the mind "reading out of itself and into the sensation ideal elements which transform the sensation and make it a part of knowledge" (Dewey, 1898, p. 142).

The mind makes sensations meaningful by apprehending them against the background of a stock of knowledge. Sensations are also made meaningful by relating them to other sensations which together comprise a whole event (Dewey, 1898, p. 85-86). Such "totalizing" (to use Sartre's term) of sensations is a teleological act which foregrounds certain aspects and relegates others to the background. It precludes any experience of pure, independent sensations, and dictates that every sensation is imbued with psychological meaning (Dewey, 1887; 1898, p. 136; Polanyi, 1966).

For Dewey, all facets of psychology are intrinsically conscious, which means that sensations do not stand apart from consciousness, generating it from afar. Rather than consciousness building up piecemeal from independent elements, psychological phenomena are differentiated parts of the same conscious essence. The whole of psychology is not the sum of parts; instead the parts are aspects of an intrinsic unity. In Dewey's words, "a sensation is not prior to consciousness or knowledge. It is but an element in the world of conscious experience. Far from being that from which all relations spring, it is itself but one relation. . . . It is but one element in an organic whole, and can no more account for the whole than a given digestive act can account for the existence of a living

body . . ." (1886a). Merleau-Ponty's work (1962, 1963) similarly elucidates the fact that sensation is "clothed with signification." It is perceived
as meaningful, as deriving from and indicating a configuration of relationships, as indicating properties of objects, as having certain uses. This
meaning determines the sensation as much as the sensation determines
perception.

Hegel devised a succinct but elegant philosophical argument to
prove the irreducibility of consciousness to pure sensation. He logically
said that a sensation must be sensed by some process or agency that is
necessarily different from the sensation per se. If there were nothing
more than the sense organ and proximal stimulus, there would be no
sensation as such, there would only be an immediate reaction to the
sense impression, but without any feeling. This is exactly the case in
nonconscious, reflexive, low organisms, and it proves that sensation devoid of consciousness cannot exist (cf. Scheler, 1961).

Recounting Hegel's explanation of this point, deVries (1988, chap.
4) makes an interesting analogy with thermostats. He says that thermostats are sensitive to temperature but they do not *sense* heat or cold
because there is no sensing agent to register them. Since input is directly
connected to output, no sensation is possible. Consequently, the mere
presence of sense receptors is insufficient for sensations. There must be
a conscious agent to sense the information provided by sense receptors.
Accordingly, consciousness cannot be built up from pure sensation in
the empiricist sense that sensation precedes consciousness; consciousness
must already exist in order for sensation to exist (be sensed, felt) at all.
If sensation requires more than sense receptors, it cannot be strictly
determined by sense receptors alone. It is necessary to (intentionally)
look in order to perceive.

Vygotsky (1987, p. 47) was quite clear about the fact that consciousness surpasses sense experience. He said, "reality is reflected in consciousness in a qualitatively different way in thinking than it is in
immediate sensation. This qualitative difference is primarily a function
of a generalized reflection of reality." Vygotsky (1987b, p. 93) explained
how the ontogenetic development of human sensory acuity rests not on
refining sensory processes per se but on the increased sophistication of
higher mental functions. He said, "A child learns to distinguish colors
better, to discriminate sounds, and to compare odors not because his
sense of smell and hearing have become more subtle, but because of
the development of his thinking, his voluntary attention, and other higher
psychological functions."

Bartlett experimentally demonstrated that psychological meaning, far
from being reducible to sensations, "constructs the sensory pattern into

something having a significance which goes beyond its immediate sensory character." This is proven by the fact that "the most immediately striking result of the experiments on perceiving was the great diversity of response which can usually be aroused by substantially constant sensory patterns, both in the same individual at different times and in different individuals" (Bartlett, 1967, p. 188ff; cf. also, Schneirla, 1972, p. 59).

More contemporaneously, Rock (1983) has reiterated this idea. He says, "While the description [of an object] is guided by and must conform to the features of the proximal stimulus, that does not mean it is nothing more than a copy or literal statement of the features of that stimulus. It may contain less or more than can be said to be physically represented in the stimulus" (p. 16). Thus,

> the local stimulus does not predict what is perceived because precisely what it represents is ambiguous, because it is subject to variability given the same outer object or event, because its effect depends upon context and not only upon its own properties, because it does not do justice to the phenomena of organization, enrichment, completion, delay, and the dependency of one perception upon another. (Rock, p. 29)

Once perception is acknowledged to depend upon more than a single, discrete proximal stimulus, and is recognized as depending upon numerous interrelated stimuli, then perception is ineluctably made dependent upon cognitive activity. For this activity determines what is relevant to the proximal stimulus, i.e., what its context is. The perceiver establishes that the object must be compared to certain things standing at certain distances in order to determine its apparent size.

Sense data are part of perception but they do not comprise it. Perceptual experience is a meaningful construction which includes acquired assumptions about the object's properties, relationships, origins, and possible appearances. The senses allow us to sense *that* something exists but not *what* it is. The study of perception can only be conducted with a sensitivity to meaningful signs, it cannot be replaced by the study of sensory acuity for signals (Volosinov, 1973, pp. 68-69; Leontiev, 1981, p. 319).

Optical illusions, reversible figures, perceptual constancy, hallucinations, and cultural differences in color perception are not determined by sense organs. Quite the contrary, sensory information is overridden by functionally different social-psychological processes. In addition to the perceptual experiments that were cited in Chapters 1 and 2, some famous examples of perceptual illusions demonstrate this clearly. Vygotsky (1987, p. 296) explained that meaningful interpretation underlies Sharpant's illusion. In this case, two objects that are identical in weight and form but differ in size are perceived to be differentially heavy: The smaller object appears heavier than the larger one. The reason is that the objects' weight is not sensed as a discrete datum but is perceived in relation to its size. A given weight compressed into a small size is perceived as denser/heavier than when it occupies a larger size. As Vygotsky put it, "the immediate perception of heaviness is subordinated to the meaningful perception of heaviness in relation to volume. This results in the distortion of the immediate perception." Immediate perception is more absolute if we insulate it from meaningful interpretation. One way to accomplish this is to reduce our understanding of the object's size by closing our eyes. Then the large and small objects are felt as equally heavy. Another way to minimize cognitive overriding of sense experience is to use as subjects young children who have not yet acquired requisite concepts. Children under 5 years of age are not susceptible to Sharpant's illusion.

Another illusion which transcends sensory data and depends upon cognitive mental operations is the illusory experience that one is moving while in reality being stationary. Most people have experienced this effect when sitting in a stationary train or automoblile while the adjacent train or car is moving. This illusory movement of the self can be induced in the laboratory by placing an observer inside a rotating drum lined with vertical stripes. Ideally only the drum is visible and the stationary floor and ceiling are not. After a short period, the drum appears to be slowing down and observers experience themselves as beginning to turn in the opposite direction. When the experiment is performed in the dark, observers do not experience themselves as moving.

Rock (1983, p. 2) contends that "the 'force' yielding induced motion of the self is the tendency to construe the surrounding environment as stationary. If this interpretation is correct, the percept can be thought of as the result of a process much like reasoning. The assumption in question is analogous to an implicit axiom. Given the acceptance of it by the perceptual system, the angular displacement of the drum is inferred to result from self-motion." Once one realizes that the surrounding environment is not stationary but moves, the sensation of self-movement ceases. The very sensation of self movement, then, is induced by cognitive assumptions about the motility of one's environment (Rock, 1984, chap. 7).

Complicating the foregoing experimental condition illuminates the cognitive basis for this perceptual effect even more strikingly. This complication involves surrounding the subject with *two* concentric cylinders of differing diameters. The outer drum can be seen through slots in the inner drum (the one nearest the subject). With the outer drum stationary and the inner one rotating, no induced motion of the self occurs. With the outer drum moving and the inner one stationary, however, such induced motion does occur. The inner stationary drum also appears to rotate along with the subject.

A cognitive explantion of these results is as follows. The outermost surrounding structure is regarded as stationary, in keeping with normal experience where such structures typically occupy fixed positions. When motion is experienced, it is attributed to interior elements which are typically more movable in everyday experience. Thus, when the outer drum moves, motion is attributed to one's self and to the inner drum which remains in a constant position relative to the subject. Both of these are then perceived (experienced) as moving. On the other hand, when the outer drum is truly stationary, and the inner drum rotates, the subject has no difficulty attributing movement to this inner section and he veridically perceives its motion against the stable framework. The subject also can see the drum rotating around himself so that no sense of motion is induced in the self (Rock, 1990). Induced motion of the self thus depends upon one's understanding of what elements of a configuration ought and ought not move.

Illusory induced motion in objects is also a function of cognitive assumptions (Rock, 1990). A familiar example is the apparent motion of the moon when viewed through a surround of moving clouds. Although the moon is stationary, it appears to move in the opposite direction to the cloud motion. The reason for this illusion is that we construe the clouds as forming a background or context to the moon. We have acquired the assumption that contexts are stabile while objects move within their contours. Since the clouds are regarded as context they appear to be stable, which means that the motion must occur in the moon. When we revise our interpretation and attend to the moon as a fixed object, the clouds are seen to move.[3]

Similar demonstrations are provided by Koffka. In laboratory conditions when two figures are made to move at the same speed, smaller objects appear to move faster than larger ones, brighter objects appear to move more slowly than darker ones, and thinner lines appear to move faster than wider ones (Koffka, 1963, pp. 288-291). In addition, when a figure and a ground are both changed in color, subjects perceive the figure as retaining its original color longer, whereas the ground appears to change color more quickly (Kohler, 1959, p. 120). These experimentally induced illusions are all premised on assumptions that are acquired in everyday life. Small, thin objects are usually lighter than larger ones, and are easier to move. Naturally, in a laboratory experiment without any other cues about speed, we assume and see smaller, thinner objects to be moving more quickly than larger, thicker ones. Similarly, since figures are usually more solid and coherent than their ground, we expect to see them as less changeable in quality. These cognitive schemata override sensory data and determine perception.

The well-known "framework effect," where objects' phenomenal position is heavily influenced by the frame in which they occur, is yet another fascinating illustration of the power of cognitive assumptions on perception. If one is upright with respect to gravity in a tilted room, one will perceive oneself as tilted. The room is taken as an upright frame of reference in relation to which the self is perceived as tilted. This proves that the body is not the natural locus of psychological experience, and that experience of one's body derives from cognitive assumptions about the world. Our learned assumption that rooms are upright makes us feel that our body is tilted, when, in fact, our body is upright and the room is tilted. Cognitive schemata about the world override sensory information about our body's position and determine our bodily sensations.

The rod-and-frame effect of Asch and Witkin similarly demonstrates how cognitive assumptions about frameworks and objects determine perception of both of these. In this case, a tilted frame induces the illusion that a rod within it is vertical when the rod is perpendicular to the frame's bottom contour. Because the frame is tilted, being perpendicular to the bottom means that the rod is not vertical with respect to the ground. However, subjects perceive the rod as vertical with respect to the ground even when it is displaced 6 degrees. Viewers perceive the rod's vertical position with reference to the frame's orientation because frames are presumed to be rectangular with respect to the ground. This presumption of rectangular regularity is evidenced in the fact that when subjects are asked to perceive the tilt of the *frame* itself, they generally *underestimate* it. Significantly, when the frame is known to be tilted it is not used to define the vertical direction, the rod is not perceived in relation to the frame's axes, and no displacement occurs.

An additional demonstration of the cognitive determinants of the rod-and-frame effect—or the degree to which the rod's perceived vertical position is displaced by the presence of a frame—is the fact that the effect depends upon the size of the frame. A small frame produces a miniscule effect while a large frame induces a substantial effect. The reason for this is that larger structures are generally found to be more regular rectangles than smaller ones and are therefore presumed to be more reliable cues for a vertical orientation. Their power to distort directionality, as in the case of the rod-and-frame test, is correspondingly greater.

The rod-and-frame effect, then, depends upon numerous cognitive assumptions regarding the relation of rod to frame and the normal orientation of frames (Rock, 1990). Rock emphasizes the fact that rod-and-frame data cannot be explained by invariant visual mechanisms. For instance, one purported mechanism is a tendency of the eye to automatically follow the direction of the frame's tilt and to locate the rod's position with reference to the rotated axes of the eye. However, research does not confirm such a visual tendency. Such disconfirmation reflects the fact that the framework effect is a psychological phenomenon which depends upon our understanding of the properties and relationships of particular objects. Perception in general is a psychological phenomenon that is not explainable by autonomous sensory tendencies independent of knowledge, motives, and emotions.

Kanizsa's (1976) subjective contours are another fascinating example of perceptual experience being generated by habitualized expectations despite the absence of corresponding, point for point, sensory data. Perceptual constancy similarly relies on knowledge of things' enduring character in order to overcome transient sensory appearances (Hochberg, 1972, pp. 404ff). For example, the retinal image of a receding object shrinks; however, we see the object as constant in size and infer that it is moving away. The size of the retinal image does not dictate perceived size; it is disregarded as a size cue and construed instead as a distance cue (Gregory, 1983). Furthermore, perception of objects' spatial coordinates is not isomorphic with cortical projections of sensory input but mentally reverses the horizontally and vertically inverted projections (Sperry, 1952). The failure to establish psychophysical laws between stimulus properties and sensation is due to the fact that the relationship is not direct but is mediated by consciousness (Bruner, 1983, p. 69).

Even pain is a psychological process, irreducible to sensory threshold elicited in isolation (Melzack, 1973, chap. 2; Wall, 1974). Although it might seem that pain should be a direct function of physiological sensitivity, pain is actually mediated by expectations, interpretations, past experiences, and memory. The pain threshold that is measured as a just noticeable difference—the minimum stimulus intensity that is detectable in isolation—is unrelated to the experience or tolerance of pain. Whereas the former is uniform and universal, psychological pain varies widely among individuals and cultural groups (Melzack, pp. 24-25).

Athletes and soldiers often experience little pain despite severe physical trauma, and pain threshold has been experimentally raised from 350 to 450 microamperes of electric shock by simply ascribing the pain to a drug that subjects had taken (Nisbett & Schachter, 1966). In addition, certain cultural practices that we regard as physical torture produce no manifestations of pain in the recipient. In the Indian hook-hanging ritual, for example, a man is suspended on steel hooks directly implanted into his back muscles while he blesses children and crops. Astonishingly, there is no evidence that the man is in pain during the ritual; rather he appears to be in a state of exaltation. This is a striking confirmation of Whorf's idea that physiological processes (Whorf's "lower" functions) are superceded by functionally autonomous social-psychological ones.

Even dogs react differentially to shock depending upon the meaning it has. Pavlov found that dogs which normally react violently to strong electric shock, develop a new response if the shock is followed by food. The shock then becomes a signal for food, and the dog responds to the shock by salivating and wagging its tail. Most important, the dog fails to manifest any indication of pain (Melzack, p. 30)!

The fact that cognitive processes mediate perception and affect its sensitivity means that perceptual deficits originally believed to be caused by sensory impairments can be due to social psychological factors. Actually these cognitive mediations are far more susceptible to refinement, correction, and education than sense organs are (Vygotsky, 1987b, p. 93). Leontiev (1969) notes that "Despite the absence of any physiological defects, tone deafness proves to be a common phenomenon in England and America, but is practically unknown among African tribes whose languages entail intoning vowel sounds" (p. 429). Leontiev reports that tone deafness can be successfully treated by teaching individuals to recognize sounds. Subjects coached to sing prescribed tones, thereby matching their *vocalization* to the tones, were, after two to six sessions, able to more accurately *hear* the tones.

Describing the relative autonomy of perception from physiological sense receptors, Norwood Hanson states:

> Seeing is an experience. A retinal reaction is only a physical state—a photochemical excitation. Physiologists have not always appreciated the differences between experiences and physical states. People, not their eyes, see. Cameras, and eyeballs, are blind. Attempts to locate within the organs of sight (or within the neurological reticulus behind the eyes) some nameable called 'seeing' may be dismissed. That [two individuals holding different expectations and assumptions, observing the same object] do, or do not, see the same thing cannot be supported by reference to the physical states of their retinas, optic nerves, or visual cortices: there is more to seeing than meets the eyeball. (Hanson, 1965, pp. 6-7).[4]

Hormones and Psychology

Psychology is as undetermined by hormones as it is by physiological sense receptors and genes. The behavior of low animals is directly controlled by hormones; however, the influence decreases in the higher animals and is unimportant in man. This is evident in sexuality, aggression, and emotionality.

Sexuality

Washburn (1960) points out that whereas sex among animals is "subject to physiological—especially glandular—controls, in man these controls are gone, and are replaced by a bewildering variety of social customs." Higher animals, of course, manifest somewhat greater independence from hormones than lower animals do, however, in most cases even nonhuman primates' sexual behavior is biologically regulated. This is demonstrated in four areas (Beach, 1947, 1958).

(1). Sexual activity is closely tied to estrus and the secretion of estrogen in the female animal, but not in the human female who is unique in being continuously receptive throughout the menstrual cycle, regardless of hormonal changes.

(2). Removal of animals' gonadal hormones through castration or ovariectomy prevents adult sexual activity if done before puberty, or eliminates it if done after puberty (Hoyenga & Hoyenga, 1979, p. 124, 126); however, reduction in hormonal levels has little if any affect on human sexual behavior. Ovariectomy and menopause in a high proportion of women produce no change in sexual desire, just as oral contraceptives, which inhibit ovarian, hypothalamic, and pituitary hormones, have no inhibiting affect on sexual activity (and, if anything, increase it!). Girls completely lacking in any kind of ovarian hormone nevertheless describe daydreams and fantasies of romantic courtship, marriage, and autoerotic genital play. Thus, significant aspects of feminine psychosexual orientation are present in girls despite the total absence of any estrogenic hormone (Hampson, 1965, p. 121).

Healthy males show a wide range of testosterone values (from about 350 to 1000 nanograms per 100 milliliters of blood) and variations within this range have no significance for sexual behavior (Rosenzweig & Leiman, 1982, p. 403). Castration of males sometimes leads to reduced interest in sex; however, many individuals maintain an undiminished sexual drive and coital ability for several decades.

(3). Addition of hormones to depleted animals restores sexual behavior regardless of the age of original removal. However, hormonal therapy to enhance sexual desire is not particularly effective in many men and women.

(4). Normal prepubescent animals (males and females) whose gonadal hormones have not begun secreting show no sexual activity (except in the case of apes where prepubertal males and females do often copulate); however, human children (especially in societies that encourage them) are known to indulge in sexual activities years before gonadal hormones have begun functioning.

Summing up the evolutionary changes which have resulted in the diminished influence of hormones on sexual activity, Beach (1947) concludes:

> Evidence pertaining to prepubertal sexual activity, to the correlation of sexual behavior with cycles of [hormonal] secretion and to the effects of ovariectomy [as well as castration] followed by replacement therapy suggests that advancing phyletic status is accompanied by progressive relaxation of rigorous hormonal control over sexual receptivity. It appears that in the course of mammalian evolution, and specifically in the development of the primate stem, the physiological basis for sexual behavior has undergone certain modifications which have tended to free . . . sexual responsiveness from complete dependence upon . . . hormones. (pp. 300, 303)

The culmination of this independence of sexuality from hormones occurs in humans where, as Rosenzweig and Leiman (1982) explain:

> in the adult human male, as in the adult female, most individual differences in sexual behavior cannot be explained by individual differences in hormonal levels. Hormones are certainly important in early development of reproductive structures and in later development of secondary sexual characteristics. They also play an activational role in facilitating the initiation of sexual behaviors and in maintaining them. But wide variations in hormonal levels do not have clear effects on the amount or quality of human sexual activities. Once the neural circuits for these behaviors have been established, other sources of stimulation can suffice even in the absence of endocrine facilitation. (p. 404)

Not only is sexual practice independent of hormones, gender orientation in the broad sense is independent also. This is the conclusion of John Hampson (1965) based on a fascinating investigation of 113 hermaphrodites. The ambiguity of the external genitalia allows parents to treat the individual as a certain gender when, in fact, gonadal, genetic, or hormonal characteristics mandate an opposite biological gender. In other words, the individual is biologically one sex but is treated socially as the opposite sex. The presence of competing social and biological characteristics within a single individual provides a fascinating natural experiment for disentangling nature versus nurture. Almost every one of Hampson's 113 cases felt comfortable with their socially assigned gender role and chose to maintain it rather than adopt a gender role that was consistent with their biological sex. Even the 5 cases that switched their orientation after hormonal secretions began at puberty did not do so *because* of the hormones, but rather because of other psychological reasons (Hampson, p. 115).

Surprisingly, 25 hermaphrodites were assigned a gender that contradicted their external genital appearance. Here one might expect the gender associated with genital organs to predominate over a socially designated gender because the individual can clearly see his sex type regardless of what others believe. However, every single such patient conformed to the assigned gender role rather than to the gender indicated by his or her sexual organs (Hampson, p. 117)!

Hampson reaches an important conclusion concerning the indeterminateness of biology for sexual orientation. He states that "an individual's gender role and orientation as boy or girl, man or woman, does not have an innate, preformed instinctive basis as some theorists have maintained. Instead the evidence supports the view that psychologic sex is undifferentiated at birth—a sexual neutrality one might say—and that the individual becomes psychologically differentiated as masculine or feminine in the course of the many experiences of growing up" (p. 119). Socially reassigning the gender of a child can be successfully imposed prior to one and one-half to two years of age without psychological damage (Hampson, p. 125). However, alterations after this age do produce psychological difficulties because they violate the child's learned sexual *identity* (self-concept).

Money and Ehrhardt (1972) arrived at the same conclusion on the basis of research into hermaphroditism. One of their cases was a boy whose penis was lost during circumcision at seven months. Female genitalia were surgically constructed and the child was treated as a girl despite being a perfectly normal biological male. Later personality and behavior were thoroughly feminine. Another unusual case was a genetically malformed male who was born with a 1 cm. long penis. At 17 months he was surgically provided with female genitalia and raised as a girl. After the operation, the baby's three and one-half year-old brother was told that the baby was really a girl. He quickly accepted the change in gender and altered his behavior accordingly. Gentleness and protectiveness replaced fighting that had occurred when he believed his sibling was a boy. The father underwent a similar change in attitude. He said, "I have completely different feelings towards this child as a girl than as a boy." The socially constructed girl baby grew up with a feminine personality.

A final case that illustrates the dominance of social treatment over hormones was a matched pair of hermaphrodites who were genetically female but, because of excessive androgens, had quasi-masculine genitalia. One such individual was raised a boy and discovered to his distress that at puberty his anatomy became feminized due to estrogen secretions from gonads and uterus. Even in the face of these female biological influences his masculine gender was unshaken. He underwent surgical removal of his uterus and gonads and was delighted to maintain his male role. The girl with andrenogenital syndrome who was raised as a girl identified with girls and hated her masculine features. She insisted on estrogen hormonal therapy to reduce these features, and went on to marry as a woman.

Money and Ehrhardt (p.161) explicitly state that these cases wreck the assumption that gender identity is preordained by the sex chromosomes, or by prenatal or postnatal hormone status. The authors agree with Hampson that biology is like clay that can be socially molded into male or female personality (p. 152). Even the few cases where gender identity was inconsistent with socially assigned sex were due to social rather than hormonal reasons. Among the cases reported, only two or three failed to achieve gender identity that was consistent with their socially assigned sex and the reason lay in the parents' ambiguous treatment of their children's gender:

> Hermaphroditic children who eventually decide that they were wrongly assigned . . . typically have a biography of uncertainty as to their sex of assignment. The biography includes such items as a change of name and declared sex, without change on the birth certificate; overt advice to the parents that the 'true sex' will not be evident until puberty [therefore keeping parents undecided throughout childhood]; and discordance between the declared sex and the genital anatomy which is allowed to remain surgically uncorrected in childhood (Money & Ehrhardt, p. 153).

According to the authors, greater parental consistency in assigning gender identity would lead to fewer deviations from this social construction.

Another study on hermaphrodites, conducted by Imperato-McGinley et al. (1979), suggests other social influences which may affect choice of gender identity. The study was done in a remote, rural area outside Santo Domingo, Dominican Republic on hermaphrodites who were members of a common family genotype. These hermaphrodites were genetically male, although an intra-utero hormonal dysfunction caused them to be born with female-like genitalia. They were raised unambiguously as girls. Seventeen out of 18 subjects choose to adopt a *masculine* identity at puberty upon the appearance of masculine sex characteristics. The researchers presume that it was the increased concentration of testosterone secreted at puberty that overrode the assigned childhood gender role and determined masculine identity. However, a social explanation can readily account for the data. The village was an extremely traditional peasant society which bestowed economic, social, and personal privileges on men, but not women. Men held social and economic power that derived from a traditional sexual division of labor (with men working at wage-earning jobs while women were confined to household chores). In addition, men had greater personal autonomy in such areas as sexual activity where a double standard gave men more freedom than women.

In such a male-dominated society, it is not surprising that adolescent "girls" who sprout male sexual characteristics would utilize this physical change as an opportunity to switch to a more favored gender identity. It is well known that many girls in male-dominated societies fantasize about becoming males. The physical changes experienced by the subjects in this study provided a possibility and rationale for making this socially conditioned desire come true.

Testosterone simply provided the possibility of changing from female to male gender. It did not determine the change. Switching identity is a psychological choice which is mediated by social values. Gender change is a response *to* hormonal change under certain social circumstances, it is not a direct by-product *of* hormonal change (Herdt, 1990; Gooren, 1990).

Aggression

The evolutionary trend toward independence from hormonal determination exists in the case of aggression. Lloyd (1975) cites several works which indicate decreased hormonal control over aggression with evolutionary ascent to the higher species. In mice, reduction in the level of circulating androgen produced by castration is associated with profound reduction in intermale aggressive behavior. Restoring testosterone by injection in castrated animals increases fighting behavior in mice in a dose-related manner. Androgens likewise enhance the social position of chickens and fish.[5]

Effects of androgen on aggression are even less pronounced in primates. Investigations done on castrated rhesus monkeys have failed to find any straightforward relationship between castration and the lessening of aggressive behavior or social dominance (Lloyd, 1975, p. 190). Among nonhuman primates hormonal levels may follow behavioral responses to environmental conditions in addition to inciting behavior. Thus, it is *after* attaining a position of social dominance and getting access to females that rhesus monkeys displayed a two- to threefold increase in testosterone levels. Introduction of these same males into groups of strange males, where they were subject to sudden and decisive defeat, resulted in declines in their levels of plasma testosterone. Subsequent presentation to the defeated males of receptive females resulted in elevations of levels of plasma testosterone in the males (Lloyd, 1975, p. 189; Hoyenga & Hoyenga, 1979, p. 122).

Likewise, manipulation of rhesus monkeys' social environment which lowers their social dominance rank and elevates stress leads to elevated levels of the hormone ACTH. Conversely, reducing the subordinate animals' social stress (e.g., by removing them from the dominance of powerful members) resulted in decreased ACTH levels among subordinates (Lloyd, 1975, p. 196). Clearly, social relationships cause hormonal changes at least as much, if not more so, as hormones determine social behavior.

Among humans, aggression is a function of consciously controlled experience, not hormones. Washburn and Hamburg (1968) observe that the entire biological basis of aggression is degraded in man relative to animals. Human adrenal glands are relatively small compared to those of nonhuman primates. And the biologically mandated agonistic bodily expressions which are so characteristic of nonhuman primate species are substantially diminished in man. In addition, "it is not clear that levels of androgens in intact men is related to aggressiveness" (Rosenzweig & Leiman, 1982, p. 535).

Anne Fausto-Sterling (1985, Chapter 5) has comprehensively reviewed and evaluated studies dealing with the relation between hormones and aggression. She effectively demolishes the belief that testosterone causes aggression and that reducing testosterone via castration or other chemical means reduces aggression. For example, one study of castrated men found the treatment so ineffective that nine out of 16 subjects subsequently died as a result of aggressive encounters. "The few studies on the effects of 'chemical castration' on violent or aggressive behavior conclude that the procedure is not particularly effective" (Fausto-Sterling, 1985, p. 127). The tremendous cultural variation in aggressive behavior among human specimens with generally the same hormonal levels further testifies to the nondetermining role that hormones play in aggression.

The nondetermining role of hormones on aggression is demonstrated in studies on the interaction of hormonal levels and social circumstances. Where the social position of individuals having varying hormonal levels is considered, social position, not hormonal level, predicts aggressive behavior. For example, Dabbs & Morris (1990) found that low socioeconomic status men with low to normal levels of testosterone were more likely to engage in antisocial behavior than were upper-class men with high levels of testosterone. Only 4% of upper-class, high testosterone men were delinquent as adults compared with 15% of lower-class men with normal testosterone levels. Four percent of upper-class, high testosterone men had been AWOL from the military, in contrast to 10% of lower-class men with normal testosterone levels. And, fourteen percent of lower-class men with normal testosterone levels were delinquents in childhood, in comparison with 11% of high testosterone, upper-class men. Clearly, high testosterone among upper-class men does not produce antisocial behavior whereas low to normal testosterone in lower-class men does produce antisocial behavior.

Emotions

Emotions generally manifest the same relative autonomy from hormonal control. Comparatively speaking, "In man, visceral processes play a far more indirect and delicate role in emotional reactions which are much more influenced by the perceptual significance of the situation than they are in lower mammals" (Schneirla, 1972, p. 79). Where hormones do activate feeling states, their secretion is caused by psychological processes (from "top-down") rather than the reverse (from "bottom-up"): Whether we become angry or amused determines hormonal levels; they do not automatically regulate themselves in response to events (cf. Mandler, 1975, for a good account of the cognitive mediation of emotions as well as a critique of naturalistic theories). For example, phobics given tasks which they felt incapable of handling secreted high levels of epinephrine and norepinephrine into their blood (as well as manifesting elevated heart rates and blood pressure); however in response to tasks which they felt confident dealing with, catecholamine levels were low, as were blood pressure and heart rate (Bandura, 1986, pp. 443-444). Similarly, adrenocorticosteroid levels of soldiers in the Vietnam war rose when the men worried about surviving an enemy attack, but fell when they felt confident about surviving (Reynolds, 1980, p. 159).[6]

The hormonal discharges which follow cognitive interpretation appear to be general innervations rather than particular correlates of single feelings. This indeterminateness of hormones makes cognitive appraisal the determinant of particular emotions. One study found that women reacted to both pleasant-amusing and aggression-provoking films with increased epinephrine levels, and ACTH release similarly occurs with a wide variety of emotional arousals (Candland et al., 1977, pp. 124-125; Mandler, 1979, pp. 296-297).

Nonhormonal physiological effects of emotionality are equally general. For instance, even the contradictory emotions mirth and sadness generate extremely similar physiological response patterns of GSR, heart rate, respiration rate, temperature, and pulse (Averill, 1969). Summarizing the current state of evidence, Mandler said, "Despite repeated attempts to demonstrate the existence of discrete patterns, there is currently no evidence that different patterns of autonomic activity occurring *prior* to the experience of an emotion determine that experience"

(Mandler, 1980, p. 227). Autonomic nervous system activity may affect the intensity of emotional experience; however, cognitive appraisal determines the emotional quality.

Autonomic activity, including hormonal secretions, has a general energizing effect which prepares the individual to make any appropriate response. As Candland stated, "these hormones all result in an increase in energy availability. It may be that this increased availability of energy is the most important function of hormonal changes following or during exposure to emotional situations, since this increase in energy would aid the individual's adaptation to the stresses of 'being emotional'" (1977, p. 127).[7] From all that we know about the volitional, cognitively mediated character of human responsiveness, such general arousal is all that physiology can or should do. A more specific arousal, leading to rigidly constrained behavior, would impede our flexibility, creativity, and adaptability. As Bandura (1986) insightfully observed:

> If the [physiological, behavioral, and psychological] modalities were totally conjoined, a fearful thought would regularly trigger flight, while an annoying one would prompt physical assault, neither of which would be especially advantageous under most circumstances. If visceral arousal and action were firmly wedded to each other, arousal would routinely trigger immobility or avoidant behavior, which would severely curtail people's ongoing activities. It is because people can confront and cope with stressful situations, despite perturbing arousal, that they are able to overcome inappropriate fears and to function adequately, even in the face of realistic threats. If, through preset linkages, actions set off corresponding thoughts, people would have limited opportunity to think about matters that differ from what they happen to be doing at the moment. Leeway for varied patterning of thought, affect, and action permits development of functional dependencies and disuniting malfunctional ones, whereas fixed coupling would be most maladaptive. (p. 191)

The foregoing discussion of hormonal indeterminacy with regard to emotions concerned the normal situation in which cognitive interpretation elicits hormonal secretion (sequentially depicted as: External stimulus—Cognitive mediation—Hormonal response—Emotional and behavioral response). Even under atypical conditions where hormones are directly *physically* stimulated, they still do not directly determine emotion. Instead, the physiological arousal itself is interpreted, and the attribution of its source and significance mediates the emotional response (sequentially depicted as: Hormonal secretion—Cognitive mediation—Emotional and behavioral response). This, of course, is Schachter's famous insight which is supported by a variety of evidence. Schachter himself demonstrated that a given physiological arousal can lead to feelings of happiness or sadness depending on the kind of situation the subject is in and depending on his knowledge of the source of the arousal. This aspect of Schachter's theory—that the arousal-emotion relationship is mediated by causal attributions—has been confirmed by other experiments as Reisenzein (1983) reports. Candland et al. (1977) similarly conclude:

> a strict interpretation of James' position that discrete physiological states evoke discrete emotions is not supported. Not only do different physiological states *not* elicit different emotions, but many different types of emotions or emotional behaviors can be affected by a single hormonal manipulation. For example, manipulations of pituitary adrenocortical activity affect emotionality, fearfulness, and aggressiveness. Similarly, manipulations of gonadal hormone levels affect both fearfulness and aggressiveness (p. 121).

Rather than hormonal manipulations directly determining specific emotions, they only affect general arousability, or the intensity with which the individual reacts, thereby leaving him with the power to decide what to respond to and how to respond.

This is confirmed by research on the premenstrual syndrome. PMS is supposed to be a complex of moodiness, irritability, depression, and ineffective behavioral performances commencing 3-5 days before menstruation and continuing into the period itself. Since its "discovery" in 1931 as premenstrual tension—which was renamed premenstrual syndrome in 1953—PMS has been regarded as caused by hormonal changes associated with menstruation. This hormonal determination is taken to be so powerful as to occasionally cause women to commit murder, as testified by the British physician Katharina Dalton.

Contrary to Dalton's fatalistic position, recent evidence casts doubt upon the existence of the syndrome itself, as well as upon the presumed hormonal cause. Several extensive reviews of the literature (Lips, 1988, pp. 174-184; Sommer, 1973; Fausto-Sterling,1985, chap. 4) conclude that no evidence has established that specific psychological symptoms regularly occur only at particular times in the menstrual cycle and are directly attributable to the menstrual cycle.

Studies which claim such a syndrome and causally connect it to hormones have serious methodological flaws which invalidate their conclusions. One common problem is the use of women's retrospective reports concerning their symptoms, a procedure which has been found to be open to tremendous subjective distortion. Symptoms may be retrospectively "recollected" when they were never experienced in the first place. For example, when Ruble (1977) misinformed women that they were in the premenstrual period and asked them to recollect their psychological and physical state during the preceding day or two, the subjects "remembered" experiencing many symptoms—such as pain, water retention, negative affect, changes in eating habits and altered sexual desire—which women who were informed that their periods were a week away, or not given any information at all, failed to remember. (In fact, all the women in the experiment were questioned a week prior to their periods.)

An extensive study by McFarland et al. (1989) asked women to keep daily records of their physical and psychological states during menstruation. Affective and physical states did not correlate with the menstrual cycle. The authors then asked subjects to recall their states at a later time when they were not menstruating. Psychological symptoms were exaggerated in recall by women who believed that menstruation causes distress. Women with a more beneficent concept of menstruation manifested more accurate recall of their affective states as being undisturbed. Psychological symptoms associated with menstruation thus appear to be more imagined than real, more a product of one's cognitive theory than a by-product of experience (cf. Ross, 1989).[8]

Another discrepancy between actual behavior and reports of PMS symptoms is the fact that mothers reporting PMS symptoms have a lower suicide rate than mothers who do not report the symptoms (Hoyenga & Hoyenga, 1979, pp. 154-159)!

Although estrogen is purported to cause physical and psychological discomfort in PMS sufferers, direct measurement of estrogen has failed to establish a correlation of estrogen levels and discomfort. Moreover, progesterone treatment fails to alleviate this discomfort, thereby further challenging the physiological basis of the symptoms (Johnson, 1987, pp. 343-344).

Objective measures find little cyclical variation in psychological and behavioral impairments. It appears that most cases of PMS are more a function of culturally conditioned memories about what women believe they should feel than actual experienced symptoms. Of course, a small percentage of women do actually sometimes experience premenstrual mood changes. However, the reason also seems far more related to socialized views *about* the physical changes—i.e., regarding them as embarrassing, frustrating, etc.—than to any natural influence that menstrual hormones have by themselves. The fact that a legacy of derogatory notions about menstruation still lingers today (Martin, 1988), and that 3/4 of adolescent girls fear menarche (Grief & Ulman, 1982, table 3; Wishnant & Zegans, 1981) casts a pall over menstruation which readily accounts for later negative emotional reactions to it.

Where menstruation is a socially sanctioned respite from social pressures, such as in India where it excuses women from household chores (or in America where menstruation brings relief from the fear of an unwanted pregnancy), it leads to many positive feelings. Thus, Chandra and Chaturvedi (1989) report only 6% of Indian women experience PMS.

Further evidence of PMS depending upon socially derived cognitive schemata is the fact that the intensity of menstrual distress among many religious women varies according to whether they have adhered to menstrual sex taboos or violated religious sexual practices such as premarital sexual activity (Paige & Paige, 1981, p. 275). All of this evidence leads Koeske to suggest that "premenstruation, like epinephrine in Schachter and Singer's study, is not sufficient to produce emotion" (1987, p. 143).[9]

Nor do biochemical changes produce psychological disturbances associated with adolescence. Social scientists have documented the fact that adolescent turbulence concerning emotions, behavior, and identity are limited to particular sociohistorical conditions despite the universality of pubescent hormonal fluctuations (Baumeister, 1986, chap. 5). The Western association between physical pubescence and psychological adolescence is an entirely spurious coincidence. It just so happens that modern Western culture initiates the transition from childhood to adulthood at the time that puberty occurs. The culturally specific social psychological stresses therefore appear to be associated with puberty when, in fact, they have nothing to do with it.

Mead's conclusion that adolescent psychological stress is a social rather than a physiological product is equally valid for PMS and other emotional reactions. Culturally induced stress is one response that may be associated with hormonal secretions. However, it is not a necessary or sole response. Attributing emotions to hormones per se creates the false impression that particular emotional reactions are natural, universal, inescapable products. This reinforces the fatalistic acceptance of these emotional responses and focuses attention away from strategies which could alter them (Koeske, 1987, p. 144).

Biochemical changes in the body are indeed a stimulus which can be discomforting. However, humans generally respond to these internal stimuli as they do to external stimuli, via mediations. Physical discomfort may be genuine; however, the psychological reaction to this is mediated by social consciousness. The fact that some individuals *become* irritable or aggressive during certain biochemical changes does not mean that biochemistry *causes* the behavior. As Dewey (1886c) picturesquely put it, the body is the spark which fires the mind to light its own flame.

Additional convincing evidence for the relative autonomy of emotions from visceral processes comes from Cannon who, in 1914, repudiated the James-Lange theory. Using a mixture of experimental findings and logical analyses, he disproved visceral determination of emotions. Among other things, he demonstrated that when the viscera are separated from the central nervous system, emotional behavior may still persist (Mandler, 1979, pp. 289-290). Reisenzein (1983) similarly notes "The frequently weak effects of arousal manipulations on the intensity of emotional states" (p. 258), as well as the fact that chemically blocking the sympathetic nervous system produces no reduction in reported anxiety (p. 246).

Echoing this general viewpoint, Mandler and Kremen (1958) report that no relationship exists between degree of autonomic activity and reported anxiety. Moreover, performance on a test was negatively related to subjects' *report* of autonomic activity but not to actual autonomic activity. This parallels Valins' (1966, 1967, 1970) work which demonstrated that one's belief about heart rate is more influential on attitudes, desires, and behavior than actual heart rate is.

The inescapable conclusion is that emotions are cognitively mediated, they are not by-products of physiology (Ratner, 1989a). Vygotsky and Luria emphasized the irreducibility of emotions in their critiques of the James-Lange theory (Van der Veer & Valsiner, 1989). Applauding Canon's repudiation of this theory, Luria (1932, p. 17) complained that "the James-Lange theory of emotion was the theoretical justification of a capitulation of psychological investigation and the transfer of the whole domain of affect to pure physiology" (ibid., p. 11). Luria argued that psychological emotions cannot be illuminated by describing physiological processes because "the [physiological] processes lie in an entirely different plane from that of our [psychological] problems" (ibid., p. 16). Emotions must therefore be studied in their own right as social psychological, rather than physiologically determined, phenomena.

The Cortex and Psychology

The reason that human psychological phenomena are not determined by genes, sense receptors, and hormones is that they are mediated by the cortex instead. Activities which in lower animals are governed by genes, hormones, and sense receptors are processed by the cortex in man. Whereas noncortical mechanisms produce innately mandated, stereotyped behavior, cortically mediated behavior is acquired and flexibly effected (Schneirla, 1972, p. 54). For example, sexual behavior that is governed by hormones in animals has a very different character from cortically processed sexuality, as Frank Beach describes:

> Heredity, as represented by the relatively stereotyped and inflexible functions or capacities of the subcortical neural mechanisms and the gonadal hormones, plays the major role in the courtship and mating of subprimate species. En-

vironment or experience, as it affects the more modifiable cortical functions and the capacity of cortical activity to alter the responsiveness of lower centers, is of primary importance in the sexual behavior of the higher mammals. (Beach, 1947, p. 310; Beach, 1958, pp. 278-279; Schneirla, 1972, p. 56)

Among humans, the endocrine processes as a whole are dominated by the cortex. Guided by conscious understanding, cortical control over autonomic processes provides for ready adjustment to changing environmental conditions. Even more important, consciously mediated cortical control allows for autonomic adjustment to *anticipated* environmental changes (Sterling & Eyer, 1981, pp. 6-10). If peripheral systems were left to function autonomously, they would be rigid and unadaptable.

When the cortex malfunctions the ensuing behavior has the stereotyped, involuntary character that is typical of lower organisms. For example, lesions in the septal, amygdala, and hypothalamus regions of the cortex often release spontaneous aggression which an intact cortex subjects to voluntary control (Candland et al., 1977, pp. 166-167). Similarly, decerebration produces rigid, stereotyped, uncomprehending behavior which is not characteristic of cortically mediated acts (Schneirla, 1972, p. 73).

Cortically mediated behavior is voluntary and flexible because the cortex enables consciousness to intercede between stimulation and response. As Hebb observed:

> the higher animal is less stimulus-bound [than lower animals]. Brain action is less fully controlled by afferent input, behavior therefore less predictable from the situation in which the animal is put. A greater role of ideational activity is recognizable in the animal's ability to 'hold' a variety of stimulations for some time before acting on them and in the phenomenon of purposive behavior. There is more autonomous activity in the higher brain, and more selectivity as to *which* afferent activity will be integrated with the 'stream of thought,' the dominant, ongoing activity in control of behavior. (cited in Geertz, 1973, p. 71)

For example, olfaction in noncortical organisms is a direct sensation of an olfactory stimulus; but it is a consciously mediated perception in higher animals. As Diamond (1985) explained, "The cortex originated only when the nonolfactory systems began to penetrate the olfactory system. The cortex thus provided new opportunities for the interaction of motivational and cognitive neural mechanisms and permitted the olfactory centers to outgrow their exclusive connection with external olfactory cues" (p. 338). Similarly, human pain is not a direct product of peripheral stimulation, but manifests substantial social psychological variation (described above) because peripheral afferent axons for pain are processed by cortical projection areas which include conscious mediation (Wall, 1974).[10]

Ontogeny manifests the same integration of sensory systems within the cortex and their subjugation to cortical, ideational control. The integration of sensory systems is revealed in the fact that whereas five-year-old children have difficulty identifying a previously seen object solely with the use of kinesthetic cues (obtained from having their arm passed over the outline of an object hidden from view), almost all 11-year-olds can make such an identification (Birch & Lefford, 1963, 1967). Rose (1976, p. 195) describes the increased cortical displacement of lower-brain functions that accompanies this integration: "There is evidence of the increasing control by the cortex over the activities of lower-brain regions, as the more primitive reflexes, such as the grasp reflex, which characterize the one-month-old child, begin to disappear, presumably as a result of inhibition of the functioning of lower motor centers by the developing cortex." The result of these changes is that "the relationship of motivated conduct to organic processes is at first insistently direct in the infant, and later steadily more indirect and devious" (Schneirla, 1972, p. 223).

The cortically mediated consciousness that makes behavior voluntary and flexible cannot be *determined* by the cortex. The cortex does not substitute its own mechanical determinism for hormonal, sensory, and genetic control. Consciousness cannot be strictly determined by any organ, because a biologically determined consciousness is a contradiction in terms. Consciousness must therefore stand in a nondetermined relation to the cortex that spawns it. It must be an emergent from, rather than a product of, the cortex. The cortex is not a predetermining, "hardwired" cause of consciousness. It rather potentiates consciousness. The cortex is the biological organ whose unique properties provide for a new functional system—consciousness—which functions according to its own principles. The cortex is a biological organ which potentiates a nonbiological realm of consciousness. Like a magnanimous parent, it spawns an offshoot which has the freedom to create its own existence.

The cortex is a biological Trojan horse which transports a foreign power—consciousness—into the biological world and allows consciousness to subjugate biological functions such as sense receptors and endocrine glands.

The way in which the physical matter of the cortex spawns a qualitatively different consciousness is explained with great sophistication by Roger Sperry (1965, 1969, 1970, 1977, 1980, 1986). Employing the dialectical notion of "emergence" with great elegance, Sperry emphasizes how, on the one hand, consciousness is composed of physiological and physiochemical elements and is not a supernatural element apart from them. Yet consciousness is a new form or organization of brain functions which possesses new "macro-properties" and laws which are subjective, mental, and volitional. The special physical properties of cortical neurones empower neuronal matter to take on mental properties. "The subjective qualities are recognized to be real and causal in their own right, as subjectively experienced, and to be of very different quality from the neural, molecular, and other material components of which they are built" (Sperry, 1980, p. 204).

Sperry (1980) describes how, in 1965, he, John Eccles, and Karl Popper all revised their earlier reductionistic conceptualizations, which explained consciousness as nothing but neurophysiological processes *without any emergent properties of its own*, into a dialectical model in which consciousness is both physical and more than physical, or mental. Sperry rejects mechanistic materialism (i.e., reductionism, or mind-brain identity) and also dualism which posits the mind apart from the brain. The mind is part of the brain but a unique *mental* part.

This is, in our terms, a "dialectical monism" (or, in Margolis's (1978) terms, a "nonreductive" or "emergent" materialism) which recognizes the mind and brain as inseparable parts of the same continuous hierarchy, yet recognizes the mind as a unique, subjective, function in this hierarchy. Pribram (1960, p. 22) similarly repudiates identity and dualistic conceptions of the mind-brain relationship and advocates a hierarchical structure in which psychological processes represent a different and more complex level of cortical processes. The mental is physical-and-more-than-physical; it is not merely physical.

The relationship of consciousness to cortical cells is analogous to the relation of water to hydrogen and oxygen. Consciousness is cortical cells, just as water is hydrogen and oxygen. There is nothing else to consciousness besides cortical cells, just as there is nothing else to water other than hydrogen and oxygen. But consciousness is no more reducible to cortical cells than water is to its elements. Properties of water are not found in hydrogen and oxygen per se. These properties only emerge from a special organization of hydrogen and oxygen. Analogously, properties of consciousness are unique to a particular organization of neural matter; these properties are not found in the neurones per se. Consciousness has unique features which operate according to principles that are entirely different from the features and principles governing nerve cells—just as water has unique properties and obeys principles that are entirely different from gasses. This functional autonomy makes it unnecessary to understand the properties of gasses in order to understand the properties of water, as it is unnecessary to understand the cortex in order to be a psychologist.

Insisting that consciousness can be understood in physiological terms is as fallacious as explaining water in terms of the properties of gasses. Identity theory is a form of atomism which is insensitive to the qualitative changes that accrue to neurones in different configurations. However, the fact that phenomena are constituted not simply by their elements but by the relationship of elements means that consciousness is irreducible to neurones, per se.

In an insightful critique of the identity theory of mind and brain, Errol Harris (1966) points out the qualitative difference between them. Brain activity has spatiotemporal and physical characteristics which are not analogous to feelings, percepts, and thoughts. For example, a perceived or imagined scene is not isomorphic with the spatial pattern of the neurones involved. And colors are perceived as existing outside our heads despite the fact that the neuronal representation is inside. Similarly, the fact that the neural process is in the brain while sensations are felt in different parts of the body is sufficient reason for denying their identity. In the same vein, memory of a past event cannot be equated with the passage of ions along nerve fibers because the latter are not endowed with intentionality that could refer to past events.

Physical and phenomenological terms do not mean or describe the same thing. Nor does physiology explain experience. We have already stated that physiological representations of things are reversed and inverted images of what is actually perceived. Perceived entities additionally differ from cortical projections in that the latter are divided into two incomplete parts, each of which is localized in different hemispheres. Even when the corpus callosum is surgically severed, thereby preventing any closure between the two projections, objects are still perceived as whole and complete.

Another reason for refusing to identify neural impulse with feeling is the well-attested fact that all neural discharges, both afferent and efferent, are alike. They differ in frequency and in the number of fibers which they invade, but there is no qualitative difference between those discharges which originate from the diverse sense organs. Yet there is a vast range of qualitative differences among the sensations which result from the impulses transmitted by these different receptors (Harris, 1965, pp. 300-302; Puccetti & Dykes, 1978).

Reductionism, or identity theory, entirely misconstrues the nature of consciousness. Consciousness is intentional in that it actively selects, interprets, and organizes information. Neurones per se do not possess this kind of agency, intelligence, comprehension, and creativity. Only mechanisms that are endowed with an emergent consciousness possess these qualities. Organisms which function entirely on a physical level are barely sentient and are not conscious (Harris, 1966, pp. 531-532). Far from mechanical physiological processes explaining mind, they preclude it. Reducing mind to physiology eliminates rather than illuminates the mental.

The self is equally irreducible to physiology. Individuality is only possible for a subject who is more than physical. A purely physical being cannot have a self any more than a computer can. Only a mediated consciousness that is differentiated from physical mechanisms can be an intentional agent. As we know from Chapter 1, organisms submerged *in* the natural world cannot be subjects who *have* or *create* a world.

As Ornstein (1970) said in a critique of the identity theory: "S may *be* B without being *reducible* to B. Sensations may be constituted by neural firings, yet it is highly misleading to say that sensations are *merely* neural firings." "To claim that persons are 'nothing but' or 'really' or 'simply' bodies is to consider the *first* word about persons to be the *last* word about them. Persons after all, are not just objects (bodies) but are subjects too" (Ornstein, pp. 166, 167). Insofar as the mental is not identical to the physical, dualism has a grain of truth, but insofar as the mental is grounded in the physical, identity theory also is partially true. However, both theories are false in their one-sidedness.

The irreducibility of consciousness to neurones per se is further demonstrated by the fact that electrical stimulation of neurones does not produce normal mental activity. Feelings, thoughts, and memories, and behavior can be electrically activated, but they are experienced as alien, mechanical acts rather than as voluntarily initiated by the subject. Penfield (1975, p. 76-77) reports that a patient who moved his hand in response to electrical stimulation of the motor cortex invariably said, "I didn't do that. You did." When electrical stimulation caused him to vocalize, he said, "I didn't make that sound. You pulled it out of me." And when memories were electrically elicited a patient said, "Things *seem* familiar," not "I have been through this before." Finally, a stimulated perception that things are growing large and coming near is so alien that it does not provoke the patient to move out of the way of the oncoming object.

Electrically stimulated responses are experienced as simulated, not as real mental activity. Intentional, willful, comprehending, interpretive mental activity cannot be electrically stimulated. In Penfield's words, "There is no place in the cerebral cortex where electrical stimulation will cause a patient to believe or to decide." An illusion of interpretation can be electrically produced, "But none of the actions that we attribute to the mind has been initiated by electrode stimulation or epileptic discharge" (Penfield, pp. 77-78). In other words, the mind cannot be activated from the bottom up, by stimulating its neural constituents. The mind can only be approached in terms of its emergent properties as a distinct conscious phenomenon.

Respecting the emergent, functionally autonomous properties of mind means that,

> Mind and consciousness are put in the driver's seat, as it were: They give the orders, and they push and haul around the physiology and the physical chemical processes as much as or more than the latter processes direct them . . . It is a scheme that idealizes ideas and ideals over physical and chemical interactions, nerve impulse traffic, and DNA. It is a brain model in which conscious mental psychic forces are recognized to be the crowning achievement of some five hundred million years or more of evolution . . . In the brain model described here, man is provided in large measure with the mental forces and the mental ability to determine his own actions. This scheme thus allows a high degree of freedom from outside forces as well as mastery over the inner cellular, molecular, and atomic aspects of brain activity. Depending on the state of one's will power, the model also allows considerable freedom from lower-level natural impulses . . . (Sperry, 1965, pp. 78, 87).

Squarely supporting this formulation, Vygotsky (1989, p 71) said, "*man regulates or controls his brain, the brain does not control man.*"[11]

Neuroanatomical properties of the cortex make it clear why consciousness is an emergent phenomenon that is not directly determined by "hard-wired" programs. Far from being a rigidly determined substance, the cortex is the most plastic part of the brain and is thoroughly molded by incoming information. As J.C. Herrick, one of the founders of comparative neurology, observed, "the cerebral cortex is the organ of the highest and most plastic correlations, which are in large measure individually acquired." "The cerebral cortex differs from the reflex centers of the brain stem chiefly in that all of its parts are interconnected by inconceivably complex systems of associational connections, many of which are probably acquired late in life under the influence of individual experience, and any combination of which may, under appropriate conditions of external excitation and internal physiological state, become involved in any cerebral process whatever" (cited in Bernard, 1924, pp. 50-51).

More recently, Nash has similarly concluded that "It is those neurones which are latest in ontogenetic maturation that retain the greatest degree of plasticity, and these comprise much of the frontal lobe and other regions concerned with 'higher' intellectual processes" (Nash, 1970, p. 99; cf. also Parker & Gibson, 1979, p. 378; Scher, 1962, p. 5).

Mark Rosenzweig and his colleagues have demonstrated the cortex's plasticity and openness to worldly experience in a serious of famous experiments (Diamond, 1988). Ironically, Rosenzweig began his research from the opposite point of view: He initially hypothesized that learning ability in rats *depends upon* the amount of acetylcholinesterase in the cerebral cortex. What he found was that learning stimulated the production of acetylcholinesterase. "Rather than cortical acetylcholinesterase being a fixed individual characteristic, as we had supposed, it could apparently be altered by experience" (Rosenzweig, 1984, p. 366)!

Rats exposed to enriched conditions (in which many rats lived together in a large cage furnished with playthings that are changed daily) and impoverished conditions (where a rat was kept alone in a cage without any playthings) produced significant differences in cortical features. The enriched rats had cortexes that weighed 6% more than their impoverished counterparts, had 8% more protein, were 6% thicker, had 14% more glial cells, 14% larger cell bodies, synaptic junctions that averaged 50% larger in cross-section, and 10% more cholinesterase (Rosenzweig, Bennett, & Diamond, 1972). In addition, experience affected the development of dendritic branching, and the number of dendritic spines per unit length of dendrite (Rosenzweig, 1984). Cortical development had practical consequences for behavior as the enriched rats learned mazes three times faster than impoverished rats (Riege, 1971). Furthermore, "early stimulation induces brain lateralization where it does not otherwise occur" (Denenberg, 1987, p. 43). Interestingly, "The capacity for plastic neural changes was found to be present not only early in life but throughout most if not all of the life span" (Rosenzweig, 1984).

The cortex, then, forms in response to experience and thereby mirrors the encountered world. Experience affects cortical structure by stimulating the growth of new axons, dendrites, synapses, and glial cells. Synapses can be generated as rapidly as 10-15 minutes after a new experience.

Denenberg (1987, p. 44) correctly points out that the effects of early experience on human brain development should be even more powerful since our brain is far more malleable than the rat's, and because we live in a more complex milieu. In addition, the human cortex matures over a long time during which it is influenced by experience. It is well known that the human association regions are the least mature part of the cortex at birth and take longer than any other part to mature. In contrast to the primary sensory and motor areas which are myelinated by 2 years of age, some layers of the association areas remain unmyelinated at 6 years. Being the most neotenous areas of the cortex, the association areas are most open to experientially acquired information. It is natural that the association areas, which underlie the highest intellectual comprehension of things, should develop in accordance with worldly experience rather than according to internal processes.

Experience not only affects the cortex by stimulating the growth of new neural components. Experience also organizes synapses that are endogenous to the cortex. Synaptic connections naturally proliferate more than tenfold from birth to two years of age. However, only those that are utilized in experience are retained. Those junctions and pathways that are not utilized—as many as 70%—degenerate, thus providing room for the development of those that are used (Edelman, 1987; Parker & Gibson, 1979, pp. 378-379; Siegler, 1989, pp. 355-359). Endogenous neurones thus come to reflect experienced reality just as experientially generated neurones do (Greenough, Black, & Wallace, 1987). For example, if neo-natal experience is restricted to vertical lines, the occipital neurons that register horizontal lines atrophy and only the vertically oriented remain (Blakemore, 1970).

Dramatic evidence for cortical plasticity among humans comes from research comparing cortical structures of deaf individuals who use sign language, and hearing individuals who use spoken speech. Sacks (1989, pp. 101-106) reports that the visual acuity which deaf people use to compensate for their lack of hearing is reflected in much faster evoked potentials to movement in the peripheral visual field—compared with the speed of evoked potentials in hearing subjects. Even more striking is the fact that perception of movement, picture identification, and the recognition of faces are registered in the left temporal lobe of deaf people which is normally devoted to auditory functions in hearing individuals. This suggests that what are normally auditory areas are *reallocated* in deaf signers for visual processing. This astonishing phenomenon means that the nervous system is so plastic that it adapts to an entirely different sensory mode from what it normally handles.

Another fascinating aspect of visuospatial perception being localized in the left hemisphere of deaf signers is that it is localized in the right hemisphere of hearing people! Sacks states that the reason for the switch is that visuospatial perception is intimately part of sign language and is therefore represented as language in left hempisphere language centers of sign users. Visuoperceptual processes in *hearing* individuals are distinct from auditory language and are consequently processed in right hemisphere areas apart from left hemisphere language centers.

Far from the brain being "hard-wired" for fixed hemispheral faculties, any psychological function can be represented in any hemisphere depending upon its full psychological character. Visuospatial perception, audition, musical performance, game playing, mathematics, and even language itself will be represented in the right hemisphere if they are impressionistic, rudimentary, and not highly codified. However, they will be represented in the left hemisphere if they are embedded in a highly organized symbolic system. As the individual becomes more accomplished in any of these activities, as these functions become more routinized and symbolically objectified in the course of an individual's experience, they evidence a shift from right to left hemisphere within a given individual's brain.

Significantly, only the cortex is neurologically plastic and subject to influence of experience. Subcortical regions are not. Thus, the cortex of enriched rats increased in weight, but the subcortex was no heavier than among the impoverished subjects (Riege, 1971). Similarly, higher-order occipital dendrite branching was significantly affected by rearing complexity whereas lower order branching was not (Volkmar, 1972).

Cortical plasticity is necessary for intelligence because plasticity opens the cortex to experience with the world so that it can understand events. A biologically programmed brain would be less sensitive to worldly events and thus less intelligent. A malleable cortex also enables the rearranging of information which is crucial to intelligence. The correlation between plasticity (receptivity) and objectivity (intelligence) underscores our frequently emphasized inverse relationship between biological determination and objectivity-intelligence. The human being is objectively oriented to the world *because* he is free from the biological constraints which limit animals (Scheler, 1961, p. 37).

Since the cortex which mediates higher mental functions is plastic and susceptible to experience, it cannot *determine* these functions. The cortex does not preexist psychological activities, but, on the contrary, is formed by them as they generate themselves. The ways in which we use our cortex determine its development, rather than the other way around. Montagu described this well when he said:

> Mind is a social product. It represents the social organization of previously unorganized nervous tissue, and the expression of that nervous tissue according to the cultural pattern of its organization, that is, in behavior. The hereditary determinants of the morphological character of the nervous system do not make a mind, but merely provide the cellular organization of such nervous cellular elements from which a mind may be organized. It is the cultural organization of such nervous cellular elements that *creates* mind. (1957, p. 251)

Actually, social life may be said to have even produced the cellular elements themselves. For as Washburn and Hamburg (1968, p. 476) stated:

> The increase in the association areas is probably the result of new selection pressures that came with the evolution of more complex forms of social life,

and is probably highly related to the evolution of language which made the new ways of life possible. Taken together the new parts of the association areas and the parts of the brain making language possible might be thought of as the 'social brain'—the parts of the brain that evolved in response to social pressures and the parts that today mediate appropriate social action.

Even when the cortex is stimulated by electrical means the effect is mediated by situational and cognitive factors. This is true in animals as well as humans. For example, when Delgado electrically stimulated aggression centers of the cortex, monkeys and cats remained docile toward individuals fiercer than themselves although they did aggress toward individuals more submissive than themselves (Delgado, 1969, p. 128ff; Candland et al., 1977, pp. 29, 167-172; Plotnik, 1974). Furthermore, in the absence of a social situation, aggressive mannerisms were not manifested at all; the animals only evidenced a general restlessness (Delgado, 1973, p. 47). Similarly, when Pribram (1976, pp. 59-63) lesioned monkeys' amygdalae, submissiveness usually followed; however, it depended upon the interaction the individual had with others. One lesioned animal became *more* aggressive because its playmate was unusually docile. Pribram describes additional caretaking conditions that interact with neurophysiological states, and he concludes that this interaction challenges the notion of brain mechanisms automatically controlling behavior.

> Postoperative monkeys were especially sensitive to the way they were treated by their cage mates and handled by their caretakers. The immediate postoperative taming could be prolonged for years by gentling procedures, whereas ordinary neglect and occasional rougher treatment would produce either an excessively fearful or an unpredictably aggressive monkey. These results make it unlikely that some fundamental mechanism responsible for aggression had been excised; rather, some brain process sensitive to the social environment seems to have been tapped." (p. 63)[12]

Rod Plotnik (1974) also challenges innate neural triggers of aggression among primates. He questions whether actions ensuing from electrical stimulation of the brain (ESB) are really aggressive. They may, after all, be random responses akin to epileptic seizures without any aggressive motivation or feeling at all. Finally, even if ESB does elicit aggression this is no evidence for innate neural pathways or triggers. In the first place, these pathways are undoubtedly acquired and organized through experience. Secondly, the aggressive acts may be responses to the pain produced by ESB rather than being direct products of the ESB itself. In other words, ESB may not directly stimulate innate neural pathways for aggression but may simply produce pain to which the animal responds by learned actions. Plotnik argues that until studies disentangle these two possibilities, it is unjustified to presume that ESB directly produces aggression through innate neural pathways.

Human electrical stimulation of the brain produces even more variable results because conscious mediations are much more diverting. As Delgado said,

> Personal identity and reactivity depend upon a large number of factors accumulated through many years of experience. . . . Language and culture are among the essential elements of individual structure. All these elements cannot be substituted for by the delivery of electricity to the brain. Memories can be recalled, emotions awakened, and conversations speeded up by ESB, but the [individuals] always express themselves according to their background and experience. It is possible to disturb consciousness, to confuse sensory interpretations, or to elicit hallucinations during excitation of the brain. It is also possible to induce fear, pleasure, and changes in aggressive behavior, but these responses do not represent the creation of a new personality—only a change in emotionality or reactivity with the appearance of manifestations closely related to the previous history of the subject. (Delgado, 1969, pp. 193-195)

ESB at most arouses a tendency toward action which is controlled by the organism according to its appraisal of the situation. "The brain processes, in other words, constitute only one, albeit often a critical one, of several classes of variables that determine the organization of behavior" (Pribram, 1960, p. 22). In view of the other variables, there is no one-to-one correlation between ESB and psychological activity. The amygdala, for instance, cannot be the aggression center or the sex center because it does not unilaterally control these acts. Instead, the amygdala has a much more general function of understanding momentary events in terms of prior events, i.e., generalizing prior experience to contemporary situations. Damage to this center interferes with the organism's general interpretation of events and produces inappropriate behavior; it is not to be conceived as some change in response mechanism per se (Pribram, 1960, pp. 23-24).[13]

ESB has such variable, imprecise effects because the neural codes for human responsiveness are not given in singular, discrete locations. Multifaceted psychological processes, shot through with creative activity and socially organized features, cannot possibly rest on discrete, localized brain functions which produce isomorphic responses. As Luria (1966, p. 25) explained,

> If all human psychological functions are complex functional systems, if they are the product of prolonged (and social) development, are complex in composition, and can be subjected to modification of their component links, then we can understand that there can be no question of localization of complex

functional systems in circumscribed areas of the brain or in individual neurons.

Once we disabuse ourselves of the reified fiction that psychological phenomena are discrete, homogeneous faculties, the notion that they can be isomorphically linked with strictly defined, discrete brain centers vanishes accordingly. The human brain is certainly specialized, however not in the form of discrete centers standing in an isomorphic relation to discrete mental faculties (cf. Efron, 1990). Instead, as Luria brilliantly describes, the specialized centers are subject to variable interrelationships according to social requirements. Since relationships constitute the very nature of all things, specialized brain centers undergo qualitative variations as a result of their socially constituted interactions. The centers do not have endogenous, fixed associations with each other or with behavior. Vygotsky pointed out the antithesis between socially constituted psychobiological processes and intrinsic neural codes or cortical centers. He said:

> If relationships among people genetically [developmentally] underlie psychological functions, then: (1) it is ridiculous to look for specific centers of higher psychological functions or supreme functions in the cortex (or in the frontal lobes; Pavlov); (2) they must be explained not on the basis of internal organic relations (regulation), but in external terms, on the basis of the fact that man controls the activity of his brain from without through stimuli; (3) they are not natural structures, but constructs . . . (Vygotsky, 1989, p. 59)

Vygotsky went on to explain that the connections between brain centers and psychological functions is created from outside the individual as a result of his social relations. Consequently, there can be no purely internal determination of psychology by endemic characteristics of brain centers. "The personality alters the role of individual psychological functions, systems, layers, and strata, establishing connections that do not, and cannot, exist in the biology of the individual. *It is not the relation of subcortical centers to cortical centers, but the social structure of the personality that determines which layers are to dominate*" (Vygotsky, 1989, pp. 64-65). In short, cortical flexibility which allows creative, socially constructed, variable activity also allows this activity to organize the cortex itself. Obviously, the cortex must be susceptible to human organization if it is to participate in creative, complex, social activity. The brain does not stand apart from the activity it empowers, it must share the characteristics of this activity. As Vygotsky (1989, p. 64) succinctly put it, "one cannot understand the activity of any nervous apparatus *without man. This brain is a man's brain.*" In short, *the human brain is a humanized brain.*

All of the foregoing evidence points to the same ineluctable general conclusion concerning psychology's relation to biology: psychological activities presuppose normal biological functioning; however, they are not specifically determined by it. Accordingly, the quest for biological causes of psychology is perversely antagonistic to the entire nature of human biology and psychology. It is especially ironic when the most creative, insightful acts are explained as biologically determined products. The popular view of scientific and artistic genius as genetically determined is a flagrant contradiction because genetic determination produces rigid, simple, automatic, nonconscious responses, whereas science, art, and intelligent activities involve the utmost novelty, and profound comprehension. Nothing could be *less* biologically determined than they. Biological determinists (reductionists) are in the untenable position of trying to explain active, creative, flexibly implemented behavior by fixed mechanisms. While such mechanisms are certainly appropriate for explaining the stereotyped, involuntary behavior of lower organisms, they are incapable of accounting for the character of human character (Bernard, 1924, 1926).

Psychology's concrete character cannot be explained biologically because it is a function of individuals' collective efforts to develop their consciousness, sociality, and technology. A deterministic biology (as animals have) cannot accommodate these mediations because it is antagonistic to them. This is why animals are unable to add these mediations onto their biology. Mediations can only emerge with the elimination of biology as a "fully armed," specific influence, and they, in turn act as a selective pressure to enforce this abatement. Human biology is therefore not a continuation of animal biology with cultural factors added to it. It is a complete transformation in which animal biology has become humanized, or, more precisely socialized. As Geertz states:

> the accepted view that mental functioning is essentially an intracerebral process, which can only be secondarily assisted or amplified by the various artificial devices which that process has enabled man to invent, appears to be quite wrong. On the contrary, a fully specified, adaptively sufficient definition of regnant neural processes in terms of intrinsic parameters being impossible, the human brain is thoroughly dependent upon cultural resources for its very operation; and those resources are, consequently, not adjuncts to, but constituents of, mental activity. (Geertz, 1973, p. 76)

Biologistic models of psychology persistently promulgate versions of biological determinism which only occurs among animals, human infants, and biologically abnormal human adults. Such caricatures of psychology can never account for the intelligence, cognition, perception, personality, learning, psychopathology, or other psychological functions of biologically normal human adults.

Notes

1. Cf. Durkheim, 1953, chap. 1, for a lucid explication of the hierarchical, irreducible relationship between the mental and the physical.

2. At our current level of medical sophistication, the crippling effects of disease are far less a function of genetic susceptibility than they are of socially mediated conditions. These conditions include hypertension, inadequate nutrition, sanitation, and access to medical care. A striking example of the social distribution of mortality is the fact that in precapitalist societies, male and female death rates were at roughly comparable levels. With modern capitalist development, the gap between male and female life expectancy widens progressively, with males dying now about eight years sooner on the average than females. "The key to understanding modern male excess mortality is to see that females have benefited much more than men from the health advance possible with capitalism, while men have suffered more from the rise of stress-induced and other risk factors" (Eyer, 1984, p. 33). Social conditions have clearly superceded genetic risk in determining mortality.

3. Induced motion has been explained in terms of physiological characteristics of the occular system. However, all such biological explanations fail because they disregard the psychological aspects of perception. Perception is not the outcome of involuntary mechanisms; it depends upon the psychological significance which the object has for the perceiver. This significance activates perceptual processes, not vice versa.

   Post and Leibowitz (1985) explain induced motion as caused by the interaction of antagonistic visual tendencies toward pursuit and stabilization. The theory is that the moving stimulus stimulates a pursuit tendency which is then stabilized by a tendency to focus on the opposite direction. This latter tendency leads to apparent movement in the opposite direction. Thus, the reason for apparent motion of the moon is that "the clouds provide an optokinetic stimulus to move the eyes reflexively in the direction of their motion. To prevent loss of fixation, a pursuit effort is required in the opposite direction" (Post & Leibowitz, p. 636). This "efferent motion signal" induces the illusory perception of movement in the opposite direction.

   Such hypothetical tendencies of the occular system disregard the psychological significance of the stimulus objects. We have seen that apparent moon motion is induced because the clouds signify a surrounding context which is assumed to be stable, and the moon signifies an object which is assumed to be mobile. When these meanings are altered, the illusion disappears. Whether the moon is regarded as a fixed object in front of which clouds move or a mobile object that is situated in a stable context may produce variations in eye movement. However, any difference in eye movement is more the consequence than the cause of psychological significance. To paraphrase Vygotsky, it is not the eye that perceives, the person perceives.

4. Our entire experience of being in the world and encountering real things is also inexplicable in purely sensory terms. It requires an intentional con-

sciousness which relates sensations to events outside. As the empiricist philosophers themselves discovered, sensory impressions in and of themselves are unaware of the external events that generate them. The causal relation of which they are a part is not given in sense impressions because sensations are simply sensory registers which cannot comprehend their own origins. Consciousness must transcend all sensory impressions to intentionally see their origins in external reality. As Hegel said, "To discover the truth in things, mere attention is not enough; we must call in the action of our own faculties to transform what is immediately before us" (Hegel, 1965, p. 43). A presumed objectivism which postulates physical sensory processes independently of consciousness actually results in gross subjectivism which cannot experience objective reality.

5. Interestingly, even in middle level animals, previous experience and current perceptions influence the strength of hormonal effects: mice that have lost their social position during dominance struggles are not emboldened to act aggressively by receiving injections of testosterone, nor do successful fighters cease their aggression after castration or ovariectomy (Hoyenga & Hoyenga, 1979, pp. 129-130).

   Maternal behavior shows the same dominance of experience. Whereas hormones strongly affect maternal behavior in inexperienced rats, the effect is minimized by experience: For example, transfusing the blood of pregnant rats into non-pregnant rats stimulates maternal behavior in the latter, and reducing estrogen in inexperienced pregnant rats causes 50% of them to reject their young after birth. However, reducing estrogen in pregnant rats which have previously borne litters results in only 5% of them rejecting their young after birth (Hoyenga & Hoyenga, 1979, p. 120-131).

   Consistent with the findings on sex and aggression, hormones have less effect on maternal behavior of primates than they do on middle mammals such as rats (ibid., p. 131).

6. Besides hormones, other physiological reactions are also normally subordinate to consciousness. This has been experimentally confirmed by Geen and Rakosky (1973) who found that subjects' interpretation of a fight they had witnessed influenced their GSR. Subjects who believed the fight to be a fictional act evidenced low GSR while subjects who believed the fight was a professional prizefight manifested higher GSR.

7. Ekman (1983) claims that autonomic nervous system activity does distinguish among emotions; however, his data do not in the least support this conclusion. He recorded several autonomic measures as subjects contorted their facial muscles according to certain instructions. These subjects were explicitly requested not to produce an emotional expression, but simply to produce muscle movements that Ekman interpreted as corresponding to various emotions. Any differences in ANS cannot therefore be interpreted as differentiating *emotions*, only as differentiating facial responses. In fact, Ekman admits that ANS changes associated with facial responses were greater than ANS changes associated with reliving emotional experiences (p. 1210). It is thus

quite unacceptable to talk about "emotion-specific autonomic activity" when this activity has nothing to do with emotions.

ANS changes associated with facial responses were quite contradictory and ambiguous. Facial responses corresponding to anger elicited a slight elevation in temperature, however "fear," "sadness," "happiness," "surprise," and "disgust" facial movements produced virtually no change in temperature. Heart rate, on the other hand, increased about 8 beats per minute under "anger," " fear," and "sadness," and remained virtually unchanged under "happiness," "surprise," and "disgust." No explanation is offered for such discrepancies in different ANS activities. According to the data, temperature does not discriminate between "sadness" and "happiness" responses, while heart rate does. What is the reason for this?

Finally, if emotions entail specific ANS activity, then ANS measures should vary among each emotion. This is not the case, however, as anger, fear, and sadness all entail the same heart rate change, and fear, surprise, and sadness all entail the same absence of temperature change. Far from specific ANS variation occurring among each facial response, most responses entail similar ANS levels. Differences in ANS activity are the exception rather than the rule.

8. McFarland's, Ross's, and Ruble's studies are interesting confirmations of Figure 2 which depicts recall as a function of socially derived cognitive schemata. See also Cordua et al. (1979), Middleton & Edwards (1990), Cohen (1989, pp. 75-76, 202-216).

9. The same lack of causal connection between hormone levels and behavior exists for menopause when estrogen is reduced. Again, contrary to popular belief, many women—75% in one study—do not have any remarkable *physical* symptoms. Nor do they undergo psychological changes directly attributable to the hormones. For instance:

> there are no data to support the idea that menopause has any relationship to serious depression in women. Postmenopausal women who experience psychosis have almost always had similar episodes premenopausally. The notion of the hormonally depressed woman is a shibboleth that must be laid permanently to rest. Some studies have related irritability and insomnia to loss of sleep from nighttime hot flashes. Thus, for women who experience hot flashes, these emotional difficulties might, indirectly, relate to menopause. But the social, life history, and family contexts in which middle-aged women find themselves are more important links to emotional changes occurring during the years of the climacteric. And these, of course, have nothing whatsoever to do with hormones. Quite a number of studies suggest that the majority of women do not consider menopause a time of crisis. Nor do most women suffer from the so-called "empty nest syndrome" supposedly experienced when children leave home. On the contrary, investigation suggests that women without small children are less depressed and have higher incomes and an increased sense of well-being. Such positive reactions depend upon work histories, individual upbringing, cultural background, and general state of health, among other things. (Fausto-Sterling, 1985, p. 119)

McKinlay et al. (1987) similarly found no increase in depression among menopausal women compared with premenopausal women. Menopausal women who become depressed did so because of stressful life events such as divorce, widowhood, financial difficulties, care of aged relatives, or poor health.

Townsend and Carbone (1980) and Beyene (1989) document substantial social variation in psychological accompaniments of menopause. Beyene (Chapter 9) found that Mayan women reported no psychological or physiological symptoms. They regard menopause as a relief from menstruation which is conceived as an illness. Menopause also brings relaxed sexual activity because it eliminates the fear of pregnancy. Mayan women report no hot flashes associated with menopause. Greek women, in contrast, reported hot flashes but unaccompanied by psychological symptoms of irritability or melancholy. A plausible cultural explanation for the lack of psychological symptoms in both cultures is the fact that both grant higher status to older than to younger women. The mother-in-law heads an extended family. This increased social status and happiness lies in direct contrast to the position of Western women entering old age. This period is usually associated with loss of the mother role as children leave the home for independent lives. In addition, retirement from work is another immanent deterioration to a woman's status. The contrasting social contexts explain the contrasting experiences women have regarding menopause. Certainly, the fact that both Greek and Mayan women experience psychological symptoms despite discrepant physical experiences of menopause indicates that physiology is not a predisposing factor of psychological discomfort.

Beyene (Chapter 10) hypothesizes that diet is responsible for the different physiological symptoms reported by Greek and Mayan menopausal women. However, she never produces any evidence to support this claim. Nor is there any evidence that diet or other physical processes cause differences in psychological symptoms.

10. Phylogenetic evolution may be characterized as a transformation of discrete, direct afferent-efferent pathways into interpenetrating sensory-motor systems within the cortex which subjects them to ideational control. Explaining the phylogenetic development of sensory integration, Birch and Lefford state:

> Starting with the fish—in which class the independence of one another of the different sensory modalities is the rule—a clear sequence of intermodal evolution can be traced through the amphibia and reptiles—in which classes partial liaison among the sense systems appears—to the mammals—among whom intersensory liaison is characteristic. . . . After a detour for birds in the evolutionary course, the mammal is characterized by an enormously expanded system of intersensory relations structurally reflected in the cerebral cortex. (Birch & Lefford, 1967, p. 6; cf. Schneirla, 1972, p. 78)

"Considerable evidence has been amassed to suggest strongly that even for relatively simple sensory functions the effects produced by the application of a stimulus to a given sense organ are continuously modified by ongoing activity in the other sense modalities" (Birch & Lefford, 1963, p. 3-4).

11. Conscious control over physical organs is obvious from everyday experience as when we decide to raise our hand, but it has also received some interesting experimental demonstration. Shaw (1940) found that imagination innervates effector neurons, and the greater the imagined responses the stronger is the innervation: Imagining oneself lifting heavy weights produces greater muscle-action currents than imagining lifting light weights.

    Powell (1973) demonstrated that mentally rehearsing an activity such as dart-throwing improved actual performance by 28%.

    Selective attention to different parts of a perceptual object produces corresponding alterations in the nerve firings associated with the different parts. Attending to a figure enhances the evoked potential in the corresponding section of the occipital cortex but attenuates the evoked potential in response to a simultaneous flash of light; conversely, attending to the flash enhances the associated evoked potential and reduces the evoked potential in response to the figure. When subjects attend to both the flash and the figure, the two evoked potentials are similar (Donchin & Cohen, 1967).

12. Pribram (1976, pp. 75-77) reports that electrical stimulation of the motor cortex produces different movements depending on body and limb position as well as physical conditions and opportunities. Thus, a rat, when stimulated, may initially drink, but if the liquid is removed and replaced by some pieces of wood, he will likely chew on them when stimulated.

13. Cortical activity not only fails to determine psychological experience. It is not even a perfect correlate, or measure, of experience. For instance, the experience of sleep or wakefulness bears little relationship to cortical activity. Sewitch (1984) found that most individuals (55%) who have been awakened from Stage 2 sleep, as defined by EEG criteria, and 27 % who have been awakened from REM sleep, report that they were *awake* just prior to being awakened.

6

Madness

If sociohistorical psychology is to be a comprehensive, coherent paradigm, it must be able to explain madness in the same framework as it explains other psychological phenomena. The task of this chapter is to demonstrate that disturbed psychological functioning follows the same sociohistorical principles that normal functioning does.

In view of the fact that the founders of sociohistorical psychology devoted relatively little attention to madness per se (as opposed to mental retardation and learning disabilities which they considered at greater length), a sociohistorical perspective on mental illness must be constructed out of the principles which have been elucidated in other areas. Vygotsky did mention that psychotic thinking grows out of disturbing social interactions. However, a fuller understanding requires searching the voluminous literature on psychosis to find material that is compatible with sociohistorical principles. This material is readily available and I shall attempt to organize it into a coherent description of psychopathology that is explicitly Vygotskian.

I have restricted the discussion of psychological dysfunction to extreme psychosis and will have little to say about milder neurosis. The reason for this, aside from constraints of space, is to test sociohistorical psychology on difficult-to-explain, bizarre behavior which appears to defy social and psychological intelligibility. If sociohistorical psychology can render madness intelligible, then the case is strengthened for contending that sociohistorical psychology is an adequate paradigm for explaining all psychological activity. Of course, less serious dysfunctions (neurosis) cannot be entirely excluded. Despite differences in degree and kind, neurosis and psychosis are part of a common universe of psychological disturbance which does not admit of clear-cut distinctions. While differences must be respected, we will occasionally draw upon research on neurosis to explain general issues that pertain to madness.

Definition of Madness

Madness shares with all psychological phenomena a fuzziness that defies precise definition. Just as consciousness, cognition, experience, personality, emotion, and even psychology itself can only be indicated but not captured in definition, the same is true for madness. And just as the other phenomena indubitably exist despite their conceptual indefiniteness, so psychosis does also. There is no question that certain individuals are tormented by uncontrollable thoughts and feelings, have severe misgivings about their veridicality, and lack a sense of sociality with other people which combine to profoundly disturb their individual and social functioning. Psychosis is not simply unconventional behavior. It is felt by the individual himself as interfering with his life activities. *He* finds it difficult to accomplish his chosen aims; *he* feels dominated by his thoughts, moods, fears; *he* finds his situation unbearable and upsetting. The individual is dispirited about himself, about his loss of agency, and his inability to understand or alter his functioning. He feels alone and confused as in a dream (Natanson, 1969, p. 103). Psychotics "do not know what is happening, and no one is likely to enlighten them" (Laing, 1967, p. 87). Psychosis is not a matter of violating particular normative behaviors. It is a rupture of sociality per se—a breakdown of communication and interaction with others that is rooted in a lack of confidence in a common social world altogether. The fact that madness is not simply nonconforming behavior means that personality disorders which are defined by aggressive, impulsive, nonconforming behavior but which are not accompanied by anxiety, distress, or psychotic disorganization, should not be included within psychiatric nosology (Gove & Tudor, 1977, p. 1328).

Nor is madness indicated by any particular activity. Any act can be psychotic or not, depending upon its social psychological character. Irrational judgments, delusions, hallucinations, and trances are not ipso facto psychotic. It is normal practice for youngsters to develop fantasy relationships with musicians, actors, or sports heroes to the point that they talk to their photographs, feel part of their lives, fall in love with them, become jealous when the star takes a lover, believe that the hero knows and cares about them ("he's singing that song for me"), and engage in other delusions (Caughey, 1984). Religion is also heavily delusional in the sense that there is no empirical referent for the belief in god. When someone says they know that god has acted in some way, when they pray and attempt to communicate with him, and when they claim to hear his voice, these unsubstantiated experiences certainly qualify as delusions and hallucinations.

However, they are not psychotic. The reason they are not is that they are socially institutionalized and psychologically bounded. This gives them some solidity and keeps them under the agent's control. If the same delusions lacked consensual validation (H.S. Sullivan's term), were free-wheeling, irrepressible, and interfered with his personal aims and social interactions, they would be psychotic.

Vygotsky (1989, p. 71) put it well:

> The difference between a mentally ill and a normal person is not so much that the laws of mental life are violated in the mentally ill, or patients have something (neoplasms) that normal people do not have (tumor). Rather, normal people have the same thing as the mentally ill: delusions, suspicions. Delusions of reference, obsessive ideas, fear, etc. But the *role* of all this, the hierarchy of the entire system, is different.

The difference between an individual who suddenly blanks out of social interaction and personal activity because "god has summoned him," and the person who intentionally allocates a certain portion of time for prayer—or the difference between the lunatic who believes himself to be a machine and the social scientist who claims that men are machines—epitomizes the difference between madness and "normalcy" (for want of a better word) quite apart from issues of rationality, contact with reality, normativeness, and benevolence.

The fact that socially institutionalized and individually controlled belief systems are not psychotic does not make them benevolent or fulfilling. They may very well be mystical, superstitious, irrational, and destructive. Freud coined the term "social neurosis" to refer precisely to deleterious consequences of normative social practices. And Eric Fromm (1955) correctly observed that many socially institutionalized beliefs and acts are "socially patterned defects" with deleterious effects which go unnoticed precisely because they are normative. Contrasting psychotic to normal does not imply that normal is good and psychotic bad. It simply distinguishes a state of free-wheeling, uncontrolled thoughts which dominate, confuse, and frighten the individual from a state where the individual retains some agency and sociality.[1]

Acknowledging madness does not endorse traditional conceptions and classifications of psychosis. Quite the contrary, these will be challenged in the following pages. Syndromes such as schizophrenia and depression are so misconceived and poorly diagnosed that they will be treated as synonymous with madness in general rather than as precise, differentiated categories. Empirical research into these syndromes will be utilized to illustrate relationships between social events, biological processes, and psychosis in general, not to uncover facts about conventionally defined categories of psychosis.

My use of the neutral terms "madness," "psychosis" (affliction of the psyche), "psychological dysfunction," "distress," and "madness" is aimed precisely at avoiding medical and behavioral connotations which permeate the conventional psychiatric language of "mental illness," "psychopathology," and "abnormal psychology." I also seek to avoid such medically-laden terms as patient, and instead refer to "psychologically dysfunctional individuals." It is sometimes difficult to avoid medical terminology because most psychiatric phenomena have traditionally been designated with medical labels and nonmedical language has been preempted. When no suitable alternative is available, the reader should understand that medical terms are used here as neutral synonyms of distress, not as designating biomedical phenomena.

On the other hand, repudiating conventional categorizations and conceptualizations does not negate the reality of psychosis. The task we face is to discover a more truthful and helpful understanding of it.

A main point of sociohistorical psychology is that general psychological features are always embedded in a concrete social context and embody its social character. Psychosis is thus a psychological reaction comprised of particular socially mediated thoughts and feelings which generate specific kinds of uneasiness. Madness is instigated by and concerned with specific social relationships, it is expressed in culturally characteristic ways, and is treatable by culturally appropriate methods and explanations. The hallmark of sociohistorical psychology is emphasizing the concrete social features of psychosis which undergird and permeate the general features. Sociohistorical psychology excavates this social character from its burial beneath abstract generalities which preoccupy psychologists and psychiatrists. Beyond the abstract description of causes of psychosis as lying in stress or poor communication, the abstract categorization of symptoms into depression, delusions, or inappropriate behavior, and abstract therapeutic techniques such as positive reinforcement and encouraging self-expression, the sociohistorical approach reveals the concrete social character of these aspects of psychosis as follows.

Sociohistorical Analysis of Madness

Causes of Madness

Since sociohistorical psychology insists that intrapersonal psychological operations derive from interpersonal relations, psychosis must be grounded in problematical social relations. It is because the social ground has been pulled from beneath the feet of individuals that individuals' thinking is socially disoriented. Devoid of social support, the individual must single-handedly constitute his world, and this effort is unsuccessful and inviable because of its asociality. Devoid of social limits and definition, psychological functions are free-floating, uncontrollable, and overwhelming. The individual has no confidence in being able to communicate his ideas and feelings, and this leads to losing confidence in the ideas and feelings themselves. As Vygotsky so often emphasized, what is not available for the other (socially) is not available for oneself. Mental illness is psychological activity that is culturally unorganized.[2]

Malevolent social relations ultimately derive from broad societal practices. The more prevalent psychosis is, the more it springs from central characteristics of the social system in which people live. A few scattered instances of dis-ease may be due to misfortunes that are incidental to the system, but when large sectors of the population suffer, something basic to the society is at work. According to latest estimates from the National Institute of Mental Health, one-third of the American population suffers from a serious psychological dysfunction (including substance abuse which afflicts 10% of the population) during their lifetime (Regier et al., 1988, Table 4). Such an incidence cannot be chiefly due to accidental misfortunes or individual weaknesses; it must primarily stem from systemic social practices which impact on individuals with debilitating effect. These practices vitiate the psychological functioning that depends on humane sociality (cf. Chapter 1).

Destructive social practices confuse, depersonalize, neglect, and frighten people, deprive them of necessary support and stability, call into question the veracity of their actions and perceptions, place them in contradictory, untenable positions, coerce them into unwanted activities, vitiate their self-confidence, and interfere with their powers of ratiocination.

Destructive social pressures foster psychosis in two ways. Firstly, caretakers fail to address their children's *psychobiological needs* by withholding recognition of their personhood, ignoring their imploring cries, failing to maintain consistent feeding schedules, placing untenable demands upon youngsters, obliquely responding to their communications, lying about their own intentions, and impugning the motives of their children. This invalidation has been vividly described by Laing, Lidz, Bateson, and Henry Massie (cf. Massie & Rosenthal, 1984).

Destructive social pressures also engender psychosis by violating *culturally derived needs* such as the need in our society for material and occupational advancement, individual autonomy and privacy, leisure time, popularity, and intimate personal relationships. Such violation occurs during childhood but also afflicts adults in the course of activities outside the family, such as work. This violation of culturally derived needs is as threatening to one's sense of reality and selfhood as the childhood violation of general psychobiological needs is. The reason, derived from Vygotskian principles, is that adults' sense of self and reality exists in and through socially defined needs. The general need of infants for any kind of support, attention, validation, or accomplishment becomes concretized into socially defined needs for particular kinds of support, attention, validation and accomplishment. Whereas infants are satisfied by any form of these, adults are only satisfied by particular forms. Frustrating these social needs disrupts psychological functioning just as dishonoring children's general psychobiological needs precludes psychological functioning from developing in the first place.

A full appreciation of the social causes of psychosis requires recognizing that violations of psychobiological and cultural needs all ultimately spring from prevalent societal practices. As Henry said, psychosis is the final outcome of all that is wrong with society (J. Henry, 1963, p. 322; Furst, 1954, pp. 129, 138). Normally, debilitating practices are mitigated by beneficent ones. As a result, most people have debilitating neuroses, or socially patterned defects, which are not too severe because of the support rendered by their positive experiences. Some fortunate individuals will have mostly positive experiences and suffer few social psychological disturbances. Less fortunate individuals will encounter mostly debilitating practices and will become psychotic. As destructive social practices become more pervasive, they will affect more people and generate more psychosis. Conversely, as humane practices expand, psychological well being will increase.

Debilitating social practices are of two types. One kind consists of particular, anomalous, disruptive events such as war, unemployment, divorce, and immigration into a foreign society. A second type of debilitating social practice is ongoing, normative behaviors such as destructive competition, alienated working conditions, poverty, and discrimination. The first sort of events has received greater documentation than the second.

Anomalous Disruptive Events. Immigration. In an interesting documentation of the disruptive effects of immigration, H.B.M. Murphy (1968, 1972) studied eight different immigrant groups in Canada. In all eight (Russian Ukrainians, Dutch, Polish, Eskimos, British, Germans, French, and Minor Europeans), Catholic males had a higher rate of mental hospital admissions diagnosed as schizophrenic than Protestant males. In accounting for this consistent cultural effect Murphy quickly discounts the possibility that Catholics are simply more prone to accept hospitalization than Protestants. Quite the opposite, Catholics are less ready to seek psychiatric help than Protestants, according to other studies. Given this reluctance, the actual incidence of psychosis among Catholics vis-à-vis Protestants is possibly even greater than Murphy reports. Murphy also rules out any genetic explanation for the Catholic-Protestant difference in psychosis. He correctly points out that there is no known or even likely genetic difference between Catholics and Protestants in eight disparate nationalities that could explain the consistent difference in psychosis.

On the other hand, all the Catholics share a common religious culture which is consistently different from that shared by all the Protestants. And, most crucial is the fact that the Catholic culture clashes more with Canadian social practices than Protestantism does. As Max Weber observed, Catholicism stresses communality, obedience, and spiritual purity, while Protestantism is more individualistic and materialistic. Catholics would therefore be expected to experience more debilitating conflict with Canadian social practices than Protestants. This greater cultural shock suffered by Catholics—which upsets the trusted social underpinning of their values, possibility of success, personal interactions, self-expression, and self-confidence—plausibly accounts for their relatively greater incidence of psychosis.[3]

Unemployment. The impact of unemployment on psychosis has been carefully studied by M. Harvey Brenner in his pathbreaking work, *Mental Illness and the Economy* (1973). Brenner found that over 127 years, from 1840-1967, a strong positive correlation exists between unemployment and admissions to mental hospitals. For most of those years, the correlation was an astounding 0.80!

Brenner's data has been replicated by other researchers. In a review of this literature Liem (1981) argues that despite the correlational nature of the studies, the causal impact of unemployment on psychosis can be inferred. Any other relationship between the two seems unlikely. It is inconceivable that a small population of mental hospital admittees could cause a significant decline in employment levels. Moreover, an upturn in mental hospital admissions typically follows, rather than precedes, a downturn in the economy. The possibility of a third factor causing the correlation between unemployment and hospital admission rates is also remote: The high correlation is persistent over such a long period of time that it transcends the ebb and flow of other events. For example, war might conceivably produce unemployment and psychosis, thereby accounting for the correlation between them; however, this is negated by the fact that the high correlation persists in peacetime.

Another objection to inferring the effect of unemployment on psychosis is the incomplete picture that hospital admissions give of mental illness prevalence. Hospital admissions account for only a small fraction of the mentally ill—in fact it is estimated that all American mental health practitioners together (including private psychiatrists and psychologists as well as those in institutional settings) only see about 20% of psychiatric disorders, in a country possessing one of the highest psychiatrist to population ratios—which makes hospital admissions a poor, and potentially biased indicator. It may be the case that unemployment impoverishes people so they send their psychotic friends and relatives to mental hospitals rather than care for them at home. If this were true, psychosis would not have increased despite the increase in mental hospital admissions.

However, this cannot be the whole story because outpatient psychiatric admissions also increase with unemployment. Outpatient status would not relieve families of caring for their psychotic relatives. Furthermore, admissions to expensive private mental hospitals increase during economic downturns. Evidently, the relatives of these patients are not admitting them in order to save money, but rather because they have developed serious symptoms.

One can never entirely rule out the possibility that the association between unemployment and psychosis is due to spurious sources. However, Brenner's (1973, pp. 178-201) refutation of many such possibilities heightens confidence in his statement that "adverse economic changes usually bring about severe social and personality disorganization for a considerable number of persons in the society" (p. 201).

Evidence from other researchers supports a causal relation of unemployment on psychological disorder (Jahoda, 1982). Banks and Jackson (1982) designed a telling longitudinal experiment which investigated the mental health of high school children, some of whom found employment after leaving school and some of whom remained unemployed. The two groups had similar scores on a mental health inventory while in school; however the group that found work manifested an improvement in mental health, while the group that went unemployed evidenced increased psychiatric distress.

Linn et al. (1985) arrived at the same conclusion on the basis of their prospective study which compared the psychiatric status of employed and unemployed men. Unemployment produced significant psychological dysfunction in men who, before they lost their job had no evidence of disturbance. While working, these men had the same level of mental health as other employed men. However, after suffering unemployment, their mental health deteriorated in comparison to those men who continued working. In the Linn et al. and Banks and Jackson experiments, pre-unemployment psychiatric status does not explain job loss. Psychological dysfunction only appears after job loss which proves the causal impact that employment and unemployment have on mental health.[4]

Numerous studies have documented the way in which unemployment contributes to psychosis. Since work in our bourgeois society is so central to success, social contact, security, self-esteem, and the organization of many life activities, unemployment ravages the cultural foundation of these and produces reduced social contact, generalized anxiety, suspiciousness, disorganization of life activities, and low self-esteem. It is not surprising that 62% of subjects experiencing a demotion or job loss experience clinically significant psychiatric distress, in contrast to 22% of those in stable work situations (Liem, 1981, p. 67).

Of course, despite the tremendous influence of unemployment on psychological dis-ease, its impact is not inevitable. The malevolent effect derives from the total social context in which it stands, including the social needs which it violates. With different needs and alternative sources of satisfaction and security, unemployment (and certain other malevolent events) would lose its traumatic quality. Even within our present society, diverse sectors of the social system may mediate unemployment. These mediating social relations include family relations, union benefits, the presence of crisis intervention agencies, community support organizations, job prospects within the individual's geographical and occupation areas, and the individual's personal history and coping mechanisms (Gore, 1978). For instance, Brown and Harris (1978) found that among women suffering a serious loss (including loss of a job, a relative, or a friend) 41% became clinically depressed if they had no intimate relationships, but only 10% became depressed if they had intimate friendships (Brown & Harris, p. 177).[5] In other words, society is heterogeneous, composed of diverse and contradictory segments. This social dynamic accounts for variable effects that any one sector has on individuals.

The relation of mediating events to unemployment can be framed according to Bronfenbrenner's model. Figure 6 depicts this.

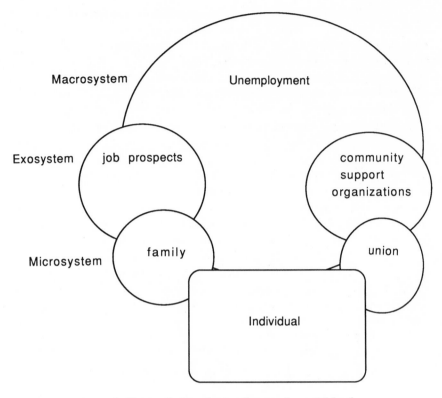

Figure 6. The mediation of unemployment by social levels.

Figure 6 highlights three points of general importance. First of all, mediations of the macroscopic level both reflect and refract it. The family, for example, reflects macroscopic societal characteristics; however, it does so through its unique position and function. The societal practices which are filtered through the family thus take on distinctive features and these latter qualities contradict the activities practiced at the macroscopic level. Heterogeneity, contradiction, and change are endemic to the social system.

A second aspect of the figure is the mutual interpenetration of all of the social levels. While lower levels mediate higher ones, the converse is equally true. For instance, macroscopic events, such as one's employment status or income, affect family relations. Family difficulties are easier to tolerate and resolve with a high income than in poverty. This makes divorce less inevitable among the upper class than among the poor.

Finally, the position that social levels occupy in Figure 6 reflect their relative power. Macro-level influences are the strongest and most pervasive, while individual action has the least power. The family has some ability to compensate for the debilitating effects of unemployment, for example; however, this ability is qualified. The family and the individual garner their ability to compensate the harmful effects of unemployment by utilizing positive practices and policies of the macrosystem. If the macrosystem has numerous destructive aspects, the positive resources will wane, leaving the family and individual with little recourse. The negative macrosystem features will increasingly destabilize and corrupt the lower levels, diminishing their oppositional power.

Family relations and friendships are part of social systems, they are not independent phenomena. Their protective capability depends upon the humaneness of the system, and it wanes under alienating pressures. For example, the stress of unemployment often causes so much family friction that support from the spouse deteriorates. This finding has led Atkinson et al. (1986) to question the whole notion of family as a buffer against stress. The same doubts can be aimed at government agencies, unions, and religious groups.

Of course, the lower levels always stand in some degree of contradiction to the macrosystem and vary its impact on individuals. Not everyone who occupies a given position in the macrosystem will be uniformly affected by it because their exo- and microsystems will differ. However, the unity of this differentiated system remains an importunate fact. Brown and Harris (1978, pp. 182-3) have documented the fact that protective mediations are class-related and consequently reflect the macrosystem. Intimate relationships, family coherence, and the presence of one and two parents during childhood are all more common in the middle class than the lower class. Whereas 70% of lower-class women reported intimate friendships, 85% of middle-class women did; and whereas 11% of lower-class women had lost their mothers before age 11, only 6% of middle-class women had.

Even a sense of control over one's life, which mediates hardship by giving individuals courage and confidence to overcome difficulties, is socially distributed, being more characteristic of the middle and upper class than the lower class. Ross and Mirowsky (1989) conclude that this social distribution in the perception of control is an important factor in the social distribution of depression. They contend that depression is more prevalent among lower-class individuals because they lack a sense of being in control of their lives. Conversely, the sense of control that middle and upper class individuals have forestalls depression in the face of adversity.

In conclusion, the very system that disproportionally generates socioeconomic hardship among the poor also provides fewer social psychological means for coping with that hardship. Conversely, the middle class experiences less socioeconomic hardship and has more social psychological means for coping. The middle class has more means for coping with less hardship while the lower class has fewer means for coping with more hardship. Individuals of low socioeconomic status develop more symptoms of psychological distress to serious, undesirable life events than middle-class individuals do (McLeod & Kessler, 1990; Williams, 1990). As individual options for coping with the system close, the need for altering the system itself intensifies.

Normative, Enduring Social Situations. Normative, enduring pressures associated with work, gender roles, socioeconomic class, ethnicity, social isolation, ruthless competition, callous individualism and profit maximization are as deleterious to mental health as anomalous, acute disruptions. The debilitating psychological effects of these enduring social influences is described in sociological and historical research but is rarely mentioned in psychological circles. A sampling of this material for the psychologically oriented reader is therefore quite warranted.

Gender Role. Feminist analyses of Victorian times have illuminated how women's gender role contributed to hysteria. Exemplifying this genre, Carroll Smith-Rosenberg (1972) argues that middle-class women's role was unbearably contradictory. On the one hand, women were required to be dependent, diffident, childlike, ethereal, and pure; however, this was contradicted by the demands of being an efficient, self-reliant homemaker and mother. The first set of requirements left women unprepared to accomplish the second set, while successfully accomplishing the second set led to guilty feelings about failing to live up to the first set. In addition, women felt great frustration over the disparity in opportunities they were afforded vis-à-vis men, especially in a society which proclaimed equal opportunity and heavily emphasized self-fulfillment and advancement. We shall discuss later on how the frustration of women's social needs and desires culminated in hysterical symptoms. For the moment we shall update Rosenberg's conclusions with contemporary findings that link gender role to psychological distress.

One such finding is that gender roles concerning marital status have definite consequences for psychological well being and distress. A higher percentage of married women are psychotic than are married men. But a higher percentage of unmarried men (including never married, divorced, and widowed men) are psychotic than are women (Gove, 1979). Gove's explanation is that women experience more difficulties in the marital social relationship than men do, whereas men experience more difficulties in being unmarried than do women.

Fox (1980) has disputed these findings on the basis that they only reflect treated cases of psychosis—cases brought to the attention of psychiatric authorities. Reviewing data on untreated cases (living at home, unseen at professional health care institutions), Fox concludes that women are more mentally disturbed than men across all marital statuses. This suggests that female gender roles are generally more stressful than male roles, and that the stress is not mitigated by any particular marital status. However, Gove's data did include community surveys of untreated cases (Gove & Tudor, 1977, p. 1329) which makes their conclusion sounder than Fox recognizes. Gove (1984) recognizes that the overall prevalence of mental illness is greater among women than men, however, he insists that particular marital statuses reverse this ratio.

Dohrenwend and Dohrenwend (1977) challenge Gove's conclusion from another direction: they dispute any gender difference in the prevalence of mental illness, claiming that Gove's conclusion rests upon faulty evidence and a restricted definition of mental illness. The Dohrenwends argue that women's greater prevalence rates are artifacts that reflect: (1) Women's willingness to seek and receive treatment, (2) their tendency to articulate psychological problems more readily than men, and (3) the tendency of health professionals to label women as more psychotic than men. Gove (1984), however cites data that refute these three contentions, and he insists that the overall greater prevalence of mental illness among women is real and due to the greater difficulty of many women's roles.

Sociohistorical psychology, it should be noted, is theoretically neutral on this point which is purely an empirical question. Sociohistorical psychology simply maintains that psychosis is engendered by destructive social pressures, leaving the designation and comparison of these pressures to empirical research. That both gender roles incorporate disturbing tendencies is undeniable; whether one role is more disturbing than the other is open to investigation. Of course, any deleterious aspects of gender role are particular to given societies, they are not intrinsic problems. The gender distribution of psychosis is reversed under conditions that make male roles more adverse than female. For instance, psychiatric surveys in rural Ghana and Nigeria find that men have higher rates of mental illness than females (Ember, 1981, p. 569).

According to Gove, the impact of gender on psychosis is not only mediated by marital status, but by childhood roles as well. The ratio of female to male psychosis (that is, the percentage of females who are psychotic divided by the percentage of males who are psychotic) parallels age-related gender roles. Whereas young boys suffer from psychosis more than girls, the reverse is true among teenagers, as the following comparison shows (Gove, 1979, pp. 35ff):

Age	Female/male ratio
5-9	0.41
10-14	0.87
15-19	1.21

Gove maintains that the reversal in psychosis rates stems from changing pressures associated with gender roles. The greater protection afforded young girls than boys plausibly accounts for the lower female rate among 5-9-year-olds. This protection would make independence difficult to negotiate at adolescence, resulting in a higher rate of female psychosis at that time. Certainly no known biological changes could produce the psychological pattern described in the above table.

Gender-linked variations in incidence of schizophrenia exist throughout the life span. The incidence of schizophrenia for white men aged 15-24 years is almost three times that of white women of the same age. After 34 years of age, the rates are identical for white men and women. These gender patterns do not hold for nonwhites, however. Nonwhite women, 25-34 years old have a higher incidence of schizophrenia than men; however, from 35 to 60 years nonwhite men have the higher rate (Warner, 1985, p. 231). Ethnicity interacts with gender role to influence the rate of madness.

Poverty. In addition to certain gender roles, another social influence that contributes to psychosis is poverty. The disproportionally large number of lower-class mental problems has been extensively documented in numerous sociological studies. Hollingshead and Redlich (1953, 1954, 1958), Dohrenwend (1975), Srole (1962, 1975), Ortega and Rushing, (1983, p. 148), and others have reported that the percentage of mental patients in the poorest one-fifth of the population is up to 40 times that of the upper one-fifth.

It is well known that some of this research on the sociology of mental illness is methodologically flawed.[6] Hollingshead and Redlich's studies are flawed by the use of hospital admissions to measure the incidence of psychosis. Hospital admissions are not only incomplete indicators of mental illness, they are also heavily skewed toward the lower-class which would practically guarantee a higher incidence of recorded psychosis among the poor.

Another flaw is the biased interpretation that almost inevitably intrudes when middle-class psychiatrists diagnose lower-class patients. Doctors' unfamiliarity with poor peoples' manners makes them appear strange, and this can easily lead to handing out more severe diagnoses than those given to more kindred middle-class patients. Redlich, Hollingshead, and Bellis (1960) report that psychiatrists are far less understanding of lower-class psychiatric problems than they are of middle-class problems. Moreover, psychiatrists liked 62% of their middle-class patients in contrast to only 17% of their lower-class patients. And they disliked 50% of their lower-class patients in contrast to only disliking 23% of the middle-class clients (cf., Loring & Powell, 1988, for additional instances of class- and gender-related diagnostic distortion).[7]

These methodological weaknesses are overcome in studies which investigate the "true prevalence" of psychosis in the nonhospitalized population. These studies, such as Srole's and Dohrenwend's, request community members at large to rate themselves on psychiatric measures and life events.[8]

Self-ratings are, of course, open to another potential problem, that of response bias—according to which, lower-class individuals, for example, may simply feel more comfortable reporting symptoms than middle-class individuals. However, Gove and Geerken's (1977) careful investigation revealed little response bias effect in self reports of symptoms. The fact that these improved investigations find an overrepresentation of psychosis in lower-class patients testifies to the veracity of the phenomenon. Srole et al. (p. 230), for example, found nearly four times as much impairment in the lowest as the highest socioeconomic stratum in New York City: 47% as compared to 13%. In their investigation of nonhospitalized community women, Brown and Harris (1978, p. 151) similarly found 25% of working class married women were clinically depressed in contrast to only 5% of middle-class married women. Schwab et al.'s (1979) community survey in Florida found 35% of lower-class respondents to be psychiatrically impaired, in contrast to 5% of upper class respondents (p. 93). Most recently, Dohrenwend (1990) reports several community studies on the true prevalence of schizophrenia, depression, antisocial personality, and substance abuse which all found an inverse relationship with socioeconomic status.

The reason for this overrepresentation of psychosis among the poor is that they experience far more disruptive, undesirable events than middle-class people do (Myers et al. 1974). Lower-class people are also less skilled at coping with these events than middle-class individuals are (Kessler, 1979; Wheaton, 1980; McLeod & Kessler, 1990). Where opportunity, success, security, knowledge, and self-confidence are utterly linked to social class, individuals in the lower class will necessarily be deprived of psychological as well as material resources.

Once lower-class people have the opportunity to become upwardly mobile, their incidence of mental disturbance decreases. Thus, as each successive immigrant group occupied the impoverished ghettos of our central cities, that particular group had the highest rates of mental retardation and mental disturbance. As each group climbed into the middle-class world, their rates of distress declined to match their middle-class counterparts while the new arrivals in the slums showed excessively high rates. At first there were the Irish, then the Scandinavians, then the Eastern European Jews, and then the Southern Italians (Albee & Gullotta, 1986, p. 211; Dohrenwend, 1975, p. 374). Conversely, as middle-class individuals slide downward into poverty, their psychological disturbances, suicide rate, and drug and alcohol consumption increase. Evidently, powerlessness is a cause of distress and a redistribution of power may be preventive.

The power of lower-class life to generate deviant behavior may be judged from the fact that its impact is even stronger than parental psychopathology. Investigating the relative importance of various risk factors for schizophrenia in children, Sameroff, Seifer, and Barocas (1983) found that parental social status was a more powerful risk factor than the presence of schizophrenic parents. In other words, poor families appear to be at even greater risk than families with maternal mental illness.

Of course, this conclusion concerning the causal influence of poverty on psychosis is disputed by the social drift theory. That hypothesis claims that psychosis develops for any number of reasons and that psychosis causes maladaptive behaviors which send individuals plummeting down the social hierarchy. Thus, psychosis contributes to poverty rather than the other way around. However, the social drift theory has been discredited. Most lower-class psychotics originate in that stratum, they do not drift there from higher levels. The Midtown Manhattan study found a negative correlation between the degree of patients' mental disturbance and their *parents'* socioeconomic status. Since the parents of psychotic patients are poor, the patients obviously did not drift down from a higher social class (Dohrenwend & Dohrenwend, 1974; Dohrenwend, 1975; cf. also, Wheaton, 1978).

Some decline in social position following a psychotic breakdown would hardly be surprising. However, the fact that most psychosis occurs among people who are already in the lower class reflects the debilitating effects of relative poverty on psychological well being. These debilitating effects are demonstrated in the fact that over a three year period from 1970-1973, lower-class individuals suffered a greater deterioration in their psychological functioning than upper class individuals did (Schwab et al., 1979, p. 187). Conversely, upper class cases are twice as likely to improve as lower-class cases. Whereas only 5% of poor psychiatric cases became normal after three years, 11% of wealthy cases did so.

Socioeconomic Practices. Although the foregoing demographic studies demonstrate the social distribution of madness, they do not illuminate the process by which social events engender psychological dysfunction. The weakness is corrected by Jules Henry's important research on the deleterious effects of normative socioeconomic practices such as intense competition, individualism, and materialism. Henry's book *Culture Against Man* (1963, Chap. 9) is a unique analysis of the manner in which normative macroscopic practices underlie parental mistreatment of children.

Employing participant observer methodology, Henry lived with disturbed families, recorded their intimate interactions, and showed how these interactions reflect the central practices and values of American society. In one scenario, a mother spent 20 minutes vacuuming a rug while her distressed daughter cried painfully. When the mother finished her housework she finally approached the girl and said to her, "Okay, you're the winner." Henry's analysis is that the mother engaged in a competitive struggle with her daughter over the time and effort she will offer to her. The less she spends on her daughter, the more she has for herself, and, conversely, spending time and energy is tantamount to losing a commodity she values for herself. The mother says quite plainly that her attending to the daughter is a victory by the girl. The mother thus introduces a central American practice, competition, into her family relationship where it has deleterious effects upon the psychological well being of her daughter.

In addition, prioritizing the cleanliness of the rug over her daughter's needs is an extreme form of materialism which is also central to the broader society. The mother's excluding personal considerations (for example, her daughter's needs) from her housework reflects yet another social practice, namely the segmenting of work and personal issues. Finally, leaving the baby to cry by herself was believed to teach independence and toughness, another core social value.

The mother's insensitivity to her daughter in this one situation thus rests upon the conjoint presence of several predominant social practices. In contrast to most families which have managed to mitigate these social practices in their homes, Henry's families have relied heavily upon these practices in dealing with their children. It is not surprising that the adverse psychological effects that these practices have in the public domain (cf. Kohn, 1986) will be manifested in the families they pervade. To the extent that these practices dominate family relations they will erode the family's ability to moderate their effects in the public sphere.

Henry identifies other disturbing parent-child interactions which reflect debilitating societal practices. A mother who drives her son to distraction by constantly shifting his feeding schedules reflects impulsiveness

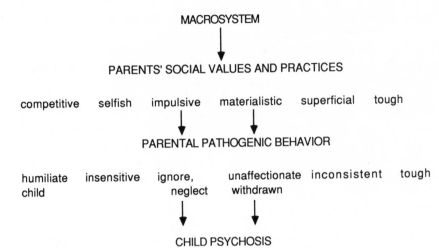

Figure 7. Societal practices which underlie pathogenic family interactions.

and egocentrism that are mainstays of the contemporary American socioeconomic system. A father's exaggerated toughness with his son, which results in physical pain as well as emotional distance, reflects a pervasive masculine norm. Force-feeding a child and shifting time schedules is motivated by the socially sanctioned desire to economize on time. A mother's stoic indifference toward her child who frantically tries to escape from a fearful haircut is motivated by a concern for his appearance that predominates consideration of his personhood—which is another typical attitude internalized from the society at large.

Henry's tracing of children's psychological disturbance to their parents' mistreatment and beyond this to parents' socially derived values and practices can be depicted in Figure 7.

Figure 7 highlights the fact that parental insensitivity to and neglect of their children have a concrete social character. In keeping with the central tenets of sociohistorical psychology, parents are insensitive, unsupportive, communicate poorly, misperceive, and behave inappropriately in definite circumstances, in definite manners, and for reasons that stem from definite social values and practices. It is because caretakers have these values that they mistreat their children. As long as parents believe and engage in these practices, they will mistreat their children, despite their best intentions to the contrary.

The reason that certain parents rely on these destructive behaviors more than others undoubtedly includes complex personal experiences.

However, the central importance and pervasiveness of these practices to society makes them increasingly available and respectable as normative models, and makes their increasing intrusion into the family inevitable. Parents' pathogenic behavior is not simply a personal or family weakness. It must not only be traced back "horizontally" to prior generations of the individual's family, it must also be traced "vertically" to other levels of the society. Illuminating the broader society which the parents reflect provides a social grounding for the parents' behavior which less complete social analyses omit. Such an omission leaves parents' behavior unexplained and it opens the door to accidental, personal, and biological explanations. Henry's explanation of parental mistreatment in terms of pervasive societal values has another virtue of explaining the prevalence of madness throughout all sectors of society. Other social explanations which highlight poverty and unemployment as important factors do not touch on the causes of psychosis among the middle and upper classes. Henry's analysis fills this gap.

Societal practices form a medium which motivates a variety of parental abuses. There is no inexorable connection between a given parental mistreatment of children and any one societal value or practice. Each social practice has variable, broad effects, just as each mistreatment has numerous social bases. Competition can lead to neglecting children, humiliating them, and treating them roughly. Conversely, parental insensitivity can derive from selfishness, materialism, or competition. As we know from earlier chapters, social influences do not act singly or mechanically. They form a context from which individuals draw in constructing their life-styles. Parents creatively combine destructive social practices in new ways and concretize them into novel forms. However, the social character that pervades these incarnations is unmistakable if one takes the trouble to look for it.

Psychiatric Practices. Any discussion of the social causes of psychosis in our society would be remiss if it overlooked the role that psychiatric practice plays in compounding psychological stress. Although psychiatry's ostensible purpose is to mitigate madness, many critics have eloquently argued that practice contradicts this lofty goal. Laing, Scheff, Sarbin, Szasz, and Goffman have all described ways in which psychiatry's medical model serves to invalidate disturbed individuals (and purportedly disturbed, but actually normal, persons as well, cf. Rosenhan, 1973).

One invalidation procedure is to construe psychosis as the victim's fault (by virtue of his psychobiological defects) and as utterly nonsensical (disconnected from reality). This assumption intensifies the victtim's distress by further undermining his already weak self-confidence, grasp of reality, and faith in interpersonal communication. Casting him into a sick role compounds the debilitation that resulted from other social sources. Several studies have found that individuals who accept the sick role suffer more prolonged and intense debilitation than individuals who reject it. Because we shall explore this medical model later on, we will not dwell on it here. For now we simply wish to call attention to the fact that psychiatric theory and practice emanates from, embodies, legitimates, and promulgates, the dominant socioeconomic system (Kleinman, 1980, p. 44), and this is why it compounds rather than ameliorates the system's other distressing pressures.

The macrosystem, then, is at the heart of all socially significant pathogenic pressures. These pressures include enduring, pervasive, normative practices; abrupt, circumscribed, traumatic events; and the health system that reinforces psychosis. These pressures may work independently or in combination to generate psychosis. That chronic destructive practices are capable of engendering psychosis is clear from many cases marked by the absence of any precipitating event such as unemployment or immigration.

On the other hand, acute events can precipitate psychosis in the absence of severe distress caused by the central, pervasive practices. As Dohrenwend (1975, p. 386) concluded from a review of the literature, "environmentally induced stress is a sufficient condition for a wide range of psychopathology." Unemployment, for instance, can overwhelm quite "normal" individuals, shatter their self-esteem and produce extreme anxiety about material survival. Of course, where the two sets of factors act in concert, their effects will be compounded. And this effect will be further aggravated if the distressed victims are treated under the framework of a reifying medical model.

Certainly, psychosis can arise from the first two kinds of social pressures in the absence of psychiatric reification. Psychosis is not entirely a product of the psychiatrists' diagnosis and it would not disappear with the abolition of psychiatry. Historically and today, many individuals are psychotic who have not been exposed to invalidating psychiatric treatment. While the power of psychiatry is formidable, it is so because of its role as handmaiden to the larger society. Possessing only derived power, psychiatry only represents and reinforces debilitating social pressures, it does not replace them.[9]

Different causes of psychosis generate distinctive psychological problems. Children treated mechanically and callously by their parents will suffer differently from children whose parents manipulate or frighten them. Children who have been terrorized into fearing spirits if taboos are violated have different worries from children whose parents surreptitiously manipulate their affections. And these problems are dissimilar from the frustrations that immigrants face in a foreign culture. Of course, different social systems may contain similar disturbing elements. Middle-class women in ancient Greece were subjected to many of the contradictory role requirements that frustrated nineteenth century European and American women. This accounts for the common occurrence of hysteria in the two societies (Simon, 1978, Chap. 13). Similarly, the Ojibwa Indians are like contemporary Americans in being a highly individualistic people strongly motivated by personal success. The Ojibwas place the same kind of stress on successful hunting that Americans place on obtaining a job. Accordingly, individual economic failure plunges males of both cultures into severe psychosis (which would not occur in cooperative societies that support the individual at critical times).

However, as we know from Chapters 2 and 3, social psychological commonalities will be shot through with differences that attend the two societies. Although individual elements may be problematical in both cultures, the overall configuration of elements in which they exist, and to which they are internally related, differ. The overall problematic that constitutes the kernel of Ojibwa *wiitiko* psychosis includes intense anxiety over starvation, extreme deprivation of social succorance in order to foster self-reliance, extreme toughening of children to endure limited food supplies (which includes fasting for two meals per day every other day throughout the winter months), intense personal isolation of men during hunting (which activity commences at twelve years of age), self-effacement in deference to supernatural spirits, and the repression of hostility. The distinctiveness of this problematic is evidenced in the peculiar symptoms that ensue, namely a delusional possession by a *"wiitiko* monster"* which eventuates in homicidal cannibalism (Parker, 1960).

The differences among social causes of psychosis are easily obscured by the striking formal uniformities in psychotic breakdowns. The strangeness of psychotic thought processes—e.g., the disorientation, bizarre delusions, collapse of self-concept, rupture in sociality, and other general characteristics of psychosis that have been described above—are so astonishing as to divert attention from the concrete, differentiating details in content. Nevertheless, psychotics are upset by particular social and psychological events. As Opler (1969, p. 102) said, while disorders are maladaptive to the human condition in general as well as to the cultural contexts represented, they are traceable to specific kinds of cultural stress systems. These particularities must be understood and overcome if the psychotic disturbances are to be comprehended and mitigated.

Symptoms

Symptoms are the forms in which psychological problems are expressed. The problem of concern over unemployment may be expressed in various symptoms such as depression, violence, delusions, paranoia, drug or alcohol addiction. Symptoms are therefore the individual's response to, or way of coping with, a psychological problem. This difference corresponds to Kleinman's (1980, pp. 71-80) distinction between disease and illness: disease is what happens to the person as a result of pathogenic conditions; illness is the manner in which the individual evaluates and affectively responds to disease. Kleinman intends his distinction to apply to physical and psychological disturbances although he recognizes important differences between the two. With physical problems, the disease is physical although illness is socially and psychologically constructed. With psychological problems, disease and illness are both social psychological phenomena. In Kleinman's words, psychosocial and cultural factors are the stuff of the disease itself, and in illness they are the behavioral and societal response to the disease that provide it with meaning (p. 78).[10]

Cultural Variations. Symptoms are the outcome of individuals' attempts at understanding the source of their distress, giving meaning to the distress experience itself, defining their identities in the face of self-doubt, and responding to (coping with) their distress. Far from symptoms being meaningless flights of fancy by a diseased brain, they are grounded in social reality and actively attempt to comprehend and order reality. The general process by which individuals construct symptoms parallels the manner in which people normally try to define the world and themselves. Of course, this process suffers obvious degradation in psychosis but madness is as meaningful (meaning-giving) as normalcy.

Since all meaning is grounded in social values and practices, psychotic symptoms are socially intelligible. Describing the incorporation of social values into psychological coping mechanisms, Joseph Furst (1954, pp. 137-8) states, "All of his types of behavior, in one form or another, reflect the types of experience that the child has undergone in our socioeconomic system. He takes up some of these, and with his individual modifications, erects them into his own style of acting and thinking . . . In this way the exploitative practices and conditions of our economic system find their individual reflection in the thinking and behavior of children." "Psychodynamics, for all its complexity, can only be understood as the reflection of the real life situations and activities which

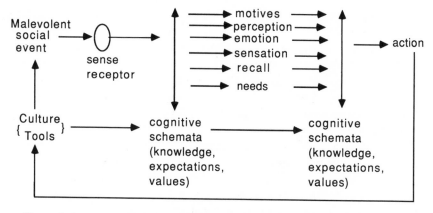

Figure 8. Cognitive schemata, derived from society and technology, as mediations between malevolent social events, psychological functions, and action.

people must engage upon, due to the specific conditions of their social, economic and political circumstances."

This account of psychological symptoms fits well within our sociohistorical model as illustrated in Figure 8.

The diagram shows that disturbances in sensation, perception and emotion, i.e., depression, delusions, hallucinations, and somatic symptoms, are constituted by cognitive mediations which derive from the social system. The fact that psychological dysfunction follows the same model as normal functioning (compare Figure 8 with Figure 3) means that the sociohistorical model encompasses both within the same consistent principles. Let us illustrate the cultural-cognitive patterning of symptoms with several examples.

Depression is a particularly good example of Figure 8. As in the case of all affect, social concepts account for the existence and quality of depression. If one considers the situations that trigger depression—loss of a loved one, failure to get a job or pass a course, despondency over an intolerable condition—it is evident that depression depends upon the unavailability of something that is highly valued. Different expectations would eliminate depression. If, for example, one was a Buddhist who believed that loss was inevitable and natural, then loss would be taken in stride rather than lead to depression. In fact, to a Buddhist, loss and suffering are construed as signs of salvation and therefore lead to a certain happiness and contentment rather than depression. This worldview actually associates success with sadness in contradistinction to our association of success with pleasure (Kleinman & Good, 1985, chaps. 2, 4).

Whereas sadness is undoubtedly universal, it only becomes intensified into depression under the aegis of appropriate social concepts. This social cognitive model of affective disorders has received considerable support from Kleinman's theoretical and empirical work. In his words, "By molding how we perceive, interpret, and react to external and internal stimuli, culture contributes to the genesis of affective disease like anxiety neurosis, depressive syndrome, and affective psychosis, as well as to normal affective experience" (Kleinman, 1980, p. 171). Accordingly, "affective disorders are really disorders of cognition . . . [That is,] affects are *cognized before* they take on the form of perceived, felt, labeled, and valuated experiences recognized as emotions" (Kleinman, 1980, p. 171ff.).

Kleinman emphasizes the point that social concepts do not simply moderate some basic, universal depression; they actually constitute depression and account for its existence and particular quality. Cultures lacking appropriate concepts will either experience depression differently from us or not experience it at all. The Kaluli people of New Guinea, for example, blame fate and external events for their failures, are free from inner guilt and low self-esteem, and therefore lack the psychological underpinnings that foster depression. No suicides have occurred since 1900, and only one case of depression was found in a recent investigation (Kleinman & Good, 1985, chap. 3).

Similarly, cultures which lack a psychological orientation to frustration will lack depression. Kleinman has shown that Chinese people generally lack this orientation and instead develop somatic rather than psychological symptoms. Kleinman (1980, pp. 133-144) explains that the centrality of social relationships in China takes precedence over personal desires and expressions. Individuals become preoccupied with the concrete situational context of personal problems rather than with their experiential effects.

This orientation to external causes of problems rather than their psychological effects is promoted through early childhood socialization which discounts individual inclinations and even has a rather impoverished vocabulary for discussing and labeling psychological phenomena. Chinese culture attends quite strongly to individuals' physical distress which threatens the physical integrity of the group. Consequently, Chinese individuals channel distress into physical rather than psychological expressions. Their illness experience involves somatic symptoms, not depression: "they feel in physical imagery in which the affect is inferred. The physical imagery rather than the affect is most real. The idiom makes the experience primarily somatic" (Kleinman, 1980, p. 141). Kleinman adds:

Chinese patients who have told me they are feeling depressed or anxious or frightened, for example, seemingly cannot go beyond naming the feeling. Unlike middle-class Caucasian-American patients with similar disorders, who will often describe the dysphoric affect in considerable detail and relate it to many different aspects of their lives, Chinese patients commonly move directly from naming the affect to the situation they believed caused it or to its somatic and interpersonal concomitants. They appear to lack more refined terminology for what they are feeling. This is not merely a function of suppression or denial, since they were willing to talk·about emotions and personal problems and were frustrated by our mutual difficulties in exploring their disturbed feelings. Indeed, an important aspect of psychotherapy with such patients is teaching them a language to communicate their intrapsychic experiences . . ." (p. 141)

Kleinman (1977) reports that even after extensive interviewing and treatment, 40% of his Chinese patients never admitted to experiencing mental illness. "They looked upon their physical complaints as their 'real' sickness, a *physical* sickness" (p. 5). In another Chinese sample, only 9% experienced depression although most manifested the signs of depression according to the Diagnostic and Statistical Manual (Kleinman & Good, 1985, chap. 13).

Of course, sadness is a universal experience but its eventuation as morbid depression is not. LIke all psychological universals, sadness is indefinite as to specific forms of expression. It therefore does not necessarily culminate in depression. Conversely, specific forms of expression are socially variable which means that depression will not be universal. Certain elements of depression may be widespread; however, their integration into a depressed syndrome—with morbid dejection, self-blame, and retreat from social interaction—is rare outside Western society. As Anthony Marsella has concluded from extensive research:

There appears to be no universal conception of depression. Indeed, many non-Western cultures do not even have a concept of depression that is conceptually equivalent to that held by Western mental health professionals. However, even among those cultures not having conceptually equivalent terms, it is sometimes possible to find variants of depressive disorders similar to those found in Western cultures. But, because the depressive experience is embedded within an entirely different cultural context, it may assume a different meaning and experience and perhaps should not be labeled as depression. (Marsella, 1980, p. 274)

Kleinman (1982, p. 132) supports this conclusion with his statement that, "even if there is an equivalent word for depression or anxiety, these emotions mean and therefore are different experiences in distinctive groups who hold particular views of the self, the body, social relations, normal behavior and illness." Confirmation of this idea is found in Binitie's (1975) study which discovered that depressives in England experienced a great deal of guilt and anxiety which were absent among Nigerian "depressives," however, the Nigerians experienced insomnia and loss of weight to a greater extent than their English counterparts.

Juris Draguns (1974) has discussed the manner in which many other North American and European symptoms rest upon Protestant values of individualism, self-control, rationalism, activism, and introspection. Catholic societies which value communalism, fateful acceptance of destiny and higher authority, manifest quite different symptomology. Whereas American patients tend toward active symptomatology with ideational distortion and elaboration, Catholic Latin patients tend toward passive symptomatology with a suspension of cognitive effort. Americans tend toward obsessional thoughts, intellectualization, guilt, and self-blame, while Latins suffer more somatic complaints, sleeplessness, and obesity. Americans are more lonely and suspicious than Latins, while Latins are more dependent.[11]

In a little-known book, *The Neurotic, His Inner and Outer Worlds,* Joseph Furst (1954) further explores the way in which disturbed thinking incorporates many normative bourgeois concepts and thought processes. His trenchant social analysis pertains to psychotic as well as neurotic symptoms. Furst shows that disturbed coping mechanisms incorporate individualism, competitiveness, superficial and fragmented thinking, over-concern with appearance, estrangement from others, concern with minutiae, and abstract thinking that are predominant in the society. In view of the fact that the disturbed individual has been one-sidedly exposed to the destructive aspects of society, it is not surprising that his consciousness tends to be a one-sided reflection of the life situations that he meets (Furst, p. 150).

For example, a classic strategy employed by schizophrenics and vividly described by Laing (1960) in *The Divided Self* involves the victim attempting to escape an untenable social reality by creating a "true self" apart from a socially presented "false self." Unhinged from reality, this true self exaggerates its own capabilities and attempts to live a fantastic existence. The self detaches from the body in order to avoid social exposure and demands. A hyperconscious meta-self is created which critically examines other people, one's own action and experience. This detached vigilance seeks freedom from threatening social interaction in an inviolate personal domain of private thoughts. From Furst's perspective, this subjective approach to life (Furst, p. 156) reflects a pervasive social philosophy, idealism. For, instead of dealing with realistic problems by the use of realistic measures, the psychotic takes a mental approach. He tries to divorce his thinking, his feelings, and the state of his happiness from the various realities of his situation.

This mentalistic approach is encouraged by Cartesian and Kantian suppositions that reality is unknowable and is a product of mind. It is also fostered by such prevalent cultural doctrines as "happiness and success are attainable by simply wanting them and putting oneself in a 'proper' state of mind," or "economic crises are caused by a lack of confidence on the part of consumers and businessmen." Ignoring objective conditions in favor of subjective attitudes is precisely what psychotic thinking does (Furst, p. 161).

The disembodied schizophrenic self reflects another prominent social value, namely an individualistic notion of freedom. Modern Western society construes freedom entirely in terms of personal choice and social disengagement, and this is precisely what the schizophrenic seeks. The detached self of the schizophrenic exaggerates normal strategies insofar as these are expressed more literally and compulsively than normal (Laing, 1969b; Ratner, 1970).

Rather than being unsocialized as most analysts believe, the schizophrenic is actually hypernormal. Consequently, the inadequacies of social values are more pronounced and debilitating among psychotics than among normals. Where individualism typically breeds loneliness and anxiety in everyday life, it fosters a debilitating sense of self-imprisonment, unreality, futility, and lifelessness in the psychotic: "the self, being transcendent, empty, and omnipotent, free in its own way comes to be anybody in phantasy and nobody in reality" (Laing, 1960, p. 142).

Disturbed thinking is characterized by other conceptual weaknesses, namely its superficial preoccupation with minutiae and its absorption in individual crises while neglecting underlying, unifying problems. This, Furst suggests, reflects another prevalent social philosophy, pragmatism. Pragmatism is a pervasive viewpoint in Western society which glorifies circumscribed, expedient, practical action at the expense of comprehensive understanding (Furst, pp. 162-163).

George Devereaux, another socially oriented psychiatrist, points out other characteristics of madness that are internalized from capitalist society. For instance, withdrawal, aloofness, and hyperactivity are attitudes that are highly valued models in our society and at the same time are characteristic of schizophrenic symptoms. "Impersonality, cold objectivity . . . the inscrutable 'poker face' of the successful diplomat or gambler, 'the great stone face' of the 'deal' administrator—these are nowadays the means by which one wins the admiration of one's fellow man and gets ahead in society" (Devereaux, 1980, p. 222). Segmentalism and partial involvement are also major schizoid traits systematically fostered by our society. "Most transactions in daily life are extremely segmental, implying little or no *total* personal involvement. Business is business and . . . must not be combined with friendship or with love, even if it must sometimes borrow their mask" (Devereaux, p. 224). Finally, depersonalization—the effort of schizophrenics to mask their real thoughts and feelings and to present a "false self" (in Laing's terms) is reinforced by the general culture which demands that

> one should be impersonal, unemotional, reticent, inconspicuous, average, neutral, and the like. All these demands amount in the last resort to saying: "Never mind who and what you really are! Just behave as expected and avoid making yourself conspicuous by being yourself, by being different." . . . Side by side with this loss of a real identity and with the taboo of displaying *real* originality goes the brute commercialization of perfectly nonfunctional and purely external "trademarks": of distinctive "packaging." This is represented by Jayne Mansfield's ample bosom, and even by the senior John D. Rockefeller's proverbial gifts of dimes, or by the famous Eisenhower smile. Similarly, a patient may refuse to discard a preposterously old and battered sweater, cap, or necktie, which he cherishes as his "trademark" precisely because only this (purely external) trademark differentiates him from the other members of the "lonely crowd." He needs a trademark because he has no shreds of a distinctive personality left and no longer has a sense of his own identity. Sometimes he is not even sure that he is real, even to himself. This is not surprising when society systematically depreciates and inhibits the functionally meaningful creative uniqueness of men, when it values only what is nonfunctional: the "trademark," the "packaging," the "image." (Devereaux, pp. 233-234).

Van den Berg (1974) sheds additional light on the social basis of fragmented self-concepts that are so characteristic of schizophrenia. The entire notion of a divided self only emerged in the late nineteenth century in conjunction with multiple, disjunctive social roles. While earlier views recognized distinct functions or components of self such as soul and body, these all revolved around one self. The nineteenth century marked a new conception of different selves or personalities within one individual. Perhaps the classic description of divided self is Robert Louis Stevenson's *Dr. Jekyll and Mr. Hyde* (1886). Dr. Jekyll is a good doctor who, when transformed into Mr. Hyde, acts out evil desires. The conception of multiple selves that arose in William James', Freud's, Janet's, and Bergson's work, as well as in the 60 publications concerning suggestion, hypnosis and the dual self in France from 1885-1887, reflected intensified division of labor in the social structure which resulted in multiple roles. This prevalent social conception is reflected in fragmentations of personality common in psychotic symptomatology.

The very feeling of personal worthlessness (i.e., the "inferiority complex"), which predominates the self-concept of psychotic individuals is a historical construct of recent origin. Previously, individuals felt a sense of sinfulness but not personal inadequacy. The notion of personal worthlessness only arose during the past century, evidently reflect a rising individualistic concern over personal inadequacy which is bred by intense competition (Burnham, 1980; Furst, p. 153). Burnham also points out that the increase of hypochondriacal delusions—ideas of illness and bodily alterations—exactly paralleled increasing popular concern with health and youthfulness, replacing concern with spiritual life.

Rieber and Green (1989) suggest that psychopathic behavior also reflects normative psychopathy of everyday life. While unconcerned with the social concepts and psychological processes that underlie psychopathic behavior, the authors nevertheless lay out the broader social basis of such deviant conduct. In their view, psychopathic antisocial behavior which lacks guilt and grandiose notions of the self's ability, only slightly exaggerates the individualistic, ambitious, competitive, ruthless, anti-social, opportunistic, materialistic ethic that is a mainstay of Western society. Deceitful, illegal, antisocial, and immoral acts are the daily fare of business leaders, advertisers, ministers, and politicians who succumb to the temptation to do whatever it takes to enrich their own coffers. Even when they are indicted and convicted they express little remorse or guilt. Reiber and Green point out the quasi-psychopathic features of Oliver North's psychology which included the pursuit of power, a penchant for risky behavior, "pathological glibness" (where speech distorts conventional meanings), paranoia, dissociation, denial ("I still think it was a neat idea"), and a complete absence of remorse. These attitudes are so pervasive that when guilt is expressed, as in the case of James McFarlane who attempted suicide over lying to Congress, it is regarded as evidence of mental disorder. Normative psychopathy provides a highly visible model for distressed individuals to imitate in their quest for self-definition.

Variations Fashioned from Psychiatric Concepts. In addition to philosophical, psychological, economic, and religious values, a final cultural pool of influences from which psychological symptoms is fashioned is psychiatric concepts about distress. As Good and Good (1981, p. 175) state: "Illness is constructed from popular medical culture, as the sufferer draws upon available theories and networks of meaning to interpret, reinterpret, and communicate a particular experience." Of course, victims are not left to their own devices to assimilate prevailing medical ideology. The professional establishment actively promotes this ideology and imposes it upon unwitting and powerless victims. This is the core of labelling theory which argues that distress is fundamentally due to the labeling of victims as psychiatric patients (Waxler, 1984; Scheff, 1975, 1984). Kleinman explains how this occurs:

Suppose a person feels dull, lacks his usual energy, becomes disinterested in work, recreation, and family, and is unhappy. If he (or his family) begins calling this state "sickness," he will start to feel sick, whereas these nonspecific complaints need not be regarded at all as symptoms of sickness but could be labeled "misfortune" or some other nebulous, general term, or they could be given a specific but nonmedical label, such as a moral, religious, or economic problem. In that case, it is highly probable that the individual will not feel ill, even if these complaints were indeed manifestations of a particular illness. (Here would be an example of a disease without an illness.) On the other hand, over the course of recent history in the West, it has become usual for individuals with the complaints described to label themselves ill— indeed to label themselves, and be labeled by others, with a psychiatric term, "depression." That in turn helps shape the problem . . . In applying the label, the afflicted person and his family make use of the explanatory accounts available to them in a particular cultural, historical, and health care sector context. (Kleinman, 1980, p. 76)

The contrast between somatic symptomatology in China-Taiwan and affective symptomatology characteristic of middle-class Americans is due in large part to the different medical ideologies which inform the formal and informal health care systems of the two countries.

The profound transformation of the self that is so characteristic of Western psychosis may partly reflect the psychological orientation of the mental illness profession. Waxler (1984, pp. 57-58) states that, "where psychiatric illnesses are believed to involve personality change and personal responsibility, the sick person receives many messages that something is seriously wrong with his self; his self-perception and behavior may conform to these messages and his illness may have a long duration." In contrast, Waxler reports that in societies such as Ceylon and Mauritius, where beliefs about mental illness center on supernatural causation, where the person is not held responsible for his illness, and where no one believes the patient is different, psychosis does not produce a radical change in self-concept which persists for long periods and is difficult to alter.

Social Class Variations. The cultural symbols which inform symptoms may be widespread throughout society, in which case the symptoms which embody these images will be randomly distributed across the social system. This is the case in the foregoing examples. But cultural symbols may also be particular to certain social sectors, in which case the symptoms will be concentrated in corresponding social groups. Class and gender role are two prominent subcultural variations in symptomatology.

Social classes within Western society evidence variation in somatization with lower classes expressing stress somatically, in contrast to ideational symptoms more characteristic of middle-class patients (Crandell

& Dohrenwend, 1967, pp. 1537-1538; Saks et al., 1970; Leff, 1977, p. 321; Kleinman & Good, 1985, chap. 13; Kleinman 1982, p. 127; Kleinman, 1980, p. 172). This distinction reflects the occupational differences among classes: middle and upper classes develop ideas and plans whereas lower-class individuals do manual, physical labor. It may well be that as lower-class jobs lose their manual character through automation the somatic model for lower-class psychotic symptoms may recede and the symptoms themselves will reflect new lower-class life styles.

Gender Variations. The pool of images which make up psychotic symptoms is not only cleaved along cultural lines but along gender lines as well. The congruence of symptoms with gender role is revealed in the fact that among the Malay people, *amok* is strictly a male phenomenon, while fright psychosis known as *latah* involves mainly women (Lee, 1981, p. 239; Opler, 1969, p. 102). Fright psychosis in all parts of the world (*susto* in Latin America, *frija* in Yemen, *kesambet* in North Bali) is almost exclusively a female affliction (Swagman, 1989; Wikan, 1989). Ojibwa wiitiko psychosis (obsessive cannibalism) is predominantly a male affliction (Parker, 1960, p. 618). Anorexia nervosa is almost entirely confined to middle- and upper-class Western women, being quite rare among men, non-Western women, and lower-class Western women (Nasser, 1988).

In a detailed analysis, Joan Brumberg (1988, chaps. 5, 7) explains the complex social reasons that Victorian women became anorexic, and her explanation is instructive for a fuller understanding of modern anorexia nervosa. Brumberg states that fasting and slimness objectified a host of cultural values which were associated with the middle-class female role. Fasting and slimness objectified such middle class, feminine values as delicacy, gentleness, demureness, purity, restraint, cleanliness, plainness, frugality, spirituality, and freedom from manual labor. Even the debilitation that attended anorexia nervosa reflected a normal condition of Victorian young women: Restricting the amount and kind of food consumed during small, irregular, light meals led most middle-class Victorian women to experience gastro-intestinal diseases. Tightly laced corsets, which were worn in order to produce the cultural ideal of an 18 inch waist, contributed headaches and fainting spells to the array of women's ailments. In fact, debilitation so epitomized the woman's role that invalidism became elevated to an ideal of feminine beauty which women routinely sought to cultivate (Banner, 1983, chap. 3). The debilitating symptoms of anorexia nervosa are only a slight exaggeration of such normal female behaviors.

Hysteria embodied similar characteristics of the female gender role. In her now classic analysis of nineteenth-century hysteria, Smith-Rosenberg (1972) explains that hysterical conversion, which deadened the senses and immobilized the limbs, reflected the middle-class feminine ideal of a weak, spiritual, person. Normal middle-class women were expected to shun physical work, take no interest in bodily pleasure, and avoid the mere mention of bodily functions. Even the breast of chicken was euphemistically called white meat to avoid reference to anatomical parts. This dephysicalized feminine ideal became the basis for the sensory and motor dysfunctions of hysteria as it was the basis for the eating dysfunction of anorexia nervosa. Although the ideal emanated from middle-class femininity it was adopted by working-class women as well (Shorter, 1986). Society, however, was intolerant of this crossing of class lines. Society acknowledged hysteria as appropriate for middle class but not working-class women. This distinction was embodied in differential therapy for women of different classes. Whereas middle-class hysterics were given the "rest cure" and confined to bed for months on end, working-class hysterics were assigned occupational therapy to motive their return to gainful employment.

The social basis of hysterical symptoms is evident from their historical specificity. Historian Edward Shorter (1986) states that

> psychogenic paraplegias and gait disturbances were relatively uncommon before the end of the 18th century. Then in the 19th century they begin to increase in frequency, culminating in the *belle epoque* in a veritable plague of "invalidism," young ladies unable to walk, or at best capable of tottering along with crutches until leg or hip pain pulled them down. After the First World War these motor disturbances vanish as swiftly and mysteriously as they arose.

With the contemporary feminine ideal being different from last century, hysterical symptoms embodying that ideal are rarely encountered. Only 0.27% of inpatient and outpatient female admissions to psychiatric hospitals were diagnosed in 1975 as manifesting conversion hysteria. Even female admissions to general hospitals only included 0.60% conversion hysteria. Yet this small population of women hysterics was six times larger than the population of male hysterics, indicating that conversion symptoms continue to be gender-linked (Winstead, 1984, Table 1).

Of course the possibility exists that such gender differences are an artifact of psychiatric diagnosis rather than a reflection of real differences. Experiments which present mental health professionals with a typical hysterical case study find that the diagnosis of hysterical personality disorder is forthcoming 76% of the time when the patient is female and only 49% when the patient is male. Interestingly, male and female clinicians are equally susceptible to the sexual bias in diagnosis (Winstead, 1984, pp. 94-95). While biased diagnosis undoubtedly accounts for some of the purported gender differences in hysterical symptoms, it unlikely is the sole reason. Gove (1984) insists that gender-based diagnostic bias is not significant in real life and that differential prevalence rates reflect genuine differences in the life experience of men and women.

Symptoms that are relatively straightforward to diagnose and which are therefore relatively free from labeling bias support the contention of real gender differences in symptomatology. Phobic symptoms are adopted more by women than by men, presumably because phobia is more congruent with women's roles. As many as 95% of animal phobics are female, while estimates of the percentage of female agoraphobics have ranged from 64% to 95% (Wolfe, 1984, p. 53). The total prevalence of phobia, estimated to be 77/1,000 population, afflicts women twice as much as men (Regier et al., 1988, Table 5). This is understandable in view of the fact that fearfulness is a normative female response to stress or danger. When casting about for a means to explain, express, and cope with problems, phobic responses appear viable for women because of their congruence with feminine ideals. In fact, most phobias arise as women waver over asserting their independence: feeling guilty over this ominous step, they retreat and explain-express this withdrawal as a fear of encountering various things. Fear of things and of open, undefined situations (agoraphobia) are metaphors for the fear of independence. One cannot be independent if (because) she is immobilized by a fear of things.

Depression is another symptom that afflicts women two to three times more often than men (Kleinman, 1982, p. 123; Regier et al., 1988, Table 5). A social constructionist view postulates this difference as due to the more passive attitude of women which makes overcoming obstacles less conceivable than it is for men. Since depression springs from the presumed inability to obtain a desired end or to overcome a loss, women's felt inability would expectedly result in more depression in women than in men.

The social construction of symptomatology may account for the greater prevalence of psychosis in women than men. When men and women are under stress, female gender-role values may contribute to expressing this stress psychologically, while male gender-role values may channel its expression into other forms such as suicide, crime, hypertension, and drug use. Accordingly, women may truly suffer psychosis more than men—not simply be labeled as psychotic more often, seek treatment more often, or complain about psychological problems more— but only because this is how their stress is socially expressed, not because they experience more stress. Gove may therefore be wrong in inferring greater female stress from greater psychosis. Psychosis is only one expression of adverse conditions. The disturbances which men suffer indicate that their role is as stressful as women's.

The cultural patterning of psychotic symptoms means that all syndromes are culture-bound. They all express the values, practices, relationships, and institutions of particular societies. Although psychotic symptoms do not obviously resemble common social practices and appear to be the most antisocial form of activity, they in fact reflect the essential values of their society. Cultural specificity is not confined to a handful of unusual symptoms such as *susto*, *koro*, *amok*, obsessive cannibalism (Parker, 1960), anorexia nervosa, *saladerra*, *dano* (deRios, 1981), and tarantism.[12] Specific symptoms found within widespread disorders of schizophrenia and depression are also culturally specific. Marsella et al. explain that psychosis must be culturally variable because the psychological processes that are involved are variable. In the authors' words,

> it is not simply the manifestation of mental disorders that varies across cultures, a fact which the research literature amply supports, but that the entire phenomenon is different. We cannot separate our experience of an event from our sensory and linguistic mediations of it. If these differ, so must the experience differ across cultures. If we define who we are in different ways, if we process reality in different ways, if we define the very nature of what is real, what is acceptable, and even what is right or wrong, how can we then expect similarities in something as complex as madness? (Marsella et al., 1985, p. 303).

Cultural specificity of symptoms has three manifestations. One is socially unique thoughts and behaviors such as obsessive cannibalism and tarantism. Another manifestation of culture bound symptoms is behavior that is common to numerous societies but which has socially unique meaning or motivation. For example, the refusal to eat, which characterizes contemporary anorexia nervosa, is analogous to a similar behavior that was characteristic of medieval women saints. However, the motives and intentions were entirely different: the saints used abstinence from eating to prove their spiritual purity to god, while contemporary young women abstain because they are preoccupied with maintaining an attractive bodily appearance (Brumberg, 1988). A third way in which dysfunctional syndromes are socially unique is when singular reactions which occur separately in diverse societies congeal into a culturally unique configuration. This is evidently true for depression whose individual components (despondence, guilt, hopelessness) are widespread across cultures but whose coalescing in a constellation or syndrome is unique. From the viewpoint of sociohistorical psychology these are ways in which personality and all psychological phenomena are culturally unique.

We take it as well established that psychotic symptoms draw upon and embody prevailing social values. We also know that these values and practices were the very ones which, employed by social authorities (from business executives to parents to psychiatrists), created the untenable situations which provoked the symptoms. *Psychological symptoms thus recapitulate the very problems they seek to escape.* This is depicted in Figure 8 where the causes of stress and the causes of cognitive schemas which constitute the symptoms (disturbances in perception, emotion, and behavior) both emanate from culture. Brown and Harris (1978, p. 22) link the causes and symptoms of depression to a common social source in much the same way except that they do not stipulate the cognitive mediations which underlie symptom formation.

Although symptoms and causes are grounded in the same cultural soil, there is no one-to-one connection between them. Socially derived cognitive schemas mediate between all stimuli and responses and this mediation precludes any strict determinism of symptoms by social problems. The same problematic can be variously interpreted and responded to depending upon the individual's social position and personal experience. For instance, a few of Opler's Irish patients manifested symptoms which resembled the Italian pattern. All of these individuals had strong fathers reminiscent of the Italian family structure. Similarly, males who develop "feminine" phobias appear to have "feminine" personality characteristics of dependency and timidity. For these men, phobias represent the same fear of autonomy that women feel (Wolfe, 1984, p. 67). In the same vein, the few Ojibwa women who manifest the cannibalism of *wiitiko* psychosis usually experienced a "masculine" training and ethos during their childhood and adolescence (Parker, 1960, p. 618). These examples suggest that symptoms which deviate from subcultural patterns are not asocial but rather reflect heterogeneous social experience within the subculture. Atypical symptomatology does not negate the cultural basis of psychosis, it simply reveals its complexity.

In conclusion, symptoms are not arbitrary expressions of psychological distress. They are rooted in values, beliefs, self-definition, emotions, and motives. The entire illness experience is saturated with cultural significance and expresses the social character of consciousness (cf., Kleinman, 1980, pp. 76-77; Good & Good, 1981). Psychotic symptoms also epitomize the tool-like function of consciousness. Like tools, symptoms are fashioned out of material made available by the environment. This material is social values. Furthermore, this material is not employed as it is found but is transformed in various ways. It is compressed, expanded, and relocated in the sense that symptoms intensify and exaggerate prevailing social values and express them in atypical situations.

Symptoms also aid the individual in coping with (adapting to) his world. In short, symptoms reflect the properties of consciousness that have been identified by sociohistorical psychology.

Treatment Therapy

Psychosis is not only social in its causation and expression, but in its response to therapy as well. Therapeutic practices alleviate symptoms because they dovetail the victim's socially mediated sense of self, social life, and belief system (including his interpretation of madness). For instance, the Latin American syndrome *susto*—or magical fright, where the victim becomes listless—is relieved by holding up the patient's shirt and shaking it in the air. Upon seeing this, the symptoms dissipate. How can such treatment be effective in Latin America when it would provoke ridicule among middle-class American psychotics? The ritual presumes that susto results from the soul becoming separated from the body and either getting lost or else being captured by a spirit. Therapy involves showing where the person is by holding up his garments so the soul can find its way back. An offering of liquor, cigarettes, and cocoa leaves is also sometimes provided as an inducement for the soul to return. Finally, the patient begs forgiveness from the spirit which may have captured his soul, to convince it to free the soul.

The effectiveness of these simple methods is entirely due to the fact that the victim *believes* his disturbance is due to soul loss. He is convinced by the curator's techniques that his soul will return, and this assurance allows his listlessness to lift. Americans' depression would be unaffected by these techniques because we have an entirely different *understanding* of depression. Consequently, we would not be assured by the curator's methods, and our depression would not abate.

Therapy for tarantism, discussed above, has the patient lie on the floor in the presence of musicians playing melodies. The patient begins wriggling and then rises up to begin dancing for ten minutes, upon which she throws herself back onto the floor. The music stops, then begins and starts the patient going through another ten minute dance cycle. After several days of dancing, the patient declares he is now cured. The therapy works on the idea that by dancing until exhaustion, the victim causes the malevolent spider to die. Obviously, the therapy is effective because it coincides with the conceptual underpinning of tarantism. No American symptom would be alleviated by this kind of therapy because it is utterly foreign to American patients' understanding of their psychosis. Variations in therapeutic practice demonstrate the socially mediated cognitive basis of madness.

Now, culturally appropriate therapy can alleviate symptoms and terminate a psychotic episode, but it does not necessarily cure the psychosis. Reports of such therapy typically express amazement at the relief which it brings to the victim. However, they do not discuss long-term results. Based on the reports it seems that local healers reinforce a fictional account of madness and utterly fail to deal with the real societal causes. In the same way, psychoanalytical, humanistic, and behavioristic therapeutic techniques are congruent with many popular notions of distress and therefore help alleviate symptoms; however, they similarly fail to achieve lasting cures.

From the point of view of sociohistorical psychology, real cure requires a social understanding of personal problems and symptoms, and it also requires corrective social action. In the first place, personal problems must be comprehended as resulting from social mistreatment. In Laing's terms, suffering must be made intelligible by tracing it to its social causes. This means linking interpersonal mistreatment at the microsystem level with its roots in the exo- and macrosystems. In order to avoid the malevolent influences that caused his suffering, the victim needs to become cognizant of these influences at all levels of social life. Otherwise his escape will only be partial, and his improvement will be incomplete.

Therapy from a sociohistorical standpoint would undertake a similar social analysis of the victim's symptoms. The social values embedded in symptoms should be exposed and critiqued. This will enable the victim to comprehend how these social values lead to self-destructive behavior and how they tend to obscure the source and nature of his psychological problems. A social analysis will facilitate uprooting these values and replacing them with more humane, fulfilling ones. In the absence of such an analysis, the social values that comprise the symptoms will persist and they will interfere with efforts to construct a more fulfilling orientation.

Sociohistorical therapy seeks to make the victim aware of the fact that the inappropriateness of his current behavior and thinking were appropriate responses—given his limited resources—to the family in which he grew up. Self-effacement, suspicion, and self-protection are effective coping strategies for avoiding invalidation by malevolent parents. They do not overcome the situation, but they do allow the victim to avoid even greater suffering while living within it. It is when the victim has to function in a different situation that his habitualized coping strategies prove to be inappropriate and ineffective. This is analogous to the habituated expectations which mediate perception and which produce optical illusions when applied to anomalous situations. Because the expectations have been successful in dealing with one's normal environment, it is particularly difficult to dispel them although they are inappropriate for the novel environment. The victim will only give up these expectations if he is supported while he develops new ones.

Given the heavily personal thrust of contemporary Western psychotherapy, social analysis of problems and symptoms undoubtedly appears inappropriate. It probably appears excessively intellectual and impersonal. However, this is a misconception. Social analysis in no way excludes personal explorations and emotional expressions. It supplements them. Certainly, the disturbed client is not subjected to a lecture on the social origins of his problems. The relaxing, supporting, and facilitating techniques of conventional therapies are tremendously useful during the initial stages of psychotherapy. However, if psychological disturbances are construed entirely in personal or interpersonal terms, and divorced from society, then the victim's understanding will be incomplete and his ability to surpass his difficulties will be impaired. (Examples of these failures will be described in the section on nonsocial approaches to therapy.) In Durkheim's terms, madness is a social fact whose origins and character reside in social relations rather than in individual minds. Personal analysis is thus insufficient to understand madness although personal analysis is certainly a necessary aspect of psychotherapy.

Sociohistorical psychology not only proposes a unique approach to psychotherapy, it also insists that therapy itself is insufficient for curing and eliminating madness. These lofty goals can only be met by truly eliminating social mistreatment not only from interpersonal relations but from the broader social system as well. All the therapy in the world is ineffective if the victims cannot escape from the malevolent influences that caused their suffering. Real pressures cause real problems, and the latter cannot be eliminated as long as the former remain intact (Egan & Cowan, 1979). It is not enough to simply interpret the world, the point is also to change it, and this is necessary for mental health as well as for economic and political improvement.

Kleinman (1988, p. 61) is quite correct to conclude that the social distribution of psychological (and medical) disorders proves the need for a social attack in order to eradicate and prevent them. Just as improved medical practices account for a small proportion of health improvements relative to social changes such as improved housing and sanitation, better diet, higher levels of education, and safer work environments, so psychotherapy must be supplemented by broader social changes that will promote mental health. As Kleinman said, "much of ill health [including mental illness] is but one domain of human misery, and the lion's share of that misery takes its origin from sociopolitical, socioeconomic, and sociopsychological affairs" (1988, p. 61).

Research has conclusively established that a beneficent social environment is critical to successful recovery from psychosis. This is true on all social levels, from family to social system. The importance of family environment has been demonstrated by research on family members' expressed emotion and affective style toward recovering patients. Miklowitz et al. (1988) found that 90% of manic-depressed patients residing in "high expressed emotion" families (where relatives were highly critical of the patient and emotionally overinvolved with him), or families characterized by negative affective style (where relatives attacked, invalidated, and guilt-tripped patients) suffered relapses. This is almost double the 50% relapse rate for patients in "low expressed emotion" or "benign affect" families. Radke-Yarrow (1989, p. 208) found similar benefits of supportive family environments in a study that is reminiscent of Emmy Werner's work. Six-year-old, psychiatrically disturbed children who were from stable homes shifted toward improved status 3 years later in 73% of the cases; however, only 33% of children from chaotic homes improved.

Employment is another social condition that aids recovery from psychosis. Mostow and Newberry (1975) found that lower-class depressed women who work show somewhat faster recovery than housewives. At recovery, workers had a greater sense of self-worth, functioned better in their activities, and felt somewhat more interested in life than the housewives. Ensminger and Celentano (1988) similarly found that unemployed individuals who returned to work suffered fewer psychiatric symptoms than their counterparts who remained unemployed. In the same vein, Warner (1985, pp. 144-145) found that the level of employment and general economic prosperity in the U.S. and Britain are clearly important for recovery. For instance, during the Great Depression, the rate of recovery from schizophrenia was half that of the decades preceding and following the economic crisis. In contrast to a complete recovery rate of 20% during the early 1920s and 1940s, the rate was only 12% during the Depression (Warner, 1985, pp. 70ff.).

Cooper's (1961) British study found that length of stay in mental hospitals, rate of discharge, clinical condition at discharge, probability of relapse, the total amount of time spent in mental hospitals are all directly related to social class. This is confirmed by Schwab's (1979) data that over a 3-year period, twice as many upper-class patients recovered from psychosis as did lower-class patients (11% vs. 5%).

The World Health Organization's Follow-Up Study on Schizophrenia (1979) provides powerful evidence that recovery differs dramatically in developing and developed countries. As Chapter 6 of the report explains, psychotic symptoms terminate fairly quickly in undeveloped countries, whereas they persist much longer in developed nations. The particular psychotic episode which brought on the initial diagnosis of schizophrenia terminated in 6 months in the undeveloped countries, compared with 11 months in the developed nations. The entire course of schizophrenia was also substantially shorter in undeveloped than developed countries. For example, only 25% of the patients in Ibadan remained psychotic after 2 years, in contrast to 61% in Aarhus. During the 2 years following the initial diagnosis, patients in developed nations spent 45% of the time in psychotic episodes, while patients in the undeveloped spent only 27% of the time in such agony. The authors of the report conclude that "for all variables considered, the schizophrenic patients in [developing countries] tended to have a better outcome on average than the schizophrenic patients in the [developed countries]."

Murphy (1978) found similar superiority in outcome for third world patients. Compared to Britons, Mauritians suffered far less psychological disturbance after being discharged from treatment. And Mauritians suffered far less chronic disability and less relapse than did Africans from similar genetic stock who were living in the U.S. Virgin Islands. For example, less than 10% of Mauritians experienced any relapse of symptoms in contrast to over 50% of their counterparts in the Virgin Islands.

These studies prove that social structure exerts a powerful effect on recovery from psychosis. The difference between recovery in developing and developed countries is far greater than that obtained for different kinds of psychotherapy within a given social system.

Nonsocial Analyses of Madness

Now that the sociohistorical approach to psychosis has been articulated, we shall contrast it with nonsocial views. The point of this comparison is not simply to reject nonsocial views out of hand. It is to explain why nonsocial views are inadequate so that the sociohistorical approach can be better appreciated. A comparison of social and nonsocial approaches also reveals the positive aspects of the latter and enables them to enrich sociohistorical psychology. My point is to illuminate the essence of nonsocial approaches to the causes, symptoms, and treatment of psychological dysfunction. Accordingly, it is sufficient to select the most important approaches to each aspect of psychosis without discussing every nonsocial theory with respect to every aspect of madness.

Causes

Diathesis-Stress Model. Perhaps the most predominant conception of the causes of psychosis is the diathesis-stress model. It proposes that psychological dysfunction results from a combination of external stress coupled with a dispositional weakness which is extraordinarily vulnerable to stress.

The concept of stress as a social-psychological phenomenon was taken from the physical notion of stress. Throughout the eighteenth and nineteenth centuries, the term stress was used in engineering and physics to refer to force, pressure, or strain. This meaning connoted disruption of ordinary functioning. During the 1940s Hans Selye promulgated this notion into biology to refer to disruptions in the life activity of organisms. From biology it was extended into psychology. As applied to explaining psychosis, stress triggers maladaptive behavior much as it does on the biological level (Pollock, 1988). Whether stressors are pleasant or unpleasant is immaterial since all that matters is the *intensity* of the disruption. In this neutral view, weddings, birthdays, and promotions are as stressful and pathogenic as divorce, war, and unemployment.

From the standpoint of sociohistorical psychology stress is certainly a causal factor in psychosis. However, the manner in which stress is conceived fails to capture the concrete malevolence of social relations. With stress referring to any disruption in ordinary behavior, the particularity of social problems is dissolved. This leads to equating the stress of preparing a wedding with that of losing a job. The abstractness of "stress" severs the stressor from particular aspects of the social system. Although investigation into the effects of stress has a ring of social concern, it is a hollow ring deprived of substance. Dohrenwend (1990) complains that most research on social stress does not connect with social class or any variable on a societal level. The shift in focus from social class to social stress means the epidemiological research into socioeconomic status will be halted in its infancy and never be allowed to enter the mainstream of social psychology and psychiatry.

Even when attention is paid to extremely pernicious forms of stress, such as unemployment, death of a loved one, and mistreatment by parents, construing these abstractly as stress obscures the reality of the psychological problems and makes this reality more difficult to alter. These are significantly different problems, are distressing in very different ways, and require different solutions. Unemployment may connote personal inadequacy and failure while widowhood is a natural occurrence which casts no aspersions on the personhood of the griever.

The naturalistic flavor of stress as violating biological needs further obscures the social psychology of mental problems. Certain kinds of stress do violate natural needs and cause serious dysfunction. The research of Laing, Bateson, Henry Massie, and others demonstrates the destructive consequences of violating needs for consistency, stimulation, and support (recognition). However, many (most) forms of stress are stressful because *social* needs have been violated. It is therefore necessary to understand *why* unemployment and divorce, for example, are stressful *in our culture*. They are so not because they disturb a natural homeostasis but because they disturb the social importance that accrues to work and family relations in our culture. In collective societies that provide for the welfare of all members, unemployment and family breakups entail no onus. Construing stressors as naturally stressful obscures the social context and the social needs that make them so. Naturalizing the stressors and their effects—i.e., making unemployment a natural cause of stress and psychological dysfunction—has the effect of naturalizing the context and needs: it appears that everyone needs to work in order to command respect from others, feel good about themselves, achieve financial security and behavioral regularity because that is how life is. No society would respect and care for able-bodied individuals who did not work, and no individual could accept himself if he did not work. In a classic case of false universalization, alternative social environments and needs are rendered unimaginable.

Construing stress as deviations from normal conditions also has an uncomfortable conservative flavor that tends to uphold the status quo. The norm is regarded as benign because it is habitual. Actually, it is the status quo which fosters psychological dysfunction in one-third of the American population. Action which redresses this state of affairs may ultimately bring relief from stress.

Identifying stressors as unusual, disruptive activity leads the stress model to focus on discrete, acute events rather than enduring, systemic values and practices (Kleinman, 1988, p. 65). After all, these latter are not unusual and involve no change from the norm because they *are* the norm. The search for stressful life changes thus inevitably focuses on sudden disruptions such as unemployment, divorce, and death. Problematic norms are beyond reproach.

The inadequacies of the stress model are greatly compounded by adding on the diathesis factor. For this factor stipulates that the organism's reaction to stress is endogenously determined. The cause of stress is thereby driven deeper inside the individual to his low threshold for stress tolerance. What is stressful is what the organism cannot tolerate, rather than ways in which the environment weakens the organism.

Stress is more a subjective than an objective problem. Selye himself held this position (Pollock, 1988, p. 388) which he adopted from numerous precursors. Nineteenth-century medical explanations of women's susceptibility to mental disorder rested entirely upon such a viewpoint. Education was considered to be debilitating to women because it taxed their fragile neuroanatomy, while men withstood the stimulation of education because their neuroanatomy was stronger.

Contemporary versions of the diathesis-stress theory follow this line of reasoning, although specific details have been changed. One of the most representative versions is Gottesman and Shields' (1982), and it deserves a thorough critique in order to illustrate the details and shortcomings of the theory.

According to Gottesman and Shields, the impact of stress on psychological functioning is mediated by biological processes. These determine the individual's vulnerability, or threshold, to stress, as well as the individual's reaction to (expression of) stress. Stress per se does not generate psychosis, stress acts to trigger off innate biological predispositions to particular forms of psychosis. As with all nativistic formulations, the environment is conceived abstractly, devoid of specific form and content. These particulars are supplied by internal mechanisms. Thus, Jon Karlsson, another advocate of genetic causes of schizophrenia, denies that "faulty environment is responsible for the origin of schizophrenia, but rather such stress seems to bring out or aggravate the symptoms in persons with a schizophrenic constitution" (Karlsson, 1966, p. 64).

Gottesman and Shields assert that genetic defects are the preponderant cause of susceptibility to psychosis. According to their model, a high genetic predisposition will produce psychosis even in the absence of environmental stress. In their words, "Individuals who happen to be at the extreme tail of a distribution of genetic liability will easily become cases and will rarely have such objectively defined stressful life events prior to their breakdowns; for those individuals almost any environment they experience appears to be sufficiently stressful" (p. 181). In the more numerous instances of a moderate rather than a high genetic liability, madness will only ensue upon encountering some particular intense stress. At the other end of the scale are individuals with a high genetic resistance to madness who won't break down under even the most stressful conditions. Extreme environmental stress will most likely produce some psychological disturbance in these individuals, but not schizophrenia (Gottesman & Shields, p. 211).

This notion of diathesis-stress minimizes the social causes of psychosis in numerous ways. Rather than impugn the quality of social life, the model places responsibility for madness on genetic defects inside the individual (Pollock, 1988, p. 389). Gottesman and Shields assume that social stress is ordinarily not sufficient to produce psychosis. Most individuals can handle social stress without breaking down. Stress will only lead to madness in genetically defective individuals. In the authors' words, "the effects of environmental risk factors may be interaction effects only that operate on the relatively few genetically predisposed individuals to produce schizophrenia but that will have no adverse effects on the population as a whole" (pp. 211, 177).

According to this viewpoint, stress is an inevitable feature of life and is not intrinsically deleterious. Consequently, psychosis cannot be attributed to stress per se, it must entail some genetic inability to deal with things that normal individuals easily negotiate. Gottesman and Shields go so far as to state that "a large and rather specific genetic 'something' interacts with nonspecific, rather *commonplace* environmental factors" (p. 210, my emphasis). They liken the genetic-environment interaction to that involved in fava bean anemia: favism occurs after eating fava beans but only among genetically susceptible individuals. There is nothing intrinsically harmful about the beans themselves; the real cause of the disease is genetic, although, of course, the stricken individual must have eaten the beans (pp. 145, 211). From this perspective, treating and preventing psychosis entails protecting the susceptible individuals from commonplace stress. It does not involve altering the given social environment in which most people live.

Obviously this conception of the interaction between genes and environment places primary responsibility for psychosis on the genes. It "means that environmental factors were relatively unimportant as causative agents of the schizophrenias" (p. 230). "Genetic factors in the puzzle [of schizophrenia] are more central and more important to its solution than environmental pieces" (p. xii). The relative importance of genes vis-à-vis environment can even be codified in a formula wherein "the genetic heritability of the liability for schizophrenia is about 70%, and the cultural-inheritance component accounts for about 20% of the combined liability" (p. 229).[13] These statements, typical of interactionist theorists, belie the claim that the diathesis-stress model acknowledges environmental as well as social causes of psychosis. The model is actually thoroughly nativistic, with social conditions as inculpable for madness as fava beans are for favism. Not only is social stress regarded as normal and innocuous; even severe and multiple stressors are presumed to have little adverse effect on the majority of the population who are genetically healthy (p. 181).

These speculative conclusions fly in the face of empirical evidence. Psychosis does not require genetic predisposition as proven by the ease with which neurosis and psychosis can be experimentally created in animals. Any animal can be driven to distraction regardless of its genetic pedigree, and this holds for humans as well. Many studies were described above which demonstrate the debilitating impact of unemployment and immigration on the psychological functioning of normal people. Banks and Jackson's, and Linn et al.'s experiments rigorously selected individuals with no indication of psychological problems who, subsequent to unemployment, developed severe impairments.

Brown and Harris (1978) similarly found that acute stress combined with unemployment, three or more children at home, early loss of one's mother, and a paucity of intimate, supportive social relationships produced depression in 100% of individuals! (Brown & Harris, p. 180). The fact that every single person falling within these social circumstance suffered psychological damage makes genetic speculations gratuitous. Moreover, improving social relationships produced a direct reduction in depression, which further obviates genetic determination. When an acute stressor is combined with only one social vulnerability factor (e.g., lack of intimate, supportive social relationships) instead of four of them (unemployment, children at home, early loss of mother, and paucity of supportive relationships), the incidence of depression drops from 100% to 41%. And when all four of the foregoing social vulnerability factors are eliminated only 10% of individuals experiencing an acute stressor became depressed—with other social factors presumably accounting for this 10% incidence (Brown & Harris, p. 177).

Sameroff et al. (1987, p. 391, Figure 1) similarly found a monotonic linear relationship between number of risk factors and severity of psychological dysfunction. The strict coincidence between degree of social vulnerability and incidence and severity of psychological dysfunction, leaves little place for genetic determinism. Evidently, psychosis is more akin to measles which can strike any non-inoculated person regardless of genetic makeup than it is to favism which only strikes those who are genetically liable.[14]

The entire notion of a genetic predisposition to schizophrenia is challenged by the low incidence the disorder among close relatives of schizophrenic individuals. Coryell (1988) found only 1.4% of first-degree relatives of schizophrenic probands suffered from schizophrenia. Surprisingly, more of the first-degree relatives of schizophrenics suffered from depression (11.4%) than from schizophrenia.

Along the same lines, Sameroff, Seifer, and Barocas (1983) found that children of schizophrenic mothers evidenced no signs of disturbance through 48 months. A genetic predisposition to schizophrenia would be inherited from schizophrenic mothers and should be obvious in their children. The fact that symptoms are not overrepresented in these children casts doubt upon the existence of such an inherited predisposition. Instead of childhood schizophrenia being a natural product of schizophrenic mothers, Sameroff et al. conclude that social relations are responsible: "Recent evidence has suggested that it may not be simply the fact of a mother's schizophrenia that predicts illness in the child, but that one must also consider the affective relation between mother and child" (p. 244). In other words, whether or not one's children will become schizophrenic has nothing to do with the presence or absence of schizophrenia, per se, in the parents. It depends upon the manner in which parents treat their children, and schizophrenics are no more likely to mistreat their children than normal parents are.

Other evidence confirms Sameroff's contention that schizophrenia follows social rather than genetic relationships. Buried within the research that is offered in support of genetic heritability of schizophrenia lie the discordant findings that the concordance rate for same-sexed DZ twins is twice that of opposite-sexed DZ twins—despite the fact that the genetic relationship between same- and opposite-sexed twins is identical—and the concordance rate for DZ twins is about three times what it is for siblings—despite the fact that the genetic relationship between DZ twins and siblings is identical (Shields, 1968, p. 98). These findings, for subjects reared together, suggest that social relations are more important than genes because we know that same-sex twins are treated more alike than their opposite-sex counterparts, and DZ twins in general are exposed to more similar treatment than sibs are. Concordance rates for schizophrenia follow social rather than genetic lines.

The social distribution of psychosis across culture, class, religion, employment, and gender is further testimony to the causative impact of social conditions (Kleinman, 1988, p. 57). It repudiates the contention that the environment is simply a trigger of individual-genetic liability. For if genetic liability were the basic cause of psychosis, then madness would show no particular social distribution. Because cultures, classes, religions, and genders evidence no differential genetic defectiveness, psychosis should, according to genetic principles, be randomly distributed throughout societies. The fact that it is not demonstrates that different social conditions—cultures, classes, roles, employment—are primarily responsible for psychological problems. While all known social conditions generate some psychological disturbances, the quantity and quality are substantially different. Even within the same society, a given event will be stressful for members of one subgroup and nonstressful for members of another (Kleinman, 1988, p. 65).

Gottesman and Shields see stressors as singular, decontextualized events which all people encounter with equal frequency and intensity. From this perspective it appears that maladaptive reactions must be due to genetic defects which reside inside the individual. However, once the social epidemiology and social context of stressors and distress are recognized, it becomes obvious that the adverse effects of stress are a function of this context rather than of individual weakness.

The sheer magnitude of psychological dysfunction in America argues against individualistic causes. The fact that 33% of Americans who suffer psychological dysfunction (along with millions more who probably would become disturbed if not for ingesting daily doses of tranquilizers and sedatives) means that madness is not a problem of a few weak individuals unable to withstand normal, commonplace conditions. It is the conditions themselves that are insufferable.

The argument for genetic vulnerability not only fails on sociological (epidemiological) grounds, it lacks support from psycho-biological data as well. There is simply no good psychobiological evidence for a genetic liability to psychosis. No genetic markers associated with psychosis have been found, despite fantastic positive claims. Articles in the British journal *Nature* (Feb. 26, 1987; Nov. 10, 1988) have enthusiastically proclaimed success in identifying genetic markers for depression and schizophrenia; however, these have been quickly repudiated by other reports in the same journal (*Nature*, Nov. 16, 1989).

No systematic neuroanatomical or hormonal abnormalities have been discovered in the bodies of psychotic individuals (see below).[15] More indirect claims for genetic predisposition, based upon twin and adoption studies are equally unsubstantiated (Ratner, 1982; Lewontin, Rose, Kamin, 1984, chap. 8; Lidz, 1976; Lidz, 1977; Lidz, Blatt, Cook, 1981; Lidz & Blatt, 1983; Gottesman & Shields, 1976).[16] Undoubtedly some cases of psychosis have a biological basis but the percentage is probably akin to the percentage of car accidents which are caused by faulty engines. With psychology being functionally autonomous of biology, it is to be expected that most psychological problems will result from distinctly social-psychological processes.

The line of thinking that presumes psychosis to be a neurophysiological malfunction fails to understand that psychosis is intelligible, socially mediated, psychological activity. The biogenetic view construes madness as originating in a natural, nonpsychological, physiological deficit when, in fact, most madness springs from thoroughly psychological disturbances including a certain sense of oneself, expectations of other people's reactions toward each other and toward oneself, attitudes, values, and emotional reactions. Madness is rendered unintelligible when it is regarded as the outcome of a physical malfunction because all sensible psychological activity is precluded.

This non-sensical conception of psychosis underlay the widely touted but now discredited dopamine theory of schizophrenia. The theory was born after learning that drugs which induce stereotyped behavior in animals—such as repetitive, licking and biting—also stimulate dopamine neural receptors (Meltzer & Stahl, 1976, p. 24). Likening stereotypical animal behavior to schizophrenia led the authors to hypothesize that human schizophrenia might be caused by the same dopamine abnormality. It was only because schizophrenia was equated with bizarre behavior of rats that the dopamine hypothesis was conceived. A more sensitive understanding of psychosis would never have associated it with rat behavior and would never have sought to explain the two by the same causes.[17]

The social-psychological character of madness that we have painstakingly described above further refutes the notion that an inadequate nervous system, incapable of processing information, causes madness. Sufferers of tarantism, for example, possess a detailed knowledge of tarantula spiders. We have seen how this knowledge is maintained and utilized by patients to give their symptoms the proper quality and to produce their symptoms at the proper time of year so as to mimic the spider's behavior. Obviously, there is no incapacity to transmit information across synapses, or any other type of mechanical failure among these individuals.

With psychological functions being qualitatively different and emergent from biological phenomena, biology cannot adequately explain psychosis. The interaction that produces madness is not between culture and biology because biology does not function at the same level as culture or psychology. The malevolent interaction that culminates in psychosis is an interaction of various facets of culture. The reasons for the vast preponderance of psychosis lie in factors internal to culture, rather than external to it. Rather than physiological abnormalities mediating between stressful events and psychosis, culture does so, as depicted in Figure 8.

The notion that psychosis results from biologically abnormal individuals confronting normal (commonplace) social conditions is incorrect. In reality, psychosis results from biologically normal individuals confronting unbearable social conditions. The diathesis-stress model misconstrues the real source of psychosis as lying within the individual instead of outside him. The conception of a predisposition to psychosis is purely speculative, ill-defined, and devoid of confirmation. Research on biological risk for psychophysiological abnormalities proves that even when tangible biological risk exists (i.e., low birth weight, poor nutrition, stressful birth and other states that have a demonstrable relation to later physical and psychological impairment) it does not constitute a strong pre-disposition to future problems but is superceded in importance by the type of environment in which the child is brought up. For instance, Werner (1982, 1989) and Gollnitz (1990) have found that infants at high biological risk brought up in normal families achieve normal psychological development. It is only when high-risk babies live in impoverished conditions that their developmental outcome is poor. And this retardation obtains even for babies who are born without biological risk. In other words, even when some abnormal predisposition to psychophysiological disorder *is* evident, its effect on future health is minimal. This will certainly be true for predispositions to insanity if they ever are discovered.

Attachment Theory. Attachment theory parallels the diathesis-stress model in muting the importance of concrete social practices for psychosis. The attachment between a baby and its mother is construed as a single variable which determines the quality of later psychological functioning. However, evidence suggests this is not true and that more encompassing social interactions have far more importance. We have already cited Kagan in Chapter 1 as saying that secure attachment offers no guarantee of happiness because it may produce a disinterest in people beyond the parent and therefore yield a social misfit. Lewis et al (1984, p. 133) similarly state that "relatively few data support the contention that attachment relationships in infancy are related to psychopathology much after the toddler period." For instance, only 15% of their 1-year-old, insecurely attached female subjects developed behavioral problems at six years. Forty percent of insecurely attached 1-year-old boys became disturbed at six years; however, the reason for the relationship is due to social mediations, not to any intrinsic, causal power that attachment has on mental illness. When the social experience of the insecure boys was investigated, it was evident that they had suffered numerous life stress events. A pooled index of stressful events correctly differentiated the insecurely attached boys who later suffered psychological disturbance from the insecurely attached boys who suffered no disturbance.

In other words, insecure attachment to parents generates no mental illness in most cases (60% of boys and 85% of girls). And the cases where insecure attachment is associated with later psychopathology are due to the unfortunate experiences these particular individuals suffered apart from their attachment problem. Insecure attachment per se does not predispose one toward mental illness, just as narrowly defined difficulties associated with toilet training or nursing have no necessary adverse consequences (Schatzman, 1973; Lichtman, 1982; Stannard, 1980;

Poster, 1976; Opler, 1969; Riesman, 1983; Barnouw, 1973, pp. 213-218; Caldwell, 1964; Orlanaksky, 1949).

Humanistic Psychology. For all of its stated opposition to the biomedical model, humanistic psychology shares with them an asocial, individualistic account of the causes of madness. Humanistic psychology focuses upon abstract characteristics of individuals and treats them as indigenous rather than as socially caused dysfunctions. Laing's early book, *The Divided Self,* is flawed by this approach, as he explains schizoid symptoms as deriving from "ontological insecurity." Why certain individuals are ontologically insecure is never addressed, and this omission produces the impression of an intrinsic weakness in the psychotic. Nor is the supposed causal impact of insecurity on schizoid symptoms explained.

Laing implicitly presumes that insecurity naturally causes individuals to form a dichotomized false and true self. However, this is neither justified by Laing nor is it a plausible assumption. In the first place, many secure individuals nevertheless form false selves for succeeding in impersonal situations. Insecurity is not the main motive for constructing a false self, nor does it necessarily produce this result. Insecurity can lead to a great diversity of symptoms depending upon the social concepts that comprise an individual's schemata. Laing never illuminates the connection between insecurity and schizophrenic symptoms, and he simply presumes what needs to be explained. The explanation needs to clarify the socially mediated, active manner in which individuals react to insecurity to construct symptoms. The failure to undertake this kind of analysis actually obscures the psychological activity that humanists so intensely glorify.

Laing eventually abandoned abstract existential categories for a more concrete description of psychotics' social relations. This enabled him to comprehend the social and psychological significance of symptoms and sympathize with the victims' oppression. Other humanists unfortunately failed to recast their analysis in such social terms. Ludwig Binswanger's classic existential analysis of Ellen West exemplifies the resulting inadequacies. Although Binswanger (1958) does provide some details of Ellen's early self-description, these are never explained in terms of her social existence. They are rather existentially paraphrased in terms of her "being-in-the-world." Binswanger uses Heideggerian categories to describe Ellen's psychology.

According to Binswanger, Ellen's problem is that from infancy her self developed in opposition to, rather than in harmony with, her social and physical environment (the *Mitwelt* and *Umwelt,* respectively). She stubbornly defied these worlds rather than accommodate to them. Rather

than comfortably being "with others" Ellen sought to dominate and attack other people. Instead of planting her feet firmly on the ground of
Being and practically *striding across* it, Ellen wistfully *flew above* Being in
a phantasy world. Ellen's unauthentic dissociation from the world was
expressed, according to Binswanger, in her romantic interest in a foreign
man, i.e., a man not from her own social world. It was also manifested
in her preoccupation with being thin, or noncorporeal and ethereal.

This description certainly creates the impression that Ellen's symptoms are due to *her* unauthentic mode of responding to people. Binswanger never mentions the manner in which people treated Ellen. He only
describes how she reacted to events. This is done out of a concern for
neutral description which "brackets" any theoretical assumptions regarding causation. However, a definite sense of explanation is created by
default. Leaving activity ungrounded in social life creates the impression
that the individual is intrinsically deficient. Ellen's antagonistic relationship to the *Mitwelt* and *Umwelt* appear, from this vantage point, to be
entirely her problem because no other explanation is given. When
Binswanger states that Ellen failed to take responsibility for her own
being, and instead sought unauthentic ways of "taking it easy" (p. 271)
is this not an undisguised criticism of her? Is not the tone of this humanistic analysis just as accusatory and insensitive as Kraepelin's
biomedically based description that humanists purportedly reject?

Binswanger does not discuss the concrete content of Ellen's relationships with others. Instead, he is exclusively concerned with abstract
features of her relationships such as whether she was with others or
separated from them. For instance, in discussing the significance of
Ellen's quest for slenderness, Binswanger denies that the wish means an
identification with youth and beauty—an identification that would reflect
aesthetic and sexual norms of her particular society. It is rather an identification with an ethereal wish-world that is crucial. The specific content
is irrelevant to existential analysis; only the general "mode of being"—
wishfulness—is important. In Binswanger's words, the fact of wishing is
more important than the specific prevailing wish and the specific prevailing dread (p. 316).

Another example of this attitude is Binswanger's granting priority
to the experience of the sequence of events rather than to the sequence
of experiences (pp. 330-331). Here, the actual sequence of experience
is less important than the general sense one has of the sequence. One's
temporal sense about "sequence" is more important than the sequence
of real events. Moreover, these abstract features of *Dasein* are presumed
to have intrinsic consequences. For instance, Ellen's early harsh separat-

ing of her self (*Eigenwelt*) from *Um-* and *Mitwelt* "exacts vengeance" throughout her whole existence (pp. 286-7).

Binswanger's Heideggerian categories are far too abstract to be serviceable descriptions of social psychology. Pinpointing the problem with this kind of existential-phenomenology, Marcuse (1969, p. 21) said, "a phenomenology of human existence falls short of the necessary clarity and completeness if it bypasses the material condition of historical existence. This is the case with Heidegger. If existence is typically historical, then it is always part of a concrete historical situation which must be penetrated before its fundamental structure can be indicated."

Symptoms

Nonsocial psychological viewpoints conceive psychiatric symptoms in the same abstract terms as their social causes. For instance, the standard definition of schizophrenic symptoms as "inappropriate affect," "delusions," "hallucinations," "thought disorder," "out of touch with reality," "flatness of affect," "distortion of self-perception," "lack of insight," or "personality change," eliminates any sense of what and how the individual is thinking. The specifics are all rendered immaterial and collapsed into abstract features. Homogenizing disparate content into abstract characteristics is useful for a general characterization of psychosis. However, the abstractions should be drawn from and grounded in specific symptomatology. It must be made clear that the abstractions have a real social psychological basis which has only been momentarily suspended from consideration for the purpose of highlighting general features. "Distortion in self concept," for example, will thereby be an abbreviation for the end product of a complex social psychological process whose richness and variation will attract future investigation.

Unfortunately, psychiatric abstractions are not conceived in this way. Duplicating the errors of other psychological abstractions described in Chapter 3, abstract notions of symptomatology ignore the social psychological basis and construe the general features as a world unto themselves. Abstract features become foregrounded with such fervor that concrete social characteristics are absented from consideration.

A good example of this error is M. Field's (1960) ethno-psychiatric study of rural Ghana. Her descriptions of psychiatric cases suggest a wealth of culturally significant psychological problems; however her diagnosis of these in terms of Western categories leads to a false sense that they are similar to Western dysfunctions. This complacency discourages investigation of the social psychological details. For example, one young man (case #33) became frightened because an amulet he bought violated a taboo against having this kind of thing. He consequently gave the amulet to his brother who promised to destroy it. However, another brother stole it and used it to bewitch an eminent man and seduce his wife. The patient then was overcome by fever and pains in his head and belly. He thought a god had found out that his tabooed amulet had been used for these malevolent purposes and that the god was punishing him. The patient became depressed and languid.

This case obviously presents fertile material for studying Ghanese taboos, witchcraft, religion, kinship relations and responsibilities, socially constructed emotional reactions, and culturally mediated psychotic symptoms. Instead, however, Field proclaims, on the basis of extremely scanty information, that this man is an incipient schizophrenic. So labeled, he is cast within familiar categories and dispensed with. Now he is just like our schizophrenics and can be understood and treated in familiar terms.

So it is that the preoccupation with abstract psychological phenomena and the search for psychological universals drive each other on. The focus on the abstract aspects of psychotic symptoms emphasizes what is universal and, conversely, the quest for universal aspects emphasizes abstract properties. This is only natural because psychological abstractions are general, and psychological universals are abstract. It is no accident that research on the universality of psychiatric symptoms, such as the World Health Organization's (1973) study of schizophrenia, employ extremely abstract criteria which can be compared across cultures. And extremely abstract definitions of psychiatric syndromes, as found in the American Psychiatric Association's *Diagnostic and Statistical Manual*, are construed as denoting universal phenomena.

We should not deny the reality of abstract universals; however, we must be aware of their limited value for psychology. Abstract universals only represent the formalized end product of complex, dynamic, variable occurrences. Thus, "thought disorder," "word salad," "distortion of self-concept," all refer to the fact that thought is disordered, self is distorted, etc.; however, they do not convey the process which generates these results. A preoccupation with the formalized abstractions detracts attention away from the process and leads to the illusion that all thought disorder is essentially the same. Details of form and content are considered secondary or irrelevant.

Focusing on abstract symptoms to the exclusion of details is as fallacious as classifying all inflammations together regardless of their specific properties. Obviously, inflammations of internal organs, of the joints, and of the skin represent radically different maladies produced by different causes and requiring different treatment. Inflammation is not a single disease, it is a common property of several different diseases.

Construing inflammation as a disease obfuscates these important concrete variations. In the same way, schizophrenic symptoms are common abstract properties of disparate processes; they do not constitute a single disease entity.

Beneath the surface, Field's Ghanese case is not really like our schizophrenics at all. His guilt over having violated a taboo is foreign to us, as is his expectation of reprisal because of malevolent acts that his *brother* committed. Americans are generally not afraid of punishment for these kinds of things, and this difference is crucial in understanding why this Ghanese man became psychotic. Conversely, the fragmented "divided self" that Laing describes would be utterly foreign to African schizophrenics. The substantial differences between Opler's Irish and Italian schizophrenics, Draguns' Catholic Latin American and Protestant American psychiatric cases, and Kleinman's Chinese neurasthenics and American depressives further testify to the folly of equating symptoms on the basis of superficial, abstract characteristics.

With schizophrenia and other diagnostic categories being abstract cover terms for diverse psychological dysfunctions, they cannot be specific disorders any more than "inflammation" is a specific physical disorder. It is extremely ironic that psychiatrists and psychologists have gone to enormous lengths to expunge concrete psychological details from their definitions of symptoms but then insist that these symptoms comprise specific dysfunctions. *The major psychiatric syndromes of symptoms are based on a serious category error of confusing abstract, general properties with specific disorders.* This tendency is the opposite of false universalization. False universalization elevates specific phenomena to universals, but psychiatric abstraction presumes that general phenomena are specific disorders.[18]

Look at the DSM's definitions of depression—loss of interest in usual activities, morbid sadness, loss of energy, feelings of worthlessness, and a diminished ability to concentrate. These are aspects of most psychosis. Likewise, the criteria of mania—restlessness, flight of ideas, and distractibility—characterize numerous dysfunctions. They do not constitute a specific disorder.

The major syndromes are so indefinite that they cannot be distinguished from each other. For instance, manic and depressive symptoms are not distinct from inadequate drive or interest, preoccupation with illogical ideas and fantasies, illogical thinking, flat or inappropriate affect which comprise schizophrenia. Even the delusions and hallucinations that supposedly identify schizophrenia are hardly confined to a single form of disturbance. As we stated at the start of this chapter, delusions are quite common in everyday life; they must therefore be at least as familiar in the various psychoses. Paranoid symptoms show a similar pervasiveness. Paranoid persecutory delusions are hardly distinguishable from delusions of persecution and control that characterize schizophrenia. And the DSM acknowledges that paranoia frequently includes mania and depression. Emphasizing the interdependence and interchangeability of these responses is not to deny that patients experience some of them more than others. However, these are not discrete disorders or syndromes. They are simply different responses which coexist in various combinations and are not separated by any hard-and-fast boundaries.

The general, abstract nature of DSM symptoms is responsible for their conceptual and empirical indistinctness. This indistinctiveness is evidenced in numerous ways. To begin with, controversy rages over where the proper boundaries between disorders lie. Is paranoia a distinctive entity, or is it really a phenotype of manic depression as Zigler and Glick (1984) contend? Similarly, are melancholia and attention-deficit disorder (which is the most frequently diagnosed childhood psychiatric disorder) coherent entities or are they artifacts as Zimmerman and Spitz (1989) and Rubinstein and Brown (1984) maintain? Such a cloud of uncertainty naturally makes diagnosing these disorders notoriously unreliable. Numerous studies have found that schizophrenics, manic-depressives, and paranoids diagnosed by one group of psychiatrists are diagnosed differently by another group (Abrams, 1974; Taylor et al., 1974; Pope & Lipinski, 1978; Lipton & Simon, 1985).[19]

The absence of specific physiological underpinnings of the various DSM disorders further testifies to their indistinguishability. Sarbin and Mancuso (1980, chap. 7) and Cohen and Cohen (1986) conclusively disprove the thesis of biological abnormalities in mental patients. And Buschbaum and Haier (1983, p. 424) are forced to conclude their *Annual Review of Psychology* survey with the statement, "The current state of the biological approaches to psychopathology is chaotic; no markers [biological abnormalities] have been accepted . . ." For instance, autonomic nervous system and limbic system changes appear to be nonspecific in depression and anxiety which means that physiological markers are common to both disorders. This is not surprising in view of the fact that anxiety often accompanies depression, so that the two are not easily separable (Kleinman, 1988, p. 60).

Another indication of the lack of specific physiological correlates of psychiatric disorders is the fact that drugs are indistinguishable in their efficacy to alleviate symptoms. Claims concerning the efficacy of one drug for treating a particular disorder have been repudiated by controlled experiments. For instance, lithium has been widely regarded as a specific treatment for manic depression while chlorpromazine was dubbed the drug of choice for treating schizophrenia. In fact, both drugs are equally effective (or ineffective) on both disorders (Pope & Lipinisky, 1978; Brockington et al., 1978; Alexander et al., 1979; Prien et al., 1972; Delva & Letemendia, 1982; Branden, 1982; Spring et al., 1970; Johnson, 1980, pp. 18, 41-43). One study (Prien et al., 1984) found that lithium was successful in preventing recurrences of depression in only 12% of severely depressed patients. In these patients, lithium was no better than a placebo. Evidently, drug-induced relief of symptoms is not due to the specific properties of drugs working on corresponding specific physiological mechanisms which underlie particular symptoms. Relief is due to the generic property of drugs which reduce the overall reactivity of the individual regardless of which symptoms he manifests.

Disorders defined by DSM and other symptomatic criteria are additionally indistinguishable in terms of outcome variables such as social isolation, role impairment, and overall outcome (Endicott et al., 1986, Table 3; Strauss & Carpenter, 1974; Zimmerman & Spitzer, 1989).

The foregoing evidence makes it clear that abstract symptoms do not constitute specific disorders; they are characteristics of psychosis in general. Any psychological distress can result in disorientation and/or self-doubt and/or morbid sadness and/or fear and/or delusion. It makes no sense to maintain these symptoms as specific syndromes.

The misguided attempt at constituting specific disorders from abstract, general symptoms is not unique to contemporary psychiatry. Neurasthenia and hysteria from last century were also nothing more than general signs of distress. They included tiredness, moodiness, agitation, pains and aches, along with convulsions and paralysis. The last two symptoms are more specific and circumscribed than the others, and shall be addressed momentarily. But, by and large, it is evident that all the major categories of madness over the past century(ies) are nothing more than different names for madness itself. They are not refinements in understanding this troublesome problem. Since virtually all psychosis includes disorientation, thought disorder, uncertainty, fear, depression, discomfort, recurrent (obsessive) troubling ideas, stereotyped familiar (compulsive) behaviors, anxiety, and physical aches and pains, the major diagnostic categories which identify these symptoms merely reiterate the general features of psychosis. They break no new ground whatsoever in conceptualizing and unraveling the mysteries of madness.[20]

Even when the DSM does mention truly specific symptoms, such as conversion reactions, it defines them in formal, behavioral terms which overlook psychological meaning (Weiss, 1989). Focusing on the physical paralysis of conversion reactions diverts answering why the victim chooses this particular symptom, what it means to her, what function it serves for her, and how it is related to the social problems that she faces? The same is true for so-called eating disorders, or drug-abuse disorders. In all of these cases, the psychological significance, motives, and underlying problems are ignored in favor of the behavior.

Actually, of course, there is no such thing as an eating disorder. Over- or under-eating is not the problem to focus on. The reasons for the behavior are the real psychological issue that must be addressed. As an analogy, imagine how preposterous it would be to proclaim a "crying disorder" for chronic, uncontrollable crying, without considering the reasons for crying. How absurd would it be to classify all criers together and presume that they should all receive the same treatment when some are crying because they stubbed their toe, some because their husband had been killed, some because they had won a beauty pageant or a ball game.

The entire attempt to categorize symptoms is misguided because the same behavior can serve to express numerous psychological problems, and numerous problems can be expressed by the same symptom. Focusing upon behavior itself obfuscates the psychological problem and the true meaning of the behavior. It forsakes difficult psychological analysis for the superficial categorization of behavior.

Vygotsky was adamantly opposed to symptomatic definitions of disorder. In his comments on psychological diagnosis, he condemned symptom-based nosologies as static, abstract, formal, and vacuous. Vygotsky explicitly criticized Kraepelin because he "told us nothing about the essence of mental disorders; he made them an unknown quantity, X" (Vygotsky,1987b, p. 87). Vygotsky pointed out that mental complexes and events are inadequately defined by their phenotypical characteristics and that psychologically meaningful problems must become the focus of analysis. Mere measurement of overt symptoms must be replaced by unraveling, interpreting, and exposing the meaningful connections between symptoms themselves and between symptoms and the problems that generate them. Progress in this direction requires overthrowing the positivistic suspicion of interpretive understanding.

> The task of a [diagnostic] procedure is not just to learn how to measure but to learn how to see, think, and make associations; and this means that an excessive fear of so-called subjective factors in interpretation and an attempt to arrive at research results in a purely mechanical and arithmetic way are wrong . . . [O]ften the immediate purpose of a scientific investigation is to establish some fact that is not given directly in the reality before us. From symptoms to what lies behind them and from the confirmation of symptoms to a diagnosis of development are the path that investigation should take. Hence the notion that a scientific truth can always be established by direct observation is false. (Vygotsky, 1987b, p. 95)

Reversing the positivistic notion of science, Vygotsky said that psychology will only become a true science when it penetrates beneath superficial appearances to phenomena that are not directly observable:

> So long as a science remains immersed in the study of the external manifestations of things, it will remain at the empirical level and will not be a science in the true meaning of the word. Saddest of all in this situation is that our knowledge not only does not rise to the level of a true science but in fact leads us directly to fallacious conclusions and inferences. This follows from the fact that the essence of things does not coincide directly with their appearance, and he who judges things solely on the basis of their incidental manifestations judges falsely and inevitably arrives at false notions about the reality he is studying, and at false practical instructions with regard to how to act upon this reality. (Vygotsky, 1987b, p. 86)

Overlooking psychologically meaningful problems and focusing on discrete symptoms eliminates any possibility of understanding and empathizing with the psychotic. With all formative process and psychological significance banished, symptoms appear totally irrational and unintelligible. This kind of abstraction not only precludes a scientific analysis of psychosis, it also dehumanizes the victim and prevents effective treatment. It is a perfect example of psychiatric ideology promulgating rather than treating disturbance.

The unscientific and dehumanizing consequences of abstract notions of symptoms are epitomized in Kraepelin's pioneering work which set the tone for the entire course of Western psychiatry. Kraepelin inherited the nineteenth century preoccupation with collapsing psychological phenomena into quasi-physical dimensions. Just as his mentors Wundt and Titchener had construed perception in terms of sensory sensitivity (reaction time and just noticeable differences), and just as they had dissolved emotion into contentless dimensions of pleasure-pain and tension-relaxation, and ideas into colorless features such as intensity, duration, and vividness, so Kraepelin construed schizophrenia as a deficit in attention. He employed psychophysical tests, such as reaction-time measures, to ascertain differences in response between disturbed and normal individuals. Kraepelin's psychophysical orientation led him to construct an entire psychiatric nosology on the basis of such de-psychologized, quasi-physical responses. The absurdity of trying to differentiate specific psychological disorders in terms of abstract features like attention deficit, affect-laden thoughts, delusions, morbid fearfulness, or sadness, can be traced back to, and also epitomizes, the bankruptcy of the entire psychophysical approach. The absence of psychological analysis—which has plagued the entire field of experimental psychology since its nineteenth century birth—made Kraepelin grossly insensitive to psychotic individuals' real problems and intentions. One of his descriptions, written in 1894, is painfully clear in this respect:

> The patient makes his statements slowly and in monosyllables, not because his wish to answer meets with overpowering hindrances, but because he feels no desire to speak at all. He certainly hears and understands what is said to him very well, but he does not take the trouble to attend to it. He pays no heed, and answers whatever occurs to him without thinking. No visible effort of the will is to be noticed. All his movements are languid and expressionless. . . . In spite of his good education he lies in bed for weeks and months, or sits about without feeling the slightest need of occupation. He broods, staring in front of him with expressionless features, over which a vacant smile occasionally plays, or at best turns over the leaves of a book for a moment, apparently speechless, and not troubling with anything. . . . He occasionally composes a letter to the doctor, expressing all kinds of distorted, half-formed ideas. . . . These scraps of writing, as well as his statements that he is pondering over the world, or putting himself together a moral philosophy, leave no doubt that, besides the emotional barrenness, there is also a high degree of weakness of judgement and flightiness, although the pure memory has suffered little, if at all. . . . Besides the mental and emotional imbecility, we meet with other very significant features in the case before us. The first of these is the silly vacant laugh, which is constantly observed in dementia praecox. . . . Then we must notice the tendency to peculiar, distorted turns of speech—senseless playing with syllables and words.

Although David Rosenthal (1970, p. 97) praises Kraepelin's description as unsurpassed in excellence, it is evident that Kraepelin's behavioral orientation depersonalizes the entire situation. The patient is made to appear as simply lazy, stubborn, stupid, disinterested in reality, and deluded. No meaning, intentionality, relation to social experience, or intelligibility is implied. Such an unfortunate interpretation is the necessary consequence of abstract, behavioral definitions because psychological significance has been expunged from consideration.

Treatment Therapy

Deleterious consequences of nonsocial approaches to psychosis are not confined to mere interpretation and description. They have painful practical manifestations in the treatment of victims. Overlooking the social causes and character of psychosis severely limits the improvement that can be effected because it obscures the full range of social values and practices which the victim must change within himself. Furthermore, problematical aspects of the social environment will also remain unchallenged. As a result, psychological improvement will be confined to minor, superficial, transient personal changes within the boundaries of the status quo. While not unimportant, these changes fall far short of what could and should be achieved.

Behavior Modification. Behavior modification simply modifies the individual's behavior through immediate reinforcements. It does not subject the social environment to analysis or change. Recalcitrant mental patients, students, or prisoners are shaped to conform to the status quo by prizes, privileges, and punishment; however, the social structure (the school, family, job, or prison) remains intact. Weaknesses in the social structure which cause psychological problems are obscured in the effort to make individuals conform. Behavior modification is thus the antithesis of a social perspective, not its epitome, as some have claimed.

Biomedical Treatment. The biomedical approach to treatment has received sufficient criticism concerning its asocial, physiological orientation as to make further comment unnecessary. However, one point bears raising. Contrary to numerous critics who attack the medical model as inherently asocial, this is not necessarily so. The medical model of physical disease does acknowledge the importance of environmental factors for disease. Controlling the source of disease through sanitation and hygiene is a well-known part of medicine that complements pharmaceutical treatment. Even social causes of physical disease are recognized in medical theory and practice, as footnotes 4 and 5 above documented. For example, social-psychological stress is the cause of hypertension which is a major contributor to diabetes, cancer, and cardiovascular disease (hypertension is involved in over 80% of cardiovascular deaths and is twice a strong a predictor as smoking or cholesterol) [Sterling & Eyer, 1981].

The biomedical model could certainly incorporate these kinds of social causes in an analysis and treatment of psychological dysfunction (Engel, 1977). Actually, the medical model of insanity employed during the nineteenth century did include "moral" causes such as the general excitement of civilized life. Unfortunately, attention shifted to the physical predispositions of madness and social causes were relegated to being the match which ignites the explosive physical predisposition. Selye emphasized individualistic rather than environmental solutions to stress (Pollock, 1988, p. 392), and the diathesis-stress model of psychosis has followed in his footsteps.

Today, biofeedback, meditation, and other forms of behavioral change occupy center stage in the treatment of stress. Eliminating environmental stressors is a theme rarely heard. This is not to deny social conscience to mental health practitioners. Some are politically active, however, their activity is usually confined to issues directly relating to mental health policy. This is insufficient because alleviating the problem of madness requires a broad transformation of the social values and practices which disturb people.[21]

Humanistic Therapy. For all its difference with the medical model, humanistic therapy shares its asocial focus. This therapy emphasizes personal change apart from societal considerations. Not only is the individual presumed to be able to improve his psychology without humanizing the broad society; he is not even encouraged to intellectually examine the ways in which his own psychology reflects it. Nor is he encouraged to consider alternative *social* values as the basis for new cognitive schemata and behavioral patterns. Instead, society is construed as intrinsically antithetical to individual freedom and fulfillment. This orients the quest for fulfillment in asocial, individualistic directions such as getting in touch with one's own feelings and "true self" which lie buried under social conventions. Freedom and fulfillment are regarded as lying inside the individual ready to be plumbed and actualized. They are not construed as requiring a new social praxis (Carl Rogers, 1964).

Sociohistorical psychology condemns this viewpoint as misguided. As we know from previous chapters, the notion of a pre- or nonsocial, personal self buried under social conventions is a fiction. The self is thoroughly social from its inception. As such, it does not contain any intrinsic, ready-made alternatives to social oppression. Instead, psychological problems can only be overcome by looking *outside* the self and understanding and altering their social character. While social deconstruction is a necessary first step in clarifying destructive social practices, it must be complemented by social reconstruction which replaces malevolent social forces with humane ones.

Humanism's indiscriminate revulsion against social order precludes any constructive social activity which is necessary for real psychological improvement. Typically, social life in general is attacked as intrinsically stultifying without specifying the particular structural problems that are at fault. This leads to a blanket suspicion of all social analysis and social relations beyond the most immediate personal relationships. Individualistic solutions are the inevitable consequence. Of course, humanistic therapists hope that their therapy will produce a caring, socially conscious individual. But they do not directly encourage this as a necessary part of personal fulfillment. In fact, the entire thrust of humanistic therapy is so individualistic as to subordinate social concerns to personal desires (Wallach & Wallach, 1983, chaps. 7, 8).

The asociality of humanistic therapy is evident in its focus on abstract, contentless psychological change which ignore the social substance of psychological problems and symptoms. Therapy urges people to heighten their expressiveness, ability to communicate, self-worth, self-awareness, and wholeness. Additional directions for psychological change include becoming more natural, more oriented toward the present rather than future or past, more accepting, less judgmental, more flexible, spontaneous, autonomous, creative, and less intellectual. These changes are all abstract in being devoid of any particular content. Humanists are peculiarly unconcerned with *what* people feel, communicate, accept, or are. The assumption seems to be that abstract acts necessarily entail positive content so that if one is expressive or communicative or independent or emotional, one will necessarily be so in beneficent ways. This, of course, is false.

As Schur (1976) has observed, merely becoming more expressive is insufficient if the content that is expressed is hurtful. An aggressive, competitive individual, for instance, will not improve his personal relations if he simply expresses himself and communicates more effectively. He needs to alter the aggressive, competitive values that he has acquired. Likewise, developing self-esteem carries no intrinsic direction for improved social psychological functioning. High esteem does not automatically prevent destructive behavior since many high-esteem individuals are hurtful. Becoming more accepting and supportive of oneself and others is similarly only praiseworthy to the extent that one accepts humane things. Accepting destructive values and practices is hardly virtuous or fulfilling.

Remaining on an abstract level of personal concerns, humanistic therapy shares a fundamental asocial orientation with the behavioristic and biomedical treatments it so adamantly opposes. However different therapies may be, they are concordant in overlooking the concrete social nature of psychological problems. This is why the Western orientation toward psychological phenomena and psychotherapy makes real psychological cure quite difficult to achieve (Waxler, 1984).

Despite its good intentions, a humane individualistic orientation cannot counteract malevolent social pressure. Western psychology's attempt to shore up personal strengths and interpersonal interactions cannot succeed in the face of chronic, widespread practices that depersonalize, frighten, antagonize, frustrate, alienate, and divide people. Under the prevailing social forces described above, efforts at enhancing self-esteem, communication, sympathy, and love will be as successful as the campaign to "say no to drugs" will be in urban slums. A few successes can be registered, but hardly enough to mitigate the problems.

Psychotherapy can only be successful in a humane social system which complements rather than contradicts therapeutic care. Ironically, a more humane society will need less psychiatry and psychotherapy because people will be more at ease. In other words, the most effective psychiatry is that which occurs in a humane society which reduces the need for psychiatry. Conversely, a malevolent society that creates psychological problems and creates a massive need for psychiatry is one where psychiatry cannot solve those overwhelming problems (Waxler, 1984).

Notes

1. Psychologically disturbed individuals may actually be more decent than normal people because they are incapable of sustained malevolence. Only psychologically normal individuals are capable of sustained malevolence (Furst, 1954, p. 154).
2. In his classic account, *The Divided Self*, Laing vividly describes how as individuals withdraw from social relations and create a non-interactive "true self," their thoughts become ungrounded, take on a life of their own, and dominate the person. The result of social withdrawal is thus the precise opposite of its aim: The intention is to gain autonomy, security, and superiority, but the outcome is domination, fear, insecurity, and rigidity. The absence of social boundaries yields cognitive disorganization, confusion, and other features of psychosis.
3. Littlewood and Lipsedge (1982, p. 93) explain the differential incidence of psychosis among immigrant groups as due to similar social psychological factors. These include the reasons for immigrating, the expectations that members of the various groups had about their new lives, the extent to which these expectations were met, particular stresses that the ethnic groups experienced in their adopted country.
4. Economic difficulties are also correlated with numerous other psychological and physical maladies such as suicide, cardiovascular diseases, cirrhosis of the liver, infant mortality, and criminal aggression.
   The correlation of these maladies with economic downturns can only be interpreted as causal relationships of economic events on psychological and somatic disturbances. It is difficult to see any other relationship between these two domains since cirrhosis, suicide, infant mortality, etc., cannot cause economic events. It is plausible to conclude, as Brenner (1979) does, that economic difficulties generate a wide range of disturbances, of which psychosis is only one.
5. Companionship also mitigates physical pathology. As Lynch (1977), and Sterling and Eyer (1981) have documented, mortality rates from most physical causes are lower among married people than among single or divorced in-

dividuals. Especially telling is the fact that the mortality rate from lung cancer for married cigarette smokers is lower than the rate for unmarried non-smokers. In other words, being unmarried is more hazardous than smoking for dying of lung cancer. The longevity that married individuals enjoy relative to unmarried people holds true for women as well as men although the relative advantage that married women have over unmarried women is less than the relative advantage which married men have over unmarried men.

Interestingly, human companionship is not unique in reducing mortality. Companionship from pets is also a significant moderator.

6. Cf. the special issue of the *Journal of Health and Social Behavior*, 1975, 16, 4 for a discussion of these problems.

7. The bias against lower-class patients intrudes into treatment as well as diagnosis. Mollica and Milic's (1986) investigation of a community mental health center found that lower-class patients were routinely given poorer treatment than upper-class patients. 45% of the upper class patients received psychotherapy in contrast to 18% of lower-class patients. Even when upper- and lower-class patients received the same diagnosis of schizophrenia, the wealthier patients were assigned to the psychotherapy unit whereas the poorer patients were assigned to drug or alcohol abuse units of the center, which were staffed by paraprofessionals rather than professional therapists.

8. The greater objectivity (or, at least, lessened subjectivity) of structured self-report indicators over psychiatrists' diagnosis is demonstrated in Dohrenwend et al.'s (1970) experiment. This important study investigated the objectivity of two psychiatric indicators: the Psychiatric Status Schedule (PSS), which is an open-ended questionnaire that allows the psychiatrist to code patients' responses, and the Structured Interview Schedule (SIS) which asks the subject to respond within a fixed range of alternatives (e.g., "true-false") to standard, explicit questions. The SIS was modelled after the questionnaire used in the Midtown Manhattan Study, so the results of this experiment reveal a good deal about the Manhattan investigation. Now, both instruments were employed by psychiatrists in direct interviews with patients, with full knowledge of the patients' class status. Written case records of these interviews were compiled, with information about the patients' social class omitted. Other psychiatrists (who had not made the initial interviews on these patients, but who had experience interviewing other patients) then rated the case records according to severity of disturbance.

The results revealed enormous differences in interrater reliability between the SIS and PSS. On the SIS, the "blind" reviewers generally agreed with the interviewing psychiatrist. But on the PSS, the interviewing psychiatrist rated lower-class patients as more disturbed than the blind reviewer did, while rating the middle-class patients as less disturbed than the blind reviewer did. For example, the interviewing psychiatrist only diagnosed 8% of the richest patients as psychiatrically disturbed, whereas the blind reviewer rated 75% of them as disturbed! The interviewing psychiatrist similarly rated 15% of the middle-income patients as severely disturbed, while the blind reviewer placed 45% of them in this category. In contrast, a sample of the poorest patients was diagnosed as severely disturbed in 18% of the cases by the interviewing psychiatrist, and only 9% of the cases by the blind reviewer (Table, 4.18).

The interviewer's knowledge of the patient's class status obviously biased his diagnosis on the PSS, but only minimally on the structured SIS.

9. Labeling theory's preoccupation with society's *response* to psychological problems and its inattention to social *causes* of those problems is therefore inadequate. While the medical community's response exacerbates distress and must be made more humane, the underlying causes cannot be disregarded in the idealistic hope that more sensitive treatment of the victims is all that is necessary. Scheff (1984) and Waxler (1984) are therefore quite wrong to believe that societies are basically benign, generating only moderate stresses, and to blame psychosis entirely on psychiatrists' treating stressful individuals as mad.

It is instructive to examine Scheff's explanation of why individuals deviate from social norms in the first place, since it is that deviance that is labeled as mad by psychiatrists. Scheff (1984, p. 41) lists four reasons for deviance: organic (biochemical or genetic), psychological (mistreatment during socialization), external stress (drug ingestion, military combat, deprivation of food and sleep), and volitional acts of innovation or defiance. None of these includes malevolent social norms! These causes of deviance are therefore outside normal social practice rather than being features of social practice itself.

10. A given behavior may be either a social problem causing psychological distress or a symptom of that distress. For instance fear may be caused by another party's harmful actions toward the individual, or it may be the paranoid by-product of a faulty interpretation of events.

Depression, however, would seem to always be an illness, a symptom of, and a reaction to a social problem. It is not imposed on the victim the way that a social crisis, neglect, or confusion are. Depression is a state that the victim develops in view of his hopeless inability to overcome malevolent conditions. It is therefore perplexing that Kleinman frequently refers to depression as a disease (e.g., 1980, p. 157; 1982, p. 181).

11. Other studies have detailed the social variation in symptomatology without identifying the social concepts that mediate this variation. Regarding somatization, Stoker et al. (1968) found that Anglos had half the number of headaches as Mexican-Americans. In his classic study on Irish and Italian male schizophrenics, Marvin Opler (1957) discovered distinct symptom patterns that differentiated most of the Irish from most of the Italians. The Irish were fearful of females, low in self-esteem, tortured by feelings of guilt and inadequacy, and sunk in paranoid delusions. The Italians, on the other hand, were hostile to male figures, extremely impulsive and excitable, subject to mood swings, sometimes assaultive and destructive. Italians typically ex-

press their suffering openly and dramatically in contrast to the Irish who deny symptoms (Good & Good, 1981, p. 172).

According to Opler, the Irish fear of women represents the structure of the Irish family in which the mother plays a dominant role. When this dominance becomes intensified to the point where it psychologically damages the son, it will inevitably be expressed—however incompletely, ambiguously, and metaphorically—in symptoms involving antipathy to women. In contrast, intensification of the typical Italian family structure will produce exaggerated male authority, and generate symptoms expressing an antipathy toward men. Italian symptoms of emotional expression and flagrant behavior likewise reflect the general emotional expressiveness of Italian culture.

12. *Tarantism* is a little known but fascinating culture-bound syndrome which is localized in a small area of Southern Italy (di Martino, 1975). Tarantism is a syndrome of symptoms which include nausea, malaise, anxiety, muscle pain, and several other general effects. It results from the belief that one has been bitten by a tarantula spider, although actually no bite has occurred. In fact, the great majority of patients are women, although men are more exposed to spider bites in the course of their work. The symbolic nature of tarantism is further manifested in the fact that it often starts in disturbing situations (death of a loved person, family conflicts) quite apart from any contact with spiders. The symptoms mimic the known effects of real bites, and even only occur during the summer harvest when the tarantula bite is most likely to occur.

13. It is not clear why Gottesman and Shields fix upon these proportions when a few years earlier they proclaimed quite different numbers. In 1976 Gottesman and Shields (1976, p. 376) stated that "The inheritability of the liability to developing schizophrenia on present evidence is in the neighborhood of 85%."

14. The social epidemiology of madness is often challenged with the question, "What about individuals from pernicious environments who manage to avoid psychosis? Doesn't this indicate a role for endogenous resistance or susceptibility to psychological dysfunction?" The answer is no. Variations in the circumstances themselves can plausibly account for individual differences in reaction. A given environment (culture, social class, social role, or family) is not homogeneous and does not subject all individuals to the same experience. Parents who mistreat a son may favor a daughter and so spare her from the problems which drive her brother to distraction. First- and second-born children are also treated differently. Solicitous baby-sitters, teachers, and peers may support and protect certain individuals but not others. Social dynamics make a given environment differentially disturbing to individuals. Merely being present in a pernicious environment does not mean that one has been treated deleteriously. A social explanation of psychosis maintains that one must have actually been victimized by mistreatment, not simply surrounded by it. Evidently, when this is the case, few individuals escape madness.

15. It is important to state that even if psychotics were found to possess neuroanatomical abnormalities this would not prove biogenetic causation of madness. In the first place, the biological abnormalities could be the *result* of social-psychological stress (Candland, 1977, pp. 127 ff.). And even if they were found to antedate madness, they might still not be its cause. A biological abnormality, e.g., leading to hyperactivity, excessive crying or irritability, or even extreme weakness, might function like a temperamental trait that parents find difficult to handle. The parents' inability leads to abusing the child and eventually to psychosis. In this case, it is not the trait that causes madness, it is the parents' mistreatment of the trait.

    Finally, any biological differences between psychotics and normals could be due to a third extraneous factor. A good example of this is the highly significant correlation (r=.80-.90) between favorable course and outcome of schizophrenia and a low percentage of total fat in the diet. An even higher correlation (r=.91-.95) exists between favorable course and outcome of schizophrenia and saturated fat in the diet. While this has led Christensen and Christensen (1988) to mistakenly assume a causal impact of diet on schizophrenia, and to ludicrously propose altering diet as a means of improving course and outcome of schizophrenia, a more plausible explanation for the relationship is that it is an entirely spurious result of another factor that underlies both diet and course of schizophrenia. A promising candidate is industrialization, which, as we shall presently see, is a major influence on the course of schizophrenia as well as on fatty diets.

16. In an important adoptive study, Tienari et al. (1985, 1987) found impressive support for environmental determinants of madness. Noting that no adoption studies have thus far directly investigated the quality of family interaction, the authors set out to investigate the adoptive families of index adoptees whose mothers were schizophrenic, and adoptive families of control adoptees whose mothers were not schizophrenic.

    Seven percent of the index Ss became psychotic in contrast to 1% of the control Ss. However, the psychosis is explainable by the disturbed family settings in which the dysfunctional subjects lived. On a range from healthy to severely disturbed, only 5% of index adoptive families were rated healthy (in contrast to 10% of control adoptive families), and 16% of index adoptive families were severely disturbed (in contrast to 8% of control adoptive families). A more specific analysis of the families of individual psychotics reveals that every psychotic individual (in both the index and control groups) grew up in a disturbed adoptive family environment. Conversely, there were no psychotic diagnoses among the offspring reared in healthy or mildly disturbed adoptive families. Looking at it from another angle, every individual who was raised in a severely disturbed adoptive family developed some psychological dysfunction (ranging from neurotic to psychotic), while not one individual raised in a healthy adoptive family developed psychological dysfunction (Tienari et al., 1985, Table 5).

These results fully confirm Emmy Werner's findings that biological risk for psychological problems pales in comparison with environmental risk. After all, none of the 43 offspring of schizophrenic mothers who were reared in a healthy family or in a mildly disturbed family environment had a schizophrenic or borderline diagnosis. The only offspring of schizophrenic mothers who became dysfunctional were reared in a severely disturbed family—and even the majority of these index subjects, whose biological and adoptive parents were severely disturbed, managed to avoid serious dysfunction (only 38% of them became psychotic or borderline).

Sameroff et al. (1983, pp. 247-248) provide another environmental explanation for the higher incidence of psychosis in index as opposed to control subjects. Adopted-away offspring of schizophrenic mothers experience inferior pre- and postnatal conditions compared with infants of normal mothers. Consequently, the index subjects are more sickly than control subjects, which could contribute to poor parenting on the part of some adoptive parents. Adoptive parents of control subjects would have an easier time dealing with their healthier children, and would be more adequate parents. Poor parenting would then be the major cause of the index children's psychological dysfunction. This scenario is quite different from genetically determined psychological deficits constituting an intrinsic predisposition to psychosis.

17. The postulated role of beta-endorphin in schizophrenia had a similar ludicrous rationale (Goldberg, 1988, pp. 115-140).

Peculiar, nonpsychological conceptions of psychological dysfunction not only underlie assumptions about causes. Such conceptions also underlie hypotheses concerning treatment of psychological dysfunction. For example, electro-convulsive (shock) therapy was conceived out of a comparison between schizophrenia and epilepsy. According to Johnson-Laird and Wason (1977, p. 437), "Epileptics seemed to be less likely to suffer from schizophrenia than non-epileptics, it was therefore considered a good idea to induce epileptic-like seizures in schizophrenics [in order to reduce schizophrenic symptoms]." According to this logic, if polio victims manifest a low incidence of schizophrenia, then doctors will induce polio-like paralysis in schizophrenics to reduce their symptoms!

18. The WHO investigation was not altogether free from false universalization. Kleinman (1988, pp. 18-22) and Higginbotham and Connor (1989) point out certain devious ways in which universalization was manufactured. The more unusual "culture-bound" symptoms were expunged from the study, and significant cultural divergences in the pattern of schizophrenic symptoms were downplayed in an effort to maximize the appearance of universal symptomatology. For instance, the WHO study asserted that for paranoid schizophrenia, "All [national] centers had high scores on experiences of control, predelusional signs, delusions, and flatness of affect." (WHO, 1973, p. 184). In fact, only 26% of the Indian paranoid schizophrenics had experiences of control, just 26% of the Czech paranoid schizophrenics manifested pre-

delusional signs, a mere 17% of the Russian paranoid schizophrenics reported delusions, and only 27% of the Colombian paranoid schizophrenics suffered flattened affect. The reason for these discrepancies is that not all patients in all cultures manifest all of the symptoms all of the time. Nevertheless, the abstractly formulated symptoms were universally present to some extent among the nations investigated. There is little doubt that most psychotics throughout the world will experience most of the abstract symptoms sometime over the course of their disturbance. In this sense the symptoms are universal.

19. The indistinctiveness of DSM disorders makes diagnosticians susceptible to relying on extraneous considerations in judging dysfunction. Race, class, and gender of the patient have all been found to influence diagnosis. Loring and Powell (1988) found that diagnosis varied enormously depending upon whether psychiatric cases were presented as male, female, white, or black. Women and black psychiatrists were no more objective than male and white psychiatrists. For example, 17% of white female psychiatrists diagnosed the record of a black male as manifesting undifferentiated schizophrenia. However, when the same case was portrayed as a black female, 50% of white female psychiatrists offered this diagnosis. Psychiatrists have also been found to offer widely different diagnoses depending upon which side of a legal case they are hired to represent (Simon & Zusman, 1983). Straightforward financial considerations, like those of gender and race, provide a clearer diagnostic basis than do the ambiguous symptoms.

20. In view of the foregoing, it is peculiar that a critic of psychiatric theory like Arthur Kleinman still attempts to operate within the standard diagnostic categories. His entire analysis of the difference between depression and neurasthenia assumes some specific reality to these entities when, in fact, none exists. It is one thing to state that Chinese symptoms are phenomenologically experiences in physical forms while middle-class American symptoms generally take psychological forms. But this does not validate depression and neurasthenia as distinctive psychological *disorders* with particular causes and outcomes. Kleinman's acceptance of other orthodox terms such as "brief reactive psychosis" (Kleinman, 1988, p. 36) is equally bewildering because the brevity of reaction certainly does not constitute a distinct psychological entity. Again, innumerable psychological problems and symptoms can occur acutely, and their acuteness is not the important issue. Their socially variable causes and meaning are what is psychologically important.

It is gratifying to see that Kleinman's latest work is moving away from inappropriate psychiatric categories to more ecologically sensitive descriptions.

21. Physical health also requires a humane social environment and is not achieved by advances in medical care alone. Thus, Sterling and Eyer (1981, p. 31) state, "The contributions of chronic arousal [hypertension] to mortality cannot be mitigated solely within a medical framework because the forces

that generate arousal are powerful and deeply ingrained in our social structure and culture." Berliner (1975, p. 577) shows how, historically,

> it was not medical services at all that led, for instance, to the improvement in death rates, but rather a combination of events, including better nutrition brought about by better transportation of food between town and country, the change from woolen to cotton clothing, and the introduction of a clean water supply. For almost every leading cause of death at the turn of the century, with the possible exception of diptheria, the mortality rate had begun to decline well in advance of the introduction of specific therapeutic measures made possible by medical science. . . . Although it is widely assumed that the introduction of antibiotics and effective immunization campaigns marked a dramatic breakthrough in the fight against infectious disease, most of the reduction in mortality rate had already occurred, and there was only a slight downward inflection in an otherwise declining curve following their introduction.

Conclusion: Political Aspects of Psychological Doctrines

Psychological doctrines have wide-ranging effects on social praxis. They influence the manner in which people think about themselves, their expectations and treatment of others, their understanding of the causes of psychological problems, the kinds of solutions they believe possible, and the public policies they endorse. Psychological descriptions and explanations are thus eminently political.

Sociohistorical psychology is politically unique in placing psychological phenomena and social praxis squarely within human management. The conception of psychology as composed of humanly produced mediations means that the most central facets of psychological activity are transformable. Psychological transformation requires altering the social and technological underpinnings of consciousness, which as human artifacts are modifiable. This ability of consciousness to refine itself through humanizing its social and technological environment is the most thoroughgoing freedom, because nothing is left outside of human control.

Sociohistorical psychology denies that the human condition is attributable to natural intra-organismic forces, because these have been superceded by mediations. Nor is the human condition due to natural external forces because these have been fundamentally mastered. Virtually all the problems which imperil man are man-made. Natural disasters occur, however, their consequences are minimal and could be further mitigated through improved technological applications.

The real perils to mankind are war, pollution, malnutrition, inadequate housing, exploitation, stress, and dangerous working conditions. All of these are fundamentally socioeconomic and technological problems that could be remedied by socioeconomic and technological reforms (Lappe, 1986, 1987). Natural *environmental* threats (such as predators, insufficient food supplies, and inhospitable climactic changes) have been

313

virtually eliminated because natural *organismic* constraints have been su-perceded. Animals are overwhelmed by environmental perils because their sensitivity, intelligence, and responsiveness are constrained by im-mutable (or, at best, slowly mutating) biological mechanisms. Animals cannot control their environments or themselves. Humans can master both. Sociohistorical psychology promotes human freedom in relation to nature, society, technology, and consciousness by emphasizing the un-naturalness of human activity.

In contrast, nonsocial psychological viewpoints absolutize the given character of psychological phenomena and of sociopolitical practices. The societal character of psychological phenomena is disregarded, which does not eliminate it but only takes it for granted and falsely universalizes it as the inevitable limit to all variations. Psychologists believe that the limits of psychological variation are either naturally imposed or naturally cho-sen ("individuals just like to do things in that way"). However, the limits are actually social because the entire character of psychological phenom-ena is social.

Disregarding the social character of psychology ensures that the way people think about themselves, treat others, understand and resolve their problems, will ultimately fall within existing, unrecognized social param-eters. Moreover, the broader social practices that engender psychology are also obscured. Obfuscated, they persist in an alien manner, beyond awareness and control. Consequently, nonsocial psychological doctrines absolutize both the sociopolitical and the psychological status quo.

There are three main schools of nonsocial psychology—naturalism, humanism, and empiricism-positivism. All three reify psychological phe-nomena and sociopolitical practices. Within each school, certain strands enthusiastically accept this dual reification. They affirm the congruence of their nonsocial postulates with the status quo, and they utilize these postulates to disavow the possibility of transforming psychological activity and societal practices. Other strands of each nonsocial school express dissatisfaction with the status quo. They seek to avoid it by postulating nonsocial characteristics and origins of psychological phenomena. How-ever escapism is not an effective opposition to social reality and social elements permeate the conceptions of escapist nonsocial doctrines. These doctrines absolutize psychological activity and societal practices as much as the affirmative nonsocial standpoints do. A few examples will sub-stantiate this contention.

The bulk of naturalistic psychology explicitly affirms the social and psychological status quo. This is not surprising in view of the fact that the naturalistic viewpoint in modern psychology was founded by Galton and other elitists who explicitly sought to justify the prevailing social distribution of cognitive and personality traits across class, gender, and ethnic groups. Contemporary advocates of naturalism, such as sociobiologists, continue to recognize that attributing monogamy and private property to indigenous organismic tendencies solidifies these customs as currently practiced. In Wilson's (1978, p. 109) words, "The biological formula of territorialism translates easily into the rituals of modern property ownership."

However, not all naturalistic psychologists are so explicitly conservative.Piaget's work exemplifies naturalistic psychological systems erected in opposition to deleterious social practices. Piaget was perturbed by social antagonisms and authoritarian social relations and he sought to evade them by postulating endemic, universal, cognitive forms. Piaget hoped that "underlying the manifold differences and vagaries of human action there is a common universal rationality which develops" (Kitchener, 1986, p. 81). This rationality was presumed to be the product of auto-regulatory mechanisms such as equilibrium which would prevail despite social perturbations. Piaget relegated social influences to a secondary role in cognitive development because he was suspicious of their impact (Elbers, 1986, p. 382). His psychological theory was thus at least partially motivated by his political orientation.

We have seen in Chapters 2 and 3 that Piaget's psychological concepts fail to evade society's imprint and are quite bound by it. Despite his abstracting cognitive form from content, these forms reflected Western modes of thought and social relations. In his quest to escape social reality, Piaget failed to realize that his asocial bastion was fashioned out of social brick and mortar. That is, the features of cognitive development that Piaget regarded as most natural were actually products of his society. Rather than escape from society into nature, Piaget made his society appear natural. Paradoxically, the very attempt to escape from society gave it an air of inescapable permanence. Piaget did not discover a common universal rationality that unifies all people. He idealistically presumed this state and ideologically imposed it upon people to whom it is actually quite foreign. The naivete of relying on nature to provide human harmony is evident in Piaget's political declarations. He went so far as to claim that biological "laws of equilibrium" tend toward increasing equality, reciprocity, and justice regardless of what any particular society is like (Mays, 1982, p. 44). This trend is presumed to stem from an originary sense of justice which is rooted in childhood reciprocity and mutual respect. The fact that harmony, justice, and equality still remain a distant goal for our society, much less our planet, demonstrates that biology is as incapable of promoting political harmony as it is of promoting uniform cognitive development. Unfortunately, naturalistic psychological theories which seek to elude social ills ultimately leave us as inexorably trapped within those ills as sociobiology does (cf., Marcuse's trenchant critique of idealist solutions to social problems in Marcuse, 1968, chaps. 2, 3).

Humanistic psychology is strongly opposed to naturalistic reification and it conceives of psychological activity as freely chosen rather than naturally mandated. Humanistic psychologists, who, for the purposes of this discussion will be considered to include existentialists and phenomenologists, presume that individuals freely invent their own psychology by drawing upon indigenous capabilities and interests. At least, individuals can exercise such autonomy if they steadfastly resist attempts by society to influence them. Certainly, this is the ideal that underlies such concepts as self-actualization, self-acceptance, self-awareness, and self-constituted perception. Exemplifying the latter, Merleau-Ponty claimed that the body has an "original intentionality" in the sense that it "secretes in itself a significance which comes to it from nowhere, projecting that significance upon its material surrounding . . ." (Merleau-Ponty, 1962, pp. 387, 197).

Ironically, humanism's preoccupation with free choice results in absolutizing psychological phenomena and sociopolitical practices. Concern about the *process* of choosing, expressing, and growing supercedes attention to *what* is chosen and expressed. The *self-analysis* involved in deciding which activity is appealing supercedes a *social analysis* of the content of activity. It doesn't matter what activity one chooses, or what content one expresses, as long as one does so whole-heartedly and feels good about it. The social values and implications of the activity are subordinated to personal feelings of pleasure, so that good and bad, fulfilling and unfulfilling, are defined in subjective terms of whether the individual feels happy or not.

Humanists fail to recognize that emotions, perceptions, and all psychological functions are socially derived. Consequently, the perceptual and emotional choices that one makes to restructure a worldview or to augment happiness are shot through with social values. Yet the social values are disregarded in humanism's preoccupation with the act of choosing. This leaves the social character of the choice unchallenged and absolute. Humanist freedom thus winds up being a choice within a socially stipulated range of alternatives. Like the situation faced by a consumer in a shopping center, the range and nature of the available choices remains beyond question.

The very goal of perceiving and acting according to what is personally gratifying reflects the predominant social value of bourgeois individualism. Taking this value for granted as the *sine qua non* of psychological fulfillment absolutizes it. The process of choosing activity thus embodies social values as much as the content of the choice does. This is one more example of the fact that the psychological processes which psychologists construe as devoid of social character typically remain fraught with it. Both the form and content of psychological phenomena are thoroughly social.

Humanists' preoccupation with personal growth and agency not only absolutizes the social character of psychological phenomena. It also absolutizes sociopolitical practices by failing to systematically examine the nature of society and the course that social restructuring should take. As Schur (1976, p. 92) said:

> In the preoccupation with 'process' (and lack of interest in specific social forms), we are never told in detail what kind of society would maximize even the possibilities for meaningful self-realization. There is, of course, the usual reference to our presently inhibiting and restricting social conditions, along with abstract proclamations favoring love, community, trust, honesty, and the like. But what specific social arrangements would make these things possible? And how are we to attain them? For many of the awareness writers, one hardly gathers that it makes much difference.

The indifference to societal change leaves the status quo as the taken-for-granted, immutable framework within which activity conforms. Such constrained freedom is the essence of humanistic philosophy and psychology. For instance, in his account of perception, Merleau-Ponty said, "The world remains the same world throughout my life, because it is that permanent being within which I make all corrections to my knowledge, a world which in its unity remains unaffected by these corrections . . ." (Merleau-Ponty, 1962, pp. 327-328). Sartre epitomized this alienated freedom in his statement, "to be free is not to choose the historic world in which one arises—which would have no meaning—but to choose oneself in the world whatever this may be" (*Being and Nothingness*, 1956, p. 521). The failure to concretely analyze, reformulate, and challenge the social system is the reason that the most apparently antisocial activities are ultimately compatible with, and co-opted by, the status quo (Ratner, 1971a, b).

Despite its antipathy to oppressive social life humanism entraps us within the status quo to the same extent as other forms of individualism which affirm it. Humanism is no more liberating than the individualistic philosophy of the Enlightenment which portrayed individual freedom and self-interested action as justifying capitalistic economic relations. Actually, the Enlightenment philosophers were more correct in depicting the conservative political implications of individualism than humanists are in asserting its liberating potential. As Ellen Wood (1972, p. 159) has argued: "because liberal doctrine assumes an antagonism between private and public, individual and community, the individual freedom it calls for can paradoxically be achieved only at the price of subjection to an external, alien public power, a power ultimately inimical to individual liberty and autonomy."

Empiricist, or positivist, epistemology absolutizes psychological phenomena and sociopolitical practices to the same extent that naturalism and humanism do. Empiricism construes psychological phenomena as independent atoms whose qualities are fixed and only vary quantitatively. According to empiricists, intelligence, love, self-concept, depression, and aggression are simple, homogeneous factors whose qualities are taken-for-granted, presumed to be universal, and thus undeserving of investigation. Research need only be conducted into the *degree* to which individuals differentially exhibit these fixed qualities. Granting priority to quantity over quality, or measurement over conceptualization, obfuscates psychology's social character. For instance, defining aggression as the number of incidences of hitting, obliterates the act's meaning, intention, and contextual conditions. It becomes impossible to perceive the social values that underlay the decision to commit the act, the difficulty or ease with which the decision was made, or the expectations about social repercussions following the act.

Contending that empiricism obfuscates social character may appear untrue in view of the fact that empiricist methodology is often employed to investigate social influences on psychology. Indeed, the whole thrust of empiricism emphasizes environmental causation. Ironically, however, its atomistic epistemology precludes comprehending society as an integral system with a definite character. Instead, society is dissolved into independent factors whose origin and character are tacitly assumed to be given. They are thus shorn of their sociohistorical character. As Bronfenbrenner was quoted as stating in the Introduction, social factors are treated as quantitative variables possessing so much "stimulation" or "stressfulness," without regard for their rich social content. Social elements or variables are singular phenomena, stripped bare of the complex of things that sustain them in a context. Accordingly, our understanding of the variable itself and its context must suffer. Blumer (1969, chap. 7) put this well in his trenchant critique of variables:

> the very features which give variable analysis its high merit—the qualitative constancy of the variables, their clean-cut simplicity, their ease of manipulation as a sort of free counter, their ability to be brought into decisive relation—are the features that lead variable analysis to gloss over the character of the real operating factors in group life, and real interaction and relations between such factors. (p. 138)

In his essay, "The Professional Ideology of Social Pathologists," C. Wright Mills (1963, pp. 525-552) echoes this idea. He states that, "The focus on 'the facts' takes no cognizance of the normative structures within which they lie."

Mills then spells out the political implications of this atomistic methodology. "The liberal 'multiple-factor' view does not lead to a conception of causation which would permit points of entry for broader types of action, especially political action . . . If one fragmentalizes society into 'factors,' into elemental bits, naturally one will then need quite a few of them to account for something, and one can never be sure they are all in. A formal emphasis upon 'the whole' plus lack of structural consideration plus a focus upon scattered situations does not make it easy to reform the status quo" (pp. 536-537). Reform is further obviated by the conceptualization of social and psychological factors as quantitatively but not qualitatively changeable.

It is well known that empiricist-positivist methodology was originally designed precisely in order to make social reform difficult. Comte intended positive philosophy to affirm the existing order against those who asserted the need for negating it. Describing social facts as obeying invariable social laws consolidates public order by fostering a sense of resignation to one's social condition. While Comte and Saint Simon by no means rejected the need to reform the status quo, they conceived positivism to combat transcendent thinking and revolutionary principles that might overthrow it. Facts were construed as existing within a social order that was itself beyond analysis. Indeed, the atomistic approach to factual inquiry necessarily immunized the social whole from investigation (Marcuse, 1960, part 2, chap. 2; Gouldner, 1970, pp. 88-108).

Liberal empiricists-positivists are as trapped within the status quo as their nineteenth century forefathers were. Speaking about the good intentions of empiricist researchers who avow their interest in reforming society, Mills says, "these writers [nevertheless] typically assume the norms which they use, and often tacitly sanction them. There are few attempts to explain deviations from the norms in terms of the norms themselves, and no rigorous facing of the implications of the fact that social transformations would involve shifts *in them*" (Mills, 1963, p. 532).

The psychological and sociopolitical inadequacies of nonsocial psychological doctrines go hand in hand. They both reflect a failure to recognize the social basis of psychological activity. It should be obvious by now that nonsocial mechanisms are no more the true source of psychology than the moon is the source of moonlight. Just as moonlight is actually the reflection of an external source, so the postulated nonsocial determinants of psychology actually reflect social relations which are the true source of psychological functions. Natural processes, individual choices, and fragmentary psychological and social elements unwittingly represent the character of concrete social systems. Just as science had to dispel the naive illusion that the moon's light originated from endogenous sources, so science must dispel the equally naive illusion that psychology stems from nonsocial sources. Such de-mystification will illuminate the nature of psychological phenomena and the nature of social practices. This will open the opportunity for improving the functioning of both.

Nonsocial views of psychology which reify psychological phenomena reify the social practices which underlie them. However, reifying social practices also reifies psychology. The inconceivability of transforming society leads psychologists to adopt an asocial view of psychology and human nature. With society taken for granted, the social character of psychology is taken for granted and ignored.

If political viewpoints truly underlie the conceptualizing and acceptance of psychological doctrines, then it follows that sociohistorical psychology will become increasingly acceptable as social change becomes more politically palatable. As social change becomes more imperative, the social character of psychology will become more obvious. It will then become evident that the actual state of psychology and society is only one of many possible conditions. The actual will be contrasted with other possibles and its specific, concrete, unique character will be illuminated. When actual social conditions are seen as improvable, individual potentiality for creativity and fulfillment will become actual. Individual potential will become actual as the social actual is conceived to be a mere potential and is superceded by that potential.

References

[Where two dates are given, e.g., 1895/1944, the initial one is the date the work was written or first published; the second is the date of the edition cited.]

Abrams, R., Taylor, M., & Gaztanaga, P. Manic-depressive illness and paranoid schizophrenia. *Archives of General Psychiatry*, 1974, *31*, 640-642.

Abravanel, E., & Sigafoos, A. Exploring the presence of imitation during early infancy. *Child Development*, 1984, *55*, 381-392.

Adamson, L., Bakeman, R., & Smith, C. Gestures, words, and early object sharing. In V. Volterra & C. Erting (Eds.), *From gesture to language in hearing and deaf children*. New York: Springer, 1990, chap. 3.

Ainsworth, M., & Bell, S. Mother-infant interaction and the development of competence. In K. Connolly & J. Bruner (Eds.), *The growth of competence*. New York: Academic Press, 1974, pp. 97-118.

Albee, G., & Gullotta, T. Fact and fallacies about primary prevention. *Journal of Primary Prevention*, 1986, *6*, 207-218.

Amir, Y., & Sharon, I. Are social-psychological laws cross-culturally valid? *Journal of Cross-Cultural Psychology*, 1987, *18*, 383-470.

Anderson, J. *The architecture of cognition*. Cambridge: Harvard University Press, 1983.

Aries, P. *Centuries of childhood: A social history of family life*. New York: Vintage, 1962.

Armon-Jones, C. The thesis of constructionism. In R. Harre (Ed.), *The social construction of emotions*. New York: Blackwell, 1986(a), chap. 3.

Armon-Jones, C. The social functions of emotions. In R. Harre (Ed.), *The social construction of emotions*. New York: Blackwell, 1986(b), chap. 4.

Arnheim, A. *Visual thinking*. Berkeley: University of California Press, 1969.

Arnold, W. *Nebraska Symposium on Motivation*, 1975, Lincoln: University of Nebraska Press, 1976.

Aronson, E. *The social animal*. San Francisco: Freeman, 1984.

Aronson, R. *Sartre's second critique*. Chicago: University of Chicago Press, 1987.

Arnove, R. *Philanthropy and cultural imperialism*. Indiana: Indiana University Press, 1980.

Asch, S. Forming impressions of personality. *Journal of Abnormal and Social Psychology*, 1946, *41*, 258-290.

Asch, S. *Social psychology*. New York: Prentice-Hall, 1952.

Atkinson, T., Liem, R., & Liem, J. The social costs of unemployment: implications for social support. *Journal of Health and Social Behavior*, 1986, *27*, 317-331.

Averill, J. Autonomic response patterns during sadness and mirth. *Psychophysiology*, 1969, *5*, 399-414.

Averill, J. Emotion and anxiety: Sociocultural, biological, and psychological determinants. In A. Rorty (Ed.), *Explaining emotions*. Berkeley: University of California Press, 1980a, chap. 2.

Averill, J. A constructionist view of emotion. In R. Plutchik & H. Kellerman (Eds.), *Emotion: Theory, research, and experience, vol. 1*. New York: Academic Press, 1980(b), chap. 12.

Baldwin, A. L. *Behavior and development in childhood*, New York: Dryden, 1955.

Baldwin, J. M. Consciousness and evolution. *Psychological Review*, 1896, *3*, 300-309.

Baldwin, J. M. On selective thinking. *Psychological Review*, 1898, *6*, 1-24.

Baldwin, J. M. *Social and ethical interpretations in mental development: A study in social psychology*, New York: Macmillan, 1897/1913 (5th ed.).

Baldwin, J. M. *The individual and society*, New York: Arno Press, 1911/1974.

Baldwin, J. M. *History of psychology* (2 vols.), New York: Putnam, 1913.

Bandura, A. *Social foundations of thought and action: A social cognitive theory*. New Jersey: Prentice Hall, 1986.

Bandura, A., Grusec, J., & Menlove, F. Observational learning as a function of symbolization and incentive set. *Child Development*, 1966, *37*, pp. 499-506.

Bandura, A., Grusec, J., & Menlove, F. Vicarious extinction of avoidance behavior. *Journal of Personality and Social Psychology*, 1967, *5*, 16-23.

Bandura, A., & Jeffrey, R. Role of symbolic coding and rehearsal processes in observational learning. *Journal of Personality and Social Psychology*, 1973, *26*, 122-130.

Bandura, A., Jeffrey, R., & Bachicha, D. Analysis of memory codes and cumulative rehearsal in observational learning. *Journal of Research in Personality*, 1974, *1*, 295-305.

Banks, M., & Jackson, P. Unemployment and risks of minor psychiatric disorder: Cross-sectional and longitudinal evidence. *Psychological Medicine*, 1982, *12*, 789-798.

Banner, L. *American beauty*. New York: Knopf, 1983.

Barclay, R. The role of comprehension in remembering sentences. *Cognitive Psychology*, 1973, *4*, 229-254.

Barnouw, V. *Culture and personality*. Ill: Dorsey Press, 1973.

Barolo, E. Acquisition of substance conservation in pre-school years: The socio-economic factors. *Italian Journal of Psychology*, 1979, *6*, 9-15.

Bartlett, F.C. *Remembering, a study in experimental and social psychology*. New York: Cambridge University Press, 1932/1967.

Bartlett, F.C. *Thinking, an experimental and social study*. London: Allen & Unwin, 1958.

Bateson, G. The frustration-aggression hypothesis and culture. *Psychological Review*, 1941, *48*, 350-355.

Baumeister, R. *Identity: Cultural change and the struggle for self*. New York: Oxford University Press, 1986.

Beach, F. A. Evolutionary changes in the physiological control of mating behavior in mammals. *Psychological Review*, 1947, *54*, 297-311.

Beach, F. A. Neural and chemical regulation of behavior. In H. F. Harlow & C. Woolsey (Eds.), *Biological and biochemical bases of behavior*. Madison: University of Wisconsin Press, 1958, pp. 263-284.

Beach F., & Jaynes, J. Effects of early experience upon the behavior of animals. *Psychological Bulletin*, 1954, *51*, 239-263.

Beck, L. Private speech: Learning out loud. *Psychology Today*, May 1986, 34-42.

Bee, H., Bernard, K., Eyres, S., Gray, C., Hammond, M., & Spietz, A. Prediction of IQ and language skill from perinatal status, child performance, family characteristics, and mother-infant interaction. *Child Development*, 1982, *53*, 1134-1156.

Bellugi, U., et al. Enhancement of spatial cognition in deaf children. In V. Volterra & C. Erting (Eds.), *From gesture to language in hearing and deaf children*. New York: Springer, 1990, chap. 21.

Berger, P., & Luckmann, T. *The social construction of reality*, New York: Doubleday, 1966.

Berland, J. *No five fingers are alike: Cognitive amplifiers in social context*. Cambridge: Harvard University Press, 1982.

Berlin, B., & Kay, P. *Basic color terms, their universality and evolution*. Berkeley: University of California Press, 1969.

Berlin, B. Ethnological classification. In E. Rosch & B. Lloyd (Eds.), *Cognition and categorization*. New Jersey: Lawrence Erlbaum, 1978, chap. 1.

Berliner, H. A larger perspective on the flexner report. *International Journal of Health Services*, 1975, *5*, 573-590.

Bernal, J.D. *Science in history*. New York: Cameron, 1954.

Bernard, L.L. *Instinct, a study in social psychology*. New York: Holt, 1924.

Bernard, L.L. *An introduction to social psychology*. New York: Holt, 1926.

Bernard, L.L. *An introduction to sociology*. New York: Crowell, 1942.

Berry, J.W. Temne and eskimo perceptual skills. *International Journal of Psychology*, 1966, *1*, 207-229.

Berry, J.W. Social psychology: Comparative societal and universal. *Canadian Psychological Review*, 1978, *19*, 93-103.

Berry, J. Imposed etics-emics-derived etics: The operationalization of a compelling idea. *International Journal of Psychology*, 1989, *24*, 721-735.

Berry J., & Bennett, J. Syllabic literacy and cognitive performance among the Cree. *International Journal of Psychology*, 1989, *24*, 429-450.

Beyene, Y. *From menarche to menopause*. Albany: SUNY Press, 1989.

Billig, M. *Ideology and social psychology*. New York: St. Martin's, 1982.

Billig, M., et al. *Ideological dilemmas: A social psychology of everyday thinking*. Beverly Hills: Sage, 1988.

Bing, E. Effect of childrearing practices on development of differential cognitive abilities. *Child Development*, 1963, *34*, 631-648.

Binitie, A. A factor-analytical study of depression across cultures (American and European). *British Journal of Psychiatry*, 1975, *127*, 559-563.

Binswanger, L. The case of Ellen West. In R. May et al. (Eds.). *Existence*. New York: Simon & Schuster, 1944/1958, chapter 9.

Birch, H., & Lefford, A. Intersensory development in children. *Monographs of the Society for Research in Child Development*, 1963, *28*, 5.

Birch, H., & Lefford, A. Visual differentiation, intersensory integration, and voluntary motor control. *Monographs of the Society for Research in Child Development*, 1967, *32*, 2.

Birken, L. *Consuming desire: Sexual science and the emergence of a culture of abundance*. Ithaca: Cornell University Press, 1988.

Blakemore, C., & Cooper, G. Development of the brain depends on the visual environment. *Nature*, 1970, *228*, 477-478.

Blanshard, B. *The nature of thought*. New York: Humanities Press, 1939/1978.

Blumer, H. *Symbolic interactionism*. New Jersey: Prentice Hall, 1969.

Bogin, B., & MacVean, R. The relationship of socioeconomic status and sex to body size, skeletal maturation, and cognitive status of Guatemala city schoolchildren. *Child Development*, 1983, *54*, 115-128.

Bornstein, M., & Sigman, M. Continuity in mental development from infancy. *Child Development*, 1986, *57*, 251-174.

Bousfield, J. The world seen as a color chart. In R. Ellen & D. Reason (Eds.), *Classifications in their social context*. New York: Academic Press, 1979, chap. 10.

Bowles, S., & Gintis, H. IQ in the U.S. class structure. *Social Policy*, Nov./Dec. 1972, pp. 65-96.

Brackbill, Y. Continuous stimulation reduces arousal level: Stability of the effect over time. *Child Development*, 1973, *44*, 43-46.

Braly, K. The influence of past experience in visual perception. *Journal of Experimental Psychology*, 1933, *16*, 613-643.

Brandon, W., Fink, E., Qualis, C., & Ho, C., Samuels W. Lithium and chlorpromazine in psychotic inpatients. *Psychiatry Research*, 1982, *7*, 69-81.

Brazelton, T. Implications of infant development among the Mayan Indians of Mexico. In P. Leiderman, S. Tulkin, & A. Rosenfeld (Eds.), *Culture and infancy, variations in the human experience*. New York: Academic Press, 1977, chap. 7.

Brazelton, T., & Tronick, E. Preverbal communication between mothers and infants. In D. Olson (Ed.), *The social foundations of language and thought: Essays in honor of Jerome S. Bruner*. New York: Norton, 1980, chap. 13.

Brenner, M. H. *Mental illness and the economy*. Cambridge: Harvard University Press, 1973.

Brenner, M. H. Influence of the social environment on psychopathology: The historic perspective. In J. Barrett et al. (Eds.), *Stress and mental disorder*. New York: Raven Press, 1979.

Brent, S. Individual specialization, collective adaptation and rate of environmental change. *Human Development*, 1978, *21*, 21-33.

Brewer, W. There is no convincing evidence for operant or classical conditioning in adult humans. In W. Weimer & D. Palermo (Eds.), *Cognition and the symbolic processes*. New Jersey: Lawrence Erlbaum, 1974, chap. 1.

Brockington, I., Kendell, R., Kellett, J., Curry, S., & Wainwright, S. Trials of lithium, chlorpromazine, and amitriptyline in schizoaffective patients. *British Journal of Psychiatry*, 1978, *133*, 162-168.

Bronfenbrenner, U. *The ecology of human development*. Cambridge: Harvard University Press, 1979.

Brooks, I.R. Cognitive ability assessment with two New Zealand ethnic groups. *Journal of Cross-Cultural Psychology*, 1976, *7*, 347-356.

Broughton, J. Piaget's structural developmental psychology: IV. Knowledge without a self and without history. *Human Development*, 1981a, *24*, 320-346.

Broughton, J. Piaget's structural developmental psychology: V. Ideology-critique and the possibility of a critical developmental theory. *Human Development*, 1981b, *24*, 382-411.

Broughton, J., Leadbeater, B., & Amsel, E. Reflections on Piaget: Proceedings of the Jean Piaget memorial conference. *Teacher's College Record*, 1981, *83*, 2, 151-217.

Broughton, J. The genesis of moral domination. In S. Modgil & C. Modgil (Eds.), *Lawrence Kohlberg, consensus and controversy*. Pa.: Falmer Press, 1985, chapter 23.

Brown, G., & Harris, T. *Social origins of depression, A study of psychiatric disorder in women*. New York: Free Press, 1978.

Brown, R., & Lenneberg, E. A study in language and cognition. *Journal of Abnormal and Social Psychology*, 1954, *49*, 454-462.

Brown, R. *Social psychology*. New York: Free Press, 1965.

Brumberg, J. *Fasting girls: The emergence of anorexia nervosa as a modern disease*. Cambridge: Harvard University Press, 1988.

Bruner, J. S. Inhelder and Piaget's "The Growth of Logical Thinking," *British Journal of Psychology*, 1959, *50*, 363-370.

Bruner, J. S. The growth of the mind. *American Psychologist*, 1965, *20*, 1007-1017.

Bruner, J. *Toward a theory of instruction*. Cambridge: Harvard University Press, 1966.

Bruner, J. *Processes of cognitive growth: Infancy*. Worcester: Clark University Press, 1968.

Bruner, J. *The relevance of education*. New York: Norton, 1971.

Bruner, J. S. *Beyond the information given, studies in the psychology of knowing*. New York: Norton, 1973.

Bruner, J. S. Early social interaction and language acquisition. In H.R. Schaffer (Ed.), *Studies in mother-infant interaction*. New York: Academic Press, 1977, chap. 11

Bruner, J. S. Afterward. In D. Olson (Ed.), *The social foundations of language and thought, essays in honor of Jerome S. Bruner*. New York: Norton, 1980.

Bruner, J. Review and prospectus. In B. Lloyd & J. Gay (Eds.), *Universals of human thought, Some African evidence*. New York: Cambridge University Press, 1981, chap. 12.

Bruner, J. *In search of mind, essays in autobiography*. New York: Harper, 1983.

Bruner, J. *Child's talk: learning to use language*. New York: Norton, 1983b.

Bruner, J.S., Olver, R., & Greenfield, P. *Studies in cognitive growth*. New York: Wiley, 1966.

Bruner, J., Caudill, E., & Ninio, A. Language and experience. In R.S. Peters (Ed.), *John Dewey reconsidered*. Boston: Routledge & Kegan Paul, 1977, chap. 2.

Bruner, J., & Sherwood, V. Thought, language, and interaction in infancy. In J. Forgas (Ed.), *Social cognition: Perspectives on everyday understanding*. New York: Academic Press, 1981, chap. 2.

Buck-Morss, S. Socio-economic bias in Piaget's theory and its implications for cross-culture studies. *Human Development*, 1975, *18*, 35-49.

Burnham, J. Psychotic delusions as a key to historical cultures: Tasmania, 1830-1940. *Journal of Social History*, 1980, 368-383.

Bushbaum, M., & Haier, R. Psychopathology: Biological approaches. *Annual Review of Psychology*, 1983, *34*, 401-430.

Buss, A. R. *A dialectical psychology*. New York: Wiley, 1979.

Cairns, R. B. *Social development: The origins and plasticity of interchanges*. San Francisco: Freeman, 1979.

Caldwell, B. The effects of infant care. In M. Hoffman (Ed.), *Review of child development research* (Vol. 1). New York: Russell Sage, 1964.

Caldwell, B. The social biology of human beings. In R. Cooke & S. Levin (Eds.), *The biologic basis of pediatric practice*. New York: McGraw-Hill, 1968, chap. 6.

Callanan, M. How parents label objects for young children: The role of input in the acquisition of category hierarchies. *Child Development*, 1985, *56*, 508-523.

Camaioni, L. The role of social interaction in the transition from communication to language. In A. D. Ribaupierre (Ed.), *Transition mechanisms in child development: The longitudinal perspective*. New York: Cambridge University Press, 1989, chap. 4.

Camras, L. Socialization of affect communication. In M. Lewis & C. Saarni (Eds.), *The socialization of emotions*. New York: Plenum, 1985, chap. 7.

Cancian, F., & Gordon, S. Changing emotional norms in marriage: Love and anger in U.S. women's magazines since 1900. *Gender and Society*, 1988, *2*, 308-342.

Candland, D., et al. *Emotion*. Belmont: Brooks/Cole, 1977.

Capek, M. Time. In P. Wiener (Ed.), *Dictionary of the history of ideas*. New York: Scribner's, 1973, vol. 4, pp. 389-398.

Carroll, J., & Casagrande, J. The function of language classifications in behavior. In E. Maccoby (Eds.), *Readings in social psychology*, 3rd ed., New York: Henry Holt, 1958, pp. 18-31.

Carter, H., & Glick, P. *Marriage and divorce: A social and economic study*. Cambridge: Harvard University Press, 1970.

Cartwright, D. Contemporary social psychology in historical perspective. *Social Psychology Quarterly*, 1979, *42*, 82-93.

Cassel, J. Physical illness in response to stress. In S. Levine & N. Scotch (Eds.), *Social Stress*. Chicago: 1970, chap. 7

Caughey, J. *Imaginary social worlds*. Lincoln: University of Nebraska Press, 1984.

Ceci, S. *On intelligence . . . more or less*. New Jersey: Prentice Hall, 1990.

Chandra, P., & Chaturvedi, S. Cultural variations of premenstrual experience. *International Journal of Social Psychiatry*, 1989, *35*, 343-349.

Chase, W., & Ericsson, K. Skilled Memory. In J. R. Anderson (Ed.), *Cognitive skills and their acquisition*. New Jersey: Lawrence Erlbaum, 1981, chap. 5.

Chiszar, D. Learning theory, ethological theory, and developmental plasticity. In E. Gosllin (Ed.), *Developmental Plasticity*. New York: Academic Press, 1981, chap. 3.

Chomsky, N. Human language and other semiotic systems. In T. Sebeok & J. Sebeok (Eds.), *Speaking of apes, A critical anthology of two-way communication with man*. New York: Plenum, 1980, pp. 429-440.

Christensen, O., & Christensen, E. Fat consumption and schizophrenia. *Acta Psychiatrica Scandanavia*, 1988, *78*, 587-591.

Cicchetti, D., & Schneider-Rosen, K. Theoretical and empirical considerations in the investigation of the relationship between affect and cognition in atypical populations of infants. In C. Izard, J. Kagan, & R. Zajonc (Eds.), *Emotions, cognition, and behavior*. New York: Cambridge University Press, 1984, chap. 12.

Clark, C. Domestic architecture as an index to social history: The romantic revival and the cult of domesticity in America, 1840-1870. *Journal of Interdisciplinary History*, 1976, *7*, 33-56.

Clark, R. The transition from action to gesture. In A. Lock (Ed.), *Action, gesture, and symbol: The emergence of language*. New York: Academic Press, 1978, chap. 10.

Clark, R. *Einstein, the life and times*. New York: Avon, 1971.

Cohen, D., & Cohen, H. Biological theories, drug treatments, and schizophrenia: A critical assessment. *Journal of Mind and Behavior*, 1986, *7*, 11-36.

Cohen, G. *Memory in the real world*. Hillsdale: Lawrence Erlbaum: 1989.

Cole, M., Gay, J., & Glick, J. Some experimental studies of Kpelle quantitative behavior. *Psychonomic Monograph*, 1968, *26*.

Cole, M., & Bruner, J. Cultural differences and inferences about psychological processes. *American Psychologist*, 1971, *26*, 867-876.

Cole, M., Gay, J., & Glick, J. *Cultural context of learning and thinking*. New York: Basic, 1971.

Cole, M., & Gay, J. Culture and memory. *American Anthropologist*, 1972, *74*, 1066-1084.

Cole, M., & Scribner, S. *Culture and thought*. New York: Wiley, 1974.

Cole, M., & Scribner, S. Theorizing about socialization of cognition. *Ethos*, 1975, *3*, 249-268.

Cole, M., Sharp, D., & Lave, C. The cognitive consequences of education: Some empirical evidence and theoretical misgivings. *Urban Review*, 1976, *9*, 218-233.

Cole, M., & Scribner, S. Cross-cultural studies of memory and cognition. In R. Kail & J. Hagen (Eds.), *Perspectives on the development of memory and cognition*. New York: Erlbaum, 1977, chap. 8.

Cole, M. An Ethnographic psychology of cognition. In R. Brislin et al. (Eds.), *Cross-cultural perspectives on learning*. New York: Wiley, 1975, pp. 157-175.

Cole, M. How education affects the mind. *Human Nature*, 1978, *1*, 50-58.

Cole, M. Introduction to the Kharkov school of developmental psychology. *Soviet Psychology*, Winter 1979-1980, *18*, 3-8.

Cole, M. Cross-cultural research in the sociohistorical tradition. *Human Development*, 1988, *31*, 137-157.

Colaizzi, P. Learning and existence. In R. Valle & M. King (Eds.), *Existential-phenomenological alternatives for psychology*. New York: Oxford University Press, 1978, chap. 6.

Collins, S. Categories, concepts, or predicaments? Remarks on Mauss's use of philosophical terminology. In M. Carrithers et al. (Eds.), *The category of the person*. New York: Cambridge University Press, 1985, chap. 3.

Condry, J., & Ross, D. Sex and aggression: The influence of gender label on the perception of aggression in children. *Child Development*, 1985, *56*, 225-233.

Conklin, H. Hanunoo color categories. *Southwestern Journal of Anthropology*, 1955, *11*, 339-344.

Cooley, C. H. *Human nature and the social order*. New York: Scribner's, 1922, 2nd ed.

Cooper, R. Social class and prognosis in schizophrenia. *British Journal of Preventive and Social Medicine*, 1961, *15*, 17-30.

Corbin, A. *The foul and the fragrant: odor and the French social imagination*. Cambridge: Harvard University Press, 1986.

Cordua, G., McGraw, K., & Drabman, R. Doctor or nurse: Children's perception of sex-typed occupations. *Child Development*, 1979, *50*, 590-593.

Coryell, W. The heritability of schizophrenia and schizoaffective disorder. *Archives of General Psychiatry*, 1988, *45*, 323-327.

Cox, M. V. *The child's point of view: The development of cognition and language*. New York: St. Martin's, 1986.

Craik, F., & Watkins, M. The role of rehearsal in short-term memory. *Journal of Verbal Learning and Verbal Behavior*, 1973, *12*, 599-607.

Craik, F., & Tulving, E. Depth of processing and the retention of words in episodic memory. *Journal of Experimental Psychology, General*, 1975, *104*, 268-294.

Crandell, D., & Dohrenwend, B. Some relations among psychiatric symptoms, organic illness, and social class. *American Journal of Psychiatry*, 1967, *123*, 1527-1538.

Cummings, E., Iannotti, R., & Waxler, C. Aggression between peers in early childhood: Individual continuity and developmental change. *Child Development*, 1989, *60*, 887-895.

Curtiss, S. *Genie: A psycholinguistic study of a modern-day "wild child"*. New York: Academic Press, 1977.

Dabbs, J., & Morris, R. Testosterone, social class, and anti-social behavior in a sample of 4462 men. *Psychological Science*, 1990, *1*, 209-211.

Damerow, P. Individual development and cultural evolution of arithmetical thinking. In S. Strauss (Ed.), *Ontogeny, Phylogeny, and Historical Development*. Norwood, New Jersey: Ablex, pp. 125-152.

D'Andrade, R. G. The cultural part of cognition. *Cognitive Science*, 1981, *5*, 179-195.

D'Andrade, R. G. Culturally based reasoning. In A. Gellatly, D. Rogers, & J. Sloboda (Eds.), *Cognition and social worlds*. New York: Oxford, 1989, pp. 132-143.

Dasen, P. Cross-cultural Piagetian research: A summary. *Journal of Cross-Cultural Psychology*, 1972, *3*, 1, 23-39.

Dawson, M. E. Can classical conditioning occur without contingency learning? A review and evaluation of the evidence. *Psychophysiology*, 1973, *10*, 82-86.

Dawson, M., & Biferno, M. Concurrent measurement of awareness and electrodermal classical conditioning. *Journal of Experimental Psychology*, 1973, *101*, 53-62.

DeFundia, T., Draguns, J., & Phillips, L. Culture and psychiatric symptomatology: A comparison of argentine and United States patients. *Social Psychiatry*, 1971, *6*, 11-20.

De Grazia, S. *Of time, work, and leisure*. New York: Doubleday, 1962.

Delgado, J. *Emotions*. Iowa: Brown, 1973, second ed.

Delgado, J. *Physical control of the mind*. New York: Harper, 1969.

Delva, N., Letemendia, J. Lithium treatment in schizophrenia and schizo-affective disorders. *British Journal of Psychiatry*, 1982, *141*, 387-400.

Demos, J. The american family in past time. *The American Scholar*, 1974, 43.

Denenberg, V. The effects of early experience. In E. Hafez (Ed.), *The behavior of domestic animals*, Baltimore: Williams & Wilkins, 1969, chap. 6.

Denenberg, V. Animal models and plasticity. In J. Gallagher & C. Ramey (Eds.), *The malleability of children*. Baltimore: Brookes Co., 1987, chap. 4.

Dennis, W. *Children of the creche*. New York: Appleton-Century-Crofts, 1973.

deRios, M. Saladerra—a culture-bound misfortune syndrome in the Peruvian Amazon. *Culture, Medicine, and Psychiatry*, 1981, *5*, 193-213.

DeRougement, D. *Love in the Western world*. New York: Harper, 1956.

Devereaux, G. *Basic problems of ethnopsychiatry*. Chicago: University of Chicago Press, 1980.

deVries, W. *Hegel's theory of mental activity*. Ithaca: Cornell University Press, 1988.

deWall, F. *Chimpanzee politics*. New York: Harper, 1982.

Dewart, L. *Evolution and consciousness: The role of speech in the origin and development of human nature*. Toronto: University of Toronto Press, 1989.

Dewey, J. The new psychology. *Andover Review*, Sept. 1884, pp. 278-289. Reprinted in J. Ratner (Ed.), *John Dewey, philosophy, psychology, and social practice*. New York: Putnam's, 1963, chap. 3.

Dewey, J. The psychological standpoint. *Mind*, 1886(a), pp. 1-19.

Dewey, J. Psychology as philosophic method. *Mind*, 1886(b), pp. 153-173.

Dewey, J. Soul and body. *The Bibliotheca Sacra*, 1886(c), pp. 239-263. Reprinted in J. Ratner (Ed.), *John Dewey, philosophy, psychology, and social practice*. New York: Putnam's, 1963, chap. 4.

Dewey, J. Knowledge as idealization. *Mind*, 1887, pp.382-396.

Dewey, J. The theory of emotion. *Psychological Review*, 1894, pp. 553-569.

Dewey, J. The reflex arc concept in psychology. *Psychological Review*, 1896, pp. 357-370.

Dewey, J. *Psychology*. New York: Harper, 1898.

Dewey, J. Interpretation of the savage mind. *Psychological Review*, 1902, pp. 217-230.

Diamond, I.T. A history of the study of the cortex. In G. Kimble & K. Schlesinger (Eds.), *Topics in the history of psychology*. New Jersey: Lawrence Erlbaum, 1985, vol 1., chap. 8.

Diamond, M. *Enriching heredity: The impact of the environment on the anatomy of the brain*. New York: Free Press, 1988.

di Martino, E. Review of *La terra del rimorso (The land of remorse)*, *Transcultural Psychiatric Review*, 1975, *12*, 73-76.

Dobzhansky, T. The present evolution of man. *Scientific American*, Sept. 1960, 206-217.

Dobzhansky, T. Cultural direction of human evolution—a summation. In S. Garn (Ed.), *Culture and the direction of human evolution*. Detroit: Wayne State University Press, 1964, pp. 93-98.

Dobzhansky, T. Unique aspects of man's evolution. In J. Pringle (Ed.), *Biology and the human sciences*. New York: Oxford University Press, 1972, chap. 6.

Dohrenwend, B. Sociocultural and social-psychological factors in the genesis of mental disorders. *Journal of Health and Social Behavior*, 1975, *16*, 365-392.

Dohrenwend, B. Socioeconomic status and psychiatric disorders: Are the issues still compelling? *Social Psychiatry and Psychiatric Epidemiology*, 1990, *25*, 41-47.

Dohrenwend, B., et al. Measures of psychiatric disorder in contrasting class and ethnic groups. In E. Hare & J. Wing (Eds.), *Psychiatric Epidemiology*. New York: Oxford University Press, 1970, pp. 159-209.

Dohrenwend, B., & Dohrenwend, B. Social and cultural influences on psychopathology. *Annual Review of Psychology*, 1974, *25*, 417-452.

Dohrenwend, B., & Dohrenwend, B. Reply to Gove and Tudor's comment on "sex differences and psychiatric disorders." *American Journal of Sociology*, 1977, *82*, 1336-1345.

Doise, W., Mugny, G., & Perret-Clermont, A. Social interaction and the development of cognitive operations. *European Journal of Social Psychology*, 1975, *5*, 367-383.

Doise, W., & Mackie, D. On the social nature of cognition. In J. Forgas (Ed.), *Social cognition*. New York: Academic Press, 1981, chap. 3.

Donahue, W.T., & Griffitts, C. The influence of complexity on the fluctuations of the illusions of reversible perspective. *American Journal of Psychology*, 1931, *43*, 613- 617.

Donchin, E., & Cohen, L. Averaged evoked potentials and intramodality selective attention. *Electroencephalography and Clinical Neurophysiology*, 1967, *22*, 537-546.

Draguns, J. Values reflected in psychopathology: The case of the protestant ethic. *Ethos*, 1974, *2*, 115-136.

Durkheim, E. *The rules of sociological method*. New York: Free Press, 1895/1938.

Durkheim, E. *Sociology and philosophy*. New York: Free Press 1898/1953.

Durkheim, E., & Mauss, Marcel. *Primitive classification*. Chicago: University of Chicago Press, 1903/1963.

Edelman, G. M. *Neural Darwinism: The theory of neuronal group selection*. New York: Basic, 1987.

Efron, R. *The decline and fall of hemispheric specialization*. Hillsdale: Lawrence Erlbaum, 1990.

Egan, G., & Cowan, M. *People in systems: A model for development in the human service professions and education*. Monterey, Cal.: Brooks/Cole, 1979.

Ekman, P. Universals and cultural differences in facial expressions of emotion. In J. Cole (Ed.), *Nebraska Symposium on Motivation*, 1971. Lincoln: University of Nebraska Press, 1972, pp. 207-283.

Ekman, P., & Oster, H. Facial expressions of emotion. *Annual Review of Psychology*, 1979, *30*, 527-554.

Ekman, P. Autonomic nervous system activity distinguishes among emotions. *Science*, Sept. 16, 1983, *221*, 1208-1210.

Elbers, E. Children's theories and developmental theory. In P. van Geert (Ed.), *Theory building in developmental psychology*, Holland: Elsevier Science Publishers, 1986.

Elias, N. *The civilizing process, the history of manners*. New York: Urizen, 1939/1978.

Ember, C. A cross-cultural perspective on sex differences. In R. Munroe, R. Munroe, and B. Whiting (Eds.), *Handbook of cross-cultural human development*. New York: Garland, 1981, chap. 16.

Endicott, J., Nee, J., Cohen, J., Fleiss, J., & Simon, R. Diagnosis of schizophrenia, prediction of short-term outcome. *Archives of General Psychiatry*, 1986, *43*, 13-19.

Engel, G. The need for a new medical model: A challenge for biomedicine. *Science*, 1977, *196*, 129-136.

Engels, F. *Dialectics of nature*, Moscow: Progress Publishers, 1886/1964.

Ensminger, M., & Celentano, D. Unemployment and psychiatric distress: Social resources and coping. *Social Science and Medicine*, 1988, *27*, 239-247.

Ervin, S. Semantic shift in bilingualism. *American Journal of Psychology*, 1961, *74*, 233-241.

Etkin, W. Social behavior and the evolution of man's mental faculties. In A. Montagu (Ed.), *Culture and the evolution of man*. New York: Oxford, 1962, pp. 131-147.

Eyer, J. Capitalism, health, and illness. In J. McKinlay (Ed.), *Issues in the polical economy of health care*. New York: Tavistock, 1984, chap. 1.

Fancher, R. *The intelligence men: Makers of the IQ controversy*. New York: Norton, 1985.

Fausto-Sperling, A. *Myths of gender: Biological theories about women and men*. New York: Basic Books, 1985.

Feinman, S. Social referencing in infancy. *Merrill-Palmer Quarterly*, 1982, *28*, 445-470.

Feldman, C., & Toulmin, S. Logic and the theory of mind. In W. Arnold (Ed.), *Nebraska Symposium on Motivation*, 1975. Lincoln: University of Nebraska press, 1976, pp.409-476.

Fernandez, J. Tolerance in a repugnant world and other dilemmas in the cultural relativism of Melville Herskovits. *Ethos*, 1990, *18*, 140-164.

Field, M.J. *Search for security: An ethno-psychiatric study of rural Ghana*. Ill.: Northwestern University Press, 1960.

Fishbein, H. *Evolution, development, and children's learning*, Cal.: Goodyear, 1976.

Fivush, R. The functions of event memory. In U. Neisser & E. Winograd (Eds.), *Remembering reconsidered: Ecological and traditional approaches to the study of memory*. New York: Cambridge University Press, 1988, chap. 10.

Fleming, E., & Anttonen, R. Teacher expectancy as related to the academic and personal growth of primary-age children. *Monograph of the society for research in child development*, 1971, *36*, 5.

Fox, J. Gove's specific sex-role theory of mental illness: A research note. *Journal of Health and Social Behavior*, 1980, *21*, 260-267.

Fraiberg, S. *Insights from the blind: Comparative studies of blind and sighted infants*. New York: Basic Books, 1977.

Frieze, I., Parsons, J., Johnson, P., Ruble, D., & Zellman, G. *Women and sex roles, a social psychologial perspective*. New York: Norton, 1978.

Fromm, E. *The sane society*. New York: Rinehart, 1955.

Fromm, E. *The anatomy of human destruction*. Conn.: Fawcett, 1973.

Fromm, E. *Greatness and limitations of Freud's thought*. London: Cape, 1980.

Fujinaga, T. Some sociogenetic determinants in human development revealed by the study of severely deprived children. In B. Bain (Ed.), *The sociogenesis of language and human conduct*. New York: Plenum, 1983, chap. 11.

Furst, J. *The neurotic, his inner and outer worlds*. New York: Citadel, 1954.

Gay, J., & Cole, M. *The new mathematics and an old culture: A study of learning among the Kpelle of Liberia*. New York: Holt, Rinehart, Winston, 1967.

Geen, R., & Rakosky, J. Interpretations of observed aggression and their effect on GSR. *Journal of Experimental Research in Personality*, 1973, *6*, 289-292.

Geertz, C. Religion as a cultural system. In M. Banton (Ed.), *Anthropological approaches to the study of religion*. New York: Praeger, 1966.

Geertz, C. *The interpretation of cultures*. New York: Basic, 1973.

Geertz, C. From the native's point of view: On the nature of anthropological understanding. In R. Shweder & R. LeVine (Eds.), *Culture theory, essays on mind, self, and emotion*. New York: Cambridge University Press, 1984, chap. 4. (Originally published 1974).

Geertz, C. Anti anti-relativism. *American Anthropologist*, 1984b, *86*, 263-278.

Geertz, H. The vocabulary of emotion: A study of Javanese socialization processes. *Psychiatry*, 1959, *22*, 225-237.

Gellner, E. *Plow, sword, and book: The structure of human history*. Chicago: University of Chicago Press, 1988.

Gellner, E. Culture, constraint, and community: Semantic and coercive compensations for the genetic under-determination of *Homo sapiens*. In P. Mellars & C. Stringer (Eds.),

The human revolution: Behavioral and biological perspectives on the origins of modern humans. Princeton: Princeton University Press, 1989, chap. 26.

Gelman, R., & Baillargeon, R. A review of some Piagetian concepts. In P. Mussen (Ed.), *Handbook of child psychology,* (4th ed.). New York: Wiley, 1983 (Vol. 3), chap. 3.

Gillis, J. From ritual to romance: Toward an alternative history of love. In C. Stearns & P. Stearns (Eds.), *Emotion and social change: Toward a new psychohistory.* New York: Holmes and Meier, 1988, chap. 4.

Goldberg, J. *Anatomy of a scientific discovery.* New York: Bantam, 1988.

Goldmann, L. Dialectical materialism and literary history. *New Left Review,* 1975, *92,* 39-51.

Goldmann, L. *Essays on method in the sociology of literature.* St. Louis: Telos Press, 1980.

Goldstein, K. *Human nature in the light of psychopathology.* New York: Schocken, 1940/1963.

Goldstein, L. *The social and cultural roots of linear perspective.* Minneapolis: MEP, 1988.

Gollnitz, G., et al. The interaction of biological and psychosocial risk factors in the etiology of child mental disorders. *International Journal of Mental Health,* 1990, *18,* 57-72.

Good, B., & Good, M. The meaning of symptoms: A cultural hermeneutic model for clinical practice. In L. Eisenberg & A. Kleinman (Eds.), *The relevance of social science for medicine.* Dordrecht: Reidel, 1981, chap. 8.

Goody, J. *The domestication of the savage mind.* New York: Cambridge University Press, 1977.

Gooren, L. Biomedical theories of sexual orientation: A critique. In D. McWhirter, S. Sanders, & J. Reinish (Eds.), *Homosexuality/heterosexuality: Concepts of sexual orientation.* New York: Oxford University Press, 1990, chap. 6.

Gore, S. The effect of social support in moderating the health consequences of unemployment. *Journal of Health and Social Behavior,* 1978, *19,* 157-165.

Gottesman, I., & Shields, J. A critical review of recent adoption, twin, and family studies of schizophrenia: Behavioral genetics perspectives. *Schizophrenia Bulletin,* 1976, *2,* 360-401.

Gottesman, I., & Shields, J. *Schizophrenia: The epigenetic puzzle.* New York: Cambridge University Press, 1982.

Gouldner, A. *The coming crisis in sociology.* New York: Avon, 1970.

Gove, W., & Geerken, M. Response bias in surveys of mental health: An empirical investigation. *American Journal of Sociology,* 1977, *82,* 1289-1317.

Gove, W., & Tudor, J. Sex differences in mental illness: A comment on Dohrenwend and Dohrenwend. *American Journal of Sociology,* 1977, *82,* 1327-1336.

Gove, W. Sex differences in the epidemiology of mental disorder: Evidence and explanation. In E. Gomberg & V. Franks (Eds.), *Gender and disordered behavior: Sex differences in psychopathology.* New York: Brunner-Mazel, 1979, pp. 23-68.

Gove, W. Gender differences in mental and physical illness: The effects of fixed roles and nurturant roles. *Social Science and Medicine,* 1984, *19,* 77-91.

Gray, H. Learning to take an object from the mother. In A. Lock (Ed.), *Action, gesture, and symbol: The emergence of language.* New York: Academic Press, 1978, chap. 8.

Greenfield, P., & Bruner, J. Culture and cognitive growth. In D. Goslin (Ed.), *Handbook of socialization theory and research.* Chicago: Rand McNally, 1969, chap. 12.

Greenough, W., Black, J., & Wallace, C. Experience and brain development. *Child Development,* 1987, *58,* 539-559.

Gregory, R. L. *The intelligent eye.* New York: McGraw-Hill, 1970.

Gregory, R. L. Visual perception and illusions. In J. Miller (Ed.), *States of mind.* New York: Pantheon, 1983, chap. 3.

Greif, E. and Ulman, K. The psychological impact of menarche on early adolescent females: A review of the literature. *Child Development,* 1982, *53,* 1413-1430.

Greven, P. *The protestant temperament: Patterns of childrearing, religious experience, and the self in early America.* New York: New American Library, 1977.

Hall, K.R.L. Tool-using performances as indicators of behavioral adaptability. In P. Jay (Ed.), *Primates.* New York: Holt, Rinehart, Winston, 1968(a), chap.4.

Hall, K.R.L. Aggression in monkey and ape societies. In P. Jay (Ed.), *Primates.* New York: Holt, 1968(b), chap.5.

Hallowell, A. I. *Culture and experience.* Philadelphia: University of Pennsylvania Press, 1955.

Hallowell, A. I. The structural and functional dimensions of a human existence. In A. Montagu (Ed.), *Culture and the evolution of man.* New York: Oxford, 1962(a), pp. 223-244.

Hallowell, A. I. Personality structure and the evolution of man. In A. Montagu (Ed.), *Culture and the evolution of man.* New York: Oxford, 1962(b), pp. 245-258.

Hallowell, A. I. *Contributions to anthropology.* Chicago: University of Chicago Press, 1976.

Halpern, D. *Sex differences in cognitive ability.* Hillsdale: Lawrence Erlbaum, 1980.

Hampson, J. Determinants of psychosexual orientation. In F. Beach (Ed.), *Sex and behavior.* New York: Wiley, 1965, chap. 6.

Hanson, N. R. *Patterns of discovery, an inquiry into the conceptual foundations of science.* New York: Cambridge University Press, 1965.

Hanson, N. R. *Perception and discovery, an introduction to scientific inquiry.* San Francisco: Freeman, 1969.

Harkness, S. The cultural context of child development. In C. Super & S. Harkness (Eds.), *New directions for child development: Anthropological perspectives on child development.* Number 8; San Francisco: Jossey-Bass, 1980, pp. 7-13.

Harkness, S., Edwards, C., & Super, C. Social roles and moral reasoning: A case study in a rural african community. *Developmental Psychology,* 1981, *17,* 595-603.

Harkness, S., & Super, C. Child-environment interactions in the socialization of affect. In M. Lewis & C. Saarni (Eds.), *The socialization of emotions.* New York: Plenum, 1985, chap. 2.

Harlow, H. Basic social capacity of primates. In J.N. Spuhler (Ed.), *The evolution of man's capacity for culture.* Detroit: Wayne State Univ. Press, 1959, pp. 40-53.

Harre, R. *The social construction of emotions.* New York: Blackwell, 1986.

Harris, E. *The foundations of metaphysics in science.* London: George Allen & Unwin, 1965.

Harris, E. The neural-identity theory and the person. *International Philosophical Quarterly,* 1966, *6,* 515-537.

Harris, E. *Fundamentals of philosophy.* New York: Holt, Rinehart, & Winston, 1969.

Harris, P., & Heelas, P. Cognitive processes and collective representations. *Archives of European Sociology,* 1979, *20,* 211-241.

Haug, W. *Critique of commodity aesthetics.* Minn.: University of Minnesota Press, 1986.

Hauser, A. *The sociology of art.* Chicago: University of Chicago Press, 1982.

Hay, D. Cooperative interactions and sharing between very young children and their parents. *Developmental Psychology,* 1979, *15,* 647-653.

Heelas, P. Emotion talk across cultures. In R. Harre (Ed.), *The social construction of emotions.* New York: Blackwell, 1986, chap. 13.

Hegel, G.W.F. *The logic of Hegel* (2nd ed.), New York: Oxford University Press, 1817/1965.

Hegel, G.W.F. *Aesthetics.* New York: Oxford University Press, 1975

Heider, E. R., & Olivier, D. The structure of the color space in naming and memory for two languages. *Cognitive Psychology* 1972, *3,* 337-354.

Heider, F. Social perception and phenomenal causality. *Psychological Review,* 1944, *51,* 358-374.

Heider, F. *The psychology of interpersonal relations.* New York: Wiley, 1958.

Heider, K. Dani sexuality: A low energy system. *Man*, 1976, *11*, 188-201.

Henle, M. An experimental investigation of past experience as a determinant of visual form perception. *Journal of Experimental Psychology*, 1942, *30*, 1-22.

Henry, J. *Culture against man*. New York: Vintage, 1963.

Herdt, G. Mistaken gender: 5-Alpha reductase hermaphroditism and biological reductionism in sexual identity reconsidered. *American Anthropologist*, 1990, *92*, 433-446.

Higginbotham, N., & Connor, L. Professional ideology and the construction of Western psychiatry in Southeast Asia. *International Journal of Health Services*, 1989, *16*, 63-78.

Hinde, R. A. *Primate social relationships*. Sunderland, Mass.: Sinauer Associates, 1983.

Hinde, R. A. The study of interpersonal relationships. In J. Miller (Ed.), *States of Mind*. New York: Pantheon, 1983(b), chap. 10.

Hochschild, A. Emotion work, feeling rules, and social structures. *American Journal of Sociology*, 1979, *85*, 551-575.

Hockett, C. The origin of speech. *Scientific American*, September 1960, 89-96.

Hogan, R., & Emler, N. The biases in contemporary social psychology. *Social Research*, 1978, *45*, 478-534.

Holender, D. Semantic activation without conscious identification in dichotic listening, parafoveal vision, and visual masking: A survey and appraisal. *Behavioral and Brain Sciences*, 1986, *9*, 1-66.

Hollingshead, A., & Redlich, F. Social stratification and psychiatric disorders. *American Sociological Review*, 1953, *18*, 163-169.

Hollingshead, A., & Redlich, F. Schizophrenia and social structure. *American Journal of Psychiatry*, 1954, *110*, 695-701.

Hollingshead, A., & Redlich, F. *Social class and mental illness*. New York: Wiley, 1958.

Holson, R., & Sackett, G. Effects of isolation rearing on learning by mammals. In G. H. Bower, ed., *The psychology of learning and motivation*, Vol. 18, New York: Academic Press, 1984, pp. 199-254.

Horkheimer, M. *Eclipse of reason*. New York: Seabury Press, 1947/1974.

Horkheimer, M., & Adorno, T. *Dialectic of enlightenment*. New York: Herder, 1944/1969.

Howe, M. *Fragments of genius: The strange feats of idiots savants*. New York: Routledge, 1989.

Hoyenga, K., & Hoyenga, K. *The question of sex differences*. Boston: Little Brown, 1979.

Humphrey, N. K. The social function of intellect. In P. Bateson & R.A. Hinde, *Growing points in ethology*. New York: Cambridge University Press, 1976, chap. 9.

Hunt, J. McV. *Intelligence and experience*. New York: Ronald, 1961.

Hunt, J. McV. Traditional personality theory in the light of recent evidence. In J. Rosenblith & W. Allinsmith (Eds.), *The causes of behavior*, 2nd ed. Boston: Allyn & Bacon, 1966, pp. 423-433.

Hunt, J. McV. Psychological development: Early experience. *Annual Review of Psychology*, 1979, *30*, 103-143.

Hunt, J. McV. *Early psychological development and experience*. Worcester: Clark University Press, 1980.

Husserl. E. *The crisis of European sciences and transcendental phenomenology*. Ill.: Northwestern University Press, 1938/1970.

Hutchins, E. *Culture and inference*. New York: Cambridge University Press, 1980.

Imperato-McGinley, J., et al. Androgens and the evolution of male-gender identity among male pseudohermaphrodites with 5a-reductase deficiency. *New England Journal of Medicine*, May 31, 1979, *300*, 1233-1237.

Isaac, G. The food-sharing behavior of protohuman hominids. *Scientific American*, April, 1978, 90-108.

Isbell, B. J., & McKee, L. Society's cradle: An anthropological perspective on the socialization of cognition. In J. Sants (Ed.), *Developmental Psychology and Society*. New York: St. Martin's, 1980, chap. 10.

Izard, C. Cross-cultural perspectives on emotion and emotion communication. In H. Triandis & W. Lonner (Eds.), *Handbook of cross-cultural psychology*, Vol. 3. Boston: Allyn & Bacon, 1980, chapter 5.

Izard, C. Emotions in personality and culture. *Ethos*, 1983, *11*, 305-312.

Jachuck, K., & Mohanty, A. Low socio-economic status and progressive retardation in cognitive skills—a test of cumulative deficit hypothesis. *Indian Journal of Mental Retardation*, 1974, *7*, 36-45.

Jahoda, G. Child animism: I. A critical survey of cross-cultural research. *Journal of Social Psychology*, 1958(a), *47*, 197-212.

Jahoda, G. Child animism: II. A study in West Africa. *Journal of Social Psychology*, 1958(b), *47*, 213-222.

Jahoda, G. The influence of schooling on adult recall of familiar stimuli: A study in Ghana. *International Journal of Psychology*, 1981, *16*, 59-71.

Jahoda, M. *Employment and unemployment: A social-psychological analysis*. New York: Cambridge University Press, 1982.

Jencks, C. *Inequality*. New York: Basic, 1972.

Jencks, C. Genes and crime. *New York Review of Books*, Feb. 12, 1987, pp. 33-41.

Johnson, F. *Handbook of lithium therapy*. Baltimore: University Park Press, 1980.

Johnson, T. Premenstrual syndrome as a Western culture-specific disorder. *Culture, Medicine, and Psychiatry* 1987, *11*, 337-356.

Johnson-Laird, P.N., & Wason, P. *Thinking*. New York: Cambridge University Press, 1977.

Kagan, J., & Klein, R. Cross-cultural perspectives on early development. *American Psychologist*, Nov. 1973, 947- 961.

Kagan, J. *The growth of the child*. New York: Norton, 1978a.

Kagan, J., et al. *Infancy, its place in human development*. Cambridge: Harvard University Press, 1978b.

Kagan, J. *The second year: The emergence of self-awareness*. Cambridge: Harvard University Press, 1981.

Kagan, J. *The nature of the child*. New York: Basic, 1984.

Kagan, J. The idea of emotion in human development. In C. Izard et al. (Eds.), *Emotions, cognition, and behavior*. New York: Cambridge University Press, 1984(b), chap. 2.

Kagan, J. The psychological requirements for human development. In A. Skolnick & J. Skolnick (Eds.), *The family in transition*. Boston, Little, Brown, 1986, chap. 22. (Originally published 1976)

Kagan, J. *Unstable ideas: Temperament, cognition, and self*. Cambridge: Harvard University Press, 1989.

Kagan, J. Commentary. *Human Development*, 1989(b), *32*, 172-176.

Kagan, J., & Moss, H. *Birth to maturity*. New York: Wiley, 1962.

Kagan, J., Reznick, S., & Gibbons, J. Inhibited and uninhibited types of children. *Child Development*, 1989, *60*, 838-845.

Kagan, J., Gibbons, J., Johnson, M., Reznick, J., & Snidman, N. A tempermental disposition to the state of uncertainty. In J. Rolf, A. Masten, D. Cicchetti, K. Nuechterlein, & S. Weintraub (Eds.), *Risk and protective factors in the development of psychopathology*. New York: Cambridge University Press, 1990, chap. 8.

Kamin, L. J. *The science and politics of IQ*. Hillsdale: Erlbaum, 1974.

Kanizsa, G. Subjective contours. *Scientific American*, April, 1976, 48-52.

Karlsson, J. *The biological basis of schizophrenia*. Springfield, Ill.: Thomas, 1966.

Kaufman, I. Charles. Learning what comes naturally: The role of life experience in the establishment of species typical behavior. In T. Schwartz (Ed.), *Socialization as cultural communication*. Berkeley: University of California Press, 1976, pp. 37-50.

Kaufman, J., Gordon, M., & Baker, A. Being imitated: Persistence of an effect. *Journal of Genetic Psychology*, 1978, *132*, 319-320.

Kay, P., & Kempton, W. What is the Sapir-Whorf hypothesis? *American Anthropologist*, 1984, *86*, 65-79.

Kaye, K. *The mental and social life of babies: How parents create persons*. Chicago: University Chicago Press, 1982.

Kelley, D. *The evidence of the senses: A realist theory of perception*. Baton Rouge: Louisiana State University Press, 1986.

Kessler, R. Stress, social status, and psychogical distress. *Journal of Health and Social Behavior*, 1979, *20*, 259-272.

Kitchener, R. Piaget's social psychology. *Journal of the Theory of Social Behavior*, 1981, *11*, 253-277.

Kitchener, R. *Piaget's theory of knowledge*. Conn.: Yale University Press, 1986.

Kleinman, A. Depression, somatization and the "new cross-cultural psychiatry." *Social Science and Medicine*, 1977, *11*, 3-10.

Kleinman, A. *Patients and healers in the context of culture*. Berkeley: University of California Press, 1980.

Kleinman, A. Neurasthenia and depression: A study of somatization and culture in China. *Culture, Medicine, and Psychiatry*, 1982, *6*, 117-190.

Kleinman, A. *Rethinking psychiatry*. New York: Free Press, 1988.

Kleinman, A., & Good, B. *Culture and depression*. Berkeley: University of California Press, 1985.

Kluckhohn, C. Universal categories of culture. In A.L. Kroeber (Ed.), *Anthropology Today*. Chicago: University of Chicago Press, 1953, pp. 507-523.

Koeske, R. Premenstrual emotionality: Is biology destiny? In M. Walsh (Ed.), *The Psychology of Women, Ongoing Debates*. New Haven: Yale University Press, 1987, pp. 137-146.

Koffka, K. *The growth of the mind*, Totawa, New Jersey: Littlefield, Adams & Co., 1924/1959.

Koffka, K., *Principles of Gestalt psychology*. New York: Harcourt, 1935/1963.

Kohler, W. *The mentality of apes*. New York: Vintage, 1917/1956.

Kohler, W. *Gestalt psychology*. New York: Mentor, 1929/1959.

Kohn, A. *No contest: The case against competition*. Boston: Houghton Mifflin, 1986.

Kolers, P. A. Experiments in reading. *Scientific American*, July 1972, 84-91.

Korner, A., & Thoman, E. Visual alertness in neonates as evoked by maternal care. *Journal of Experimental Child Psychology*, 1970, *10*, 67-78.

Kosok, M. The dialectics of nature. *Telos*, 1970, *6*, 47- 103.

Kuhn, T. *The structure of scientific revolutions*. Chicago: University of Chicago Press, 1962.

LaBarre, W. *The human animal*. Chicago: University of Chicago Press, 1955.

LaBarre, W. The development of mind in man in primitive cultures and society. In F. Richardson (Ed.), *Brain and intelligence*. Md.: National Educational Press, 1973.

Laboratory of Comparative Human Cognition. Culture and Cognitive Development. In W. Kessen (Ed.), *Handbook of child psychology*, (Vol. 1). New York: Wiley, 1983, chap. 7.

Ladygina-Kots, N., & Dembovskii, Y. The psychology of primates. In M. Cole & I. Maltzman (Eds.), *A handbook of contemporary Soviet psychology*. New York: Basic, 1969, pp. 41-70.

La Fontaine, J. Person and individual: Some anthropological reflections. In M. Carrithers, S. Collins, & S. Lukes (Eds.). *The category of the person*. New York: Cambridge University Press, 1985, chap. 6.

Laing, R.D. *The divided self*. New York: Pantheon, 1960.

Laing, R.D. *Sanity, madness, and the family.* New York: Basic Books, 1964.

Laing, R.D. *The politics of experience.* New York: Pantheon, 1967.

Laing, R.D. *Politics of the family.* New York: Pantheon, 1969.

Laing, R.D., *The self and others.* New York: Pantheon, 1969b.

Lakoff, G. *Women, fire, and dangerous things: What categories reveal about the mind.* Chicago: University of Chicago Press, 1987.

Lakoff, G., & Kovecses, Z. The cognitive model of anger inherent in American english. In D. Holland and N. Quinn (Eds.), *Cultural models in language and thought.* New York: Cambridge University Press, 1987, chap. 8.

Lancaster, J. Primate communication systems and the emergence of human language. In P. Jay (Ed.), *Primates.* New York: Holt, Rinehart, & Winston, 1968, chap.16.

Lantz, D., & Stefflre, V. Language and cognition revisited. *Journal of Abnormal and Social Psychology,* 1964, *69,* 472-481.

Lantz, H. Romantic love in the pre-modern period: A sociological commentary. *Journal of Social History,* 1982, *15,* 349-370.

Lappe, F. M. *World hunger: 12 myths.* New York: Grove, 1986.

Lappe, F. M. *Betraying the national interest.* New York: Grove, 1987.

Lashley, K. In search of the engram. In P. Tibbetts (Ed.), *Perception.* Chicago: Quadrangle, 1950/1969, pp. 49-80.

Lauer, R., & Handel, W. *Social Psychology, The theory and application of symbolic interactionism.* Boston: Houghton Mifflin, 1977.

Lazarus, R., Averill, J., & Opton, E. Towards a cognitive theory of emotion. In M. Arnold (Ed.), *Feelings and emotions.* New York: Academic Press, 1970, chap. 14.

Lazarus, R., Kanner, A., & Folkman, S. Emotions: A cognitive-phenomenological analysis. In R. Plutchik & H. Kellerman (Eds.), *Emotion: Theory, research, and experience* (Vol. 1). New York: Academic Press, 1980, chap. 8.

Leakey, R., & Lewin, R. *Origins.* New York: Dutton, 1977.

Lee, B., Wertsch, J., & Stone, A. Towards a Vygotskian theory of the self. In B. Lee and G. Noam (Eds.), *Developmental approaches to the self.* New York: Plenum, 1983, pp. 309-342.

Lee, B., Hickmann, M. Language, thought, and self in Vygotsky's developmental theory. In B. Lee and G. Noam (Eds.), *Developmental approaches to the self.* New York: Plenum, 1983, pp. 343-378.

Lee, D. The conception of the self among the Wintu Indians. In D. Lee, *Freedom and culture.* New Jersey: Prentice Hall, 1959.

Lee, R. Structure and anti-structure in the culture-bound syndromes: The Malay case. *Culture, Medicine, and Psychiatry,* 1981, *5,* 233-248.

Leff, J. The cross-cultural study of emotions. *Culture, Medicine, and Psychiatry,* 1977, *1,* 317-350.

Lenneberg, E., & Roberts, J. The language of experience: A study in methodology. *Indiana Publications in Anthropology and Linguistics, Memoir 13,* 1956. (Also referenced as: Supplement to International Journal of American Linguistics, 1956, 22, 2, April, 1956).

Leontiev, A.N. On the biological and social aspects of human development: The training of auditory ability. In M. Cole (Ed.), *A handbook of contemporary Soviet psychology.* New York: Basic, 1969, chap. 15.

Leontiev, A.N. Studies on the cultural development of the child. *Journal of Genetic Psychology,* 1932, *40,* pp. 52-83.

Leontiev, A.N. *Problems of the development of the mind.* Moscow: Progress, 1981.

Lepowsky, M. Gender in an egalitarian society. In P. Sanday & R. Goodenough (Eds.), *Beyond the second sex: New directions in the anthropology of gender.* Philadelphia: University of Pennsylvania Press, 1990.

Lerner, R. *On the nature of human plasticity.* New York: Cambridge University Press, 1984.

Levina, R.E. L.S. Vygotsky's ideas about the planning function of speech in children. In J. V. Wertsch (Ed.), *The concept of activity in Soviet psychology.* New York: M.E. Sharpe, 1981, pp. 279 ff.

Levins, R., & Lewontin, R. *The dialectical biologist.* Cambridge: Harvard University Press, 1985.

Levine, R., Klein, N., & Owen, C. Father-child relationships and changing life-styles in Ibadan, Nigeria. In H. Miner (Ed.), *The city in modern Africa.* New York: Praeger, 1967, chap. 9.

Levy-Bruhl, L. *Primitive mentality.* Boston: Beacon, 1923/1966.

Lewis, M. Social development in infancy and early childhood. In J. Osofsky (Ed.), *Handbook of infant development.* New York: Wiley, 1987 (2nd ed.), chap. 8.

Lewis, M., Feiring, C., McGuffog, C., & Jaskir, J. Predicting psychopathology in six-year-olds from early social relations. *Child Development,* 1984, *55,* 123-136.

Lewis, M., & Michalson, L. *Children's emotions and moods: Developmental theory and measurement.* New York: Plenum, 1983.

Lewontin, R.C. *Human diversity.* New York: Freeman, 1982.

Lewontin, R.C. Biological determinism. In S. McMurrin (Ed.), *The Tanner lectures on human values.* (Vol. 4). Salt Lake City: University of Utah Press, 1983.

Lewontin, R.C., Rose, S., & Kamin, L. *Not in our genes: Biology, ideology, and human nature.* New York: Pantheon, 1984.

Lichtman, R. *The production of desire: The integration of psychoanalysis into Marxist theory.* New York: Free Press, 1982.

Lidz, T. Commentary on "a critical review of recent adoption, twin, and family studies of schizophrenia: Behavioral genetics perspectives," *Schizophrenia Bulletin,* 1976, *2,* 402-412.

Lidz, T. Reply to Kety et al., *Schizophrenia Bulletin,* 1977, *3,* 522-526.

Lidz, T., Blatt, S., & Cook, B. A critique of the Danish-American studies of the adopted-away offspring of schizophrenic parents. *American Journal of Psychiatry,* 1981, *138,* 1063-1068.

Lidz, T., & Blatt, S. Critique of the Danish-American studies of the biological and adoptive relatives of adoptees who became schizophrenic. *American Journal of Psychiatry,* 1983, *140,* 426-434.

Liem, R. Economic change and unemployment: Contexts of illness. In E. Mishler et al. (Eds.), *Social contexts of health, illness, and patient care.* New York: Cambridge University Press, 1981, chap. 3.

Light, P. Context, conservation, and conversation. In M. Richards & P. Light (Ed.), *Children of social worlds: Development in a social context.* Cambridge: Harvard University Press, 1986, chap. 8.

Lin, P., Schwanenflugel, P., & Wisenbaker, J. Category typicality, cultural familiarity, and the development of category knowledge. *Developmental Psychology,* 1990, *26,* 805-813.

Linn, M., Sandifer, R., & Stein, S. Effects of unemployment on mental and physical health. *American Journal of Public Health,* 1985, *75,* 502-506.

Lips, H. *Sex and gender.* Palo Alto: Mayfield, 1988.

Lipton, A., & Simon, F. Psychiatric diagnosis in a state hospital: Manhattan State Revisited. *Hospital and Community Psychiatry,* 1985, *36,* 368-373.

Littlewood, R., & Lipsedge, M. *Aliens and alienists: Ethnic minorities and psychiatry.* New York: Penguin, 1982.

Lloyd, J. Social behavior and hormones. In B. Elftheriou & R. Sprott (Eds.), *Hormonal correlates of behavior.* (Vol. I). New York: Plenum, 1975, chap. 4.

Lock, A., ed. *Action, gesture, and symbol, the emergence of language.* New York: Academic, 1978.

Logan, R. Historical change in prevailing sense of self. In K. Yardley & T. Honess (Eds.), *Self and identity: Psychosocial perspectives.* New York: 1987, chap. 2.

Longstreth, L. A cognitive interpretation of secondary reinforcement. In J. Cole (Ed.), *Nebraska Symposium on Motivation,* 1971. Nebraska: University of Nebraska Press, 1972, pp. 33-80.

Loring, M., & Powell, B. Gender, race, and DSM-III: A study of the objectivity of psychiatric diagnostic behavior. *Journal of Health and Social Behavior,* 1988, *29,* 1-22.

Lovejoy, C. O. The origin of man. *Science,* 1981, *211,* 341-350.

Lowenthal, L. *Literature and the image of man.* Boston: Beacon Press, 1957.

Lowith, K. Mediation and immediacy in Hegel, Marx, and Feuerbach. In W. E. Steinkraus (Ed.), *New studies in Hegel's philosophy.* New York: Holt, Rinehart, & Winston, 1971, Chap. 8.

Lucy, J., & Shweder, R. Whorf and his critics: Linguistic and nonlinguistic influences on color memory. *American Anthropologist,* 1979, *81,* 581-615.

Lucy, J., & Wertsch, J. Vygotsky and Whorf: A comparative analysis. In M. Hickmann (Ed.), *Social and functional approaches to language and thought.* Orlando: Academic, 1987, chap. 4.

Luong, H. Language, cognition, and ontogenetic development: A reexamination of Piaget's premises. *Ethos,* 1986, *14,* 7-46.

Luria, A.R. The problem of the cultural behavior of the child. *Journal of Genetic Psychology,* 1928, *35,* 493-506.

Luria, A. R. Speech and intellect among rural, urban, and homeless children. *Soviet Psychology,* Fall 1974, *13,* 5-39. (Originally published 1930.)

Luria, A.R. *The nature of human conflicts.* New York: Liveright, 1932.

Luria, A.R. The development of mental functions in twins. *Character and Personality,* 1936-1937, *5,* 35-47.

Luria, A.R. *The role of speech in the regulation of normal and abnormal behavior.* New York: Pergamon Press, 1961.

Luria, A.R. The variability of mental functions as the child develops. *Soviet Psychology and Psychiatry,* 1963, *1,* 3, 17- 22.

Luria, A.R. *Human brain and psychological processes.* New York: Harper, 1966.

Luria, A.R. *Speech and the development of mental processes in the child.* London: Staples Press, 1968.

Luria, A.R. Speech development and the formation of mental processes. In M. Cole (Ed.), *Handbook of contemporary Soviet psychology.* New York: Basic, 1969 (chapter 4).

Luria, A.R. Towards the problem of the historical nature of psychological processes. *International Journal of Psychology,* 1971, *6,* 259-272.

Luria, A.R. Scientific perspectives and philosophical dead ends in modern linguistics. *Cognition,* 1974/5, *3,* 4, 377-385.

Luria, A.R. *Cognitive development: Its cultural and social foundations.* Boston: Harvard University Press, 1976.

Luria, A.R. Paths of development of thought in the child. In M. Cole (Ed.), *The selected writings of A. R. Luria.* New York: Sharpe, 1978a, pp. 97-144.

Luria, A.R. The development of constructive activity in the preschool child. In M. Cole (Ed.), *The selected writings of A. R. Luria.* New York: Sharpe, 1978c, pp. 195-228.

Luria, A.R. Vygotsky and the problem of functional localization. In M. Cole (Ed.), *The selected writings of A. R. Luria*. New York: Sharpe, 1978d, pp. 273-281.

Luria, A.R. *Language and cognition*. New York: Wiley, 1982.

Lutz, C. The domain of emotion words on Ifaluk. In R. Harre (Ed.). *The social construction of emotions*. New York: Blackwell, 1986a. Chap. 14. (Originally published in 1982.)

Lutz, C. Emotion, thought, estrangement: Emotion as a cultural category. *Cultural Anthropology*, 1986b, *1*, 287-309.

Lutz, C. *Unnatural emotions*. Chicago: University Chicago Press, 1988.

Lutz, C., & White, G. The anthropology of emotions. *Annual Review of Anthropology*, 1986, *15*, 405-436.

Lynch, J. *The broken heart: Medical consequences of lonliness*. New York: Basic, 1977.

Maccoby, M., & Modiano, N. Cognitive style in rural and urban Mexico. *Human Development*, 1969, *12*, 22-33.

Malcolm, N. The conceivability of mechanism. *Philosophical Review*, 1968, 77, 45-72.

Mandler, G. *Mind and emotion*. New York: Wiley, 1975.

Mandler, G. Emotion. In E. Hearst (Ed.), *The first century of experimental psychology*. New Jersey: Lawrence Erlbaum, 1979, chap. 7.

Mandler, G. The generation of emotions: A psychological theory. In R. Plutchik & H. Kellerman (Eds.), *Emotion: Theory, research, and experience* (Vol. 1). New York: Academic Press, 1980, chap. 9.

Mandler, G., & Kremen, I. Autonomic feedback: A correlational study. *Journal of Personality*, 1958, *26*, 388-399.

Marcuse, H. *Reason and revolution, Hegel and the rise of social theory*. Boston: Beacon Press, 1954/1960.

Marcuse, H. *One-dimensional man*. Boston: Beacon Press, 1964.

Marcuse, H. Negations: Essays in critical theory. Boston: Beacon Press, 1968.

Marcuse, H. Contributions to a phenomenology of historical materialism. *Telos*, 1969, *4*, 3-34. (Originally published in 1928.)

Marcuse, H. *Studies in critical philosophy*. Boston: Beacon Press, 1973.

Marcuse, H. *Hegel's ontology and the theory of historicity*. Cambridge: MIT Press, 1932/1987.

Margolis, J. *Persons and minds*. Boston: Reidel, 1978.

Marsella, A. Depressive experience and disorder across cultures. In H. Triandis and J. Draguns (Eds.), *Handbook of cross-cultural psychology* (Vol. 6). Boston: Allyn & Bacon, 1980.

Marsella, A., DeVos, G., & Hsu, F. *Culture and self: Asian and Western perspectives*. New York: Tavistock, 1985.

Martin, L., & Halverson, C. The effects of sex-typing schemas on young children's memory. *Child Development*, 1983, *54*, 563- 574.

Martin, E. Medical metaphors of women's bodies: Menstruation and menopause. *International Journal of Health Services*, 1988, *18*, 237-254.

Marx, K. *Grundrisse, foundations of the critique of political economy*. New York: Random House, 1857/1973.

Maslow, A. *Toward a psychology of being*. New York: Van Nostrand, 1968.

Mason, W. The effects of environmental restriction on the social development of rhesus monkeys. In C. Southwick (Ed.), *Primate social behavior*. New York: Van Nostrand, 1963, chap. 14.

Massie, H., & Rosenthal, J. *Childhood psychosis in the first four years of life*. New York: McGraw-Hill, 1984.

Matson, F. *The broken image: Man, science, and society*. New York: Braziller, 1964.

Mays, W. Piaget's sociological theory. In S. Modgil & C. Modgil (Eds.), *Jean Piaget, consensus and controversy.* New York: Praeger, 1982, chap. 3.

McCall, R. Commentary. *Human Development,* 1989, *32,* 177-186.

McFarland, C., Ross, M., & DeCourville, N. Women's theories of menstruation and biases in recall of menstrual symptoms. *Journal of Personality and Social Psychology,* 1989, *57,* 522-531.

McKinlay, J., McKinlay, S., & Brambilla, D. The relative contributions of endocrine changes and social circumstances to depression in mid-aged women. *Journal of Health and Social Behavior,* 1987, *28,* 345-363.

McLeod, J., & Kessler, R. Socioeconomic status differences in vulnerability to undesirable life events. *Journal of Health and Social Behavior,* 1990, *31,* 162-172.

McNamee, G. The social interaction origins of narrative skills. *Quarterly Newsletter of the Laboratory of Comparative Human Cognition,* Oct. 1979, *1,* 4, 63-68.

McNeil, L. *Contradictions of control: School structure and school knowledge.* New York: Routledge & Kegan Paul, 1986.

McNeil, T., & Persson-Blennow, I. Stability of temperament characteristics in childhood. *American Journal of Orthopsychiatry,* 1988, *58,* 622-625.

Mead, M. An investigation of the thought of primitive children, with special reference to animism. *Journal of the Royal Anthropological Institute,* 1932, *62,* 173-190.

Mead, M. Socialization and enculturation. *Current Anthropology,* 1963, *4,* 184-188.

Mead, M. *Sex and temperament in three primitive societies.* New York: Morrow, 1935/1963b.

Meacham, J. The social basis of intentional action. *Human Development,* 1984, *27,* 119-124.

Mednick, M. On the politics of psychological constructs. *American Psychologist,* 1989, *44,* 1118-1123.

Meltzer, H., & Stahl, S. The dopamine hypothesis of schizophrenia: A review. *Schizophrenia Bulletin,* 1976, *2,* 1.

Meltzoff, A., & Moore, M. Imitation of facial and manual gestures by human neonates. *Science,* 1977, *198,* 75-78.

Melzack, R. *The puzzle of pain.* New York: Basic Books, 1973.

Merleau-Ponty, M. *The structure of behavior.* Boston: Beacon, 1942/1963.

Merleau-Ponty, M. *The phenomenology of perception.* London: Routledge & Kegan Paul, 1945/1962.

Merleau-Ponty, M. *Consciousness and the acquisition of language.* Evanston: Northwestern University Press, 1973.

Middleton, D., & Edwards, D. (Eds.). *Collective remembering.* Newbury Park: Sage, 1990.

Miklowitz, D., et al. Family factors and the course of bipolar affective disorder. *Archives of General Psychiatry,* 1988, *45,* 225-231.

Milgram, N.W., MacLeod, C., & Petit, T. *Neuroplasticity, learning, and memory.* New York: Liss, 1987.

Miller, G. Information and memory. *Scientific American,* 1956, *195,* pp. 42-46.

Miller, G. The background to modern psychology. In J. Miller (Ed.), *States of mind.* New York: Pantheon, 1983, chap. 1.

Miller, J. Culture and the development of everyday social explanation. *Journal of Personality and Social Psychology,* 1984, *46,* 961-978.

Miller, R.E., Caul, W., & Mirsky, A. Communication of affects between feral and socially isolated monkeys. *Journal of Personality and Social Psychology,* 1967, *7,* 231-239.

Mills, C.W. *Power, politics, and people.* New York: Oxford, 1963.

Minick, N. *L.S. Vygotsky and Soviet activity theory: New perspectives on the relationship between mind and society.* Unpublished doctoral dissertation, Northwestern University, 1985.

Mintz, S. *Sweetness and power: The place of sugar in modern history.* New York: Penguin, 1985.

Mischel, T. Piaget: Cognitive conflict and the motivation of thought. In T. Mischel (Ed.), *Cognitive development and epistemology*. New York: Academic Press, 1971, pp. 311-355.

Mitzman, A. The civilizing offensive: Mentalities, high culture, and individual psyches. *Journal of Social History*, 1987, *20*, 663-687.

Mollica, R., & Milic, M. Social class and psychiatric practice: A revision of the Hollingshead and Redlich model. *American Journal of Psychiatry*, 1986, *143*, 12-17.

Money, J., & Ehrhardt, A. *Man and woman, boy and girl*. Baltimore: Johns Hopkins University Press, 1972.

Montagu, A. *Anthropology and human nature*. Boston: Porter Sargent, 1957.

Montagu, A. (Ed.), *Culture and the evolution of man*. New York: Oxford, 1962.

Montagu, A. Brains, genes, culture, immaturity, and gestation. In A. Montagu (Ed.), *Culture, man's adaptive dimension*. New York: Oxford University Press, 1968, pp. 102-113.

Montagu, A. (Ed.), *Race and IQ*. New York: Oxford, 1975.

Moore, B. *Privacy, studies in social and cultural history*. New York: Sharpe, 1984.

Moskowitz, B. The acquisition of language. *Scientific American*, November, 1978, pp. 92-108.

Mostow, E., & Newberry, P. Work role and depression in women: A comparison of workers and housewives in treatment. *American Journal of Orthopsychiatry*, 1975, *45*, 538-548.

Murphy, C.M., & Messer, D.J. Mothers, Infants and pointing: A study of a gesture. In H.R. Schaffer (Ed.), *Studies in mother-infant interaction*. New York: Academic Press, 1977, chap. 13.

Murphy, H.B.M. Cultural factors in the genesis of schizophrenia. *Journal of Psychiatric Research*, 1968 (Vol. 6), supplement #1, pp. 137-153.

Murphy, H.B.M. The evocative role of complex social tasks. In A.R. Kaplan (Ed.), *Genetic factors in schizophrenia*. Springfield, Ill.: Thomas, 1972.

Murphy, H.B.M. Cultural influences on incidence, course, and treatment response. In L. Wynne (Eds.), *The nature of perception*. New York: Wiley, 1978, chap. 52.

Mwamwenda, T., & Mwamwenda, B. Sequence of transitivity, conservation, and class inclusion in an African culture. *Journal of Cross-Cultural Psychology*, 1989, *20*, 416-433.

Myers, J., Lindenthal, J., & Pepper, M. Social class, life events, and psychiatric symptoms: A longitudinal study. In B.S. Dohrenwend & B.P. Dohrenwend (Eds.), *Stressful life events: Their nature and effects*. New York: Wiley, 1974, chap. 12.

Nash, J. *Developmental psychology, a psychobiological approach*. Englewood Cliffs: Prentice Hall, 1970.

Nasser, M. Eating disorders: The cultural dimension. *Social Psychiatry and Psychiatric Epidemiology*, 1988, *23*, 184-187.

Natanson, M. Philosophy and psychiatry. In E. Strauss, M. Natanson, & H. Ey (Eds.), *Psychiatry and philosophy*. New York: Springer-Verlag, 1969, pp. 85-110.

Neisser, U. *Cognition and reality*. San Francisco: Freeman, 1976.

Neisser, U. Memory: What are the important questions? In U. Neisser (Ed.), *Memory observed: Remembering in natural contexts*. New York: Freeman, 1982, chap. 1

Newson, J. The growth of shared understandings between infant and caregiver. In M. Bullowa (Ed.), *Before speech: The beginnings of interpersonal communication*. New York: Cambridge University Press, 1979, chap. 10.

Nisbett, R., & Schachter, S. Cognitive manipulation of pain. *Journal of Experimental Social Psychology*, 1966, *2*, 227-236.

Novikoff, A. The concept of integrative levels and biology. *Science*, March 2, 1945, 209-215.

Oberschall, A. *The establishment of empirical sociology*. New York: Harper, 1972.

Ochs, E. *Culture and language development*. New York: Cambridge University Press, 1988.

Ogbu, J. Cultural influences on plasticity in human development. In J. Gallagher & C. Ramey (Eds.), *The malleability of children*. Baltimore: Brookes, 1987, chap. 13.

Opler, M. Schizophrenia and culture. *Scientific American*, August, 1957.

Opler, M. Anthropological contributions to psychiatry and social psychiatry. In S. Plog & R. Edgerton (Eds.), *Changing perspectives in mental illness*. New York: Holt, 1969, pp. 88-105.

Orlansky, H. Infant care and personality. *Psychological Bulletin*, 1949, *46*, 1-48.

Ornstein, J. *A critique of the mind-brain identity theory and a defense of a multi-aspect theory of mind*. Unpublished dissertation for Doctor of Philosophy, University of California, San Diego, 1970.

Ortega, S., & Rushing, W. Interpretation of the relationship between socioeconomic status and mental disorder. *Research in Community and Mental Health*, 1983, *3*, 141-161.

Ortner, S., & Whitehead, H. *Sexual meanings: The cultural construction of gender and sexuality*. New York: Cambridge University Press, 1981.

Ortony, A., Clore, G., & Collins, A. *The cognitive structure of emotions*. New York: Cambridge University Press, 1988.

Ortony, A., & Turner, T. What's basic about basic emotions? *Psychological Review*, 1990, *97*, 315-331.

Ottaway, H. *Mozart*. Detroit: Wayne State University Press, 1980.

Paige, K., & Paige, J. *The politics of reproductive ritual*. Berkeley: University of California Press, 1981.

Palardy, J. N. What teachers believe, what children achieve. *Elementary School Journal*, 1969, *69*, 370-374.

Pannekoek, A. *Anthropogenesis, a study of the origin of man*. Amsterdam: North-Holland Publishing Co., 1944/1953.

Park, R. *Principles of human behavior*. Chicago: Zalaz, 1915.

Parker, S. The Wiitiko psychosis in the context of Ojibwa personality and culture. *American Anthropologist*, 1960, *62*, 603-623.

Parker, S., & Gibson, K. A Developmental model for the evolution of language and intelligence in early hominids. *Behavioral and Brain Sciences*, 1979, *2*, 367-408.

Parker, S. Higher intelligence as adaptation for social and technological strategies in early *Homo sapiens*. In G. Butterworth et al. (Eds.), *Evolution and developmental psychology*. Sussex: Harvester Press, 1985, chap. 7.

Pastore, N. *The nature-nurture controversy*. New York: King's Crown Press, 1949.

Pawlby, S.J. Imitative interaction. In H.R. Schaffer (Ed.), *Studies in mother-infant interaction* (pp. 203-224). London: Academic Press, 1977.

Penfield, W. *The mystery of the mind*. Princeton: Princeton University Press, 1975.

Pepitone, A. Toward a normative and comparative biocultural social psychology. *Journal of Personality and Social Psychology*, 1976, *34*, 641-653.

Pepitone, A. Lessons from the history of social psychology. *American Psychologist*, 1981, *36*, 979-985.

Pepitone, A. Culture and the cognitive paradigm in social psychology. *Australian Journal of Psychology*, 1986, *38*, 245-256.

Pepitone, A., & Triandis, H. On the universality of social psychological theories. *Journal of Cross-Cultural Psychology*, 1987, *18*, 471-498.

Perrin, S., & Spencer, C. The Asch effect—a child of its time? *Bulletin of the British Psychological Society*, 1980, *32*, 405-406.

Piaget, J. *Comments on Vygotsky's critical remarks concerning "the language and thought of the child" and "judgement and reasoning in the child."* Cambridge: MIT Press, 1962.

Piaget, J. *Biology and knowledge, an essay on the relations between organic regulations and cognitive processes*. Chicago: University of Chicago Press, 1967/1971.

Pichert, J., & Anderson, R. Taking different perspectives on a story. *Journal of Educational Psychology*, 1977, *69*, 309-315.

Plomin, R., & Daniels, D. Why are children in the same family so different from one another? *Behavioral and Brain Sciences*, 1987, *10*, 1-60.

Plotnik, R. Brain stimulation and aggression: Monkeys, apes, and humans. In R. Holloway (Ed.), *Primate aggression, territoriality, and zenophobia.* New York: Academic Press, 1974, pp. 389-416.

Plutchik, R. A general psychoevolutionary theory of emotion. In R. Pluthcik & H. Kellerman (Eds.), *Emotion: Theory, research, and experience* (Vol. 1). New York Academic Press, 1980a, chap. 1.

Plutchik, R. *Emotion, a psychoevolutionary synthesis.* New York: Harper & Row, 1980b.

Poirier, F. Socialization and learning among nonhuman primates. In S. T. Kimball et al. (Eds.), *Learning and culture.* Seattle: University of Washington Press, 1973, pp. 3-41.

Polanyi, M. *Personal knowledge.* New York: Harper & Row, 1958.

Polanyi, M. *The tacit dimension.* New York: Anchor, 1966.

Pollock, K. On the nature of social stress: Production of a modern mythology. *Social Science, and Medicine*, 1988, *26*, 381-392.

Pope, H., & Lipinski, J. Diagnosis in schizophrenia and manic-depressive illness. *Archives of General Psychiatry*, 1978, *35*, 811-828.

Posner, J. The development of mathematical knowledge in two West African societies. *Child Development*, 1982, *53*, 200- 208.

Post, R., & Leibowitz, H. A revised analysis of the role of efference in motion perception. *Perception*, 1985, *14*, 631-643.

Poster, M. Freud's concept of the family. *Telos*, 1976, *30*, 93-115.

Powell, G. Negative and positive mental practice in motor skill acquisition. *Perceptual and Motor Skills*, 1973, *37*, 312.

Premack, A., & Premack, D. Teaching language to an ape. *Scientific American*, October, 1972, 92-99.

Premack, D. The codes of man and beasts. *Behavioral and Brain Sciences*, 1983, *6*, 125-167.

Premack, D. Upgrading a mind. In T. G. Bever et al. (Eds.), *Talking minds: The study of language in cognitive science.* Cambridge: MIT Press, 1984, pp. 181-206.

Premack, D., & Premack, A. *The mind of an ape.* New York: Norton, 1983.

Preteceille, E., & Terrail, J.P. *Capitalism, consumption, and needs.* New York: Blackwell 1977/1985.

Pribram, K. A review of theory in physiological psychology. In P. Farnsworth & Q. McNemar (Ed.), *Annual Review of Psychology.* Berkeley: Annual Reviews, 1960 (Vol. 11), chap. 1.

Pribram, K. H. Self-consciousness and intentionality. In G. Schwartz & D. Shapiro (Eds.), *Consciousness and self-regulation.* New York: Plenum, 1976 (Vol. 1), chap. 2.

Price-Williams, D.R. (Ed.), *Cross-cultural studies.* Baltimore: Penguin, 1969.

Prien, R., Caffey, E., & Klett, J. Comparison of lithium carbonate and chlorpromazine in the treatment of mania. *Archives of General Psychiatry*, 1972, *26*, 146-157.

Prien, R., et al. Drug therapy in the prevention of recurrences in unipolar and bipolar affective disorders. *Archives of General Psychiatry*, 1984, *41*, 1096-1104.

Puccetti, R., & Dykes, R. Sensory cortex and the mind-brain problem. *Behavioral and Brain Sciences*, 1978, *3*, 337-375.

Radke-Yarrow, M. Developmental and contextual analysis of continuity. *Human Development*, 1989, *32*, 204-209.

Ratner, C. The critical psychology of R.D. Laing. *Telos*, 1970, *5*, 98-114.

Ratner, C. Totalitarianism and individualism in psychology. *Telos*, Spring 1971(a), *7*, 50-72.

Ratner, C. Principles of dialectical psychology. *Telos*, Fall 1971(b), *8*, 83-109.

Ratner, C. Review of Schutz's reflections on the problem of relevance, and Berger & Luckmann's "The social construction of reality." *Insurgent Sociologist* , 1973, *4*, 1, 85-90.

Ratner, C. Do studies on identical twins prove that schizophrenia is genetically inherited? *International Journal of Social Psychiatry*, 1982, *28*, *3*, 175-178.

Ratner, C. A social constructionist critique of naturalistic theories of emotion. *Journal of Mind and Behavior*, 1989a, *10*, 211-230.

Ratner, C. A sociohistorical critique of naturalistic theories of color perception. *Journal of Mind and Behavior*, 1989b, *10*, 361-372.

Ratner, C., & McCarthy, J. Ecologically relevant stimuli and color memory. *Journal of General Psychology*, 1990, *117*, 369-377.

Redlich, F., Hollingshead, A., & Bellis, E. Social class differences in attitudes toward psychiatry. In D. Apple (Ed.), *Sociological studies of health and sickness*. New York: McGraw-Hill, 1960, chap. 10.

Regier, D., et al. One-month prevalence of mental disorders in the United States. *Archives of General Psychiatry*, 1988, *45*, 977-985.

Reisenzein, R. The Schachter theory of emotions: Two decades later. *Psychological Bulletin*, 1983, *94*, 239-264.

Reynolds, V. *The biology of human action*. New York: Freeman, 1980.

Rheingold, H. Hay, D., & West, M. Sharing in the second year of life. *Child Development*, 1976, *47*, 1148-1158.

Rieber, R., & Green, M. The psychopathy of everyday life: Anti-social behavior and social distress. In R. Rieber (Ed.), *The individual, communication, and society. Essays in honor of Gregory Bateson*. New York: Cambridge University Press, 1989, chap 3.

Riege, W. Environmental influences on brain and behavior of year-old rats. *Developmental Psychobiology*, 1971, *4*, 157-167.

Riesman, P. On the irrelevance of child rearing practices for the formation of personality. *Culture, Medicine, and Psychiatry*, 1983, *7*, 103-130.

Robbins, L. The accuracy of parental recall of aspects of child development and of child rearing practices. *Journal of Abnormal and Social Psychology*, 1963, *66*, 261-270.

Robinson, B. Anatomical and physiological contrasts between human and other primate vocalizations. In S.L. Washburn & P. Dolhinow (Eds.), *Perspectives on human evolution* (Vol. 2). New York: Holt, Rinehart, & Winston, 1972, chap. 17.

Rock, I. *The logic of perception*. Cambridge: MIT Press, 1983.

Rock, I. *Perception*. New York: Scientific American, 1984.

Rock, I. The frame of reference. In I. Rock (Ed.), *The legacy of Solomon Asch: Essays in cognition and social psychology*. Hillsdale: Lawrence Erlbaum, 1990, chap. 15.

Roediger, H., & Crowder, R. A Serial position effect in recall of United States presidents. In U. Neisser (Ed.), *Memory observed: Remembering in natural contexts*. New York: Freeman, 1982, chap. 22.

Rogers, C. Toward a modern approach to values: The valuing process in the mature person. *Journal of Abnormal and Social Psychology* 1964, *68*, 160-167.

Rorer, L., & Widiger, T. *Personality structure and assessment*. Annual Review of Psychology, 1983.

Rosaldo, M. Toward an anthropology of self and feeling. In R. Shweder & R. LeVine (Eds.), *Culture theory, essays on mind, self, and emotion*. New York: Cambridge University Press, 1984, chap. 5

Rosch, E. Natural categories. *Cognitive Psychology*, 1973, *4*, 328-350.

Rosch, E. Universals and cultural specifics in human categorization. In R. Brislin, S. Bochner, & W. Lonner (Eds.), *Cross-cultural perspectives on learning*. New York: Wiley, 1975.

Rosch, E., et al. Basic objects in natural categories. *Cognitive Psychology*, 1976, *8*, 382-439.

Rosch, E. Principles of categorization. In E. Rosch & B. Lloyd (Eds.), *Cognition and categorization*. New Jersey: Erlbaum, 1978, chap. 2.

Rosch, E. Coherences and categorization: A historical view. In F. Kessel (Ed.), *The development of language and language researchers, essays in honor of Roger Brown*. New Jersey: Erlbaum, 1988, chap. 18.

Rose, S. *The conscious brain*. New York: Vintage, 1976.

Rose, S., Feldman, J., & Wallace, I. Individual differences in infants' information processing: Reliability, stability, and prediction. *Child Development*, 1988, *59*, 1177-1197.

Rosenhan, D. L. On being sane in insane places. *Science*, 1973, *179*, 250-258.

Rosenthal, D. *Genetic theory and abnormal behavior*. New York: McGraw-Hill, 1970

Rosenthal, R., & Jacobson, L. Teacher's expectations for the disadvantaged. *Scientific American*, April, 1968, pp. 19-23.

Rosenthal, T., & Zimmerman, B. Social learning and cognition. New York: Academic Press, 1978.

Rosenzweig, M., Bennett, E., & Diamond, M. Brain changes in response to experience. *Scientific American*, February 1972, 22-29.

Rosenzweig, M. Experience, memory, and the brain. *American Psychologist*, 1984, *39*, 365-376.

Rosenzweig, M., & Leiman, A. *Physiological psychology*. Lexington, Mass.: Heath, 1982.

Ross, C., & Mirowsky, J. Explaining the social patterns of depression: Control and problem-solving—or support and talking? *Journal of Health and Social Behavior*, 1989, *30*, 206-219.

Ross, M. Relation of implicit theories to the construction of personal histories. *Psychological Review*, 1989, *96*, 341-357.

Rothbart, M., & Macereby, E. Parents' differential reactions to sons and daughters. *Journal of Personality and Social Psychology*, 1966, *17*, 113-120.

Rothman, E. *Hands and hearts: A history of courtship in America*. New York: Basic, 1984.

Rozin, P. The evolution of intelligence and access to the cognitive unconscious. *Progress in Psychology and Physiological Psychology*, 1976, 6, 245-280.

Rubin, J., Provenzano, A., & Luria, Z. The eye of the beholder: Parents' view on sex of newborns. *American Journal of Orthopsychiatry*, 1974, *44*, 512-519.

Rubinstein, R., & Brown, R. An evaluation of the validity of the diagnostic category of attention deficit disorder. *American Journal Orthopsychiatry*, 1984, *54*, 398-414.

Ruble, D. Premenstrual symptoms: A reinterpretation. *Science*, 1977, *197*, 291-292.

Ryan, M. *Womanhood in America*. New York: Watts, 1983.

Sacks, O. *Hearing voices*. Berkeley: University of California Press, 1989.

Sahlins, M. The social life of monkeys, apes, and primitive man. In J.N. Spuhler (Ed.), *The evolution of man's capacity for culture*. Detroit: Wayne State University Press, 1959, pp, 54-73.

Sahlins, M. Colors and cultures. *Semiotica*, 1976, *16*, 1- 22.

Sahlins, M. *The use and abuse of biology: An anthropological critique of sociobiology*. Michigan: University of Michigan Press, 1977.

Sahlins, M. *Islands of history*. Chicago: University of Chicago Press, 1985.

Saks, M., Edelstein, J., Draguns, J., & Fundia, T. Social class and social mobility in relation to psychiatric symptomatology in Argentenia. *Revista Interamericana de Psicologia*, 1970, *4*, 105-121.

Salomon, G. Television is "easy" and print is "tough": The differential investment of mental effort in learning as a function of perceptions and attributions. *Journal of Educational Psychology*, 1984, *76*, 647-658.

Sameroff, A., Seifer, R., & Elias, P. Sociocultural variability in infant temperamental ratings. *Child Development*, 1982, *53*, 164-173.

Sameroff, A., Seifer, R., & Barocas, R. Impact of parental psychopathology: Diagnosis, severity, or social status effects? *Infant Mental Health Journal*, 1983, *4*, 236-249.

Sameroff, A., Seifer, R., Zax, M., & Barocas, R. Early indicators of developmental risk: Rochester longitudinal study. *Schizophrenia Bulletin*, 1987, *13*, 383-394.

Sampson, E.E. Cognitive psychology as ideology. *American Psychologist*, 1981, *36*, 7, 730-743.

Sampson, E.E. Deconstructing psychology's subject. *Journal of Mind and Behavior*, 1983, *4*,2, 135-164.

Sampson, E.E. The debate on individualism. *American Psychologist*, 1988, *43*, 15-22.

Sapir, E. *Language.* New York: Harcourt, Brace, & World, 1921.

Sapir, E. *Selected writings of Edward Sapir in language, culture, and personality.* D. Mandelbaum (Ed.), Berkeley: University of California Press, 1951.

Sapir, E. The unconscious patterning of behavior in society. In B. Blount (Ed.), *Language, culture, and society.* Mass.: Winthrop, 1974. pp. 32-45.

Sarason, S. *Psychology misdirected.* New York: Free Press, 1981.

Sarason, S. An asocial psychology and a misdirected clinical psychology. *American Psychologist*, 1981, *36*, 827- 836.

Sarbin, T. The scientific status of the mental illness metaphor. In S. Plog & R. Edgerton (Eds.), *Changing perspectives in mental illness.* New York: Holt, Rinehart, & Winston, 1969, pp. 9-31.

Sarbin, T., & Mancuso, J. *Schizophrenia: Medical diagnosis or moral verdict.* New York: Pergamon, 1980.

Sartre, J. *Being and nothingness.* New York: Philosophical Library, 1943/1956.

Sartre, J. *Search for a method.* New York: Knopf,1963.

Saxe, G., & Posner, J. The development of numerical cognition: Cross-cultural perspectives. In H. Ginsburg (Ed.), *The development of mathematical thinking.* New York: Academic Press, 1983, chap. 7.

Saxe, G., et al. Social processes in early number development. *Monographs of the society for research in child development*, 1987, *52*, 2.

Saxe, G. Developing forms of arithmetical thought among the Oksapmin of Papua New Guinea. *Developmental Psychology*, 1982, 18, 583-594.

Saxe, G. The mathematics of street vendors. *Child Development*, 1988, *59*, 1415-1425.

Scarr, S. An evolutionary perspective on infant intelligence. In M. Lewis (Ed.), *Origins of intelligence.* New York: Plenum, 1983, 2nd edition, chap. 6.

Schaff, A. *Language and cognition.* New York: McGraw-Hill, 1973.

Schaffer, H.R. *The growth of sociability.* New York: Penguin, 1971.

Schaffer, H.R. *The child's entry into a social world.* New York: Academic Press, 1984.

Schatzman, M. *Soul murder.* New York: New American Library, 1973.

Scheff, T. *Labeling madness.* Engelwood Cliffs: Prentice Hall, 1975.

Scheff, T. *Being mentally ill.* Chicago: Aldine, 1984.

Scheler, M. *Man's place in nature.* New York: Schocken, 1961.

Scheper-Hughes, N. Mother love and child death in Northeast Brazil. In J. Stigler, R. Shweder, & G. Herdt (Eds.), *Cultural psychology: Essays in comparative human development.* New York: Cambridge University Press, 1990, chap. 19.

Scher, J. M. *Theories of the mind.* New York: Free Press, 1962.

Schieffelin, B. *The give and take of everyday life: Language socialization of Kaluli children.* New York: Cambridge University Press, 1990.

Schieffelin, B., & Ochs, E. A cultural perspective on the transition from prelinguistic to linguistic communication. In R. Golinkoff (Ed.), *The transition from prelinguistic to linguistic communication.* Hillsdale: Erlbaum, 1983, chap. 7.

Schieffelin, E. The cultural analysis of depressive affect: An example from New Guinea. In A. Kleinman & B. Good (Eds.), *Culture and depression*. Berkeley: University of California Press, 1985, chap. 3.

Schiff, M. Intellectual status of working-class children adopted early into upper-middle-class families. *Science*, 1978, *200*, June 30, pp. 1503-1504.

Schiff, M., & Lewontin, R. *Education and class: The irrelevance of IQ genetic studies*. London: Clarendon, 1986.

Schiller, P. Innate constituents of complex responses in primates. *Psychological Review*, 1952, *59*, 177-191.

Schiller, P. Innate motor action as a basis of learning: Manipulative problems in the chimpanzee. In J. Bruner et al. (Eds.), *Play–its role in development and evolution*. New York: Penguin, 1976, chap. 22.

Schneirla, T.C. *Selected writings*. L. Aronson et al. (Eds.), San Francisco: Freeman Co., 1972.

Schneirla, T.C., & Piel, G. The army ant. *Scientific American*, June, 1948, 16-23.

Schur, E. *The awareness trap: Self-absorption instead of social change*. New York: McGraw-Hill, 1976.

Scull, A. *Museums of madness: The social organization of insanity in 19th century England*. New York: St. Martin's Press, 1979.

Scull, A. *Social order/mental disorder*. Berkeley: University of California Press, 1989.

Schur, E. *The awareness trap, self-absorption instead of social change*. New York: McGraw Hill, 1976.

Schutz, A. *Reflections on the problem of relevance*. Conn.: Yale University Press, 1970.

Schwab, J., Bell, R., Warheit, G., & Schwab, R. *Social order and mental health*. New York: Brunner/Mazel, 1979.

Scribner, S., & Cole, M. Cognitive consequences of formal and informal education. *Science*, Nov. 9, 1973, *182*, 553-559.

Scribner, S., & Cole, Michael. Literacy without schooling: Testing for intellectual effects. *Harvard Educational Review*, 1978, *48*, 448-461.

Scribner, S., & Cole, Michael. *The psychology of literacy*. Cambridge: Harvard University Press, 1981.

Scribner, S. Recall of classical syllogisms: A cross-cultural investigation of error on logical problems. In R. Falmagne (Ed.), *Reasoning: Representation and process in children and adults*. New Jersey: Lawrence Erlbaum, 1975, chap. 6.

Scribner, S. Modes of thinking and ways of speaking: Culture and logic reconsidered. In P.N. Johnson-Laird & P. Wason (Eds.), *Thinking, readings in cognitive science*. New York: Cambridge University Press, 1977, chap. 29.

Sebeok, T., & Sebeok, J. *Speaking of apes, a critical anthology of two-way communication with man*. New York: Plenum Press, 1980.

Segall, M., et al. *The influence of culture on visual perception*. Indianapolis: Bobbs-Merrill, 1966.

Segall, M. *Cross-cultural psychology*. Belmont: Wadsworth, 1979.

Seligman, M. On the generality of the laws of learning. *Psychological Review*, 1970, *77*, 406-418.

Sewitch, D. The perceptual uncertainty of having slept: The inability to discriminate electroencephalographic sleep from wakefulness. *Psychophysiology*, 1984, *21*, 243-259.

Shaw, W.A. The relation of muscular action potentials to imaginal weight lifting. *Archives of Psychology*, 1940, *35* (No. 247).

Shea, J., Ogaiea, B., & Bagara, B. Conservation in community school children from the Madang, Southern Highlands, and North Solomons Provinces of Papua, New Guinea. *International Journal of Psychology*, 1983, *18*, 203-214.

Sherman, J. *Sex-related cognitive differences*. Springfield, Ill.: Thomas, 1978.

Shields, J. Summary of the genetic evidence. *Journal of Psychiatric Research*, 1968, *6*(1), 95-126.

Shorter, E. Paralysis: The rise and fall of a "hysterical" symptom. *Journal of Social History*, 1986, *19*, 549-582.

Shweder, Ri. Scientific thought and social cognition. In W. Collins (Ed.), *Development of cognition, affect, and social relations*. (The Minnesota Symposium on Child Psychology (Vol. 13), New Jersey: Erlbaum, 1980, pp. 263-272.

Shweder, R. On savages and other children. *American Anthropologist*, 1982(a), *84*, 354-366.

Shweder, R. Liberalism as destiny. *Contemporary Psychology*, 1982(b), *27*, 421-424.

Shweder, R. Beyond self-constructed knowledge: The study of culture and morality. *Merrill-Palmer Quarterly*, 1982(c), *28*, 41-69.

Shweder, R. Menstrual pollution, soul loss, and the comparative study of emotions. In A. Kleinman & B. Good (Eds.), *Culture and depression, studies in the anthropology and cross-cultural psychiatry of affect and disorder*. Berkeley: University of California Press, 1985, chap. 6.

Shweder, R. Cultural psychology—What is it? In J. Stigler, R. Shweder, & G. Herdt (Eds.), *Cultural psychology: Essays on comparative human development*. New York: Cambridge University Press, 1990, pp. 1-43.

Shweder, R. Ethical relativism: Is there a defensible version? *Ethos*, 1990(b), *18*, 205-218.

Shweder, R., & Bourne, E. Does the concept of the person vary cross-culturally? In Shweder & LeVine (Eds.), *Culture theory: Essays on mind, self, and emotion*. New York: Cambridge University Press, 1984, chap. 6.

Shweder, R., & LeVine, R. (Eds.), *Culture theory: Essays on mind, self, and emotion*. New York: Cambridge University Press, 1984.

Shweder, R., & Miller, J. The social construction of the person: How is it possible? In K. Gergen & K. Davis (Eds.), *The social construction of the person*. New York: Springer-Verlag, 1985, chap. 3.

Shweder, R., Mahapatra, M., & Miller, J. Culture and moral development. In J. Kagan & S. Lamb (Eds.), *The emergence of morality in young children*. Chicago: University of Chicago Press, 1987.

Siegel, L., & Hodkin, B. The garden path to the understanding of cognitive development: Has Piaget led us into the poison ivy? In S. Modgil & C. Modgil (Eds.), *Jean Piaget, consensus and controversy*. New York: Praeger, 1982, chap. 4.

Siegel, R. Mechanisms of cognitive development. *Annual Review of Psychology*, 1989, *40*, 353-379.

Sigman, M., Neumann, C., Carter, E., & Cattle, D. Home interaction and the development of Embu toddlers in Kenya. *Child Development*, 1988, *59*, 1251-1261.

Silva, E., & Slaughter, S. *Serving power, the making of the academic social science expert*. Westport, Conn.: Greenwood Press, 1984.

Silverman, I. *The human subject in the psychological laboratory*. New York: Pergamon, 1977.

Simon, B. *Mind and madness in ancient Greece: The classical roots of modern psychiatry*. Ithaca: Cornell Univesity Press, 1978.

Simon, H. A. Using cognitive science to solve human problems. In J. Rubenstein & B. Slife (Eds.), *Taking sides: Clashing views on controversial psychological issues*. Guilford, Ct.: Dushkin, 1988 (5th ed.), pp. 118-122.

Simon, J., & Zusman, J. The effect of contextual factors on psychiatrists' perception of illness: A case study. *Journal of Health and Social Behavior*, 1983, *24*, 186-198.

Skeels, H. Adult status of children with contrasting early life experiences: A follow-up study. *Monographs of the society for research in child development*, 1966, *31*,3,1-65.

Smith-Rosenberg, C. The hysterical woman: Sex roles and role conflict in 19th century America. *Social Research*, 1972, *39*, 652-678.

Snyderman, M., & Rothman, S. Survey of expert opinion on intelligence and aptitude testing. *American Psychologist*, 1987, *42*, 137-144.

Solomon, R. C. Emotions And Choice. In A. Rorty (Ed.), *Explaining emotions*. Berkeley: University of California Press, 1980. chap. 10. (Originally published in 1973.)

Solomon, R. C. Getting angry. In R. Shweder & R. LeVine (Eds.), *Culture theory*. New York: Cambridge University Press, 1984, chap. 9.

Sommer, B. The effect of menstruation on cognitive and perceptual-motor behavior: A review. *Psychosomatic Medicine*, 1973, *35*, 515-533.

Sperry, R. W. Neurology and the mind-brain problem. *American Scientist*, 1952, *40*, 291-312.

Sperry, R. W. Mind, brain, and humanist values. In J. Platt (Ed.), *New views of the nature of man*. Chicago: University of Chicago Press, 1965, chap. 4.

Sperry, R. W. A modified concept of consciousness. *Psychological Review*, 1969, *76*, 532-536.

Sperry, R. W. An objective approach to subjective experience: Further explanation of a hypothesis. *Psychological Review*, 1970, *77*, 585-590.

Sperry, R. W. Problems outstanding in the evolution of brain function. In R. Duncan & M. Weston-Smith (Eds.), *The encyclopaedia of ignorance*. New York: Pergamon Press, 1977, pp. 423-433.

Sperry, R. W. Mind-brain interaction: Mentalism, yes; Dualism, no. *Neuroscience*, 1980, *5*, 195-206.

Sperry, R. W. Macro- versus micro-determinism. *Philosophy of Science*, 1986, *53*, 265-270.

Spitz, H. H. *The raising of intelligence: A selected history of attempts to raise retarded intelligence*. New Jersey: Lawrence Erlbaum, 1986.

Spring, G., Schweid, D., Gray, C., Steinberg, J., & Horwitz, M. A double-blind comparison of lithium and chlorpromazine in the treatment of manic states. *American Journal of Psychiatry*, 1970, *126*, 140-144.

Srole, L., et al. *Mental health in the metropolis: The midtown Manhattan study*. Springfield, Ill.: Thomas, 1962.

Srole, L. Measurement and classification in sociopsychiatric epidemiology: Midtown Manhattan study (1954) and midtown Manhattan restudy (1974). *Journal of Health and Social Behavior*, 1975, *16*, 347-364.

Stannard, D. *Shrinking history: On Freud and the failure of psychohistory*. New York: Oxford University Press, 1980.

Stearns, C., & Stearns, P. *Anger, the struggle for emotional control in America's history*. Chicago: University of Chicago Press, 1986.

Stearns, P. *Jealousy, the evolution of an emotion in American history*. New York: New York University Press, 1989.

Stefflre, V, Vales, V., & Morley, L. Language and cognition in Yucatan: A cross-cultural replication. *Journal of Personality and Social Psychology*, 1966, *4*, 112-115.

Steiner, I. Whatever happened to the group in social psychology? *Journal of Experimental Social Psychology*, 1974, *10*, 94-108.

Sterling, P., & Eyer, J. Biological basis of stress-related mortality. *Social Science and Medicine*, 1981, *15E*, 3-42.

Stern, E. Problems of cultural psychology. *Quarterly Newsletter of the Laboratory of Comparative Human Cognition*, 1990, *12*, 1, 12-24. (Originally published in 1920.)

Stoker, D., Zurcher, L., & Fox, W. Women in psychotherapy: A cross-cultural comparison. *International Journal of Social Psychiatry*, 1968, *15*, 5-22.

Stone, L. *The family, sex, marriage in England, 1500-1800*. New York: Harper, 1977.

Strauss, A. (Ed.). *The social psychology of George H. Mead.* Chicago: University of Chicago Press, 1956.

Strauss, J., & Carpenter, W. Characteristic symptoms and outcome in schizophrenia. *Archives of General Psychiatry,* 1974, *30,* 429-434.

Sullivan, E.V. A study of Kohlberg's structural theory of moral development: A critique of liberal social science ideology. *Human Development,* 1977, *20,* 352-376.

Super, C. Cross-cultural research on infancy. In H. Triandis & A. Heron (Eds.), *Handbook of cross-cultural psychology* (Vol. 4). Boston: Allyn & Bacon, 1981, chap. 2.

Super, C. Behavioral development in infancy. In R.H. Munroe, R.L. Munroe, & B. Whiting (Eds.), *Handbook of cross-cultural human development.* New York: Garland STPM Press, 1981b.

Super, C., & Harkness, S. The development of affect in infancy and early childhood. In D. Wagner & H. Stevenson (Eds.), *Cultural perspectives on child development.* San Francisco: Freeman, 1982, chap. 1.

Swagman, C. Fija: Fright and illness in highland Yemen. *Social Science and Medicine,* 1989, *28,* 381-388.

Swetz, F. *Capitalism and arithmetic.* LaSalle, Illinois: Open Court, 1987.

Swindler, A. Love and adulthood in American culture. In N. Smelser & E.H. Erikson (Eds.), *Themes of work and love in adulthood.* Cambridge: Harvard University Press, 1980.

Tajfel, H. Quantitative judgement in social perception. *British Journal of Psychology,* 1959, *50,* 16-29.

Tajfel, H., & Wilkes, A. Classification and quantitative judgement, *British Journal of Psychology,* 1963, *54,* 101-114.

Tajfel, H., & Forgas, P. Social categorization: Cognitions, values, and groups. In J. Forgas. *Social Cognition.* New York: Academic Press, 1981, chap. 5.

Taylor, C. *Human agency and language.* New York: Cambridge University Press, 1985a.

Taylor, C. *Philosophy and the human sciences.* New York: Cambridge University Press, 1985b.

Taylor, C. The person. In M. Carrithers et al. (Eds.), *The category of the person.* New York: Cambridge University Press, 1985c.

Taylor, M., Gaztanaga, P., & Abrams, R. Manic-depressive illness and acute schizophrenia: A clinical, family history, and treatment-response study. *American Journal of Psychiatry,* 1974, *131,* 678-682.

Terrace, H.S., et al. Can an ape create a sentence? *Science,* Nov. 23, 1979, 891-902.

Terrace, H. S. Nim: *A chimpanzee who learned sign language.* New York: Knopf, 1980.

Terrace, H. Thought without words. In C. Blakemore & S. Greenfield (Eds.), *Mindwaves.* New York: Blackwell, 1987, chap. 9.

Thelen, M., Dollinger, S., & Roberts, M. On being imitated: Its effects on attraction and reciprocal imitation. *Journal of Personality and Social Psychology,* 1975, *31,* 467-472.

Thomas, A., & Chess, S. *Temperament and development.* New York: Brunner Mazel, 1977.

Thompson, E.P. Time, work-discipline, and industrial capitalism. *Past and Present,* 1967, *38,* 56-97.

Thomson, G. *The first philosophers.* London: Lawrence & Wishart, 1955.

Tienari, P., et al. The Finnish adoptive family study of schizophrenia. *Yale Journal of Biology and Medicine,* 1985, *58,* 227-237.

Tienari, P., et al. Genetic and psychosocial factors in schizophrenia: The Finnish adoptive family study. *Schizophrenia Bulletin,* 1987, *13,* 477-484.

Tikhomirov, O.K. The formation of voluntary movements in children of preschool age. In M. Cole (Ed.), *The selected writings of A.R.Luria.* New York: Sharpe, 1978, pp. 229-269.

Tinsley, V., & Waters, H. The development of verbal control over motor behavior: A replication and extension of Luria's findings. *Child Development,* 1982, *53,* 746-753.

Tolman, E.C. Habit formation and higher mental processes in animals. *Psychological Bulletin*, 1927, *24*,1,1-35.

Toulmin, S. The Mozart of psychology. *The New York review of books*, Sept. 28, 1978.

Toulmin, S. Epistemology and developmental psychology. In E. Gollin (Ed.), *Developmental plasticity*. New York: Academic, 1981, chap. 8.

Toulmin, S. The concept of "stages" in psychological development. In T. Mischel (Ed.), *Cognitive development and epistemology*. New York: Academic Press, 1971, pp. 25-60.

Townsend, J., & Carbone, C. Menopausal syndrome: Illness or social role—a transcultural analysis. *Culture, Medicine, and Psychiatry*, 1980, *4*, 229-248.

Triandis, H. Individualism and social psychological theory. In C. Kagitcibasi (Ed.), *Growth and progress in cross-cultural psychology*. Lisse: Swets and Zeitlinger, 1989.

Tulviste, P. On the origins of theoretic syllogistic reasoning in culture and the child. *The Quarterly Newsletter of the Laboratory of Comparative Human Cognition*, 1979, *1*, 4, 73-80.

Tulviste, P. L. Levy-Bruhl and problems of the historical development of thought. *Soviet Psychology*, 1987, *25*, 3, 3-21.

Turner, R. Role-Taking: Process versus conformity. In A. Rose (Ed.), *Human behavior and social processes, an interactionist approach*. Boston: Houghton Mifflin, 1962, chapter 2.

Unger, R. *Male and female, psychological perspectives*. New York: Harper, 1979.

Valins, S. Cognitive effects of false heart-rate feedback. *Journal of Personality and Social Psychology*, 1966, *4*, 400-408.

Valins, S. Effects of cognitive desensitization on avoidance behavior. *Journal of Personality and Social Psychology*, 1967, *7*, 345-350.

Valins, S. The perception of labeling of bodily changes as determinants of emotional behavior. In P. Black (Ed.), *Physiological Correlates of Emotion*. New York: Academic Press, 1970, chap. 11.

Valsiner, J. Ontogeny of co-construction of culture within socially organized environmental settings. In J. Valsiner (Ed.), *Child development within culturally structured environments*. Norwood: Ablex, 1988, Vol. 2, pp. 283-296.

Valsiner, J., & Van der Veer, R. On the social nature of human cognition: An analysis of the shared intellectual roots of George Herbert Mead and Lev Vygotsky. *Journal for the Theory of Social Behavior*, 1988, *18*, 119-136.

Van den Berg, J.H. *Divided existence and complex society*. Pittsburgh: Duquesne University Press, 1974.

Van der Veer, R, & Ijzendoorn, M. Vygotsky's theory of the higher psychological processes: Some criticisms. *Human Development*, 1985, *28*, 1-9.

Van der Veer, R. Vygotsky's developmental psychology. *Psychological Reports*, 1986, *59*, 527-536.

Van der Veer, R., & Valsiner, J. Lev Vygotsky and Pierre Janet. On the origin of the concept of sociogenesis. *Developmental Review*, 1988, *8*, 52-65.

Van der Veer, R., & Valsiner, J. Overcoming dualism in psychology: Vygotsky's analysis of theories of emotion. *The Quarterly Newsletter of the Laboratory of Comparative Human Cognition*, 1989, *11*, 124-131.

Volkmar, F., & Greenough, W. Rearing complexity affects branching of dendrites in the visual cortex of the rat. *Science*, June 30, 1972, *176*, 1445-1447.

Volosinov, V. *Marxism and the philosophy of language*. Cambridge: Harvard University Press, 1929/1973.

Vygotsky, L.S. The problem of the cultural development of the child. *Journal of Genetic Psychology*, 1929, *36*, 415-434.

Vygotsky, L.S. Play and its role in the mental development of the child. In J. Bruner et al. (Eds.), *Play—its role in development and evolution.* New York: Penguin, 1976, chap. 53. (Originally published 1933).

Vygotsky, L.S. The development of higher psychological functions. *Soviet Psychology,* 1977, *15,* 60-73.

Vygotsky, L.S. *Mind in society, the development of higher psychological processes.* Cambridge: Harvard University Press, 1978.

Vygotsky, L.S. Consciousness as a problem in the psychology of behavior. *Soviet Psychology,* 1979, *17,* 4, 3-35.

Vygotsky, L.S. The Development of Higher Mental Functions. In J. V. Wertsch (Ed.), *The Concept of Activity in Soviet Psychology.* New York: Sharpe, 1981a, pp.144-188.

Vygotsky, L.S. The development of higher forms of attention in childhood. In J. V. Wertsch (Ed.), *The concept of activity in Soviet psychology.* New York: Sharpe, 1981b, pp. 189-240.

Vygotsky, L.S. *Collected works* (Vol. 1). New York: Plenum, 1987.

Vygotsky, L. S. Diagnosis of the development and pedological clinical care of difficult children. *Soviet Psychology,* Fall 1987b, *26,* 1, 86-101. (Originally published 1936).

Vygotsky, L. S. Concrete human psychology. *Soviet Psychology,* 1989, *27,* 2, 53-77. (Originally published 1929).

Vygotsky, L.S. Imagination and creativity in childhood. *Soviet Psychology,* 1990, *28,* 84-96 (Originally published in 1930).

Wagner, D. Culture and memory development. In H. Triandis & A. Heron (Eds.), *Handbook of cross-cultural psychology* (Vol. 4). Boston: Allyn & Bacon, 1981, chap. 5

Wagner, D. Ontogeny in the study of culture and cognition. In D. Wagner & H. Stevenson (Eds.), *Cultural perspectives on child development.* San Francisco: Freeman, 1982, chap. 5.

Wagner, D., & Spratt, J. Cognitive consequences of contrasting pedagogies: The effects of Quranic preschooling in Morocco. *Child Development,* 1987, *58,* 1207-1219.

Wald, H. Reflections on language and thought. *Dialectical Anthropology,* 1975(a), *1,* 51-60.

Wald, H. *Introduction to dialectical logic.* Amsterdam: Gruner, 1975(b).

Wall, P. "My foot hurts me": An analysis of a sentence. In R. Bellairs & E. Gray (Eds.), *Essays on the nervous system.* New York: Oxford University Press, 1974, chap. 16.

Wallach, M., & Wallach, L. *Psychology's sanction for selfishness: The error of egoism in theory and therapy.* San Francisco: Freeman, 1983.

Warner, R. *Recovery from schizophrenia: Psychiatry and political economy.* Boston: Routledge & Kegan Paul, 1985.

Washburn, M.F., Reagan, C., & Thurston, E. The comparative controllability of the fluctuations of simple and complex ambiguous perspective figures. *American Journal of Psychology,* 1934, *46,* 636-638.

Washburn, S.L., & Hamburg, D. The study of primate behavior. In I. Devore. *Primate behavior.* New York: Holt, 1965a, chap. 1.

Washburn, S.L., & Hamburg, D. The implications of primate research. In I. DeVore. *Primate behavior.* New York: Holt, 1965b, chap. 18.

Washburn, S.L., & Hamburg, D. Aggressive behavior in old world monkeys and apes. In P. Jay (Ed.), *Primates: Studies in adaptation and variability.* New York: Holt, Rinehart, & Winston, 1968, chap. 17.

Washburn, S.L., & Jay, P. (Eds.), *Perspectives on human evolution* (Vol. 1). New York: Holt, Rinehart, & Winston, 1968.

Washburn, S.L., & Moore, Ruth. *Ape into human, a study of human evolution* (2nd ed.). Boston: Little, Brown, 1980.

Washburn, S.L. Tools and human evolution. *Scientific American,* Sept. 1960, 63-75.

Waxler, N. Culture and mental illness: A social labelling perspective. In J. Mezzich & C. Berganza (Eds.), *Culture and psychopathology*. New York: Columbia University Press, 1984.

Weisberg, R. *Creativity: Genius and other myths*. New York: Freeman, 1986.

Weiss, K. Advantages of abandoning symptom-based diagnostic systems of research in schizophrenia. *American Journal of Orthopsychiatry*, 1989, *59*, 324-336.

Werner, E. E. Infants around the world: Cross-cultural studies of psychomotor development from birth to two years. *Journal of Cross-Cultural Psychology*, 1972, *3*, 111-134.

Werner, E.E., & Smith, R. *Vulnerable but invincible*. New York: McGraw-Hill, 1982.

Werner, E. Children of the Garden Island. *Scientific American*, April, 1989, *260*, 106-111.

Wertsch, James V. The concept of activity in Soviet psychology. In J. Wertsch (Ed.), *The Concept of Activity in Soviet Psychology*. New York: Sharpe, 1981, pp. 3-36.

Wertsch, J. V. *Vygotsky and the social formation of mind*. Mass.: Harvard University Press, 1985.

Wertsch, J. V. (Ed.) *Culture, communication, and cognition: Vygotskian perspectives*. New York: Cambridge University Press, 1985(b).

Wheaton, B. The sociogenesis of psychological disorder: Re-examining the causal issues with longitudinal data. *American Sociological Review*, 1978, *43*, 383-403.

Wheaton, B. The sociogenesis of psychological disorder: An attributional theory. *Journal of Health and Social Behavior*, 1980, *21*, 100-124.

Whitrow, G. Time and measurement. In P. Wiener (Ed.), *Dictionary of the history of ideas*. New York: Scribner's, 1973 (Vol. 4), pp. 398-406.

Whorf, B. Language, thought, and reality. Mass: MIT Press, 1956.

Wikan, U. Illness from fright or soul loss: A North Balinese culture-bound syndrome? *Culture, Medicine, and Psychiatry*, 1989, *13*, 25-50.

Wilder, R. Relativity of standards of mathematical rigor. In P. Wiener (Ed.), *Dictionary of the history of ideas* (Vol. 3). New York: Scribner's, 1973, pp. 170-177.

Will, J., Self, P., & Datan, N. Maternal behavior and perceived sex of infant. *American Journal of Orthopsychiatry*, 1976, *46*, 135-139.

Williams, D. Socioeconomic differentials in health: A review and redirection. *Social Psychology Quarterly*, 1990, *53*, 81-99.

Willis, P. *Learning to labour: How working class kids get working class jobs*. London, England: Gower, 1977.

Wilson, E. O. *On human nature*. Cambridge: Harvard University Press, 1978

Winstead, B. Hysteria. In C. Widom (Ed.), *Sex roles and psychopathology*. New York: Plenum, 1984, chapt. 4.

Winter, W. Size constancy, relative size estimation and background: A cross-cultural study. *Psychologia Africana*, 1967, *12*, 42-58.

Wishnant, L., & Zegans, L. A study of attitudes toward menarche in white middle-class american adolescent girls. In E. Howell & M. Bayes (Eds.), *Women and mental health*. New York: Basic, 1981, chap. 23.

Wishy, B. *The child and the republic*. Philadelphia: University of Pennsylvania Press, 1968.

Wolfe, B. Gender ideology and phobias in women. In C. Widom (Ed.), *Sex roles and psychopathology*. New York: Plenum, 1984, chap. 3.

Wood, E. M. *Mind and politics*. Berkeley: University of California Press, 1972.

World Health Organization. *Report of the international pilot study of schizophrenia* (Vol. 1). Geneva: World Health Organization, 1973.

World Health Organization. *Schizophrenia: An international follow-up study*. New York: Wiley, 1979.

Wundt, W. *Elements of folk psychology: Outlines of a psychological history of the development of mankind.* New York: Macmillan, 1912/1921.

Yerkes, R., & Nissen, H. Pre-linguistic sign behavior in chimpanzee. *Science,* June 23, 1939, *89,* 585-587.

Zajonc, R.B. Feeling and thinking: Preferences need no inferences. *American Psychologist,* 1980, *35,* 151-175.

Zigler, E., & Glick, M. Paranoid schizophrenia: An unorthodox view. *American Journal of Orthopsychiatry,* 1984, *54,* 43-70.

Zimmerman, M., & Spitzer, R. Melancholia: From DSM-III to DSM-III-R. *American Journal of Psychiatry,* 1989, *146,* 20-26.

Zinchenko, V. The problems of involuntary memory. *Soviet Psychology,* 1984, *22,* 55-111. (Originally published in 1939.)

Author Index

355

Subject Index

Abstract social features
  concrete features and, 116
  individual development and, 155
  univerals and, 114
Abstract thought
  decontextualized vs. contextualized
    mental processes, 89-96
  particular/universal and, 132-137
  sociality and, 96-103
  tool use and, 51
Action and activity
  consciousness and, 46
  culture and, 44
  genetics and, 202
  thinking and, 70
  tool use and, 47
Advertising, 104
Aggression
  cortex and, 234-235
  hormones and, 217-219
Anger, culture and, 77-79
Animals. *See also* Primates
  biology and, 11-12, 14
  consciousness and sociality among, 21
  emotion and, 77
  evolution and, 19, 203
  hormones and, 212-213
  infant behavior and, 150
  instinct/consciousness and, 19-20
  nature and, 18
  sense receptors, 204
  sexuality, 213
  tool use and, 52-54

Animism, particular/universal and,
    124-126
Anthropology
  genetics and, 202
  universals and, 116
Anxiety
  cultural variation and, 267
  hormones and, 224
Asociality, animal instinct and, 20
Atomism
  critique of, 5
  holism and, 103-104
  politics and, 319
Attachment, cultural mediation of, 14
Attachment theory, of madness, 291-292
Attention, developmental issues and, 159,
    162-163
Auditory perception, culture and, 72-73
Automation, consciousness and, 50

Basic psychological features, universal
    features contrasted, 119, 129-130
Behavior, biology and, 11-12
Behavior modification, critique of, 302
Biological reductionism, 85
Biology, 199-242
  animals and, 14, 19
  behavior and, 11-12
  cortex and, 224-237
  culture contrasted, 29-30
  diathesis-stress model of madness,
    285-289
  genetics, 202-204. *See also* Genetics

361